AN ANTHOLOGY OF

American Folktales and Legends

AN ANTHOLOGY OF

American Folktales and Legends

Frank de Caro, **editor**

M.E.Sharpe
Armonk, New York
London, England

Library of Congress Cataloging-in-Publication Data

An anthology of American folktales and legends / edited by Frank de Caro.
    p. cm.
  Includes bibliographical references and index.
  ISBN 978-0-7656-2129-0 (hardcover : alk. paper)
  1. Tales—United States. 2. Legends—United States. 3. Folklore—United States.
I. De Caro, F. A.

  GR105.A67 2009
  398.20973—dc22
                                                2008007917

Cover Image: Sarah Ann Garges Appliqué Bedcover; Sarah Ann Garges (c. 1834-c. 1887);
Doylestown, Bucks County, Pennsylvania; 1853; Cotton, silk, wool, and wool embroidery, with
muslin backing; h. 98 w. 96"; Collection American Folk Art Museum, New York; Gift of Warner
Communications Inc.; 1988.21.1; Photo by Schecter Lee, New York. Used with permission.

Pages 339-350 shall constitute a continuation of the copyright page.

Printed in the United States of America

The paper used in this publication meets the minimum requirements of
American National Standard for Information Sciences
Permanence of Paper for Printed Library Materials,
ANSI Z 39.48-1984.

BM (c)   10   9   8   7   6   5   4   3   2   1

Contents

Preface

The tales and legends included in this book represent a number of ethnic groups and American regions. They also represent the work of a number of folklorists who have endeavored to document the narrative traditions of the nation. They are primarily from folklore journals (in a few cases reprinted there from earlier publications, such as nineteenth-century newspapers) and the book-length collections of folklorists. The editor's intention is to present authentic, authoritative texts that have been recorded by collectors concerned with ethnographic accuracy.

Such accuracy, however, is at best a relative thing. Folklore collectors have had various intentions and methods. Some of the texts included here were actually recorded by sound-recording equipment. Other collectors recorded their texts directly into writing, and the correspondence between what was actually said and what was written down necessarily varies from case to case. Some folklorists got their informants to themselves write out stories or relied on their students to produce written texts. Some collectors no doubt unconsciously or consciously "improved" on what they heard. In the case of legends in particular, such may be the case, for legends as told are often fragmentary, nonchronological, and narrated collectively, whereas many printed legend texts are offered as complete, organic narratives. This variety in the fidelity to actual spoken language will not concern most readers. Folklore scholars may want to think further about how varied has been the precision in collecting the record of American folk narrative.

In some cases, texts have been used from collections—such as those of Richard Chase and Marie Campbell—that folklore scholars have found problematic (Chase because of composite texts, Campbell because her stories are often so close to versions of tales in the Grimm Brothers' famous book that folklorists suspected her informants or their forebears had merely read the stories and therefore did not represent a true oral tradition). These texts, however, are historically important and representative of significant aspects of American storytelling and of the presentation of folktales to the reading public, as are texts from such earlier sources as newspapers. Narrators often do not have titles for their stories; titles given here usually were provided by collectors or, in a few cases, by the editor.

No text in this volume is being "retold" by the editor. Rather, each is reprinted as originally published, except for a few minor changes, usually minimal editing to make them consistent in terms of the mechanics of style. In a very few, dialectical language has been modified, mostly for the sake of readability. The use of dialect in printing folk texts is problematic for the reasons noted in the Introduction. However, a number of texts with some form of dialect rendering have been included here unchanged from the original. To change them seemed unnecessary for readability and at odds with wanting to insure the integrity of the originals, published when ideas about the presentation of folk texts were different from standards and techniques of today.

Folk narratives exist in multiple variants or versions. Tale "types" and particular elements ("motifs") found within many tales have been cataloged and numbered by folklorists. Notes to the tales provide the relevant numbers for each story. Although these are mostly of interest to folklorists, others may be interested in comparisons or in finding other versions of particular stories. The designation AT before a number refers to a type number for a whole tale (like Cinderella) and to the system established in *The Types of the Folktale: A Classification and Bibliography* by Stith Thompson and Antti Aarne (Helsinki: Suomalainen Tiedeakatemia Academia Scientiarum Fennica, Folklore Fellows Communications, 184, 1961), referred to as the Type Index (though that term may also refer to the whole system of classification). A letter before a number references motifs established in Stith Thompson's *Motif-Index of Folk Literature,* 6 vols. (Bloomington: Indiana University Press, n.d.). There are specialized indexes for particular regions, including one for North American stories by Ernest Baughman (see the notes to the Introduction). An asterisk before a motif number indicates a newly established motif that does not appear in Thompson's compilation, and in a few instances, Baughman has modified the original numbering system of tale types to better fit American circumstances. Original sources may also include much information on comparative material, which for the most part is not provided here.

Tale types were devised by folklorists to classify folktales (that is, stories considered fictions by those who tell them), and the term *tale type* refers to a complete story like Cinderella. This system, including numbers for various types, was devised mostly to apply to the oral narratives of the Old World cultures of Eurasia and the Middle East. Thus legends (stories considered as conveying factual information) do not fit the Type Index designations. And stories from other cultures, such as those of Native America, usually do not fit either. Motifs were designed to classify not whole, fictional stories like Cinderella, but smaller parts of stories of many kinds, folktales and legends both; motifs are more inclusive of narrative elements, whether seen as fictional or factual, and many more stories can be compared in terms of motifs than in terms of types. Legends here are provided with motif rather than type numbers, as are stories that derive from cultures different from those for which the Type Index was derived. A tale type includes individual motifs (and these may be listed in the Type Index), but if a tale type number is given for a story in this book, there seemed no need to also include the motif numbers that constitute that tale type. Sometimes there is no applicable type or motif for a folk story, although in most cases one or more can be given.

The editor extends his gratitude to those who assisted him in compiling the collection, including the publishers and individuals who granted permission to reprint material. Thanks especially to those such as Hap Houlihan, who were especially helpful with advice and information regarding permissions. And thanks to M. E. Sharpe, to Todd Hallman for his support of this project, and to Cathleen Prisco and Stacey Victor for ably shepherding it through the editing process.

American Tales and Legends: An Introduction

In 1959, Richard M. Dorson, the doyen of American folklorists in his day, declared that the modern American is "a tremendous storyteller and story-listener."[1] His point was that even in the middle of the twentieth century, with such powerful media as television, radio, film, and the various forms of print to vie for our attention, the art of telling stories orally still had great vitality in American culture (as did other kinds of folklore). But his assessment was an accurate one in more general terms—Americans have had and continue to have a significant store of orally told tales, including many "traditional" folk stories that have been told, reshaped, and told again, often over very long spans of time.

This book presents a cross section of American folktales and legends—types of narrative that are in many ways distinctly different. These stories are drawn from the wide selection of published sources in which folk stories have appeared in print. Although these stories are presented for our predominantly literate twenty-first-century culture on the printed page, they represent a vernacular tradition, a tradition of the spoken word that is both ancient and potent.

Storytelling, whether oral or through other media, is a fundamental form of human communication. Cognitive scientist Mark Turner goes so far as to suggest that "story . . . is the fundamental instrument of thought,"[2] while linguist Charlotte Linde calls narrative "perhaps the most basic of all discourse units."[3] Stories provide us with a certain kind of coherence; with a record of events (whether real or imaginary); with a way of explaining, summarizing, and remembering our existence and those happenings that make up active existence. It is impossible to imagine our human lives without stories—of all kinds—to communicate with, to remember with, to amuse ourselves with, and to guide our very thoughts and actions.

Seen against the background of the importance of narrative, any collection of traditional folk stories raises questions about why certain stories have been frequently repeated, why certain recurring patterns of plot or episode or theme have had such appeal that they have been so readily reused. And to present a collection of *American* traditional narratives is to raise questions about how and what such stories tell Americans about themselves.

Although folktales and legends are both important genres of orally told narrative, in many ways they are decidedly different. As folklorists use the term, folktales are fictional stories; that is, they are regarded as fictions by those who tell and listen to them. They are the folk equivalents of novels and short stories, though as a group they may range from long, episodic, "classic" fairytales to shorter, simpler humorous stories to "formula" tales like story 88 ("Johnny-Cake") in this volume in which the same language is repeated with additions or in which an endless loop of narrative is created.[4]

Legends, on the other hand, are "true" narratives; that is, they are regarded by their tellers and listeners as recounting events that actually took place, although to say so is an oversimplification. The folklorist Robert Georges, among others, has questioned whether legends were always regarded as true or whether they were even necessarily always narrative, and in doing so he called attention to some of the complexities of legend as a type of folklore.[5] But to say that legends are orally told "true" stories is a reasonable starting-point characterization of the genre. Legends are historical accounts (such as the account of Daniel Boone's encounters with Indians, story 219); or they are sorts of news accounts (as with "contemporary" or "urban" legends in which, for example, it is asserted that a madman with a hook arm recently attacked parked teenagers somewhere nearby; see story 284); or they are attempts to discuss human interactions with other worlds, whether in the present day or in the past (as in the ghost stories included in this volume, stories 116 to 146, the large number of which attests to the widespread diffusion of ghost legends in American culture).

However, in the social contexts in which legends are told, attitudes toward the veracity of any given narrative may differ; some people may accept its truth, others may deny it, still others may keep an open mind but not commit themselves. Legends are not necessarily told as chronological stories or by a single narrator. They may be told collectively and haphazardly, with a number of people contributing bits and pieces.[6] In some cases, the "legend" may be no more than the belief or the statement that something happened (such as that doomed lovers leaped from a certain cliff). Thus traditional storytellers may regard legends as much less artful than fictional tales, may see them merely as matter-of-fact recollections of local happenings (and, indeed, the dividing line between legend and rumor cannot always be sharply drawn).

Despite their differences, folktales and legends are both key modes of oral storytelling and hence the focus of this volume. Both genres are central to American traditions of oral narrative, and the selections in this volume allow for an overview of the component parts of these traditions. Other genres, such as the joke, the historical anecdote, and the personal narrative, are not included here, although certainly some of the Native American and Native Hawaiian narratives are myths or border on the mythic, and a few stories may border on falling into other categories.

Given the multicultural character of the United States, the nation's web of narrative is also culturally diverse, drawing upon Native American, African, European, Asian, and trans-Pacific strands. Indeed, several traditions of storytelling, like much else, merge in America, although the extent to which distinct cultural traditions of story in America have influenced and borrowed from each other is complex and often difficult to ascertain.

To speak of "American stories" at all and to include in that category whatever stories have been told within the confines of the United States (the criteria for inclusion in this volume) is of course to draw artificial boundaries. Certainly many of the English-language folktales collected by American folklorists over the years have clear Old World antecedents, while the tales of French Louisiana and French Missouri or of the Hispanic Southwest also have much in common with those of, respectively, French Canada and Mexico. Yet in many ways, the tales found in America form a sort of American "canon" despite pronounced cultural differences of origin or of group. In complex ways, they constitute a national heritage in that they are attempts by Americans to consider the nature of their world through narrative.

Although it is difficult at best to date oral traditions, most **Native American stories** (and out in the fiftieth state, Native Hawaiian stories) obviously predate African- or European-derived stories at least in terms of their presence on American soil. Certainly some Native American oral narratives can be determined to be very ancient indeed. "Stealing Fire" (story 2), for example, is a story with worldwide distribution, suggesting that it came across the Bering Strait from the Eurasian land mass with early migrations into North America. And as early as the 1630s, Jesuit missionaries were recording Indian narratives such as "The Sun Snarer" (not included in this book), in which the hero temporarily captures the sun with a thread made from his sister's pubic hair, so certainly there were well-developed groups of Native American stories in the seventeenth century beginning to be known to Europeans.

A vast number of Native American stories have, in fact, been collected—that is, written down and often published—by anthropologists, folklorists, and others. The *Journal of American Folklore,* which began publication in 1888, is full of Native American materials, published especially during the years when pioneer anthropologist Franz Boas was its editor, though much material had been published even earlier. In 1879, the Bureau of American Ethnology was founded by the federal government to study American Indians, and its publications also include many tale texts. Stith Thompson, a great scholar of Indo-European folktales, would later say that "both in respect to the faithfulness of recording and to the relative number of texts available to the student, we are better prepared for a study of the North American Indian tale than for even those of Europe and the Near East."[7]

Yet despite Thompson's optimism about their study, Native American narratives can be difficult for non–Native Americans to come to terms with. Karl Kroeber, a professor of English whose parents both contributed mightily to our knowledge of Native American narratives and cultures, writes that in teaching about Indian stories, he has found "that most people familiar only with Western writing are baffled by traditional Indian narratives. . . . [T]heir strangeness is frustrating to readers."[8] The stories may seem to work from worldviews and conceptions quite puzzling to those outside Native cultures. The tale characters called "tricksters," for example—Coyote is probably the best known, though tricksters go by many other names—startlingly combine bumbling foolishness with great supernatural power. They may bring terrible calamity upon themselves and others, yet create important parts of existence, and such juxtaposition may be difficult for readers with a background in Euro-American culture to comprehend. The circumstances in which characters in a tale violate proper standards of behavior may be difficult to understand, as may be the seemingly thin dividing line between animal and human actors. Non–Native American readers may misunderstand other elements. For example, the interest shown in Native American stories in the origins of customs of physical features may seem to represent a childish attempt to explain cosmology when in fact it is an effort to re-enact in story some reality that is recognized as a part of existence. To complicate matters, Native American narratives do not fit neatly into the categories conveniently used by folklorists to classify Indo-European stories—myth, legend, folktale, jocular tale, fable—but often seem to spill across such boundaries.

Yet Native American narratives such as those included in this volume can be greatly enjoyed and appreciated by the rest of us. We can, of course, even when we find them puzzling and do not understand the cultural contexts out of which they come, enjoy their elements of adventure, fantasy, conflict, and humor. But beyond that, literary critics, folklorists, and anthropologists have begun to look at Native American narratives and to attempt explication of their meanings for the rest of us; they have, in fact, commented on several of the narratives in this volume.

For example, the Lakota Sioux story "Stone Boy" (story 5) has been discussed by Elaine Jahner, who also provided the translation given here. In this story, the action moves the characters from vulnerability and incompleteness (brothers who lack a sister and in their need let a monstrous, threatening woman into their lives) to the creation of a stable social unit (the strong structures built by Stone Boy and his uncles that thwart the buffalo attack suggest social durability, as does the name and manner of birth of Stone Boy himself). In the end, the brothers (Stone Boy's uncles) have their sister and powerful nephew as well as Buffalo wives and a culture (signified by the magic Stone Boy receives to rescue and restore the uncles to life). Their situation may still be vulnerable (the buffalo attack "when the yellow clouds are here above us"—that is, during winter storms when the group is most exposed), but the story dramatizes the strength that comes from social coherence as well as from the prowess of a hero.[9]

"Coyote and the Shadow People" (story 8) is a tale in which a husband goes to the land of the dead to bring back his deceased wife, like in the Greek myth of Orpheus. But here the husband is Coyote, whose inability to control his own impulses is the essence of his character in countless tales. He is told that to successfully retrieve his wife he must follow certain injunctions, and that Coyote is who he is foreshadows his ultimate failure when he impulsively violates an injunction and loses the wife he thinks he has regained. The story reminds listeners of the truth that they are mortal and fallible. In other stories, Coyote thinks he can do things merely by imitating some ritual or formula, and so he does here. His failure is a reminder that he is often ridiculous (and not to be emulated). Yet we can also see in his action the heroism and devotion of a husband who loves his wife, however futile his effort to find her.[10]

In the Navajo story here called "Coyote's Eyes" (story 7), Coyote performs his usual role of someone whose actions are inappropriate. He wants to be able to see like birds, though of course he is not a bird. He oversteps his proper boundaries and disaster ensues. The listener is given a message about behavior appropriate to one's nature. The story does "explain" why Coyote has yellow eyes, but the explanation is just a reminder about how impulsive Coyote is.

Such insights into Native American narratives are helpful to the rest of us and may help us to think about possible meanings for other tales (though always cultural context is important). Barre Toelken, who collected "Coyote's Eyes" from his friend Yellowman, suggests that we see Native American stories as meant to embody or dramatize something.[11] The trickster's attempting to do things beyond his own nature dramatizes for humans the truth that they must not try to exceed their own capacity.

Toelken's use of the concept of dramatization also calls our attention to the fact that the actual telling of Native American stories is often rather dramalike. The many volumes that print "texts" of these stories present them conventionally as "prose" pieces. In fact, in the actual telling, they often are more like poetry in terms of language use and like drama in terms of structure. Beginning in the 1970s, anthropologist Dennis Tedlock led a movement toward presenting Native tales in new, more poetic ways, and several of the texts in this volume (such as story 14, "The First Meeting of the Indians and the Europeans") reflect the influence of that movement.

Native Hawaiian narratives, several of which are also included in this volume because they have an importance in the cultural makeup of one American region, parallel Native American stories in that they too represent a body of material predating a Euro-American presence. However, Euro-American contact with Native Hawaiians was historically more limited than with Native Americans, and though Hawaiian narratives have many relations with those of greater Polynesia and the Pacific, they never stretched across the American continent as Native American tales did. Indeed, the store of recorded Hawaiian stories is much less extensive. Literacy and print were introduced very aggressively to Hawaii by the nineteenth-century

American missionaries who colonized the islands, and traditional Hawaiian culture suffered as a result. Nonetheless, beginning in the 1860s, attempts were made to record Native oral narratives, and there are published versions of many (though in many cases these are presented in rather literary styles). Native Hawaiian narratives include many historical legends of kings and chieftains (such as story 15, "A Story of Kamahemeha I"), as well as mythological stories. Legends of the volcano goddess Pele constitute one popular cycle. Many Pele legends involve retribution visited by the goddess upon those who offend her, whether by boasting (story 16, "Ke-lii-kuku"), by slighting her (story 17, "Pele and Kahawali," in which she is mistaken to be an easily ignored local woman), or in other ways. Pele's cultural vitality can be seen in that in recent years she has become a character in Hawaiian versions of the contemporary legend of "The Vanishing Hitchhiker" and in the lore told to tourists that Pele punishes those who attempt to take away local rocks as souvenirs.

Although there has been considerable interest in collecting and publishing Native American oral narratives over a long period of years, the recording and publication of **folktales told by European Americans** got off to a slower start and has had a more erratic history. We can surmise that tale-telling was a popular form of entertainment from colonial times. In 1824, a certain Reverend Joseph Dodderidge, looking back on his childhood in the 1760s, remembered the popularity of "dramatic narrations, chiefly concerning Jack and the Giant," stories that were "lengthy, and embraced a considerable range of incident."[12] Eighteenth- and nineteenth-century almanacs also include a broad selection of jokes and humorous tales suggestive of their popularity in oral circulation. And in the nineteenth century, folktales got into print for other reasons. The humorists who produced the pre–Civil War comic literature of the frontier of the "Old Southwest" drew extensively on orally told tales. For example, Harden Taliaferro's *Fisher's River (North Carolina) Scenes and Characters,* published in 1859, uses traditional folktales in a number of its sketches, including story 28, "The Pretended Corpse," in this volume. Also in this volume, story 40, "The Boat That Went on Land and Sea," appeared in Creole in a Louisiana French newspaper in 1878; story 42, "Nor'west Wind and Jack," comes from a Texas manuscript of stories told in the 1850s; and several others come from other nineteenth-century newspapers or from early issues of the *Journal of American Folklore.*[13]

Nonetheless, interest in extensively collecting Euro-American folktales—especially magic tales, as folklorists often call oral fairytales—for a long time was limited. Perhaps this was because the great influence of the Grimm Brothers' famous collection made such tales seem so thoroughly European, or because American collectors placed such great emphasis on collecting ballads—narrative folksongs—especially after the pioneering expeditions of the English collector Cecil Sharpe in the Southern mountains. Or it may be that because by the time folklore collectors started to seek out oral lore, magic tales had become a form primarily

told to children and thus may have been too associated with intimate domestic set-
tings to be readily shared.

It was not until the 1920s that a sizeable group of Anglo-American magic tales
appeared in print, collected by a sociologist named Isabel Gordon Carter from the
narrator Jane Gentry in the mountains of North Carolina. Several of Gentry's tales
are included in this volume, including story 25, "Jack and the Fox," and story 29,
"Old Foster." As early as 1912, Emelyn Elizabeth Gardner was collecting folklore,
including märchen (a German term folklorists have used to mean magic tales),
in upstate New York. In 1926, Marie Campbell, working as a teacher in a then-
remote part of Kentucky, began to collect folklore, including a large store of folktales (including story 37, "The Girl That Weren't Ashamed to Own Her Kin"). In
the 1930s, the Federal Writers' Project sponsored folklore-collecting projects that
gathered some magic tales (such as those collected in Virginia, notably by James
Taylor Arms, including story 112, "The Longest Tale"), and in the spring of 1939,
Herbert Halpert actually took recording equipment through a number of Southern
states to record folklore. Traveling in a converted ambulance in Tennessee, he
managed to record magic tales told by Samuel Harmon and his daughter, as well
as other narratives.[14]

Richard Chase, however, really brought American magic tales to wide public
awareness. Alabama-born, Harvard-educated Chase did this in 1943 by the publication of his book, *The Jack Tales*. This book, produced by a prominent commercial
publisher, received wide attention.[15] Chase had evidently stumbled upon the existence of the trove of tales he would tap into after meeting tale-teller Marshall Ward
at a conference for teachers in North Carolina. Ward directed him to members of
his own family who told traditional tales, Chase found other narrators as well both
in North Carolina and Virginia, and *The Jack Tales* was the eventual result of his
labors. Many of the informants were in fact related to Carter's and Halpert's informants, a large extended family (usually called the Hicks-Harmon family) whose
members have been particularly devoted to preserving traditional tale-telling, even
to the present day.

Chase not only had popular success but also initially found some favor with
folklore scholars, although more recently they have been highly critical of his work.
He has been accused of misappropriating stories he was told (or sometimes given in
manuscript), and indeed he seems to have become unpopular in the area of North
Carolina where he settled, in fact being pressured to leave. Beyond that, however, he
extensively reworked the stories, often creating composite versions from the several
he had been told, shaping his versions according to his own style and perspectives
rather than that of the actual narrators. Hence the extent to which his tales (such
as story 31, "Mutsmag") actually reflect the narrative traditions of his informants
is at best unclear.

Chase did have a powerful impact on making widely known the existence of
vital traditions of märchen-telling in the United States. Others were to come along

to more carefully record and examine the Southern mountain folktale and its tellers. Vance Randolph had visited the Ozark Mountains in the first decade of the twentieth century, lived there for much of his life, and first collected folktales there in 1920, although his book-length collections with scholarly notes were not published by Columbia University Press until the 1950s. Leonard Roberts was a teacher in Berea, Kentucky, in the 1950s when a student from the hill country led him to his tale-telling family; later, teachers who came to Roberts's folklore courses at Union College pointed him toward other local narrators. Maud Long, another member of the Hicks-Harmon family, recorded tales for the Library of Congress that were released as long-playing records in 1955. Marie Campbell, who had been collecting Kentucky folktales since the 1920s, published her tales in 1958. In 1987, Charles L. Perdue published a volume of tales that had been collected by the Federal Writers' Project in Virginia, including some that had been used by Richard Chase. Most recently, Carl Lindahl has been not only collecting stories but also unearthing many recorded decades ago and archived in the Library of Congress, including some by Herbert Halpert (who himself collected extensively, particularly in the New Jersey Pine Barrens and Newfoundland).[16]

Folklorists have also begun to consider the meaning and significance of American magic tales, although their attention has been focused on the Southern mountain tales and particularly on what has come to be known as the Jack tale. That term was probably little known until Chase used it as the title of his book, and what the term actually means is debatable. Chase seems to have seen his stories as constituting a unified cycle, like medieval narrative cycles, but *Jack tale* may be used as loosely as to mean virtually any folktale with a main character called Jack. In general, it refers to a hero tale with a young male protagonist, usually though not always called Jack, who ventures out into the world, has adventures, and finds some form of success.

Why the Jack tale should have taken such a central position is an interesting question. In part it was because Chase called so much attention to the genre with the title of his collection. In addition, however, the figure of an often unpromising young hero who makes his way in the world and overcomes adversity may have particular appeal to American values and sensibility. But, as the tales in this volume make clear, there certainly is a much broader spectrum of traditional magic tales (as well as other stories) than is represented by the Jack tales alone. The venturesome male Jack is an interesting American hero, but what of the many brave and resourceful women who are protagonists in American magic tales?

The differences between European tales and their American variants can be instructive in considering the meanings of Euro-American tales. Looking primarily at Jack tales, Carl Lindahl has noted differences in certain elements in British and American stories that may be instructive. Whereas in British tales the hero often gets magical help, in American tales it is Jack's opponents who wield the magical powers. Whereas in British tales the "donor" who helps Jack is a magical being such as a dwarf, in American tales he is more likely to be "a rich landed man" with whom Jack enters into a sort of alliance. The first of these traits might be read as expressing a faith in the abilities of the ordinary "can-do" person to succeed, without magic and in fact in the face of it. The second trait might be seen as expressing an American social solidarity across class lines and a willingness of the rich to cooperate with and even instruct others as they work toward success.[17]

And, although most recent interest from folklorists in American magic tales has been in Anglo-American materials, notably those of the Southern mountains, a significant number of tales have been collected from other Euro-American traditions, particularly Spanish and French ones. As early as 1911, Aurelio M. Espinosa published New Mexican Spanish folktales in the *Journal of American Folklore* (he had published New Mexican legends the year before).[18] Others, including his son José Manuel Espinosa and his student Juan B. Rael, followed his lead in collecting Hispanic tales, many of which have appeared in folklore journals and books.[19] Alcée Fortier published a collection of Louisiana French tales as early as in 1895, and other collectors subsequently undertook the recording of Franco-American oral narratives, in Missouri as well as Louisiana.[20] The work of these collectors suggests that there are many talented American tellers of folktales who represent rich traditions from a number of European cultures. In the 1940s and 1950s, college professor Ruth Ann Musick was able to record tales exclusively from West Virginia miners whose ancestors had peopled a number of European countries.[21] The present volume includes folktales and legends told by Irish, Polish, German, Italian, and Armenian American narrators as well as by those from Hispanic, Franco-American, and other groups. Like much of the rest of American society and American folklore, American tale-telling traditions are decidedly multicultural.

Of course, magic tales constitute only one type (though a rather varied and broad type) of Euro-American tale. Animal tales, for example—stories in which the characters are animals but behave in effect as human beings—have been popular with American narrators. Although such stories have important European antecedents, they have been particularly noticed in African American tradition.

Humorous folktales, usually fairly short ones, also abound in both Euro-American and African American tradition. Folklore scholars had long thought that in American tradition, short, humorous tales were far more numerous than other kinds of folktales. This was borne out by the systematic study of Ernest Baughman, who examined a vast number of English and American stories.[22] He examined motifs (component parts of tales, which scholars have isolated and classified) and found that American tales had more humorous motifs than English tales had motifs of any kind, suggesting an American preponderance for the humorous in storytelling. Indeed, magic tales may have humorous elements, and some in their American redactions have in effect been made over into largely humorous narratives. But in addition, there is an abundance of funny tales that satirize lawyers or preachers or spouses, glorify clever tricks, or poke fun at stubbornness or greed or easy virtue.

For example, Story 75, "A Death Bed Scene," punctures the avariciousness of both attorneys and priests; story 69, "Singing Her Warning," skirts the troubles of an unfaithful spouse; story 62, "The Tricky Yankee," plays with the nineteenth-century image of the Yankee peddler as a sharpster well able to part the locals from their worldly goods. Besides the obvious production of laughter, some of these stories may express a kind of American egalitarianism in which community notables like lawyers and ministers are brought down to earth. Those in which tricksters triumph suggest an American admiration for those who can get ahead by using their wits, even if they take some advantage of others in so doing.

But perhaps the type of folktale most central to American narrative tradition, at least in some respects, is the tall tale, also called the lie or the windy and by other names. Carl Lindahl says that this subgenre perhaps "can claim the title of America's definitive folktale,"[23] and it has been extremely popular in the United States, predominantly in rural areas and on the frontier.[24]

A tall tale often begins realistically and moves toward ever greater fantasies: large numbers of animals slain with a single shot, mosquitoes who carry off people, speech that freezes and thaws. In the actual telling, a windy is likely to be narrated in a deadpan manner, the teller seeming to present it as serious truth; commonly, although not always, it is told in the first person, the narrator presenting it as personal experience, lending it eyewitness veracity.[25] Hence there is a practical-joke aspect to the relating of these stories, the teller attempting to put one over on the listener. In part, they may appeal to the American fascination with con men and the clever con, for the teller becomes a trickster trying to fool his audience. Tall tales may in particular be tried on outsiders to a local community—the tourist to a rural area, the Easterner "dude" on the Western frontier—and such stories became incorporated into the antebellum frontier humor writing in which frontiersmen often tried to "fetch" (that is, deceive) genteel travelers.[26] Local listeners may well understand the dynamic of the situation, and some may delight in coming back with other, equally outrageous stories of their own. The great popularity of the tall tale in America may derive from some sense that America itself is a place of fantastic things or from a cultural appreciation for the cleverness that tricking someone represents.

Euro-American and **African American** narrative traditions are very much intertwined. African American servants told stories to Whites, but doubtlessly Blacks heard White storytellers as well. Beyond that, there was to some degree an Old World stock of stories shared by Europe and Africa in ways that are still little understood. The stories brought by European colonizers and African slaves to America may have been in many ways different but there were still common threads. Certainly one should not draw sharp boundaries between the stories told by Blacks and Whites in the United States, and in this volume they are mixed together, organized thematically and generically, not according to their ethnic origins.[27]

Nonetheless, distinctively African American traditions of storytelling and story types have circulated largely within Black communities. Although animal stories are well known in Europe, for example, animal stories in America have been particularly popular with African Americans. Indeed, animal trickster figures—particularly well known because of widespread publication of the Brer Rabbit stories—have been recorded in great numbers from African American narrators. This profusion of stories with animal characters may reflect the heritage of African narrative in which animal characters have important roles or may reflect that animal stories could be adapted by slaves to express disguised social criticism of Whites. It may also reflect the interests and expectations of those mostly White collectors who recorded the tales. Because of the influence of the Uncle Remus books by Joel Chandler Harris (1848?–1908), American readers came to think of animal stories, and particularly animal trickster stories, as a defining element of Black folklore. These stories were found to be particularly charming by readers, though they may also have reinforced conscious or unconscious racist stereotypes of Blacks as child-like purveyors of tales about cute little animals (or perhaps even stereotypes of Blacks as beasts themselves).[28]

If the collecting of Euro-American folktales got off to rather slow beginnings, the collecting of African American folk stories had more of a jumpstart through the early popularity of Harris's Uncle Remus books. An Atlanta newspaperman for much of his life, Harris began publishing in the Atlanta *Constitution* a series of humorous sketches in which the character Uncle Remus, the wise and kindly elderly Black man, developed. At one point, Uncle Remus began telling stories to the son of the owners of the plantation where he lived, and these popular sketches were collected in book form in 1880 as *Uncle Remus: His Songs and Sayings*.[29] Harris used stories he recollected having heard on a Georgia plantation during his own youth. Extremely popular as a fictitious storyteller, Uncle Remus reappeared in other books, and Harris started a periodical called *Uncle Remus' Magazine* in 1906. The name Uncle Remus was at one point trademarked by Harris's publishers, and much later Walt Disney, who said that the Uncle Remus stories were "familiar . . . since boyhood,"[30] produced a popular movie, *Song of the South* (1946), in which the stories became animated cartoons.

Harris re-created the Uncle Remus stories as part of a literary endeavor, so he was not exactly a folklore collector (though he did belong to the American Folklore Society and was cognizant of the work and ideas of folklorists). But he did stimulate others to record African American folklore. In the first issue of the *Journal of American Folklore*, the editor, William Wells Newell, also urged the collecting of "Lore of Negroes in the Southern States."[31] The texts of African American tales began to appear in its pages but also in more mainstream periodicals like the *Atlantic Monthly* and in a number of books assembled by emulators of Harris. In the 1890s, there was a folklore society at historically Black Hampton Institute; students collected stories that were published in the *Journal of American Folklore* and the *Southern Workman*.[32]

Part of the appeal of these stories, at least for Whites, lay in the popularity of reading literature that used dialect, for the tales almost invariably were published in what has been called "Remus dialect," an attempt to approximate on the page Negro language and speech patterns. This practice makes the stories problematic, indeed often impenetrable, for twenty-first-century readers, who are apt to find such dialectical renderings unreadable or patronizing. Nor were attempts to use dialect informed by a desire to provide linguistically accurate renderings through careful phonetic transcription. Rather they were merely a stab at approximating "how Negroes talk" in the service of providing something colorful and amusing. In trying to render nonstandard speech, dialect implies difference from educated, proper speech and hence social inferiority, though some of those folklore collectors who employed it surely meant only to suggest the social realities of speech and culture. Certainly, Black collectors such as J. Mason Brewer and the celebrated Zora Neale Hurston also use dialectical renderings of spoken language in their published work.

A central issue for African American tales is their origins and whether they stem from African or other sources. Early collectors assumed that the stories, with their many animal characters such as Brer Rabbit and Brer Fox, had an ultimate African provenance. In the 1930s and 1940s, anthropologist Melville J. Herskovits and his disciples intensively investigated African American and African cultures to stress both the connections that Black American culture, including stories, had to African antecedents and, in the face of stereotypes that cast Africa as a place only of savagery and backwardness, the high degree of African civilization. Prominent collectors such as Elsie Clews Parsons worked from the idea of African origins. Then, in the 1950s, Richard M. Dorson energetically collected African American folktales both in the South and in Michigan and in analyzing his own materials began to question whether these stories went back to the West Africa from which American slaves had come.

Dorson was devoted to the type and motif indexes that scholars have compiled to catalog types of folk stories and individual elements in these stories, indexes that referenced particular regions. When he examined his own stories in terms of the indexes, he found that his tales traced back not simply to African sources (though the African indexes were and continue to be underdeveloped at best). In essence, he argued that the oral stories of New World Blacks do "not indeed come from any one place but from a number of dispersal points" and that these "story stocks draw from multiple sources," but he certainly called into question the widely accepted Africanness of American Black narrative.[33] His contentions were challenged by anthropologist William Bascom, who spent years studying the African origins of such stories as those represented by story 86, "Talking Turtle," in this volume.[34] Ultimately, we must conclude that the cultural history of Black American folk stories is still incompletely understood and certainly complex and that there has been a great intermixing of narrative traditions among American ethnic groups.[35]

Whatever the origins of particular African American tales, we can certainly see something of why they developed in America as they did. It is easy to see, for example, how the animal stories so familiar from Harris's Brer Rabbit or the less well-known stories about the slave John and his master (such as story 64, "John, His Boss-Man, and the Catfish") could function to recommend certain behavior and help to insure survival under the very difficult conditions of slavery. Some stories, for example, reinforce the need to control what historian Lawrence Levine calls "undue pride and self-assertiveness," dangerous personality traits under an oppressive social system.[36] Abe, in story 67, "Abe and Dinah," gets himself into great trouble through arrogant self-confidence when he tries to take advantage of his master's property while the master is away, rejecting his wife Dinah's warnings that he is about to be found out; only Dinah's more prudent behavior prevents greater harm. "Talking Turtle," in story 86, makes the point that it might literally be very unwise for a slave to talk too much; powerful White people might hear things it was best they not know, with unfortunate consequences.

The plethora of tricksters, whether animal or human, points to a central need for powerless people in a system where they are controlled by the powerful: the need to live by wits and craftiness and guile to survive and get by. The trickster provides a model for survival strategies. John, in "John, His Boss-Man, and the Catfish," thinks fast and comes up with an explanation for his forbidden activity. Brer Rabbit, in story 63, "How Brer Rabbit Brought Dust Out of the Rock," gets the girl in the face of stronger rivals by his trick. In the famous tar baby story (so well known from Harris and from Disney's animated version, here represented by story 55, a field-collected version), Brer Rabbit, though caught by Brer Fox's trickery, manages to escape through greater cleverness of his own. Although animal stories are by no means the sum total of African American oral narrative, they have played a significant role in the African American past, and their meanings point to the seriousness of folk narrative as a guide for thought and behavior.

Legends are not limited to any particular American cultural, regional, or social group (though different groups may express quite different things through their legend telling), and the term *legend* covers a broad spectrum of narratives. Many legends are stories about the supernatural or supernormal—ghosts, witchcraft, magic, the inexplicable—and reflect human interest in (and anxieties about) other realities beyond the everyday world and the (sometimes thin) boundaries that separate us from them. Folklorists like the term *belief legend* for such stories. Another broad category of legendry is the *historical legend*, stories about noteworthy events and people, often local ones that have remained in memory. Thus legends in the case of belief legends may provide a discourse upon the "unknown," or in the case of historical legends, simply provide history (though not necessarily history as understood by historians). Those who tell belief legends may be believers or skeptics, may tell their tales with utter seriousness or inject broad notes of humor. Those who recount oral traditional history may tell variant accounts of the same events, either adding to or contradicting other accounts. And some legends do not fall neatly into the belief or historical category. "Urban" or contemporary legends seem more like news accounts, commenting on current situations and happenings.[37] A story such as "How Railroad Bill Chased Himself to His Girl's House" (story 258) tells us about a historical outlaw but gives him supernatural powers.

Whereas a folktale requires a certain level of oral artistry to work out plot and characters, legends may be told more casually, matter-of-factly, even haphazardly. As Jacob Grimm put it, "The folktale flies, the legend walks."[38] Sometimes a legend may be little more than a statement of fact, and contemporary legends may veer close to the realm of rumor. Nonetheless, legends are an important means of human expression and a significant form of narration. People use legends to talk about human relationships with mysterious, unseen, or even divine forces; to remember events that tie them in important ways to local contexts; or to examine what are perceived as threats to their existence, such as crime, the powers of nature, or people unlike themselves. Putting such things into narrative may make them easier to talk about, and legends may sometimes express themes not otherwise discussed or express fears and concerns that are otherwise unconscious. Families have their legends, which tell them in some way who they are through accounts of ancestral events and personalities, and ethnic or regional groups may have legends that somehow embody their senses of identity.

American legends have been collected for a long time. At the end of the nineteenth century, for example, Charles F. Skinner published thick, multivolume collections of legends that he in turn drew from earlier published sources,[39] and the *Journal of American Folklore* contains a variety of legends in earlier issues. The folklore collectors of the New Deal agency the Federal Writers' Project recorded legends in the 1930s.[40] The genre interested such folklorists as Richard Dorson, Archer Taylor, and William Hugh Jansen. But it was not until relatively recently that American folklorists began to look carefully at the characteristics and meanings of legends with the work of Jan Harold Brunvand, Bill Ellis, Janet Langlois, William Nicolaisen, Elizabeth Tucker, Sylvia Grider, and others, notably the very influential scholar Linda Dégh, who moved from Hungary in the 1960s to teach at Indiana University. In 1970, Wayland Hand organized a conference on the legend at the University of California–Los Angeles, and since that time folklorists in the United States have paid increasing attention to the genre and its significance and meanings, although as Dégh and James P. Leary have both argued, they have tended to show more interest in some types of legends than in others.[41]

Of course, as with folklore generally, the meanings of legends may vary from person to person and from situation to situation of their being told, so that understanding specific social contexts is important to understanding meaning. Nonetheless, we can often see what American legends are telling us and revealing about American ideas and concerns.

Take, for example, what have been called the legends of "Indian tragedies," a group that includes stories 214, "The Legend of Lover's Leap," 215, "The Legend of Turkey Hill," and 216, "The Annihilation of the Pascagoula." These are stories about how Indians perished or disappeared, usually before the coming of Europeans. These legends seem to have become popular among European Americans in the later nineteenth century, especially in parts of the nation where there was no longer a large or obvious Native American presence. No longer a threat to White settlement, Indians had become romantic figures. Yet it was understood by Whites that Native Americans had once been ubiquitous in the land. They were no longer there (at least not so far as most Whites noticed). But what had happened to these interesting, noble people? Of course, in historical reality, they had been defeated and pushed away and even exterminated by Euro-American advance. However, a more psychologically satisfying view was that they had somehow "vanished," and indeed the trope of the "vanishing red man"—the Indian who fades away—permeates nineteenth-century American art and popular literature. The "Indian tragedy" legends carry a similar perspective, suggesting that Native Americans were destroyed by forces for which Whites bear no responsibility: nature or their own violence or self-destructive customs.[42] Another type of legend very popular in the United States involves lost or buried treasure. The West is full of its lost mines and Spanish gold; the coastal areas of the Atlantic East and Gulf South have their many sites associated with pirate loot. Treasure legends may tell the story of a treasure's origins, but in particular they focus on attempts to recover the lost cache. That may reflect the American penchant for seeking wealth; we do, after all, admire those who have done something that makes them rich. However, what happens in most American treasure legends is that the lost loot is *not* found.[43] In "Bluebeard's Treasure" (story 236), the protagonist is too frightened to take away the loot. Jean Lafitte's Gulf Coast hoard, scuttled with his ship, is still looked for but has never been found (story 237, "Buried Treasure of Jean Lafitte"). Treasure often has guardian spirits who chase away searchers, whether the spirits are pigs ("Phantom Pigs Guard a Treasure," story 238) or mysterious, unseen "enemies" ("The Treasure of Cacapan," story 241). Larsen, in "Larsen's Vein" (story 240), can't find again the spot "or even the hill" where he once found gold encased in quartz.

The preponderance of failure to locate treasure in American legends (in contrast to those of, for example, Mexico, where the treasure is likely to be found) may seem puzzling. America is, after all, a nation that values the quest for wealth, and we like to imagine that those who strive are rewarded. But there are reasons the legends present the case as they do. Alan Dundes has suggested that because America is perceived as the land of opportunity, the treasure is not found because it must always be there for the next person, must provide perpetual opportunity.[44] It may be more likely that, as Patrick Mullen has said, the failure to find the gold offers a message about other American values, namely that wealth is the result of ingenuity and hard work, not something that can be attained simply by being found.[45] The legends stress the importance of the American work ethic over the quick, chance

efforts of mere fortune hunters. Those who would merely spend a little time looking for a sudden windfall will not succeed.

The legends that Americans of the twenty-first century are most likely to be
familiar with are the urban or contemporary legends (stories 284 to 296). Not only
do we hear them in circulation (or sometimes encounter them on the Internet,
where they have become a staple) but we have been made aware of them through
such films as *Urban Legend,* television documentaries, and books such as those
written by folklorist Jan Harold Brunvand.[46] These stories, which often have ironic
twists or tell of terrible things that befall someone (usually someone not far away
and to whom the teller may have a supposed connection), circulate widely in modern society. In urban legends, maniacs with hook arms threaten parked teenagers,
deadly snakes appear in department stores or at amusement parks, the bodies of
deceased relatives disappear with stolen cars. The appeal of such stories seems
widespread, and that fact certainly invites wondering about their meanings, for
surely they provide more than entertainment. Surely many of them provide a narrative discourse upon the things that worry and concern us today or even offer warnings about those aspects of modern life that are especially threatening. They speak,
for example, of the forces that may invade and imperil us, whether a burglar who
breaks into our home, as in "The Choking Doberman" (story 290), or "The Killer
in the Back Seat" (story 292), the criminal who slips into the rear seat of a woman's
car and tries to strangle her from behind.

Others of course may speak to more elemental fears. In the very well-known
story of "The Hook" (story 284), a teenaged couple barely escapes the depredations
of a maniacal killer with a hook arm when the girl of the couple insists on being
taken home from the lover's lane where they are parked for "making out." Linda
Dégh suggests that the story reflects a fear of the handicapped, the crippled. More
psychoanalytically oriented Alan Dundes offers an explanation that has the hook
arm as a phallus symbol; it represents not an external threat but, symbolically, the
threat posed by the sexual urges of the boy of the couple.[47]

Certainly many American urban legends have close ties to what are perceived
to be American social realities and our concerns about them. The well-known story
of the individual (usually a woman) who finds parts of a rat in the fried chicken
she has bought at a fast food joint (story 289, "The Fried Rat") may reflect our dis-
trust of the quality of fast food and of the giant corporations that sell it to us. Gary
Alan Fine has suggested that such legends may reflect what he calls the "Goliath
effect," the feeling that Americans have toward the large, dominating corporations
that seem to control important things in our lives and are accordingly mistrusted.[48]
Thus there are stories about contaminated products (not only the rat in the chicken
but worms in hamburgers, spider eggs in gum, and mice in soft drinks) and others
that contend a certain company is owned by evil forces such as a satanic cult. Other
legends may reflect other kinds of economic fears. A persistently told story about
a woman bitten by deadly snakes hidden in clothing imported from Asia reflects

anxiety about imported goods "poisoning" homegrown manufacturing and flooding our markets.

Urban legends, however, also provide the opportunity for seeing how different Americans may assign different meanings to the stories they tell and focus on different groups of stories. Fine and Patricia Turner have persuasively analyzed how Blacks and Whites shape their legends and rumors quite differently (they argue that urban legends and rumors are often closely related phenomena and that legends may be "solidified rumor"). They note, for example, that Whites may see corporations controlled by satanic cults, whereas Blacks will see the Ku Klux Klan as the evil controlling force. Whites have stories about Black gang members targeting and attacking Whites as group initiations, while Blacks tell of conspiracies to use Blacks in horrible medical experiments.[49] Legends certainly can be very revealing about cultural attitudes, though again, the complexity of American narrative must be taken into account in attempting to understand what stories mean to us. Those legends that deal with the supernatural and the supernormal may address more universal questions, as Linda Dégh suggests they do, about the order of the world: "If there are unknown forces, can they be identified, changed, avoided, or exploited to our benefit?"[50] But we still can consider how tales of the supernatural fit into American culture. For example, Yvonne Milspaw has noted differences between American and British witch legends and argues that Appalachian witch legends suggest the stories sometimes reveal that poor and powerless people, especially older women, may have used local beliefs about witches to give themselves an aura of power as a means of self-protection.[51] Such possibilities do at least raise questions about poverty and social status in America, and other legends of the supernatural may convey other truths about American society. Why do we love to hear about strange happenings even in our "postmodern" world? How is it that ghosts still haunt our houses and our consciousness?

In writing about a member of the noted Hicks-Harmon family of tale-tellers, one who achieved a measure of fame among those interested in storytelling, Robert Isbell notes: "Written words could never grasp the fidelity of Ray Hicks's narrative. . . . One must sit before him in his old parlor, hear the resonance in his speech, see the flame in his eyes, watch the impassioned gestures of his great hands."[52] Writing about **reproducing folk stories in writing**, the great Ozark collector Vance Randolph says: "Oral narratives are difficult to bring off [in writing] . . . because the timing is often fouled up in type; written sentences fail to reproduce the significant pauses and rhythms."[53]

Folklorists certainly have thought about how to better make the "translation" from the oral to print, especially as they have become increasingly aware that speaking folklore is a kind of performance, even if that does not always involve the theatricality we associate with that term. Early on, noted Texas folklorist J. Frank Dobie created fictional contexts in which tale-telling took place, and he remade his tales as literary recreations, an approach that has not found favor with many scholarly folklorists.[54] Randolph both used recording equipment borrowed from the Library of Congress and employed a stenographer to take tales down precisely in shorthand, yet he wound up deciding that "a literal rendering is less important in the case of folktales" than for other kinds of folklore.[55] Dennis Tedlock's moving from the old way of reproducing Native American narratives as blocks of prose to being more poetically rendered on the page and suggestive of the rhythms of actual speech is one solution to the problem. More recently, those interested in Jack tales have similarly tried to print stories in ways that reflect some of the rhythms and style of tale-telling.[56]

A printed tale can be enjoyed by the reading of it and as a cultural "artifact" from which we can learn about life and about society and its interests and concerns, and the tales contained in this volume constitute a record of a great American heritage. But we should keep in mind as we read a folk story that we are reading a descendant of a different experience, a shadow of a real narration by a living storyteller. A reader can pleasurably supplement the experience of reading tales with recordings and videos of traditional tale-tellers, although unfortunately there are relatively few.[57] Or we can turn to those narrators of the modern "revivalist" storytelling movement, which in part grew up as a response to the need for stories actually to be told and to provide more possibilities for the enjoyment of actually listening to tales.

Revivalist storytellers are those who came to telling stories not through their immersion in an older oral tradition of narration but through other means (for example, there is a long history of librarians telling stories). Often they are "professionals" in that they may undertake paid performances, and they may be active in the National Association for the Preservation and Perpetuation of Storytelling (NAPPS) and its annual National Storytelling Festival in Jonesborough, Tennessee.[58] (It is essential to remember, however, that professional storytellers who participate in what has been called this "storytelling revitalization movement" have styles, aesthetics, and influences quite different from those of traditional folk narrators and that they represent something quite different in terms of social and cultural history: more an interpretation of that history, less a continuity with it; more a wide constituency, less a local community.)[59]

Another way in which we can understand something about the living reality of folk storytelling and the dynamics of the oral tradition is to look briefly at a few of the **"master" narrators** from whom folklorists have collected tales. Historically, folklorists were more intensely interested in the tale than in the teller, often in fact recording little or no information on the people who gave them the stories that were published in journals or in books; it seems only right that America's traditional narrators be recognized as verbal artists and as guardians of cultural wealth that has come down to us because of their memories and their gifted speech, and that so far as is possible they be known as talented and significant individual contributors to the American cultural matrix. Fortunately, some folklorists have provided details about their valuable informants.

The collector Richard Dorson, for example, provided such information on the people he collected from, and he published information about some of the narrators whose tales he recorded, such individuals as John Blackamore, James Alley, Mary Richardson, Joe Woods, and J. D. Suggs.[60] African American narrator James Douglas Suggs (who told story 20, "Mr. Snake and the Farmer") obviously intrigued Dorson, and the folklorist collected about 175 tales from him (in addition to some songs). Suggs (1887–1955) had been born on a Mississippi plantation still owned by the same family that had once worked it with slaves who had stayed on as sharecroppers and tenants after the Civil War. A man of many trades in many places, he told Dorson that he had learned his tales from his father on the nights when they had nothing else to do; his father had learned the stories from *his* father and from others on the plantation. Clearly, J. D. Suggs liked to perform, and in 1907 he joined the cast of a minstrel show, traveling with over twenty other Black entertainers as far as the Dakotas. Later he entertained the wealthy Whites he served on their hunting trips in Arkansas. When Richard Dorson showed up at his door in Michigan in 1952 looking for stories, Suggs was able to more than oblige, telling stories for the collector sometimes literally from morning until midnight.

Another of Dorson's informants, in this case someone representing European tale-telling traditions and in fact born in Eastern Europe, was Joe Woods (who told story 30, "The Millman's Daughter"), whom Dorson found in the Upper Peninsula of Michigan in 1946. In Polish Galicia, Woods's father had been a bureaucrat, not a peasant, and Woods said that he first learned stories from a wandering beggar, Andrew Bakus, who had stopped at their house and told tales in exchange for food and a little money; young Joe was not supposed to even listen, but he heard the stories through a crack in the door. "I hear it once," he told Dorson, "and I remember it. I was hungry for stories." In the United States, he moved around, working in mines or in lumber camps or harvesting crops, and he apparently loved to "go see the country." At one mine, he reveled in having the "easy job" of telling the boss stories, and in lumber camps, he would tell stories at night and not finish a tale so that the next night his coworkers would ply him with cigarettes and chewing tobacco to finish. When Dorson met him, Joe Woods was "stocky, arthritic and cross-eyed" and no longer able to work, but he was still able to tell some remarkable magic tales in his Polish-accented English.[61]

Old World master narrators, especially male master narrators, have often been travelers, men who moved around often because of their occupations and who found audiences over a wide swath of countryside. Both J. D. Suggs and Joe Woods fit that mold. Although both had homes and families, at certain times in their lives, they moved around. The opposite seems true of some of the best American taletellers, however. The narrative tradition of the Hicks-Harmon family was preserved in part because it became the domestic tradition of family members settled across a relatively small area. And, in general, female narrators are less likely to roam and more likely to engage in domestic storytelling.

Jane Muncy Fugate (born 1938) is one of our most interesting storytellers, and though she eventually moved to Florida, she learned her stories and first exercised her verbal artistry in her small home community in the mountains of eastern Kentucky. In 1949, the collector Leonard Roberts, at the invitation of a local teacher, set up his equipment at the Hyden School in Leslie County to spend a day recording the students telling stories. Children are often not skilled raconteurs, and Roberts, though he thought some of his youthful narrators "excellent," was apologetic about using so many youthful informants.[62] But among those at the session was Jane Muncy, age 11, whose skill as a storyteller was already well developed. She told Roberts several tales that he included in his book *South from Hell-fer-Sartin*, tales that were recognized as well formed and well told. In 1955, Roberts returned to the area, encountered Jane, then 17, and recorded her (including story 43, "The King's Well") again.[63] That she told him different stories indicated that her repertoire of tales was not small.

Roberts published little information about her, but years later folklorist Carl Lindahl tracked her down in Florida, where she recorded tales for him and also an account of how she learned them. Her divorced father sent Jane to live with his mother, Sidney Farmer Muncy, whom Jane barely knew. Among the things that gave Jane great comfort during this difficult time was listening to her grandmother's stories, family histories as well as fictional tales. She particularly liked tales in which the youngest son triumphed. She would tell Lindahl: "The message to me was, you can be little, and you can be frail, and you can be the youngest, and you can be alone, but you can also be the smartest. And . . . you could be happy. You could be happy and you could be wise, and you can overcome. And so I thought of myself as that overcomer." She obtained a master's degree in social work, and in her therapy practice she sometimes used her stories to "help my clients see [themselves] through the words that are about something else, or someone else."[64] Her experiences with the comforting and healing powers of stories not only offer us a sense of one important way in which narratives function for individuals but may also explain something about her own storytelling skills; stories had power and were thus worth learning to tell well.

Abraham "Oregon" Smith (1796–1893) was a narrator whom no folklorist ever met, let alone collected from, but he made such an impact on the Indiana and Illinois communities where he lived that the man and his stories were remembered for many years after his demise. Although not a wanderer in the same sense as J. D. Suggs or Joe Woods, who worked as itinerant laborers, Smith lived in several places, including Bloomington, Indiana. Because Bloomington was later the home of the Indiana University folklore program, Smith became known to folklorists, and William Hugh Jansen, who had heard local stories about the man, wrote a dissertation about him.[65] A sojourn in Oregon in the 1850s and the fact that some of Smith's stories were about Oregon provided the origin of his nickname (though he was also known as Sassafras Smith, because he promoted remedies containing sassafras, and Lying Abe Smith because of his tall tales). In his later years, he would hold court at various locations in the towns where he lived, telling his stories, in particular tall tales. And although his stories that came down to later generations (stories 96, "The Peach Tree Deer," and 106, "Turnip and Kettle," for example) are told as third-person accounts, Smith clearly was, like many other tall-tale raconteurs, a Munchhausen, someone who cast himself as the hero of the fantastic adventures in the stories (a term taken from the famous German Baron Munchhausen, who did the same thing in his own stories) and told the stories as first-person events. That his stories were taken up by younger narrators and passed down for years testifies to his impact as a raconteur, and Smith is representative of the storytelling local character who could entrance with "lies" local audiences of "loafers" around the stove or cracker barrel of the general store. If he had not lived in a place where folklorists later came to be very active, he might have been forgotten, and no doubt many other folk narrators have been largely forgotten. We therefore have all the more reason to celebrate those whom we do know something about—Ray Hicks, Maud Long, Marshall Ward, Samuel and Alberta Harmon, John Darling, Mary Richardson, Sara Cleveland, Wilson "Ben Guiné" Mitchell, Enola Mathews, Bel Abbey, Clementina Todesco, Joshua Alley, and many others—whose artistry has been recorded and whose contributions to America's cultural heritage should be more widely recognized than it has been. The editor of this volume hopes that readers will use the stories printed here to discover or reacquaint themselves with these American tale tellers and the American traditions of oral narration. Those traditions constitute a form of vernacular expression that talks about—through story—a great variety of subjects, and ideas, and events, and personalities integral to America's past and present.

Notes

1. Richard M. Dorson, *American Folklore* (Chicago: University of Chicago Press, 1959), p. 245.

2. Mark Turner, *The Literary Mind* (New York and Oxford: Oxford University Press, 1996), p. 4.

3. Charlotte Linde, *Life Stories: The Creation of Coherence* (New York and Oxford: Oxford University Press, 1993), p. 67.

4. As though to complicate matters, folklorists sometimes have used the term folktale to encompass all oral prose narratives. This usage is no longer common, however.

5. Robert A. Georges, "The General Concept of Legend: Some Assumptions to Be Reexamined and Reassessed," in Wayland D. Hand, ed., *American Folk Legend: A Symposium* (Berkeley: University of California Press, 1971), pp. 1–19.

6. Linda Dégh and Andrew Vázsonyi provide an excellent example of these tendencies in legend-telling from Hungarian fieldwork, "Legend and Belief," in Dan Ben-Amos, ed., *Folklore Genres* (Austin: University of Texas Press, 1976), pp. 103–09.

7. Stith Thompson, *The Folktale* (New York: Holt, Rinehart and Winston, 1946), p. 299.

8. Karl Kroeber, "An Introduction to the Art of Traditional American Indian Storytelling," in Karl Kroeber, ed., *Traditional Literatures of the American Indian: Texts and Interpretations* (Lincoln: University of Nebraska Press, 1997), p. 1. Richard Erdoes and Alfonso Ortiz, eds., *American Indian Myths and Legends* (New York: Pantheon, 1984), p. xii, add: "To those used to the pattern of European fairy tales and folktales Indian legends often seem chaotic, inconsistent or incomplete. Plots seem to travel at their own speed, defying conventions and at times doing away completely with recognizable beginnings and endings." (Kroeber's father was the anthropologist Alfred Kroeber, and his mother was Theodora Kroeber, author of the widely read *Ishi in Two Worlds*.)

9. Elaine Jahner, "Stone Boy: Persistent Hero," in Brian Swann, ed., *Smoothing the Ground: Essays in Native American Oral Literature* (Berkeley: University of California Press, 1983), pp. 71–186.

10. Jarold Ramsey, *Reading the Fire: Essays in the Traditional Indian Literatures of the Far West* (Lincoln: University of Nebraska Press, 1983), pp. 47–59.

11. Barre Toelken, *The Anguish of Snails: Native American Folklore in the West* (Logan: Utah State University Press, 2003) discusses Native American narratives as dramatizing cultural elements, pp. 110ff; "Coyote's Eyes" is discussed, pp. 133–35.

12. Quoted by Charles L. Perdue Jr., *Outwitting the Devil: Jack Tales from Wise County Virginia* (Santa Fe: Ancient City Press, 1987), p. 97.

13. Such as story 51, "The Bride of the Evil One." Story 36, "The Talking Eggs," is from an American Folklore Society monograph, Alcée Fortier's *Louisiana Folk-Tales,* although Fortier collected primarily from Creole-speaking African Americans.

14. Isabel Gordon Carter, "Mountain White Folk-Lore: Tales from the Southern Blue Ridge," *Journal of American Folklore* 38 (1925): 340–74; Emelyn Elizabeth Gardner, *Folklore from the Schoharie Hills, New York* (Ann Arbor: University of Michigan Press, 1937); Marie Campbell published her tales much later, *Tales from the Cloud Walking Country* (Bloomington: Indiana University Press, 1958) with illustrations by the noted artist Claire Leighton; Perdue publishes tales from the Virginia WPA project; for Harmon's tales and some information on Halpert's collecting, see Carl Lindahl, ed., *American Folktales from the Collection of the Library of Congress,* 2 vols. (Armonk, NY, and Washington: M.E. Sharpe and the Library of Congress, 2004), I: 7ff.

15. Richard Chase, *The Jack Tales* (Cambridge: Houghton Mifflin, 1943).

16. For information on the work of some of these collectors, see n. 14; works by Randolph and Roberts are discussed below; for Long's recordings, see n. 57.

17. Carl Lindahl, "Introduction; Jacks: The Name, the Tales, the American Tradition," in William Bernard McCarthy, ed., *Jack in Two Worlds: Contemporary North American Tales and Their Tellers* (Chapel Hill: University of North Carolina Press, 1994), pp. xxvi ff; see also Kevin J. Hayes, *Folklore and Book Culture* (Knoxville: University of Tennessee Press, 1997), pp. 67ff.

18. Aurelio M. Espinosa, "New-Mexican Spanish Folk-Lore, III, Folk-Tales," *Journal of American Folklore* 24 (1911): 397–444.

19. José Manuel Espinosa, *Spanish Folk-Tales from New Mexico* (New York: American Folklore Society, 1937); Juan B. Rael, *Cuentos españoles de Colorado y Nuevo Méjico* (Stanford, CA: Stanford University Press, 1957). Américo Paredes, ed. and trans., *Folktales of Mexico,* foreword Richard M. Dorson (Chicago: University of Chicago Press, 1970), is a monumental collection of tales that includes stories collected from Mexicans in the United States.

20. Alcée Fortier, *Louisiana Folktales in French Dialect and English Translation* (Boston: Houghton Mifflin, 1895); Joseph Médard Carrière, *Tales from the French Folklore of Missouri* (Evanston: Northwestern University Press, 1937); Corinne Saucier, *Folktales from French Louisiana* (New York: Exposition, 1962); Calvin Claudel, *Fools and Rascals: Louisiana Folktales* (Baton Rouge: Legacy, 1978); Barry Jean Ancelet, *Cajun and Creole Folktales: The French Oral Tradition of South Louisiana* (New York: Garland, 1994).

21. Ruth Ann Musick, *Green Hills of Magic: West Virginia Folktales from Europe* (Lexington: University Press of Kentucky, 1970).

22. Ernest W. Baughman, *Type and Motif Index of the Folktales of England and North America* (The Hague: Mouton, Indiana University Folklore Series 20, 1966).

23. Lindahl, *Folktales from the Collections of the Library of Congress,* I: lx.

24. Baughman, p. xvii, calls the tall tale "an overwhelmingly American form." He found 3,710 examples in American printed sources, only 29 in English sources.

25. Carolyn S. Brown, *The Tall Tale in American Folklore and Literature* (Knoxville: University of Tennessee Press, 1987), pp. 1–2, offers the observation that "the tall tale is a comic fiction disguised as fact, deliberately exaggerated to the limits of credibility or beyond."

26. Vance Randolph, *We Always Lie to Strangers: Tall Tales from the Ozarks* (New York: Columbia University Press, 1951), pp. 3–13, provides an informal and illuminating description of the tall tale contexts of the Ozarks. The importance of "fetching" in frontier humor is noted by James H. Justus, *Fetching the Old Southwest: Humorous Writing from Longstreet to Twain* (Columbia: University of Missouri Press, 2004).

27. Several of the magic tales in this volume, such as story 51, "The Bride of the Evil One," and story 36, "The Talking Eggs," were told by African American narrators, the American märchen being by no means a purely Euro-American phenomenon.

28. Certainly African American animal stories are not relics from the nineteenth century, and narrators have continued to tell them, as such twentieth-century collections as Richard M. Dorson, ed., *American Negro Folktales* (Greenwich, CT: Fawcett, 1967), and Daryl Cumber Dance, ed., *Shuckin' and Jivin': Folklore from Contemporary Black Americans* (Bloomington: Indiana University Press, 1978) attest. In some cases, the stories have been updated, Brer Rabbit taking on more assertive characteristics in line with changing Black attitudes.

29. Joel Chandler Harris, *Uncle Remus: His Songs and Sayings; The Folk-Lore of the Old Plantation* (New York: D. Appleton, 1880).

30. "Walt Disney on the Appeal of the Theme," © 1946 by RKO Radio Pictures, Inc. *Song of the South* Web site, http://www.songofthesouth.net/movie/background/index.html.

31. "On the Field and Work of a Journal of American Folklore," *Journal of American Folklore* 1 (1888): 3.

32. See Donald J. Waters, ed., *Strange Ways and Sweet Dreams: Afro-American Folklore from the Hampton Institute* (Boston: G. K. Hall, 1983).

33. Dorson, *American Negro Folktales,* pp. 15, 17.

34. William Bascom, *African Folktales in the New World* (Bloomington: Indiana University Press, 1992).

35. Bascom found, for example, that tales of indisputably African origin had been recorded from British-, French-, Hispanic-, and Native American tellers.

36. Lawrence W. Levine, *Black Culture and Black Consciousness: Afro-American Folk Thought from Slavery to Freedom,* paperback ed. (Oxford: Oxford University Press, 1978), p. 96.

37. See Elliott Oring, "Legend, Truth, and News," *Southern Folklore* 47 (1990): 163–77.

38. As quoted by William Bascom, "The Forms of Folklore: Prose Narrative," *Journal of American Folklore* 78 (1965): 18, although Bascom quotes from a late nineteenth-century English translation of Grimm's *Teutonic Mythology,* but with a few changes.

39. Charles M. Skinner, *Myths and Legends of Our Own Land,* 2 vols. (Philadelphia: Lippincott, 1896); *American Myths and Legends,* 2 vols. (Philadelphia: Lippincott, 1903).

40. However, often these were not published until more recently, in such anthologies as Ronald L. Baker, ed., *Hoosier Folk Legends* (Bloomington: Indiana University Press, 1982); Thomas E. Barden, *Virginia Folk Legends* (Charlottesville: University Press of Virginia, 1991).

41. Linda Dégh, *Legend and Belief: Dialectics of a Folklore Genre* (Bloomington: Indiana University Press, 2001), p. 95; James P. Leary, "*Storviken* in the Old World and the New," *Journal of American Folklore* 118 (2005): 141ff.

42. F. A. de Caro, "Vanishing the Redman: Cultural Guilt and Legend Formation," *International Folklore Review* 4 (1986): 74–80.

43. To be sure, there are stories in which great wealth is found, such as story 236, "Bluebeard's Treasure," in which a spirit leads a family to money.

44. Alan Dundes, "Folk Ideas as Units of Worldview," in Américo Paredes and Richard Bauman, eds., *Toward New Perspectives in Folklore* (Austin: American Folklore Society and University of Texas Press, 1974), pp. 96–98.

45. Patrick B. Mullen, "The Folk Idea of Unlimited Good in American Buried Treasure Legends," *Journal of the Folklore Institute* 15 (1978): 209–20.

46. Such as *The Vanishing Hitchhiker: American Urban Legends and Their Meanings* (New York: W.W. Norton, 1981), and *Too Good to Be True: The Colossal Book of Urban Legends* (New York: W.W. Norton, 1999).

47. Linda Dégh, "The Hook," *Indiana Folklore* I (1968): 98; Alan Dundes, "On the Psychology of Legend," in Hand, pp. 29–31.

48. Gary Alan Fine, *Manufacturing Tales: Sex and Money in Contemporary Legends* (Knoxville: University of Tennessee Press, 1992), especially pp. 141ff.

49. Gary Alan Fine and Patricia A. Turner, *Whispers on the Color Line: Rumor and Race in America* (Berkeley: University of California Press, 2001). See also Patricia A. Turner, *I Heard It through the Grapevine: Rumor in African-American Culture* (Berkeley: University of California Press, 1993).

50. Linda Dégh, *Legend and Belief: Dialectics of a Folklore Genre,* p. 2.

51. Yvonne J. Milspaw, "Witchcraft in Appalachia: Protection for the Poor," *Indiana Folklore* 11 (1978): 71–86.

52. Robert Isbell, *The Last Chivaree: The Hicks Family of Beech Mountain* (Chapel Hill: University of North Carolina Press, 1996), pp. 36, 38.

53. Vance Randolph, *The Talking Turtle and Other Ozark Folktales* (New York: Columbia University Press, 1957), p. xvii.

54. Regarding Dobie's frustration with trying to represent oral stories on the printed page, see Frank de Caro and Rosan Augusta Jordan, *Re-Situating Folklore: Folk Contexts and Twentieth-Century Literature and Art* (Knoxville: University of Tennessee Press, 2004), pp. 245ff.

55. Randolph, *The Talking Turtle,* p. xvi.

56. See William Bernard McCarthy, ed., *Jack in Two Worlds: Contemporary North American Tales and Their Tellers* (Chapel Hill: University of North Carolina Press, 1994).

57. But there are, for example, Maud Long, "Jack Tales" (LP AAFS 47, 48; Library of Congress, 1955); and Pat Mire, dir., *Swapping Stories* (Louisiana Public Broadcasting, 1998).

58. The NAPPS divided in 1998 into the National Storytelling Network and International Storytelling Center.

59. Joseph Daniel Sobol, *The Storytellers' Journey: An American Revival* (Urbana: University of Illinois Press, 1999), p. 49. Jack Zipes, *Creative Storytelling: Building Community, Changing Lives* (New York and London: Routledge, 1995), writes of the importance of storytelling particularly in modern educational contexts and offers strategies for telling tales as well as some traditional tales adapted for today's needs. A noted scholar of the fairy tale, Zipes brings his knowledge of traditional tales to this endeavor.

60. Dorson discussed his narrators in various contexts but brought together discussion of several of them in "Oral Styles of American Folk Narrators," in Horace Beck, ed., *Folklore in Action: Essays for Discussion in Honor of MacEdward Leach* (Philadelphia: American Folklore Society, 1962), pp. 77–100.

61. Richard M. Dorson, "Polish Wonder Tales of Joe Woods," *Western Folklore* 8 (1949): 26–28. .

62. Leonard W. Roberts, ed., *South from Hell-fer-Sartin: Kentucky Mountain Folk Tales* (Lexington: University of Kentucky Press, 1955), p. 9.

63. These he included in *Old Greasybeard: Tales from the Cumberland Gap* (Detroit: Folklore Associates, 1969).

64. Lindahl, *Folktales from the Collection of the Library of Congress,* I: 286, 287.

65. Published as *Abraham "Oregon" Smith: Pioneer, Folk Hero and Tale-Teller* (New York: Arno Press, 1977).

AN ANTHOLOGY OF

American Folktales and Legends

I

Native American and
Native Hawaiian Narratives

The oral narratives of Native Americans have been recorded in writing and print by Europeans for centuries, and these stories have intrigued Euro-American culture for many reasons. Like European myths and folktales, they are full of fantastic happenings and magical beings and events: people who transform into animals and vice versa, parallel worlds in the sky or under the sea, seemingly mysterious figures who appear from nowhere to aid a hero on his way in the world. But they may also be baffling from the standpoint of "Western" culture. Characters may seem to lack motivations. Things may happen suddenly for obscure reasons. For example, why does a bear suddenly show up in "Blood-Clot-Boy," asking for meat? Cultural details certainly can be easily misunderstood, and non–Native American readers may not have the requisite knowledge of cultural backgrounds to understand the basic elements of Native American life. Our version of "Blood-Clot-Boy," for instance, begins with a man and his wife leaving their group and going to live alone: Would that behavior have been usual or—given that theirs is probably a society of close-knit groups in which people are highly dependent on each other—would it be a monumental action? In a related vein, in "The Boy Who Became a Mink," what is the significance of the boy and his grandmother living in isolation from other *barrabaras* (that is, settlement structures)? Does their isolation single them out in some special way as members of their society? The world of humans and that of animals seem closely related in many Native American stories, but is there any particular significance in the sexual relations between a man and a buffalo cow in "The Buffalo-Wife"? The very idea may seem bizarre and repellent to some readers: What is the story's social or moral meaning? Even a seemingly historical account such as the Koasati "The First Meeting of the Indians and the Europeans," may puzzle readers as to why these monumental events are narratively developed as they are with an emphasis on the Europeans providing strong liquor to the Indians. In the Modoc "Stealing Fire," why must fire be stolen not once, but twice, from two different groups of brothers? Is the story action contrived solely to allow discourse on the introduction into the world of both sickness and the seasons, as well as fire? And who is Black Fox-Kumush, a character who has almost the same name as the chief protagonist?

From the standpoint of folklorists, Native American stories do not easily fit the genres that scholars are used to from their knowledge of oral narratives of Europe or Africa or Asia. Native American stories may tend to fall across the conventional generic boundaries, mixing elements of myth, legend, and folktale. And, although a wealth of narrative texts have been written down and published, folklorists cannot even be sure how carefully or how completely many story texts were recorded. Often, information beyond the text itself—even things as simple as who told a story and exactly where—may be missing from the record. Who told Jeremiah Curtin the important story "Stealing Fire," for example? Was it the same informant as for many of his stories, or was it someone else? He doesn't say for sure.

These stories have the power not only to charm and intrigue the present-day reader but also to challenge and to pose questions. It is hoped that readers will appreciate them on many levels and that part of the enjoyment of these stories will be found in the questions they raise and in thinking about the answers.

Understanding Native American narratives offers a window into larger cultural meanings (the great anthropologist Franz Boas urged the collecting of these stories precisely because they could be, to use a slightly different metaphor, a "mirror of culture," telling us about many elements of Native American society, if perhaps rather obliquely). Folklorists, literary critics, and others have begun to analyze Native American story elements—the rich metaphors, the unlikely characters, the seemingly illogical actions—to gain insight into their cultural implications. A few of their attempts to do so are discussed in the introduction, and their future efforts should bring greater understanding to us all.

Native Hawaiian stories present another corpus of tales that are part of the rich collection of U. S. folklore yet stem from a culture that preceded the Euro-American presence. Like Native American stories, they have sometimes been imperfectly perceived by the Western mind-set, and we are certainly in need of a fresh approach to comprehending their full meaning. A few are included here to call attention to them as part of the great American cultural mix and as cultural "artifacts" to be interpreted as well as enjoyed.

1. The Origin of Stories

This story was narrated by Hebry Jacobs and collected by Jeremiah Curtin in the 1880s during fieldwork among the Seneca in Versailles, New York. Motifs A1400, A1464, A1590.

This happened long ago, in the time of our forefathers. In a Seneca village lived a boy whose father and mother died when he was only a few weeks old. The little boy was cared for by a woman, who had known his parents. She gave him the name of Orphan.

The boy grew to be a healthy, active little fellow. When he was old enough, his foster mother gave him a bow and arrows and said, "It is time for you to learn to hunt. Tomorrow morning go to the woods and kill all the birds you can find."

Taking cobs of dry corn the woman shelled off kernels and parched them in hot ashes and the next morning she gave the boy some of the corn for his breakfast and rolled up some in a piece of buckskin and told him to take it with him for he would be gone all day and would get hungry.

Orphan started off and was very successful. At noon he sat down and rested and ate some of the parched corn, then he hunted till the middle of the afternoon. When he began to work toward home he had a good string of birds.

The next morning Orphan's foster mother gave him parched corn for breakfast and while he was eating she told him that he must do his best when hunting, for if he became a good hunter he would always be prosperous.

The boy took his bow and arrows and little bundle of parched corn and went to the woods; again he found plenty of birds. At midday he ate all his corn and thought over what his foster mother had told him. In his mind he said, "I'll do just as my mother tells me, then some time I'll be able to hunt big game."

Orphan hunted till toward evening, then went home with a larger string of birds than he had the previous day. His foster mother thanked him, and said, "Now you have begun to help me get food."

Early the next morning the boy's breakfast was ready and as soon as he had eaten it he took his little bundle of parched corn and started off. He went farther into the woods and at night came home with a larger string of birds than he had the second day. His foster mother praised and thanked him.

Each day the boy brought home more birds than the previous day. On the ninth day he killed so many that he brought them home on his back. His foster mother tied the birds in little bundles of three or four and distributed them among her neighbors.

The tenth day the boy started off, as usual, and, as each day he had gone farther for game than on the preceding day, so now he went, deeper into the woods than ever. About midday the sinew that held the feathers to his arrow loosened. Looking around for a place where he could sit down while he took the sinew off and wound it on again, he saw a small opening and near the center of the opening a high, smooth, flat-topped, round stone. He went to the stone, sprang up on to it, and sat down. He unwound the sinew and put it in his mouth to soften, then he arranged the arrow feathers and was about to fasten them to the arrow when a voice, right there near him, asked, "Shall I tell you stories?"

Orphan looked up expecting to see a man; not seeing anyone he looked behind the stone and around it, then he again began to tie the feathers to his arrow.

"Shall I tell you stories?" asked a voice right there by him.

The boy looked in every direction, but saw no one. Then he made up his mind to watch and find out who was trying to fool him. He stopped work and listened and when the voice again asked, "Shall I tell you stories?" he found that it came from the stone, then he asked, "What is that? What does it mean to tell stories?"

"It is telling what happened a long time ago. If you will give me your birds, I'll tell you stories."

"You may have the birds."

As soon as the boy promised to give the birds, the stone began telling what happened long ago. When one story was told, another was begun. The boy sat, with his head down, and listened. Toward night the stone said, "We will rest now. Come again tomorrow. If anyone asks about your birds, say that you have killed so many that they are getting scarce and you have to go a long way to find one."

While going home the boy killed five or six birds. When his foster mother asked why he had so few birds, he said that they were scarce; that he had to go far for them.

The next morning Orphan started off with his bow and arrows and little bundle of parched corn, but he forgot to hunt for birds, he was thinking of the stories the stone had told him. When a bird lighted near him he shot it, but he kept straight on toward the opening in the woods. When he got there he put his birds on the stone, and called out, "I've come! Here are birds. Now tell me stories."

The stone told story after story. Toward night it said "Now we must rest till tomorrow."

On the way home the boy looked for birds, but it was late and he found only a few.

That night the foster mother told her neighbors that when Orphan first began to hunt he had brought home a great many birds, but now he brought only four or five after being in the woods from morning till night. She said there was something strange about it, either he threw the birds away or gave them to some animal, or maybe he idled time away, didn't hunt. She hired a boy to follow Orphan and find out what he was doing.

The next morning the boy took his bow and arrows and followed Orphan, keeping out of his sight and sometimes shooting a bird. Orphan killed a good many birds; then, about the middle of the forenoon, he suddenly started off toward the East, running as fast as he could. The boy followed till he came to an opening in the woods and saw Orphan climb up and sit down on a large round stone; he crept nearer and heard talking. When he couldn't see the person to whom Orphan was talking he went up to the boy, and asked, "What are you doing here?"

"Hearing stories."

"What are stories?"

"Telling about things that happened long ago. Put your birds on this stone, and say, 'I've come to hear stories.'"

The boy did as told and straightway the stone began. The boys listened till the sun went down, then the stone said, "We will rest now. Come again tomorrow."

On the way Orphan killed three or four birds.

When the woman asked the boy she had sent why Orphan killed so few birds, he said, "I followed him for a while, then I spoke to him, and after that we hunted together till it was time to come home. We couldn't find many birds."

The next morning the older boy said, "I'm going with Orphan to hunt, it's sport." The two started off together. By the middle of the forenoon each boy had a long string of birds. They hurried to the opening, put the birds on the stone, and said, "We have come. Here are the birds! Tell us stories."

They sat on the stone and listened to stories till late in the afternoon, then the stone said, "We'll rest now till tomorrow."

On the way home the boys shot every bird they could find, but it was late and they didn't find many.

Several days went by in this way, then the foster mother said, "Those boys kill more birds than they bring home," and she hired two men to follow them.

The next morning, when Orphan and his friend started for the woods the two men followed. When the boys had a large number of birds they stopped hunting and hurried to the opening. The men followed and, hiding behind trees, saw them put the birds on a large round stone, then jump up and sit there, with their heads down, listening to a man's voice; every little while they said,

"Un!"

"Let's go there and find out who is talking to those boys," said one man to the other. They walked quickly to the stone and asked, "What are you doing, boys?"

The boys were startled, but Orphan said, "You must promise not to tell anyone."

They promised, then Orphan said, "Jump up and sit on the stone."

The men seated themselves on the stone, then the boys said, "Go on with the story, we are listening."

The four sat with their heads down and the stone began to tell stories. When it was almost night the stone said "Tomorrow all the people in your village must come and listen to my stories. Tell the chief to send every man and have each man bring something to eat. You must clean the brush away so the people can sit, on the ground near me."

That night Orphan told the chief about the story telling stone, and gave him the stone's message. The chief sent a runner to give the message to each family in the village.

Early the next morning every one in the village was ready to start. Orphan went ahead and the crowd followed. When they came to the opening each man put what he had brought, meat or bread, on the stone; the brush was cleared away, and everyone sat down.

When all was quiet the stone said, "Now I will tell you stories of what happened long ago. There was a world before this. The things that I am going to tell about happened in that world. Some of you will remember every word that I say, some will remember a part of the words, and some will forget, them all—I think this will be the way, but each man must do the best he can. Here after you must tell these stories to one another.

Each man bent his head and listened to every word the stone said. Once in a while the boys said "Un!" When the sun was almost down the stone said, "We'll rest now. Come tomorrow and bring meat and bread."

The next morning when the people gathered around the stone they found that the meat and bread they had left there the day before was gone. They put the food they had brought on the stone, then sat in a circle and waited.

When all was quiet the stone began. Again it told stories till the sun was almost down, then it said, "Come tomorrow. To-morrow I will finish the stories of what happened long ago."

Early in the morning the people of the village gathered and, when all was quiet, the stone began to tell stories, and it told till late in the afternoon, then said, "I have finished! You must keep these stories as long as the world lasts; tell them to your children and grandchildren generation after generation. One person will remember them better than another. When you go to a man or a woman to ask for one of these stories carry something to pay for it, bread or meat, or whatever you have. I know all that happened in the world before this; I have told it to you. When you visit one another, you must tell these things, and keep them up always. I have finished."

And so it has been. From the Stone came all the knowledge the Senecas have of the world before this.

2. Stealing Fire

One of a complex of widespread "theft of fire" stories, this narrative is found among Native American groups from Labrador and the far north of Canada to California and the Southwest. It is one of many stories that tell of the human acquisition of basic elements of life, here not only fire but also sickness and the seasons. Jeremiah Curtin recorded this version from the California Modocs and published it in the early twentieth century. He does not specify who told him the story, but many in this collection were narrated by Ko-a-lak-ak-a in 1884. Motifs A1415, A1415.2.

The ten Sickness Brothers, who lived in the east at the edge of the world, and the ten Sun brothers, who lived in the west, where the sky touches the earth, were the owners of fire.

Other people had no fire, they ate their meat raw; but they knew about fire, and were thinking how to get it; they knew that those men owned it.

At last Black Fox called a council of all the people in the world. When they had assembled, he said: "I feel sorry for the people who are to come." (He had heard that people would come soon, and that he and his people would no longer be persons.) He called the people who were to come People to Come.) "It will be hard for them in the world if they have no way of keeping warm. I know where fire is, and if you will help me I will get it."

All promised to help, then Black Fox said: "You must stand in a line, one person a long running distance from another, and the line must reach from here to within one running distance of the place where the Sickness Brothers have their house. I will go to the house and steal fire, but you must bring it home."

Black Fox sent the best runner to the farthest station, the second fastest runner to the second station and so on, till near home he placed men who could run only a little, men who soon tired out. The Rattlesnake family he sent underground. People who traveled in the air formed a line above the earth.

"We will tell you how the Sickness Brothers live," said the people of the air, "for we see them often. Every morning they build fires on the mountains to drive deer to their snares. When you see a big smoke, you will know that you are near their house. Two Squirrel brothers are the servants of the Sickness Brothers. The Squirrels never hunt; they stay in the house and watch that no one steals fire."

Black Fox traveled toward the east for a good many days. At last he reached the Sickness Brothers' house without being seen by the brothers, or by their servants. When he went through the smoke hole into the house, the Squirrel brothers were terribly scared; one ran out to call the Sickness Brothers but Black Fox drove him back.

"Why are you frightened?" asked he. "I have come to talk to you. Sit down. Why don't you have your faces painted? You would look nice. I know how to paint; I will paint them for you."

He took dead coals, drew long lines across their faces and said: "Go to the spring and look at yourselves." (From that time those people have stripes on their faces.)

As soon as they were out of the house Black Fox took the largest piece of fire, put it behind his ear and ran off as fast as he could. When he picked up the coal, the fires on the mountains died down.

"Somebody is in our house," said the Sickness Brothers.

"Somebody has stolen fire!" And they hurried home.

When Black Fox had fire behind his ear, he ran a long distance, ran till he met Mink. Mink took fire and ran till he came to Kaiutois; the next man to carry fire was Lion. Lion carried it till he came to Bull Snake, who was stationed under the ground.

The Sickness Brothers were fast runners and they nearly caught Bull Snake. He was so scared that he was just going to drop fire and run off when he met Red Squirrel and gave it to him. The next to carry fire was Bear. Bear was a slow runner and the Sickness Brothers nearly came up to him before he met Squirrel, a fast runner. When Squirrel was getting tired, and was running slower, he came to Lizard. Lizard sprang away and was soon far ahead. When he reached Black Marten the

9

Sickness Brothers were a long way off, but Black Marten was not a good runner, and the Sickness Brothers gained on him fast. They got so near that he hid in the bushes and gave out a frightened call. Otter was waiting right there; he snatched fire and ran as fast as he could till he was tired and was thinking: "Where is the man who is going to take fire? I can't hold out much longer."

Then he met Skunk. Eagle took fire from Skunk; he went up in the air and carried fire a long distance, until Swallow took it. When darkness came, Owl was there to carry fire, and he and his people carried it till daylight. Then Dawn took it, and afterward Kawhas. Kawhas was about to drop it, when he saw Turkey Buzzard and called: "Take it quick! I am tired! I can't hold it; I shall let it drop."

Turkey Buzzard looked back as he started. The Sickness Brothers were so near that his head turned yellow from fright, but he reached the next man—and so they carried fire day after day, till the ocean was not far off. Only a few runners were left, and some of them couldn't run ten steps.

At last Wood Dove took fire, but the Sickness Brothers were so near that he hid in the bushes. He thought: "Now they will kill me, and then people will never have fire." It made him feel lonesome; and he cried, not loud, but down in his throat.

The Sickness Brothers heard his cry, and said: "We can never overtake these people; that cry is far off. We can't get fire back, but the people who have stolen it will have us with them always. We will stay in their country; we won't go back to our old place; we will scatter and live everywhere in the world."

Till that time the Sickness Brothers had lived by themselves, and had never troubled people. After fire was stolen, they were everywhere in the world. People had fire, but they had sickness too.

Black Fox-Kumush saw this race, but he didn't help, for at the council, when he told the people what would happen, they wouldn't listen to his words. They liked the words of Black Fox better.

Now Black Fox called a second council of all the people in the world, and when they came he said: "What else shall we do for the people who are coming? I think we should steal fire from the brothers who live in the west, at the edge of the world. I can go there and get it."

"Stork, Sun brother's servant, will see you," said the people; "you will never get there."

"Oh, I can get there," said Black Fox. "I will kill the ten brothers and come back. It will not be hard."

"What will you do when you get to the house? No person has ever been there."

"Don't kill all the brothers," said Black Fox-Kumush. "If you do it will be dark here. There will never be any light again. It will always be night."

"You will freeze to death," said some of the people. " There is deep snow along that trail."

"I will build ten houses, where I can rest and get warm."

"Before you get to Sun brother's house there is a long, broad flat," said Eagle.

"The brothers dig roots there. I often see them when I am up in the air. Near the house there is a high mountain. You must go to the top of it and watch the brothers from there. When they start for home, there is always a terrible snowstorm. The eldest brother goes first, and one follows another. In the morning, when they start to hunt for roots, the youngest goes first."

When Black Fox came to the mountain he talked to it and asked it for help; then he watched for the brothers. Soon he saw the youngest brother come out of the house and start toward the flat. One brother followed another till all ten had gone to dig roots; then Black Fox went toward the house. The house was made of dirt and covered with turf. Stork didn't see Black Fox coming; when he sprang in at the smoke hole Stork screamed out. Black Fox jumped on him, choked him and scolded him; then he threw him into a corner, and said: "When I come to see you, what makes you scream? I want to talk nice to you; I want you to go home with me. This is a bad place. I will give you shells and nice beads."

"I will go out and make just a little noise," said Stork, "and then the brothers won't come home; that is the way I do."

Black Fox let him go out, but he followed him so he wouldn't scream loud.

The brothers heard Stork and one said: "What's the matter? I heard something." When they heard him the second time they said: "Oh, that is Stork at play."

"How do these men live?" asked Black Fox.

"Every morning they go early to dig roots; they dig all day, then one brother comes home. When he gets to the house, he puts down his basket of roots, comes to the smoke hole and looks all around to see if any one is here; then he comes in. Each brother comes in the same way; each one brings a basketful of roots, and each looks around the house before he comes in. The five oldest brothers come first, then the five youngest follow. As each one starts for home, there is a terrible snowstorm. I build a big fire from that pile of sticks outside the house. The snow and cold almost put the fire out, but I keep putting on sticks."

"Where can I hide, so that they won't see me when they look around?" asked Black Fox.

"They don't look toward the east," said Stork. "You must hide in the east part of the house, in the hole where we keep roots."

"Hide me there," said Black Fox. "I am going to take you home with me. You must tie up a bundle of roots for us to eat on the road. You will have to eat a good deal or you will give out. It is a long road."

The eldest brother was coming, so Stork built a great fire. When the man got to the house he put down his basket of roots and looked in at the smoke hole; he looked all around, then asked: "Why did you scream?"

"It was getting late; I wanted you to come home," said Stork.

Just then Black Fox sprang at Sun brother and cut off his head. He and Stork pulled the body in and hid it; then they put the head in the hole where the roots were.

Again it began to snow; the second brother was coming. Soon he looked in at the smoke hole, and asked: "Why did you scream?"

"I missed the step and fell into the house," said Stork.

"We have always told you to be careful," said Sun brother.

That moment Black Fox sprang up. Sun brother screamed, but Black Fox cut his head off and dragged the head and the body to the hole where the roots were.

When the third brother came he asked: "What noise was that? I thought I heard my brother scream."

"I was screaming," said Stork. "I wanted to hurry you home."

Black Fox killed the third brother, as he had the other two.

Again it began snowing; the fourth brother was coming. Black Fox told Stork that he must work around as he always did. "You must not talk," said Stork; "he will hear you. He is stronger than the other brothers."

Sun brother looked in at the smoke hole, and asked: "Why don't you brush up the snow? What makes it so yellow?"

"I've been walking in the ashes," said Stork.

Sun brother was just going to draw his head up out of the smoke hole and come down into the house, when Black Fox sprang at him and cut his head off. That time a good deal of blood was left. Stork couldn't clean it up; it made the snow yellow.

Black Fox was afraid the fifth brother would see the blood. "I will go outside and kill him," said he.

"You mustn't do that," said Stork. "If you do the other brothers will see you."

Sun brother was at the house now; he left his basket outside and looked in. "Why does it look so yellow around here?" asked he. "It looks queer."

"Oh, I've worked around a good deal," said Stork, "That is why it looks queer."

Sun brother stretched half his length in to see that no one was there and Black Fox sprang at him and cut his head off.

"Now the other five brothers will come," said Stork. "They come quicker, for it is getting late." The fifth brother had screamed louder when Black Fox killed him. His brothers had heard his scream and they were running.

Black Fox jumped out of the house and started for home. Stork picked up the bundle, put it on his back and followed. Both ran as fast as they could; sometimes Stork got ahead of Black Fox, then Black Fox was ahead. The wind blew terribly. Black Fox's ears were filled with snow, and he was almost frozen. They were giving out when they reached the last house that Black Fox had built; the fire was still burning. They had just got warm when they heard the brothers coming, and started off again. They ran till Stork said: "I'm so tired I can't run any farther!"

"Hurry," said Black Fox. "They won't overtake us. We are near the next house." They reached the ninth house, and the fire was burning.

"Look and see if they are coming," said Black Fox.

"Not yet."

After a while Stork looked again. "They are coming!" called he. And off the two ran as fast as they could. When they got near the eighth house, the brothers were close behind.

"I am afraid!" said Stork.

"I am not," said Black Fox, but he kept on running, though snow was in his ears and in his hair; he was almost frozen. They stopped at the seventh house, but Stork looked back and said: "They are coming; they are not far away!"

The brothers were tired. They began to think that they couldn't overtake Black Fox and Stork. They still carried their baskets. Black Fox didn't stop at the sixth or fifth house.

"Don't open your mouth so wide," said Stork; "if you do, it will fill with snow."

"No matter," said Black Fox, "that will help me to run."

When the brothers reached the fifth house and found it empty, the elder said: "Let us be only five. We can never catch up with the man who killed our brothers, and stole our servant. Let us go back, but we will always watch this country. We won't let any one come here again. I thought we were the strongest people in the world. I wonder who this man is."

They didn't know the people of this world; they had always lived by themselves. The only man they knew about was Stork.

When the people saw Black Fox coming, they went to one place to wait for him. They talked about him, and said: "Black Fox is a smart man; we couldn't have done what he has done." When Black Fox came up to them, they saw that he had Stork with him. Stork still had his bundle of roots, for he hadn't had time to eat many. Everybody was glad now, for there was summer and winter. Up to that time people had had only clouds and storms.

After a while Black Fox said: "We must do another thing for the People to Come. We have done a good deal—they will have two kinds of fire—but there is too much cold. We must hold a council and decide how much cold they can have, how long winter will be."

Black Fox sent for all the people in the world. Every one came; every one thought: "What will Black Fox say?" But nobody talked; they all sat still waiting. At last Black Fox said: "There should be ten months of cold." Then everybody began to talk. Nobody wanted ten months. Some said: "If there are ten months of cold, people will starve to death; they can't lay up roots and seeds enough. Let us have five months." Others said: "Two months are enough." Black Fox kept saying: "There should be ten." When they couldn't agree, someone said: "Let the oldest man here decide." There was one very old man there—the oldest of all, but he only listened, he didn't say a word. Again Black Fox said: "There should be ten months."

The council lasted all night; then people asked: "Where is Kanoa? Why doesn't he talk?" It was getting daylight, and Black Fox still insisted on ten months. "The months can be short," said he, "not many days long." Now the people said to Kanoa:

"Speak, old man; maybe you have something in your mind to say." He started to go, and just then he called out: "Three months."

Black Fox was mad, but the other people were glad, and said: "The old man is right. There will be three months of winter."

"I am afraid people will not be thankful for what we have done," said Hedgehog, "and will eat us." Porcupine was afraid, too, but others said: "We have got fire for them; we have killed five of the Sun brothers; we have made winter short; they will be thankful."

The council broke up, and soon after all those people turned to common animals, for real people were coming.

The five Sun brothers lived in their house in the west, but they watched the world. And since then things have been as they are now.

---

3. Djogeon (Dwarf-Man) and His Uncle

This hero tale was collected from a Seneca informant early in the twentieth century by the anthropologists Jeremiah Curtin and J. N. B. Hewitt for the Bureau of American Ethnology. The Bureau was founded in the nineteenth century as a federal government agency that gathered information on Native American groups. Motifs D1962.2, H310.

Djogeon lived in the woods with his uncle. When the boy was old enough to learn, his uncle taught him how to shoot; for this purpose he took him out to hunt. When the uncle grew too old to hunt the nephew then went alone.

About noon one day while following an elk, a woman sitting on a log at the edge of an opening in the forest called to Djogeon, saying "Come here and rest; I know you are tired." At first he paid no attention to her, but after she had called to him the third time he went to her and sat by her side. She talked to him, and before he realized it she had his head in her lap and had begun searching therein for vermin.

He soon fell asleep, and when she was satisfied that he was sleeping soundly she put him into a basket which she placed on her back and started off with great speed, traveling until the sun had almost set. Then stopping, she put her basket down and roused the young man asking him, "Do you know, this place?" "Oh, yes," said he, "my uncle and I used to hunt here. I know the place very well." They spent the night there.

The next morning she searched again in his head until he fell asleep; then putting him into the basket again, she hurried on as before until late in the afternoon. She stopped at a lake and, putting the basket down, she again awakened the young man, asking him, "Do you know this lake?" "Yes; I have fished here many times with my uncle," replied the young man. Then, taking out of her basket a canoe no larger than a walnut, she struck it with her hand repeatedly until it became large enough to hold both. Then they both boarded it and paddled across the lake. "We will now go home," said she. "I have a mother and three sisters; all the latter are married and live in the same lodge. We will go to them," she declared.

Djogeon and his companion traveled on until they reached her mother's lodge. When they stood at the door her mother saw the stranger with her daughter and cried out, "Welcome, son-in-law. I am glad you have come." Djogeon became the young woman's husband, and they lived happily until one night the old woman had a frightful dream, rolling out of her couch and over the floor to the edge of the fire. Then her son-in-law jumped up and asked his mother-in-law, "What is the matter? Are you dreaming, mother-in-law?" She paid no attention to him but rolled about, muttering to herself. Then he said, "I will make her listen," and, taking the pestle for pounding corn, he hit her a heavy blow on the head. She started up, saying. "Oh! I have had such a bad dream. I dreamed that my son-in-law would kill the Ganiagwaihegowa." "Oh," said he "I will attend to that in the morning. Now go to sleep, mother-in-law." The next morning the old woman told her son-in-law he must kill the bear and bring it back quickly. So he sought and killed the bear without much trouble and brought it home.

The next night she dreamed that he must make a great feast for the Dagwanoenyent, and that he must invite them all to a feast and provide so much food that they would not be able to eat it all. The next day he hunted and killed a great many elk, deer, and bear. There was an abundance of food, the lodge being full of meat, and still there was more. Then he went out and called all the Dagwanoenyent to come to a great feast prepared for them to eat their fill. They answered him, all agreeing to be at the feast. Soon they began to appear one after another: they came in such numbers that the shelves, the floor, and the seats were filled with them. They began to eat and ate with a terrible appetite. The old woman went around urging them, saying, "Eat, eat your fill. I want all to have plenty to eat in my lodge." They ate, and the old woman still urged them, hoping that the supply would run short and her son-in-law would be killed. The son-in-law, with his wife, her three sisters, and their husbands went out to have more food brought in case of need.

At last the Dagwanoenyent ate until their jaws could move no longer and their tongues refused to stir. They said, "We have had enough. Mother, mother, enough." When he heard these words the young son-in-law motioned to the walls and roof, saying, "I want the roof and walls of this lodge to become flint." The old woman and the Dagwanoenyent, seeing that they were caught, flew around in every direction. The old woman begged for mercy. "Mother-in-law, you had no mercy on me, so I will not let you out," answered Djogeon. Then he said, "I want this house to become red hot." As it grew hot the Dagwanoenyent flew about with terrible speed, knocking around the walls and making such a noise as had never been heard in the world before. At last all was still in the lodge.

Then the nephew with his wife and her three sisters and their husbands set out for the lodge of Djogeon's uncle. They went by the road over which he and his wife had come. When they reached the lake it was covered with thin ice, which could barely hold up a small bird. The young man took eight puffballs from an oak tree and, making himself and his friends small, each one entered a ball; and when the eight balls stood, side by side on the ice by the edge of the lake, he said, "Let the west wind blow," and the west wind obeyed, sweeping them over the lake to the other side. Then they came out of the balls and, resuming their natural size, continued their way until they reached the lodge of Djogeon's uncle.

4. Blood-Clot-Boy

"Blood-Clot-Boy" is a very well-known story and one of a number of Native American hero tales in which the main characters have such designations as Dirty-Boy, Thrown-Away, or, as in story 5, Stone Boy. Although this story discourses on a variety of themes, readers will want to note the great cultural concern it expresses over having a supply of meat for food. Our version was told by Good-Chief in Oklahoma, though the ancestral home of his tribe, the Skidi Pawnee, is in Nebraska. Motifs A560, B16.2.5, D2074.1.1, F831, F836, T541.1.1; cf K914.1.

A long time ago there were people in the south who lived in a village. The women cultivated the fields and looked after their crop, while the men hunted and brought meat into the camp.

In this village was a poor man and a poor woman. They were living together as man and wife. One day the man said to the woman: "Let us go from this village; the people do not care for us. I shall make my arrows, and I will hunt game and buffalo, so we can have plenty to eat and plenty to wear." The woman said: "It is well, let us go." So the man made many arrows. They started and went north. They came to a stream of water and made a grass lodge.

Here they lived, and the man found plenty of game. They now had plenty to eat and wear. So they left their lodge and went to another place. Now they made another grass lodge, and here they stayed. The man found plenty of buffalo, so he did not have to go far. He killed many buffalo, so that now they had many parfleches [rawhide holders] filled with dried meat.

One day, when they were happy, a visitor came to their lodge. It was a bear. The man was about to fight, when the bear said: "No, you must not fight me, for you cannot kill me. All I want is some of the meat you have." So the man said: "You can have the meat." But the bear said: "You must carry the meat for me, for I have young ones to feed." So the man had to carry the dried buffalo meat on his back for the bear. The bear and man now walked on to a cedar country. Now they came to a den of bears. These bears were the children of this bear with the man. The bear told the man to cut the dried meat and give the pieces of meat to the bears. This the man did; and then the man was told to sit down. After the bears had eaten all the meat, the man was told to lead the bears to his home, the bear following. The bear had told the man that he himself was the one who had been killing the people; that he did not like the people. Now the man and the bears had arrived at the man's home.

The man was then made to build a grass house for the bears. The bear was cruel to the man, and would not let him eat. The man made the grass lodge for the bears. Then he was told to bring all of his meat to the bear's lodge. So the man took all of his meat over to the bear's lodge. The man and the woman became very hungry; they had nothing to eat. Every day the bear would come to the man's lodge and would say: "Get your bow and arrows; I want you to go hunting with me." The man would go with the bear. When they came to a buffalo, the man would kill it, skin it, and would have to pack all the meat to the bear's lodge. The bear never divided any meat with the man. The bear did not even give them a small piece of meat, so that they might eat. The woman and man were both alarmed, for the bear seemed to know their thoughts. If they talked of flight, the bear would say: "You cannot run away from me."

One day the bear took the man with him on a hunt. While they were gone the least of the bears came to the woman and said: "Woman, are you hungry? I have brought you meat that my mother gave me to eat; if you desire, you may save a piece for your husband." The woman patted the young bear upon the head. Every day the young bear used to bring a little meat to the woman. The man was now getting thin, for he got but little meat. The man and woman felt badly, for they could not get any meat, and they could not escape, as the bear was watching them all the time.

One day the bear came and said to the man: "Come, get your bow and arrows and we will go hunting together, for my children are hungry; they have nothing to eat." So the man took his bow and arrows, and the man went with the bear to hunt buffalo. They came to a drove of buffalo. The man crawled to the place where the buffalo were and saw one fat cow. This he picked out, and shot an arrow at her. He hit the cow in the side, so that the arrow went through the heart. As the buffalo staggered and was ready to fall, the man saw it throw up a large-sized clot of blood. He ran and pulled up some grass and took up the blood, saying to himself, "My wife will boil this blood, and we can have blood soup." So he placed the blood in his robe before the bear noticed what he had done. So the man skinned the buffalo, while the bear sat at one side watching him, to prevent him from taking any of the meat. The man now packed the meat, and they went home. After the man threw the meat upon the ground in front of the bear's lodge, he walked fast to his own lodge.

As he entered his lodge he said: "Woman, set this blood back of the lodge and cover it with grass. Tonight, when the bears have gone to sleep, you can boil this blood, and make blood soup." The woman took the blood and set it back in the lodge at the south side. The woman divided the meat the young bear had brought to them. In the night the woman reached after the blood, and, instead of a blood-clot, the blood had turned into a baby. The woman called her husband and he saw the child, but he was afraid that the bear might hear its crying and would kill it; so the woman hid the baby away.

The next day, while hunting with the bear, the man took courage, and when he killed a [buffalo] cow took the cow's bag [udder] and hid it. This he took home to his woman, and she let the child suck the bag. The child grew up fast. The man was thin and looked badly. The bear kept telling the man to hunt with him.

One day, as the man returned, he noticed that the child had grown to a good size. So he said: "I will make the boy a bow and arrows, so that he can play and not cry." So the man made a little bow and arrows for the boy. When the man and bear were absent the boy would go out to play, and the young bear would come and play with the boy. The boy would ride the bear around, and the other young bears would say, "Mother, our brother lets Straight-up-Person ride him," but the bear-mother would say, "Let them alone, they are poor: let them play." The little bear used to steal meat for the boy, so that the boy grew up fast. Blood-Clot-Boy said one day to the man: "Father, I know we are poor. I want you to make me a strong bow; a bow that will be as strong as the tail of the mountain lion; make the sinew stout, so it will not break when I pull it; the arrow must be made of the finest dogwood; do not put anything at the ends of your arrows, but just sharpen them. When you make the bow, let it stand in the sun for several days to harden; get sumach leaves and boil them, and pour the liquid upon the bow, so that it will turn black. The arrows must all be red. I am not human. I am the child of all the animals. The animals know the treatment the bears gave you. They are sorry for you and your woman, so they sent me to help you. I am going to kill the bear, so make the bow and arrows, and do as I have asked you."

The man was glad to hear what the boy said, and when the bow and arrows were made he said: "My son, here are the bow and arrows." So the boy took the bow and arrows and went far away into a thickly timbered country. There in the timber he found many animals and birds. The animals talked to the boy and told him how to kill the bear. The arrows were breathed upon by the birds; the bow was taken by the mountain lion; the mountain lion then took it to a large black snake; the bow was breathed upon by all the animals. The birds decked the boy with downy feathers. From the creek the beavers brought up sweet grass to the boy. The otters brought up flagroot stems. These stems and grasses the boy twisted, and put them about his neck. The boy went home, for it was now night.

When he arrived he found his father and mother both at home. He woke them, and told them that he was now prepared to kill the bear. The boy told the man to sit up and hear what he had to say. Then he said: "Father, tomorrow the bear is coming for you to go hunting; accompany him as usual. When you take your choice from the herd, kill it; do not be afraid. When you skin and cut up the meat, pretend that you want the bear to carry the meat. The bear will not like it, and will threaten to kill you;

do not mind, for I will be with you. As soon as the bear raises his paws toward the Sun, I will shoot one of my arrows into his right paw, then another into his left; he will be conquered, but I shall shoot him again, in the side, so that he will die."

The next morning the bear came and said: "You man sitting within, come, go with me and hunt buffalo; my children have no meat." So the man went out, leaving the boy and woman at home. The bear and the man went a long way from their lodge. Finally they came to a drove of buffalo, and the bear said: "Kill this bull," but the man said: "No, I want to kill a cow." Finally the bear yielded. They went on, until they came to a drove of buffalo cows, when the man shot at a cow and killed it. Then he cut it up. The bear would try to make the man cut the meat in a different manner, but the man would not listen. "Why," said the bear, "you do not do as I tell you?" "You have had your way since we came out, now you must carry this meat," said the man.

The bear was angry and stood on his hind legs, as if to tear the man to pieces, but the man was not alarmed. Close by was a thicket, and here the boy lay hid, for he could travel and not be seen. As the bear raised his paws a second time, the boy came out from the thicket, took aim, and the arrow struck the bear's paw; another arrow was sent, and this time it struck the bear's other paw. The bear gave a squeal and rolled over, and as he did so the boy was upon him, and sent another arrow into the bear's side, killing him.

The man went up to the boy and hugged him. The man then put the meat upon his back and they went home. The she-bear and the young ones went away as soon as they found out that the bear was killed. The bear that was killed had been feared all over the land, for he killed not only people, but also animals.

When the man and the boy came home they told the woman that the bear had been killed, and she was glad. The young bear returned to their lodge and made its home with them. These people remained at the same place and killed many buffalo, so that they had plenty of meat. As soon as all became fat, they packed their meat and started for their village, taking the young bear. The young man said: "Father, I will go in advance, so that I can find a place for us to live." The man said: "Very well, you may go on." So the young man disappeared. The young bear then left, and went back to the cedar country. The young man arrived at the village and went about it.

Every one who saw him took him to be Burnt-Belly, a boy who lived with his grandmother outside of the village. (The name "Burnt-Belly" was given to the boy because he had no shirt, and, as he sat by the camp-fire all the time, his belly was burnt.) But this young boy went on, noticing nobody. He was poor, wore no clothes except a piece of robe, and his hair was never combed. He went to a tipi that was at a distance from the village. Burnt-Belly went out and saw the strange boy coming. He went into the tipi, and told his grandmother that a strange boy was coming into their tipi. So the old woman went out and said to Burnt-Belly: "You must tell the boy to go elsewhere, for we have little to eat." But the boy said: "No, grandmother, I want this boy to stay with us." So Blood-Clot-Boy was allowed to go into the tipi.

The old woman asked the boy whence he came, and the boy said: "I am poor, I have no home." So the old woman let the boy stay. Every day the boy used to go out with Burnt-Belly and hunt rabbits. The boys finally made bows and arrows, so that they killed small game. Blood-Clot-Boy then said that he was going to make a ring, and bade Burnt-Belly tell his grandmother to go through the camp and pick up rawhide scraps. The boy told his grandmother what Blood-Clot-Boy had said. So the old woman went through the village, and found trimmings of a buffalo hide. These she brought to the boys. Blood-Clot-Boy then boiled the trimmings, so that the hide became soft. Then he cut them into a long string. Then Blood-Clot-Boy hung the strings up. Now he went and cut an ash-tree and brought it home. He peeled off the bark, then twisted the stick, so that the stick became a ring where the ends met. Now he took the string and wound it around the ring, so that the ring looked like a spider's web. In the center was an open space. The boy then took from his belt a sack, from which he drew a pinch of dry maw-ball taken from the paunch of a buffalo bull. He pounded this into dust, then got water, which he sprinkled on the dust so that it became mud. This he put all over the ring; then he hung it up on a tree outside the tipi.

Blood-Clot-Boy said: "Now let us go into the timber; I want a better bow than this." So the boys went into the timber. Blood-Clot-Boy found a large ash-tree, cut it, and took it home. He worked on the stick several days, until at last he finished the bow. The bowstring was now made. The arrows were to be the same they had used before.

One day Blood-Clot-Boy bade Burnt-Belly tell his grandmother to roll the ring out toward the entrance. The old woman took down the ring and rolled it out, and as it came rolling, Blood-Clot-Boy shot, and the arrow went through the ring. As the arrow passed through, Blood-Clot-Boy gave a war-cry. The other boy went out of the tipi, and lying outside he saw a young buffalo calf with Blood-Clot-Boy's arrow through the flank. The boy came running out, shouting, "Grandmother! My brother has killed a young buffalo calf!" When the old woman heard her grand-child, she said: "My poor boys, how could they kill a young buffalo when there are none near?" But as she thrust her head out of the tipi, she saw the calf lying; then she went out. She asked where it came from, and Blood-Clot-Boy said nothing, but went and got the ring, and hung it in the tipi. Blood-Clot-Boy said: "Grandmother, skin the calf and get me tallow to grease my ring, so that it will not harden." So the old woman went to work and skinned the calf. The meat they took into the tipi, and roasted most of it, for they had no large pot in which to boil it.

Every fourth day the boy would say: "Tell grandmother to take the ring down and roll it out again, and I will stand outside, so that I can shoot at it." When the boy bade his grandmother roll the ring she did so; and when she heard the boy give the war-cry she knew that the boy had shot at the ring. Then she would thrust out her head, and there, in front of her grass tipi, would be a buffalo, larger than the one killed before. The old woman would then skin it and cut up the meat. Then she would pile the meat in her tipi. Every time the boy killed a buffalo, the first thing the old woman did was to get tallow, then grease the ring. She now had many hides, so she made a skin tipi. She had no tools to tan the hides. The old woman now knew that the boy was wonderful. He kept on killing buffalo, so that they had plenty of meat.

While they were having plenty, the people in the village were starving. One day a man was passing by the old woman's tipi, and he smelled burnt meat. He walked quietly, and saw the three eating meat. So he went in, and a piece of roasted meat was given him. The man went home, and told nobody, but every day would visit the tipi.

One day, when the man was at the tipi, Blood-Clot-Boy commanded the old woman to roll the ring outside. This she did and as the boy gave a war-cry, the old woman went to see what he had killed. The boy brought the ring and said: "Grandmother, go skin the buffalo, and when you cut up the meat give some to this man, for he is of my kin."

Therefore the man asked the boy why he called him a relative. So the boy told the story, about the man and woman far away, about his father picking him up (as blood) when he was born, and how he scratched him on the side of the face.

The man received his meal, then invited the chief to eat with him. So the man told the chief of the wonderful boy. The chief invited the poor Blood-Clot-Boy, and asked him to help the people kill buffalo, so they might get meat. Blood-Clot-Boy said "Chief, I can help the people. My kindred are far away. I shall go after them, and when I return, I will help the people."

So the boy went, and found the man and woman. There were all his things— robe, leggings, quiver, and cap. The cap was made from the heads of red-headed woodpeckers. He now put on his clothing, and told the father and mother that he had come after them, for he had found their people. So they all set out.

When they reached the village they went to the place where the old woman and grandson lived, and here they made their tipi. When Burnt-Belly saw them he invited them to his tipi. But Blood-Clot-Boy said: "No." So they made a new tipi of grass. The poor boy kept the ring which the boy gave to him.

A few days after, Blood-Clot-Boy said to his father and mother: "Build me a lodge, for I shall try to help the people." So the father and mother went to work, and built a great lodge. The boy entered and sat there. Every day he bade the poor boy hang up the door cover so that he could shoot. This time there was no rolling of the ring. Now Blood-Clot-Boy told Burnt-Belly that he himself was a buffalo; that his mother had vomited him up; that it was done for a purpose; that he had turned to a child; he was picked up by the man, who was under fear of the bear all the time; that he was to kill the bear so that the man and woman might go back to their people.

Now as he killed one buffalo after another, at the entrance, he was calling the buffalo to the people. One day the boy put on his leggings, his moccasins, his cap of woodpeckers' heads, and sat down in his lodge with the poor boy. Blood-Clot-Boy then sent his father after the chief. The chief came, and when he saw the boy dressed up with birds and other animals he begged him to help the people. So the boy said: "Do you stay here; sit down by me." The chief sat down, and the boy arose and went out to his father's tipi. There he took down his quiver and slung it over his breast. He started to travel over the country. In a little while he came into the tipi, where sat the chief. Blood-Clot-Boy reached under his robe and brought out a piece of kidney covered with fat. "Eat this," said Blood-Clot-Boy. "As you eat this (and I have brought it from far) the buffalo will come from a long distance, so that the people will be fed." The chief ate the kidney. While he did so the boy said: "Send men out upon the hills in the west and try if they can see anything." So the chief sent for his men, and he told them to go out upon the hills and see what they could see. The men went, and when they returned they reported that they had seen many buffalo and killed many.

Blood-Clot-Boy was upon the hill. When the people found out what he had done they said: "Chief, the boy should marry one of your daughters." So the chief said: "I am willing." But the boy would not go anywhere, so the girls never had a chance to see him.

One day Blood-Clot-Boy dressed up, slung his quiver over his shoulder, and went out. He came to a stream of water where sat a poor woman, who said: "My son, take pity on your poor grandmother; take me across." So when he went across the boy put her upon his back. The woman stuck on the boy's back. He tried to get her off but could not. The birds upon the boy's cap began to peck at her head. The bow turned into a large black snake. The arrows were all snakes. The birds upon the leggings began to make a noise, but the old woman did not mind the snakes. At last the quiver became alive, and turned to a mountain lion. The lion ran, then turned quickly, and before the woman could turn her head, had wound his tail round her neck, and pulled off her head and breast. The lion then took the other pieces her arms and legs—and scattered them over the timber, turning them into weeds covered with burrs.

The chief's youngest daughter was going after water, when she met Blood-Clot-Boy. The girl loved him; so when she went home she took her robe and went to Blood-Clot-Boy's lodge. Blood-Clot-Boy would not let her stay. But every day she came. So Blood-Clot-Boy said to the girl: "You must not look at me, for I am not a man; I shall soon depart; look at my brother, who belongs here; when I am gone he shall have my clothing." The girl said: "I wish to be with you, to see for myself that what you say is true." So Blood-Clot-Boy said: "It is well, you shall go with us."

So one day Blood-Clot-Boy told Burnt-Belly that he should accompany him to a certain lake, saying: "It is now time for me to return to my own people. I have killed the bear, and brought home the man and woman. I have fed the people and killed the old witch-woman, so that now the people may live happily."

One day the girl came to their tipi, and Blood-Clot-Boy said: "Come, my brother, and you, my sister; go with me." So they all went, Blood-Clot-Boy, Burnt-Belly, and the girl. Burnt-Belly kept asking Blood-Clot-Boy where they were going, but he would say nothing. They came to a large pond. Blood-Clot-Boy said: "Now let us sit down." So they sat down by a high cliff by the lake.

Blood-Clot-Boy said: "Burnt-Belly, you are to take my place. I am going to throw into the lake this clothing, my leggings, my robe, my cap, and my quiver; you are to dive after them. If the animals favor you, you will find these clothes; your hair will be like mine; and you shall also receive a scar as you dive." So Blood-Clot-Boy threw the clothing into the lake. Burnt-Belly leaped into the lake. For a long time Blood-Clot-Boy and the girl watched; but Blood-Clot-Boy said: "Nawa, there he comes, on the other side of the lake." The girl looked, and she saw Burnt-Belly coming, all dressed up. Blood-Clot-Boy and the girl went and met the boy. Then they went home.

Blood-Clot-Boy now sent for the chief, and said to him when he had come: "This young man whom you see shall now take my place. He has my clothing. Send your men again upon the hills to see what they can see."

The men went, and when they returned they said: "We saw many buffalo." So the people were ordered to surround the buffalo. Therefore the people went out. Blood-Clot-Boy, Burnt-Belly, and the girl went upon the hill. As the people attacked the buffalo, Blood-Clot-Boy disappeared; the girl and boy looked at the place where he had been standing, and there was a clot of blood instead of the boy. The boy and girl glanced at one another, and when they looked again there was no blood, and from them was running a young buffalo bull. They knew it was the young man, so the boy and girl went home.

The boy took the girl to her home, promising to ask for her. The boy did ask the father for the girl, and the chief gave her to him. The boy called the buffalo several times, and the people all believed that he was Blood-Clot-Boy. He died soon after, leaving no children.

5. Stone Boy

This hero tale was narrated in Lakota, a Siouan language, by George Sword. Its meanings are discussed briefly in the introduction, following the ideas of Elaine Jahner, the scholar of Native American culture who studied it. Motifs A500, A530, D55.2.5, D150, E50.

Four young men dwelt in the same tipi and one of them was called Hakela.
So they tell.
And then, from way out there, someone came and stood. They heard something; so they told Hakela to look. He peeked out and there was a young woman, more beautiful than any he had ever seen. The front part of her hair was bound and she had a great big work bag. Like that, she came and stood. Hakela saw her and he said, "Brothers, a young woman is there; she has arrived and she is standing; the front part of her hair is bound and she has a great big work bag. Really." That's what he said.

So they tell.

And the oldest brother, that one, said this, they say.

So they tell.

"Invite her into the tipi. We have no woman who can be a sister, so she can be our elder sister," he said.

So they tell.

Then Hakela peeked out and said, "Sister, come in and live with us."

So they tell.

"Our oldest brother says we have no elder sister so you can be our sister."

The woman said, "fine," and then she moved into their home. They gave her food but she didn't eat. She just kept on sitting there. Those four young men thought that she really wanted to eat but she was too bashful; so they felt sorry for the woman.

Then the oldest brother said this.

So they tell.

"My brothers, let's go for a walk. Hakela and our sister will stay here and she'll get back her appetite," he said. They went for a walk while Hakela stayed behind. The woman told him, "My brother, go hunting in the woods." Hakela took his arrows and went hunting.

So they tell.

Near the woods, he sat down. Soon that woman came out of the tipi and stood, looking all around. Then she went back inside. Next the smell of roasting meat came from the tipi, but the smoke odor was unusual. Hakela made himself into a chickadee and flew to the top of the tipi, alighting on the tipi pole. Then he peeked down into the tipi. Down there was a big metal container and it was full of crushed up scalps. The woman was saying, "I don't want the three young men around on the border so I'll put them over there."

Hakela, at the top of the tipi, peeking in, heard it all. Then the woman went on, "Anyway, Hakela's hair is awful so it will go here at the bottom."

Hakela fainted from fright. That great big bag really was filled with human heads. She roasted and then ate them. That's what he saw.

About that time, his brothers were all coming back home so he started to fly down to them.

So they tell.

He had made himself into a chickadee; then halfway down, he turned back into a man and ran to them.

So they tell.

The brothers were coming back to their own home so he told them, "Brothers, that very woman who is our sister told me to go hunting so I went hunting in the woods. From there I watched. She came out and stood looking around and then she went back in and smoke came from within with an unusual odor, so I made myself into a chickadee and perched on the tipi poles and all of a sudden she took her great big metal shield with scalps tied all over it and then she said, 'The three young men are not for this particular border. I'll put them there. That's where I'll put their hair.' Then she said, 'Even though Hakela's hair is nasty, I'll put it at the end.' That's what she said."

So those brothers decided, "We'll go home, just like always; but it is true that that food brings us no joy," they said.

So they tell.

The older sister went on acting right at home but she didn't pay any attention to them in the tipi, they say. Together the brothers secretly helped each other, and this is what they did.

So they tell.

They boiled a pack-strap and softened it. They told her to bring a bundle of wood. "As soon as she leaves, we'll go," they said. Only Hakela stayed behind in the woods.

So they tell.

That woman broke the pack strap as she was going along.

So they tell.

That's why she took so long to come home. After some time, Hakela could go back into that tipi of theirs, and he took the container full of men's heads and the metal shield and threw them into the fire.

All the while, the brothers were fleeing to get back their home; then Hakela too got moving. He looked back and saw the woman re-enter the tipi and the very things that Hakela had thrust into the fire, she took back out for herself. Immediately she started the attack on them.

So they tell.

And she caught up with them.

So they tell.

They shot arrows at her but she had that metal shield and they hit only that.

So they tell.

Then she went to the oldest of the young men and cut off his head with a mysterious knife.

So they tell.

And then she caught up to the remaining three and chopped their heads off, one by one.

So they tell.

And she killed all of them.

So they tell.

Hakela was the only one left so she came after him in quick pursuit. Then a chickadee appeared, flying above them and they said it said this, "Hakela, on the forelock," it said.

Then he shot right in the middle of the forelock and only then did he kill the woman, they say.

Next Hakela hurried to find wood and right away he made a sweat lodge.

So they tell.

And all those brothers of his, he dragged them there and then he put them in that sweat lodge and immediately poured water on the stones, they say.

Then all of them groaned and said, "Keep on, you who are so gracious but be good enough to open the door," they said.

So they tell.

Hakela heard them and opened the door.

So they tell.

And they all stood there, alive. They continued the flight to return to their home.

So they tell.

And they kept on coming home to carry on their life in their tipi.

So they tell.

Again a very beautiful young woman, wearing a lot of quill work and carrying a big bag came to their place.

So they tell.

But her forelock was not bound. That is how she arrived there and stood. Of course the brothers were terribly frightened but once again the oldest of the brothers spoke, they say.

"Hakela, ask her to come inside. We have no elder sister so we will have her as a sister," he said.

"I am very happy to have brothers," she said, and came into the tipi and made herself at home.

So they tell.

Quickly they gave her food and, this one, she just as quickly ate.

So they tell.

Then she opened the bag she was carrying and right there in plain view, she finished good moccasins for them, they say.

Then the oldest one of them said, they say, "It is not proper for you to be here alone, so I'll go," he said.

And he started to go somewhere, they say.

Then all of them said the same thing. Now that sister of theirs was all alone and she was heartbroken; all she did was lament, they say.

She stood atop a hill and wept as she walked along looking downward when she saw a transparent stone, so very beautiful. Because she was lamenting, she put it in her mouth.

So they tell.

Because she was completely exhausted, she slept and she swallowed the stone in her mouth.

So they tell.

However, she didn't know this and at once that woman got pregnant, they say, and very quickly the child was born.

So they tell.

His mother said this, they say. "My son, I want you to walk" and she took him by the hand and he walked, they say. She did that four times and now he became a young man, they say. He observed the customs of the tipi and he saw fine visions, they say. And this is what he said.

So they tell.

"Mother, whose beds are these?"

This is what his mother told him, they say. "My son, your four relatives are all uncles so these are their beds."

So they tell.

"They went on a journey and they did not come home," she said.

"Mother, make me arrows, I'm going to go to look for my uncles," he said. So his mother made him arrows, they say. Now, from there, he started to go seeking his uncles, they say.

He came near the lodge of an old woman.

"Stone Boy, my grandson, where are you going, my grandson?"

"To a ball game."

"I will give you my powers," she said. She made a yellow ball club and said, "Take this and you'll thank yourself for it," she said.

He went on from there and again he came to a lodge. An old woman said, "Grandson, I will give you one of my powers to use in the contest." And she gave him a kingfisher's feather, they say.

He went along and again he came to a lodge and an old woman said, "Stone Boy, grandson, take one of my powers for the contest." He went to her and she gave him a turtle.

So now he went on to look for his uncles, they say. He was going along when he saw a lot of people so he stood on a hill and they said, "Greetings, Stone Boy, come play ball."

These people were the buffalo tribe. They told an old woman to play with Stone Boy, he said.

So they tell.

The ball game was going along and all of a sudden he took that yellow club of his and the yellow eagle plume and he struck. An eagle started to fly.

So they tell.

Again they struck the ball but a large hawk flew by Stone Boy.

That's how Stone Boy won again.

So they tell.

Once again they struck the ball but Stone Boy hit the kingfisher's feather and a kingfisher started to fly.

Ho. That's the way Stone Boy won again.

So they tell.

Now they hit the ball into the water but Stone Boy struck the turtle and won again. Then the old Buffalo woman who had played against him said, "Well now, my son-in-law, shoot me."

He took his arrow and shot her in the neck. She died.

There, he found his uncles' bones, gathered them up and joined them together. He made a sweat lodge and he put them in there and poured water on them until they groaned and came to life.

So they tell.

He had won four very beautiful young buffalo women. His uncles seized them and brought them back home with them.

So they tell.

As they returned, he gave back their powers to the four old women.

When they got back to their own tipi, the mother of Stone Boy hugged and kissed her adopted relatives.

So they tell.

All were of good heart.

So they tell.

One time, though, Stone Boy went traveling again.

So they tell.

He met four really beautiful young women and they had a sled. So he made himself into a little boy with sore eyes and he stood there in front of where the buffalo girls were sitting. One buffalo had black hair, another grey, another had brown hair and the last had yellow hair. That's all there were.

Stone Boy said he wanted to sit where the first one was. But she said, "Oh no!" So they tell.

He said to the last one in line, "I'll come and sit there," they say.

"All right," she said.

There he was, in the last place. Now they started to slide down together when Stone Boy became a huge boulder and that's how he started to smash the four white buffalo girls, they say.

He took their tongues, they say. And he went home with them, they say.

Another time, he went traveling and he saw a buffalo sharpening the tips of his horns so he asked, "Grandfather, why are you sharpening the tips of your horns?"

That buffalo said, "Grandson, that Stone Boy killed four of my children so I'm going to go attack him," he said.

"Grandfather, when will you go to attack him?" Stone Boy asked.

The buffalo answered, "When the yellow clouds are here above us, then I'll attack." So Stone Boy answered, "Grandfather, this is who I am," and he shot him.

So they tell.

The buffalo died.

So they tell.

Just like that, Stone Boy killed four buffalo, one by one and took their tongues and went back home with them. Then he told his uncles to make arrows and he told them to make four wooden enclosures.

So they tell.

"Make them strong," he said. They did just that.

So they tell.

Now it was time for the yellow clouds to come and from all over the world the buffalo arrived, just as expected.

So they tell.

Stone Boy brought a great big piece of metal into the wooden enclosure.

So they tell.

And he stood on it. Then an old buffalo ornamented with pure white shells came to the top of the hill and said this.

So they tell.

"Stone Boy, get out of the way. A buffalo with long horns is coming there."

The long-horned buffalo came and gored the wooden structure.

They killed him.

So they tell.

Again he said, "Stone Boy, get out of the way! The Yellow Buffalo is going to try."

He ran up to the wooden enclosure and hit it head-on.

They killed him.

So they tell.

Again, "Stone Boy, get out of the way! The Crazy Buffalo is going to try," he said.

Then he ran up to the wooden enclosure and hit it head-on.

He was killed too. Well then, the buffalo came like a flood of water and Stone Boy and his uncles pursued them and sent them into a confused retreat.

Then that old buffalo who wore a pure white shell said, "That's why."

So they tell.

"That was the last time to come to this place of ours. We will not get the life of Stone Boy."

Then the men finished off the buffalo, they say.

Afterwards they went back home and they were very prosperous, they say.

This is the end.

So they tell.

6. The Boy Who Became a Mink

In this hero tale, the protagonist specifically disobeys an injunction to not do something and is forced to deal with the consequences of his action. It was originally narrated in Russian by Nicoli Medvednikoff, Corneil Panamaroff, and Mrs. Reed on Kodiak Island in Alaska. Motifs C615, C617, D110, G301.

In a small barrabara, away from other barrabaras and other people lived an old woman and her young grandson. While the boy was small, the grandmother supplied both with food and clothing by hunting and fishing. She also taught him how to hunt and fish and when nearly full grown, she surprised him one morning by telling him that a one-hatch bidarka (which she had made unbeknown to him) was on the beach ready for him.

It was there, sure enough, equipped and ready for hunting. He was supremely happy; for he had obtained that which for years he had been looking forward to. Every morning he went out hunting and fishing, and in the evening returned loaded with fish and game. In a little while he became very skillful in the handling of the bidarka, and daily ventured farther and farther out to sea.

His grandmother called him one morning, and said to him: "Son, you may go anywhere, except into yonder bay, and you will be safe; if you ever go there, you will never return to me. Take this mink skin, put it into the nose of your bidarka; this bag containing four tiny bows and arrows keep about your person. Should you ever be in trouble, turn to them, and they will help you."

He promised never to venture inside the bay, accepted the gifts, and disposed of them as he was told.

In those days, when this boy lived, there were no winds at all; the waters were always smooth and calm. One could go long distances from shore, and not be in danger of the winds and the waves. Not many days after the promise to his grandmother, the boy, while pursuing a seal, went much farther from shore than one would dare go now, and when he finally stopped paddling, after killing the seal, he found himself at the mouth of the bay.

The interior of the bay looked so inviting and alluring that he laughed at his grandmother's fears, and steered for the beautiful island in the middle of the bay. He beached his bidarka, took the mink skin, and started for the summit of a hill where he noticed a barrabara. As he began to ascend, large rocks came rolling down, blocking his way and nearly crushing him. The farther up he went the more difficult and dangerous it became. In order to save himself he jumped into a hole. The rocks fell over the hole, covered and blocked it.

He tried vainly to get out; the rocks were too heavy to be pushed off, and the openings too small to crawl through. While thinking over the situation, the mink skin occurred to him. Seizing it, he commenced chewing and stretching it until he pulled it over his head. As he did that, he changed into a mink. By scratching and squeezing, leaping and dodging, he escaped from his prison, and reached the summit, where he was surprised to see that all the rocks came from the barrabara.

Taking off the mink skin and becoming a boy again, he went into the barrabara. On the floor sat a very large woman making mats. When she saw him, she screamed in a loud and angry voice:

"Who told you to come here!"

Reaching behind her, she pulled out a long, sharp spear and threw it at him.

Before the spear reached him, he changed himself into a mink; the spear went over his head, sticking into the wall. Quickly assuming his boyish shape, he grabbed the spear, and called to her: "Change and save yourself if you can!" and hurled it at her, cutting her in two.

A loud report and earthquake followed his action. The barrabara trembled, tumbled in, and he was again a prisoner. His mink skin came into good use; by scratching and dodging he managed to crawl out and run down to the shore, and, after pulling off the skin, pushed the bidarka out and started homeward.

He had not gone very far when he heard someone calling, and on looking around saw people on the shore motioning to him. An old man greeted him as he landed, and taking him by the hand, led him into a barrabara where sat several girls. Pointing to one of them, he said: "You can have her for a wife."

This made him very happy, and glad he did not obey his grandmother. A dish of seal meat was placed before him, and after eating, they all lay down to sleep. The following morning the old man asked him to go to the woods, and bring wood for sled runners. In his position of prospective son-in-law he could not refuse any request of his prospective father-in-law, so he went.

A gruesome sight met his gaze on entering the woods. Human bones and skeletons were scattered everywhere; and he began to fear lest another trap was laid for him. He went about his work, however, and the woods soon rang with the reports of his axe.

A very frightful and horrible noise coming from the interior of the woods made him stop. The nearer it came the more terrible it sounded. "It must be a wild beast coming to eat me up," he thought.

Soon a very ferocious beast appeared and came running towards him. The boy looked for his mink skin; it was not about him, for he had left it in the bidarka; but still he had his bows and arrows. Quickly pulling them out of the bag, he sent one tiny arrow into the side of the monster, knocking him over; and when another arrow pierced the other side, he ceased kicking. Approaching him to withdraw the arrows, the boy found him dead.

On his return to the barrabara, after finishing his work, the old man looked surprised and uneasy—the old man was a shaman, and had been in the habit of sending strangers into the woods to be killed by the monster, and then eating them—and asked the boy:

"Did you see or hear anything strange in the woods?"

"No, I did not," the boy replied.

The morning of the second day, while the boy was eating breakfast, the old shaman from outside called to him:

"The girls want you to come out and swim with them!"

To refuse would have been unmanly, so he went to the beach, undressed himself, taking, however, the mink skin; for he suspected trouble, and swam after the girls, who were some distance from him. As he advanced, they retreated; and when almost up to them, a big whale appeared between them, and before he knew what to do, he was in the whale's mouth. In there, the boy put on the mink skin, and when the whale appeared on the surface, the boy escaped through the blow-hole, and swam for the shore.

When the shaman saw him, he was vexed and troubled, saying to himself: "He is the first one that I could not overcome, but I will."

That evening he had again a supper of seal meat; his bride sat where he could see her, but he dared not talk to her.

Early next morning the old man called him to have another swim with the girls. On the beach was a large whale, and the girls were climbing on his tail. When they were all on, he switched his tail, sending them through the air some distance into the sea.

The girls dared the boy do likewise. Stripping himself, and unnoticed by them—they were quite a distance from him—he took a tiny arrow in each hand. Instead of at once climbing on the tail, he approached the head of the whale. Sticking the arrows into the head, he asked the girls:

"Am I to get on here?"

"No, further down," they answered.

He stuck the arrows into the whale, as he moved down towards the tail, repeating the same question and receiving the same answer. When he finally stood on the tail, it did not move; for the whale was dead. The girls, after waiting some time, swam to the shore to report to the shaman, who returned with them only to find the whale lifeless. Furious was the shaman; and in his heart he swore he would yet eat the boy.

The following morning the old man asked the boy whether he had any relatives, mother or grandmother, whom he would like to go and see before he settled down with them.

"I have a grandmother," said the boy, and went off that day.

Paddling first on one side of the bidarka, and then on the other, he was making good progress, when all of a sudden the mink skin startled him by calling to him: "Look out, you are in danger!" He looked ahead; there was nothing dangerous there, so he paddled on. Again the mink skin called to him: "Look out, you are in danger!" Ahead everything was safe; but as he looked behind, he was almost overcome with fear; for a huge wave, high as a mountain, was coming his way, and would soon overtake and overwhelm him. As quickly as he could, he shot one of his arrows into the wave, breaking it, and he was once more safe.

Towards evening he steered for the shore, in order to eat and rest there, and when near the shore, a large sea monster appeared and swallowed him, bidarka, and all. He pulled out and put on the mink skin, and when an opportunity offered itself, he escaped through the monster's gills, and swam to the shore.

His grandmother, who was also a shaman, had been watching the grandson's doings, though far away, punished the monster by sending two large ravens to peck his eyes out.

Being on shore, and without a bidarka, the boy started to walk home. He did not take off the mink skin, and so was still a mink. On the way he came to a large lake, abounding in fish; there he stopped, fed on the fish he caught, and in a short time became acquainted with the minks of the neighborhood. This easy life pleased him so well that he decided to remain there; and there (in the neighborhood of Kodiak) he is at present. The shamans, only, can tell him apart from the other minks.

7. Coyote's Eyes

This story about the well-known Indian trickster figure Coyote was recorded by folklorist Barre Toelken, who has given particular attention to Native American materials. He recorded it by jotting it down on paper as his Navajo friend Yellowman told it to his own family in 1956. Toelken had heard the story before, and Yellowman's "delivery was very slow," so Toelken had a fairly accurate version; he added particulars about the performance of the story, given in parentheses, which, along with the arrangement of lines, provide a sense of the dynamic of the oral narration. This story is discussed in the introduction. Motifs J2423, K333.3.

Ma'i [Coyote] was going along there just as he has always been going along.
　[pause of several seconds; the audience is smiling]
Up ahead, near some trees, some junipers, in some junipers, he could see birds flying up.
　[slight pause]
They were flying up and looking all around;
　they could see everywhere.
　[pause; the audience is smiling in anticipation]
Ma'i said to them, "Come here, my relatives, give me your eyes
　so I can see as far as you can."
　[longer pause; some children are laughing quietly]
"No, you're not a bird. You can't fly."
　[general laughter, including narrator]
Ma'i said to them, "My relatives, please give me your eyes.
　Take mine out and give me yours."
　[pause; smiling]
"No [emphatically]! You're not a bird!"
　[pause; smiling]
Ma'i said, "My relatives, I want to see like you;
　please take my eyes out and put yours in!"
　[pause, deep breath]

"No! You're not a bird. You can't fly!"

    [pause; some laughter]

Ma'i said, "My relatives, please take my eyes out and give me yours!"

    [pause; smiling]

"*Yaahdilah!* [no translation; an expletive]"

    [general prolonged laughter]

They came to him. They took sticks and pried out his eyes.

    [loud laughter]

"Aah!" he was screaming. He cried. "That hurts!"

    [louder laughter, including narrator]

They pried out his eyes.

    [mild laughter]

They flew away.

    [smiling, nodding heads]

He was blind. He couldn't see anything.

    [pause; smiles]

He stumbled around in the junipers, feeling his way.

    [pause]

He was crying.

    [pause]

Ma'i felt some lumps on the side of the juniper,

    that pitch that grows there.

    [pause; someone says, "Hmm."]

He felt those lumps, and he pulled them off the tree:

    Two lumps of pitch, the same size as his eyes, perhaps.

    [short pause]

He put them into his sockets.

    [pause; several people expel air through their noses]

Now Ma'i has yellow eyes; his eyes are pitch.

    [long pause, several seconds]

That's what they say.

8. Coyote and the Shadow People

Although this particular story is from the Nez Perce of the Northwest Plateau country, Native American narratives that parallel the classical Orpheus story—of the man who goes to the land of the dead to bring back his deceased wife to the living but who violates a prohibition and thus fails—are told by a number of tribes. That the trickster Coyote is the protagonist here adds a dimension to the story, for he is a character who habitually makes grievous errors through impulsive actions. This story is discussed briefly in the introduction. Motifs F81.1, J2400; cf J2460.1.

Coyote and his wife were dwelling there. His wife became ill. She died. Then Coyote became very, very lonely. He did nothing but weep for his wife.

There the death spirit came to him and said, "Coyote, do you pine for your wife?"—"Yes, friend, I long for her . . ." replied Coyote. "I could take you to the place where your wife has gone, but, I tell you, you must do everything just exactly as I say; not once are you to disregard my commands and do something else."—"Yes," replied Coyote, "yes, friend, and what else could I do? I will do everything you say." Then the ghost told him, "Yes. Now let us go." Coyote added, "Yes, let it be so that we are going."

They went. There he said to Coyote again, "You must do whatever I say. Do not disobey."—"Yes, yes, friend. I have been pining so deeply, and why should I not heed you?" Coyote could not see the spirit clearly. He appeared to be only a shadow. They started and went along over a plain. "Oh, there are many horses; it looks like a round-up," exclaimed the ghost. "Yes," replied Coyote, though he really saw none, "yes, there are many horses."

They had arrived now near the place of the dead. The ghost knew that Coyote could see nothing but he said, "Oh look, such quantities of service berries! Let us pick some to eat. Now when you see me reach up you too will reach up and when I bend the limb down you too will pull your hands down."—"Yes," Coyote said to him, "so be it, thus I will do." The ghost reached up and bent the branch down and Coyote did the same. Although he could see no berries he imitated the ghost in putting his hand to and from his mouth in the manner of eating. Thus they picked and ate berries. Coyote watched him carefully and imitated every action. When the ghost would put his hand into his mouth Coyote would do the same. "Such good service berries these are," commented the ghost. "Yes, friend, it is good that we have found them," agreed Coyote. "Now let us go." And they went on.

"We are about to arrive," the ghost told him. "There is a long, very, very long lodge. Your wife is in there somewhere. Just wait and let me ask someone." In a little while the ghost returned and said to Coyote, "Yes, they have told me where your wife is. We are coming to a door through which we will enter. You will do in every way exactly what you see me do. I will take hold of the door flap, raise it up, and bending low, will enter. Then you too will take hold of the door flap and do the same." They proceeded now in this manner to enter.

It happened that Coyote's wife was sitting right near the entrance. The ghost said to Coyote, "Sit here beside your wife." They both sat. The ghost added, "Your wife is now going to prepare food for us." Coyote could see nothing, except that he was sitting there on an open prairie where nothing was in sight; yet he could feel the presence of the shadow. "Now she has prepared our food. Let us eat." The ghost reached down and then brought his hand to his mouth. Coyote could see nothing but the prairie dust. They ate. Coyote imitated all the movements of his companion. When they had finished and the woman had apparently put the food away, the ghost said to Coyote, "You stay here. I must go around to see some people."

He went out but returned soon. "Here we have conditions different from those you have in the land of the living. When it gets dark here it has dawned in your land and when it dawns for us it is growing dark for you." And now it began to grow dark and Coyote seemed to hear people whispering, talking in faint tones, all around him. Then darkness set in. Oh, Coyote saw many fires in a long-house. He saw that he was in a very, very large lodge and there were many fires burning. He saw the various people. They seemed to have shadow-like forms but he was able to recognize different persons. He saw his wife sitting by his side.

He was overjoyed, and he joyfully greeted all his old friends who had died long ago. How happy he was! He would march down the aisles between the fires, going here and there, and talk with the people. He did this throughout the night. Now he could see the doorway through which he and his friend had entered. At last it began to dawn and his friend came to him and said, "Coyote, our night is falling and in a little while you will not see us. But you must stay right here. Do not go anywhere at all. Stay right here and then in the evening you will see all these people again."— "Yes, friend. Where could I possibly go? I will spend the day here."

The dawn came and Coyote found himself alone sitting there in the middle of the prairie. He spent the day there, just dying from the heat, parching from the heat, thirsting from the heat. Coyote stayed here several days. He would suffer through the day, but always at night he would make merry in the great lodge.

One day his ghost friend came to him and said, "Tomorrow you will go home. You will take your wife with you."— "Yes, friend, but I like it here so much, I am having a good time and I should like to remain here."— "Yes," the ghost replied: "nevertheless you will go tomorrow, and you must guard against your inclination to do foolish things. Do not yield to any queer notions, I will advise you now what you are to do. There are five mountains. You will travel for five days. Your wife will be with you but you must never, never touch her. Do not let any strange impulses possess you. You may talk to her but never touch her. Only after you have crossed and descended from the fifth mountain you may do whatever you like."— "Yes, friend," replied Coyote.

When dawn came again, Coyote and his wife started. At first it seemed to him as if he were going alone, yet he was dimly aware of his wife's presence as she walked along behind. They crossed one mountain, and, now, Coyote could feel more definitely the presence of his wife; like a shadow she seemed. They went on and crossed the second mountain. They camped at night at the foot of each mountain. They had a little conical lodge which they would set up each time. Coyote's wife would sit on one side of the fire and he on the other. Her form appeared clearer and clearer.

The death spirit, who had sent them, now began to count the days and to figure the distance Coyote and his wife had covered. "I hope that he will do everything right and take his wife through to the world beyond," he kept saying to himself.

Here Coyote and his wife were spending their last night, their fourth camping, and on the morrow she would again assume fully the character of a living person. They were camping for the last time and Coyote could see her very clearly as if she were a real person who sat opposite him. He could see her face and body very clearly, but only looked and dared not touch her.

But suddenly a joyous impulse seized him; the joy of having his wife again overwhelmed him. He jumped to his feet, and rushed over to embrace her. His wife cried out, "Stop! Stop! Coyote! Do not touch me. Stop!" Her warning had no effect. Coyote rushed over to his wife and just as he touched her body she vanished. She disappeared—returned to the shadow-land.

When the death-spirit learned of Coyote's folly he became deeply angry. "You inveterate doer of this kind of thing! I told you not to do anything foolish. You, Coyote, were about to establish the practice of returning from death. Only a short time away the human race is coming, but you have spoiled everything and established for them death as it is."

Here Coyote wept and wept. He decided, "Tomorrow I shall return to see them again." He started back the following morning and as he went along he began to recognize the places where he and his spirit friend had passed before. He found the place where the ghost had seen the herd of horses, and now he began to do the same things they had done on their way to the shadow-land. "Oh, look at the horses; it looks like a round-up." He went on until he came to the place where the ghost had found the service berries. "Oh, such choice service berries! Let us pick and eat some." He went through the motions of picking and eating berries.

He went on and finally came to the place where the lodge had stood. He said to himself, "Now when I take hold of the door flap and raise it up you must do the same." Coyote remembered all the little things his friend had done. He saw the spot where he had sat before. He went there, sat down, and said, "Now, your wife has brought us food. Let us eat." He went through the motions of eating again. Darkness fell, and now Coyote listened for the voices, and he looked all around. He looked here and there, but nothing appeared. Coyote sat there in the middle of the prairie.

He sat there all night but the lodge didn't appear again nor did the ghost ever return to him.

9. Fox and Kingfisher

Although Coyote probably is the best known of the so-called trickster figures in Native American narratives, others fill the role, as does Fox in this story, collected by Frank Russell from Laforia, "a very old woman," whose grandson Gunsi interpreted. It was recorded in New Mexico while Russell undertook fieldwork among the Jicarilla Apache. Here the trickster attempts to imitate the powerful, transformative actions of others, but, not understanding his limitations, fails. Motif J2425.

As Fox went on his way he met Kingfisher, whom he accompanied to his home. Kingfisher said that he had no food to offer his visitor, so he would go and catch some fish for Fox. He broke through six inches of ice on the river and caught two fish, which he cooked and set before his guest. Fox was pleased with his entertainment, and invited the Kingfisher to return the call. In due time the Kingfisher came to the home of the Fox, who said, "I have no food to offer you"; then he went down to the river, thinking to secure fish in the same manner as the Kingfisher had done. Fox leaped from the high bank, but instead of breaking through the ice he broke his head and killed himself. Kingfisher went to him, caught him up by the tail, and swung Fox around to the right four times, thereby restoring him to life. Kingfisher caught some fish, and they ate together. "I am a medicine-man," said Kingfisher; "that is why I can do these things. You must never try to catch fish in that way again."

After the departure of Kingfisher, Fox paid a visit to the home of Prairie-dog, where he was cordially received. Prairie-dog put four sticks, each about a foot in length, in the ashes of the camp-fire; when these were removed, they proved to be four nicely roasted prairie-dogs, which were served for Fox's dinner. Fox invited the Prairie-dog to return the visit, which in a short time the latter did. Fox placed four sticks in the fire to roast, but they were consumed by it, and instead of palatable food to set before his guest he had nothing but ashes. Prairie-dog said to Fox, "You must not attempt to do that. I am a medicine-man; that is why I can transform the wood to flesh." Prairie-dog then prepared a meal as he had done before, and they dined.

Fox went to visit Buffalo, who exclaimed, "What shall I do? I have no food to offer you." Buffalo was equal to the emergency, however; he shot an arrow upward, which struck in his own back as it returned. When he pulled this out, a kidney and the fat surrounding it came out also. This he cooked for Fox, and added a choice morsel from his own nose. As usual, Fox extended an invitation to his host to return the visit.

When Buffalo came to call upon Fox, the latter covered his head with weeds in imitation of the head of the Buffalo. Fox thought he could provide food for their dinner as the Buffalo had done, so fired an arrow into the air; but when it came close to him on its return flight, he became frightened and ran away. Buffalo then furnished meat for their meal as on the previous occasion. "You must not try this," said he; "I am a medicine-man; that is why I have the power."

Some time afterward, as Fox was journeying along, he met an Elk, lying beside the trail. He was frightened when he saw the antlers of the Elk moving, and jumped to avoid what seemed to be a falling tree. "Sit down beside me," said the Elk. "Don't be afraid."

"The tree will fall on us," replied Fox.

"Oh, sit down; it won't fall. I have no food to offer you, but I will provide some."

The Elk cut steaks from his own quarter, which the Fox ate, and before leaving Fox invited the Elk to return the visit. When Elk came to see Fox, the latter tried unsuccessfully to cut flesh from his own meager flanks; then he drove sharpened sticks into his nose, and allowed the blood to run out upon the grass. This he tried in vain to transform into meat, and again he was indebted to his guest for a meal. "I am a medicine-man; that is why I can do this," said Elk.

10. The Buffalo-Wife

This narrative is from the Crow of the western Plains, but stories of humans marrying animal wives or husbands are common to many Native American groups. This particular story was recorded in the early decades of the twentieth century by Robert Lowie, one of the most eminent American anthropologists. Motifs B600, B630.

Some young men were on the warpath, one of them retraced his steps. He came to a coulee [ravine]. A buffalo cow was stuck in the mud. He came up to her, touched her vulva and lay with her. After he was through, he helped her out of the mud, and both went off. He came home and lived in the camp. This cow got to be pregnant. She gave birth to a calf, a little male, which was the child of the Crow.

The buffalo cow told the other buffalo, "The father of my child is a human being, I'll take it to him." She brought the child to the edge of the camp. They heard in the camp that a nice young woman and child were there. The cow said to her son: "Go out where that young man is, and say 'father' to him. He'll take you up and ask you, 'Son, when was I your father?' He looks like you. Tell him, 'At the time of the mud.' Then he will know."

The young boy came over to the young man and addressed him, "Father."

"Son, when was I your father?"

"At the time of the mud, at that time."

"Where is your mother?"

"Over there."

"Let us go to your mother."

They came up to her. She said, "Your child wanted to come so badly, I have brought him."

"Let us go to my tipi."

They stayed there, and everything was well.

The woman said to her husband, "I don't care whether you beat me, but do not call me any names."

She stayed there for a long time. The young man married again. The woman got into a quarrel and the husband said to the buffalo cow, "You are like a ghost."

"I told you not to call me names—you have done it." At night they went to bed, the husband on the right side, the woman on the left. At night he always watched both wives. He woke up and touched the side, and the cow and her child were gone. He went outside, they were not there. He looked for them, but they were gone. He tried to find their tracks, at the edge of the camp he found the tracks of a buffalo and a calf. Thinking it was their tracks, he tried to follow. A winter sparrow came and said, "That's your wife's track, they have got to a big herd now."

He went home and had moccasins made, got a lot of arrows, came to the tracks, and met a little wolf who took him to the big herd of buffalo saying, "Your wife is in that herd." He went to a knoll close by and began to cry.

From the herd came a young calf running. This was his son, "Father, you are always crying, I do not like it, stop crying. Tomorrow we'll have a lot of calves pass by you, if you can pick me out, they'll let me go with you. When we pass, I'll shake my left ear, by that you'll know me. A whole lot of calves all looking alike will pass. If you don't know me the bulls will trample on you."

When the calves really passed by and came opposite the man, the calf moved its left ear and he knew it as his own.

"Tomorrow they'll have the cows pass and if you don't pick out my mother, they'll trample on you. Tomorrow when we go to the water, I'll get into the mud and play with my mother, climb on her, and from her tail down her legs will be all mud. I'll mark her."

The cows came the next day. The man watched. As the cows passed, he saw the mark on her thigh. "This is my wife." He picked her out. "You have found both, you may take them back." So he brought her back. Now he did not call her names any more.

11. The Woman Who Married the Merman

Stories of parallel worlds in the sky (as in story 12) or under the sea (as in this one) are hardly limited to Native American cultures, but they are a popular theme in the stories of many American tribes. Often they involve finding a lover or mate in the other world. This particular story is from the Coos of the Oregon coast. Motifs B82, B82.1, F133, F725.3.3.

In an Indian village named Takimiya there lived five brothers and a sister. Many men from different places wished to marry the girl, but she did not want to get married. It was her custom to go swimming every day in a little creek. One day, while returning from her daily swim, she noticed that she was pregnant. Her brothers demanded to know how this had happened, but she could not give them any answer, because she did not know. After some time she gave birth to a boy, who was in the habit of crying all the time. Everything was attempted to stop the crying of the baby, but was of no avail. Her brothers therefore advised her to put it outdoors.

As soon as this was done, the baby stopped crying. After a little while the mother went out to look after her boy, and noticed, to her surprise, that he was eating some seal-meat, which was strung on a small stick. She looked around to see who could have given him the meat, but could not find anybody. So she took the child into the house. But the boy started crying again, and would not let anybody sleep.

Her brothers told her to take the child outside, and advised her to conceal herself and watch it. A whole day she remained outside without seeing anyone. Suddenly, towards evening, a man appeared and told her to follow him, because he was her husband. At first she refused to go with him, fearing that her relatives would not know where she had gone; but after he had assured her that she would be permitted to see her people, she took the baby in her arms and followed him. They were going into the water. Her husband told her to hang on to his belt and to keep her eyes closed. She did so, and they arrived at a village at the bottom of the sea, which was inhabited by many Indians. Her husband was one of the five sons of the chief of this village. They lived here happy and satisfied.

The boy grew up in the meantime, and acquired the habit of playing with arrows. His mother would make them for him, and tell the child at the same time, that his five uncles, who lived above them, had lots of arrows. One day the little fellow asked his mother whether she would not take him to his uncles to get some arrows. To this the father of the boy objected, although he allowed his wife to go alone. She put on five sea-otter hides, and started on her way early in the morning. As soon as her brothers saw her, they thought she was a real otter, and began to shoot at her with arrows. The otter seemed to have been hit repeatedly but it would come up again, so that they did not know what became of their arrows. The otter was swimming up and down the river, followed by many people in canoes, who were shooting at it, but nobody could hurt it. Seeing the fruitlessness of their efforts, everybody gave up the hunt—with the exception of the oldest brother, who followed the otter until it reached the beach.

There he saw someone moving around close to the shore. Approaching nearer, he noticed that it was a woman, and recognized her at once as his lost sister. She told him that she was the sea-otter, and showed him the arrows with which they had been shooting at her. She said, "I came here to get some arrows for my boy. My husband is the son of a chief. We are living not very far from here. Whenever the tide is low, you can see our house right in the middle of the ocean. I brought you these sea-otter skins that you might exchange them for some other things." Her brother gave her as many arrows as she could carry, and she went back to her husband. But before going down in the water, she said to her brother, "You will find tomorrow morning a whale on the beach, right in front of your landing." And so it came to pass. The whale was divided among the people.

A few months afterwards the woman visited her relatives with her husband and child, and her brothers noticed that part of her shoulders were turning into those of a dark-colored sea-serpent. She stayed a little while, and then returned home.

Long afterwards many of these sea-serpents came into the harbor; but the woman never came ashore again, and was seen no more. These sea-serpents had come after arrows; and people kept on shooting at them, thereby giving them what they desired. They never returned again; but every summer and winter they would put ashore two whales as a gift to their kinsmen above the sea.

12. A Tale of the Sky World

This Seneca story includes a sky world that exists in conjunction with an earthly one—common to other Native American narratives such as "The Star Husband," a story studied in great detail by the noted Stith Thompson—but really is about the creation of the world known to humans. It incorporates the internationally circulated story of an Earth Diver, an animal who dives to the bottom of a primordial ocean to bring up the earth that begins to form a land mass; and it includes the emergence of twin culture heroes who create other features of ordinary life. Motifs A515.1.1, A800, A812, C330, F50, F62.2; cf F56.

A long time ago human beings lived high up in what is now called heaven. They had a great and illustrious chief.

It so happened that this chief's daughter was taken very ill with a strange affection. All the people were very anxious as to the outcome of her illness. Every known remedy was tried in an attempt to cure her, but none had any effect.

Near the lodge of this chief stood a great tree, which every year bore corn used for food. One of the friends of the chief had a dream, in which he was advised to tell the chief that in order to cure his daughter he must lay her beside this tree, and that he must have the tree dug up. This advice was carried out to the letter. While the people were at work and the young woman lay there, a young man came along. He was very angry and said: "It is not at all right to destroy this tree. Its fruit is all that we have to live on." With this remark he gave the young woman who lay there ill a shove with his foot, causing her to fall into the hole that had been dug.

Now, that hole opened into this world, which was then all water, on which floated waterfowl of many kinds. There was no land at that time. It came to pass that as these waterfowl saw this young woman falling they shouted, "Let us receive her," whereupon they, at least some of them, joined their bodies together, and the young woman fell on this platform of bodies. When these were wearied they asked, "Who will volunteer to care for this woman?" The great Turtle then took her, and when he got tired of holding her, he in turn asked who would take his place. At last the question arose as to what they should do to provide her with a permanent resting place in this world. Finally it was decided to prepare the earth, on which she would live in the future. To do this it was determined that soil from the bottom of the primal sea should be brought up and placed on the broad, firm carapace of the

Turtle, where it would increase in size to such an extent that it would accommodate all the creatures that should be produced thereafter. After much discussion the toad was finally persuaded to dive to the bottom of the waters in search of soil. Bravely making the attempt, he succeeded in bringing up soil from the depths of the sea. This was carefully spread over the carapace of the Turtle, and at once both began to grow in size and depth.

After the young woman recovered from the illness from which she suffered when she was cast down from the upper world, she built herself a shelter, in which she lived quite contentedly. In the course of time she brought forth a girl baby, who grew rapidly in size and intelligence.

When the daughter had grown to young womanhood, the mother and she were accustomed to go out to dig wild potatoes. Her mother had said to her that in doing this she must face the west at all times. Before long the young daughter gave signs that she was about to become a mother. Her mother reproved her, saying that she had violated the injunction not to face the east, as her condition showed that she had faced the wrong way while digging potatoes. It is said that the breath of the West Wind had entered her person, causing conception. When the days of her delivery were at hand, she overheard twins within her body in a hot debate as to which should be born first and as to the proper place of exit, one declaring that he was going to emerge through the armpit of his mother, the other saying that he would emerge in the natural way. The first one born, who was of a reddish color, was called Othagwenda; that is, Flint. The other, who was light in color, was called Djuskaha; that is, the Little Sprout.

The grandmother of the twins liked Djuskaha and hated the other; so they cast Othagwenda into a hollow tree some distance from the lodge.

The boy that remained in the lodge grew very rapidly, and soon was able to make himself bows and arrows and to go out to hunt in the vicinity. Finally, for several days he returned home without his bow and arrows. At last he was asked why he had to have a new bow and arrows every morning. He replied that there was a young boy in a hollow tree in the neighborhood who used them. The grandmother inquired where the tree stood, and he told her; whereupon then they went there and brought the other boy home again.

When the boys had grown to man's estate, they decided that it was necessary for them to increase the size of their island, so they agreed to start out together, afterward separating to create forests and lakes and other things. They parted as agreed, Othagwenda going westward and Djuskaha eastward. In the course of time, on returning, they met in their shelter or lodge at night, then agreeing to go the next day to see what each had made.

First they went west to see what Othagwenda had made. It was found that he had made the country all rocks and full of ledges, and also a mosquito which was very large. Djuskaha asked the mosquito to run, in order that he might see whether the insect could fight. The mosquito ran, and ticking his bill through a sapling, thereby made it fall, at which Djuskaha said, "That will not be right, for you would kill the people who are about to come." So, seizing him, he rubbed him down in his hands, causing him to become very small; then he blew on the mosquito, whereupon he flew away. He also modified some of the other animals which his brother had made. After returning to their lodge, they agreed to go the next day to see what Djuskaha had fashioned.

On visiting the east the next day, they found that Djuskaha had made a large number of animals which were so fat that they could hardly move; that he had made the sugar-maple trees to drop syrup; that he had made the sycamore tree to bear fine fruit; that the rivers were so formed that half the water flowed upstream and the other half downstream. Then the reddish-colored brother, Othagwenda, was greatly displeased with what his brother had made, saying that the people who were about to come would live too easily and be too happy. So he shook violently the various animals—the bears, deer, and turkeys—causing them to become small at once, a characteristic which attached itself to their descendants. He also caused the sugar maple to drop sweetened water only, and the fruit of the sycamore to become small and useless; and lastly he caused the water of the rivers to flow in only one direction, because the original plan would make it too easy for the human beings who were about to come to navigate the streams.

The inspection of each other's work resulted in a deadly disagreement between the brothers, who finally came to grips and blows, and Othagwenda was killed in the fierce struggle.

13. The Siege of Courthouse Rock

This White River Sioux account was told by Jenny Leading Cloud, White River, Rosebud Reservation, in South Dakota in 1967 and was recorded by Richard Erdoes. Motifs K500, K650.

Nebraska is green and flat, a part of the vast corn belt. There are farms everywhere, and silos, and the land does not look like the West at all. But as you travel on toward the setting sun, you find three great, wild rocks which rise out of the plains. First you come to Chimney Rock, towering like a giant needle on the prairie. It was a famous landmark for the settlers in their covered wagons as they traveled west on the Oregon trail or took the more southerly route to the Colorado goldfields.

Then you come to the twins—Courthouse Rock and Jailhouse Rock. Formed of yellowish stone, they are covered with yucca plants and sagebrush. Mud swallows nest in the rock faces. If you climb one of the twins, there is a wonderful view of the plains all around. And westward beyond the plains rise the chalk cliffs and the sandhills of Nebraska, home of many western Sioux.

A long time ago a Sioux war party surprised a war party of Pahani near

Courthouse Rock. We Sioux had been fighting many battles with the Pahani. The whites had pushed nations like ours, whose homeland was further east near the Great Lakes, westward into the prairie and the hunting grounds of other tribes. Maybe the Pahani were there before us; who knows? At any rate, now we were hunting the same herds in the same place, and naturally we fought.

I guess there must have been more of us than of the Pahani, and they retreated to the top of Courthouse Rock to save themselves. Three sides of Courthouse Rock go straight up and down like the sides of a skyscraper. No one can climb them. Only the fourth side had a path to the top, and it could be easily defended by a few brave men.

Thus the Pahani were on the top and the Sioux at the foot of Courthouse Rock. The Sioux chief told his warriors: "It's no use trying to storm it. Only three or four men can go up that path abreast, so even women and children could defend it. But the Pahani have no water, and soon they'll run out of food. They can stay up there and starve or die of thirst, or they can come and fight us on the plain. When they climb down, we can kill them and count many coups on them." The Sioux settled down to wait at the foot of the rock.

On the summit, as the Sioux chief expected, the Pahani suffered from hunger and thirst. They grew weak. Though there was little hope for them, they had a brave leader who could use his head. He knew that three sides of the rock were unguarded but that one would have to be a bird to climb down them. On one of the three steep sides, however, there was a round bulge jutting out from the rock face. "If we could fasten a rope to it, we could let ourselves down," he thought. But the outcropping was too smooth, round, and wide to hold a lasso.

Then the Pahani leader tried his knife on the rock bulge. He found that the stone was soft enough for the knife to bite easily into, and he began patiently whittling a groove around the bulge. He and his men worked only at night so that the Sioux wouldn't see what they were up to. After two nights they had carved the groove deep enough. When they tied all their rawhide ropes together, they found that the line would reach to the ground.

On the third night the Pahani leader tied one end of the rope around the bulge in the rock. He himself tested it by climbing all the way down and then up again, which took most of the night.

On the next and fourth night, he told his men: "Now we do it. Let the youngest go first." The Pahani climbed down one by one, the youngest and least accomplished first, so that a large group could belay them, and the older and more experienced warriors later. The leader came down last. The Sioux did not notice them at all, and the whole party stole away.

The Sioux stayed at the foot of the rock for many days. They themselves grew hungry, because they had hunted out all the game. At last a young, brave warrior said: "They must be all dead up there. I'm fed up with waiting; I'll go up and see." He climbed the path to the top and shouted down that nobody was up there.

That time the joke was on us Sioux. It's always good to tell a story honoring a brave enemy, especially when the story is true. Are there any Pahani listening?

14. The First Meeting of the Indians and the Europeans (Thátkak ilá:ci:fó:kok)

This involved historical narrative was told by Bel Abbey of the Koasati (Coushatta) tribe of Louisiana, February 1982, and recorded by Geoffrey Kimball. Here the story is rendered in a method pioneered by the anthropologist Dennis Tedlock and others, which attempts to convey the poetic and dramatic character of the original narration. Motif A1386.

Prologue:
The Indians once were dwelling,
here in this land they dwelt.
When the white people arrived,
after the white people came,
they existed, so it is said,
and they knew that the Indians might run and hide from them.

But to change the subject for a moment, the Indians were dwelling,
the Indians dwelt here, and they hunted for game,
and lived by killing and eating various sorts of things.

Scene 1: The Meeting and Flight
Wherever the white people were going on about on our side of the ocean they
    arrived,
It seems to also have been the first meeting.
On first arriving, they also came to trade with them.

When the white people arrived,
when within a boat they arrived over the water,
the Indians dwelling there, on seeing them, ran from them, so it is said.
When they ran from them,
after they ran from them, they did not meet them.
"Whatever could it be? Why must they run off?" the white people said, so it is
    reported.
And then, they kept on fleeing from them so,
sometimes they all ran from them, at other times they all hid from them.
The Indians were afraid of them, because they had never seen such people as
    those.

It is said that they were afraid of them.
They kept on fleeing from them.

Scene 2: The Dilemma of the Europeans
Then the white people said,
"How can we get to know them before we speak to them?"
as they all ran hiding from them.
If they looked into their dwelling,
(those they had were somewhat sunken in the earth),
they who were the openers of their houses,
that those others dwelt in,
if the white people looked into the Indians' own dwellings;
people's own dwelling were looked into,
but contrary to expectation, there were no Indians of any kind,
they had gone out and run and hidden from them and disappeared.
And then, "However would it be possible for us to meet and speak with them?"
they kept on thinking.
It was impossible; the white people did not know how they might do it.

Scene 3: The Leaving of the Whiskey
They [the white people] went around with liquor, they carried whiskey with them.
They brought over one keg and went and laid it down for them, so it is said.
When they laid it down for them, as for the drinking glass, if it were not such,
it was more or less like a coffee cup, but I don't know.
How many they laid down for them I don't know,
but having laid them down for them, they returned [to their ship], so it is said.

Scene 4: The Return and Debate of the Indians
And then, the Indians who had gone off,
these Indians returned and came arriving,
and when they saw it, the Indians kept on returning.
There were many Indians there.
Having returned and arrived back, they who said it [the keg] lying with it [the
    liquor],
upon seeing the one keg lying there,
when they saw it, they said, "What is it?
No! Do ye not approach it!
Whatever it is will hurt you!
Whatever it is will kill ye!" they said,
forbidding the rest, so it is reported.
But then, contrary to expectation, they kept on turning and looking at it, turning
    and looking at it,

and they kept on so—so it is said, they kept on so;
thereupon [one said], "What is it?"
"I not know, but it is lying there with it [the liquor] just like that," said another.
Thereupon, when one person said, "Let me test it by drinking!"
"No! Do not drink it! It is bad by nature!"
"As it is a bad thing, upon your drinking it, you will die," the other said.

Scene 5: The Intervention of the Orphan
Thereupon, "I shall be the one!
I shall be the one!" said the orphaned man who was passing by, so it is reported.
Being without living relatives,
he was completely and utterly alone.
He used to live by joining up with people;
his relatives were no more.
It is as an orphan that he lived.
"Well, I will be the one!"
when he said, "I might just drink it,"
"Nay!" said another. "Do not drink it!"
As it is something bad by nature, you will die."
When he said this, the orphan man would not quit begging to try drinking it, so it
        is said.
"But all the same, let it be drunk,
because my relatives no longer exist,
no one at all can feel sorry about anything.
Nothing will sadden anyone.
Because I have been habitually alone,
no one sorrows for me.
It will be a good thing if I err in drinking it.
I want to know and tell you how it is," he said.

The leader said, "Nay!
Please do not drink even a little bit.
You as well deserve to live."
When he forbade him, the other did not listen, and just did not quit pleading.
"All right, drink it then," he said, and the other left off [begging].
"Take a drink of it that you might tell us how it is," he said.

Scene 6: The Results of Drinking
Thereupon, having left off with him,
the orphan man filled up a container and drank, so it is said.
He drank, and continued to drink,
and now, when he was completely dizzy, it is said that he was insensible.

He was in a state of insensibility, as it is reported.
Thereupon, when he was completely dizzy,
now also, he made noise
and what he said was unintelligible,
but he went on, so it is said.
Now also they said, "Drinking does so to us!"
"Listen! That is completely and utterly what will happen to ye!"
Now you see it," they said.
It is said that he was in a state of insensibility.
He drank, went on drinking, and became drunk.
Thereupon, they watched him as he drank, got drunk, fell down, and lay down on
   the ground;
they all were really keeping on watching him.
"He is almost dead.
He will die,
he is dying on us;
such is the case, he is going to die," they said.
On watching him, they kept on waiting for it, so it is said.
Thereupon, they kept on watching him in the same way;
he was lying on the ground, so it is said.
He really lay there;
I do not know how long he lay there before he regained consciousness,
but he just lay there, and he awoke;
he just lay there, woke up, and moved.
"Look! Lo! He is about to awaken!"
He was continuing to rub himself as he was awakening.
Thereupon, as he was awakening, it is said that they asked him,
"How is it?
What is it like?
How was it for you?
How are you?" they said.
Then, this one here, contrary to expectation said, "It was a very good soporific.
It was an extremely good soporific.
This being so, drink ye it!
If we were to drink it,
it would be a very good soporific.
I liked it very much;
it was an extremely good sleep," he said.

Scene 7: The Drinking Bout
Thereupon, the remainder of them,
thinking it to be the truth,

some drank
and others drank;
each lay about on the ground
drinking, as it is reported.

Thereupon, as they were doing so,
as the Indians were doing so,
the Indians were lying on the ground,
they did so and lay on the ground.

Scene 8: The Return of the Europeans and Capture of the Indians
The aforementioned white people, upon arriving,
came and caught some of them, about two in number.
They caught them, returned with them and
getting over there to the boat put them into it.
After they regained consciousness,
when the other spoke to them,
they tried to run away,
but because they could tell that they were on the water, they were unable to do so.
Their having given up [trying to escape],
now they spoke to them and taught them.
They spoke to them, and dressed them in things such as clothing;
they would have dressed them completely.
The rest also would tell them nothing more than,
"Belt on the clothing and so forth that we made and gave you."
Having spoken to each other, all the white people went along accompanying the
    Indians.
They gave them things such as clothing and made friends with them with it [clothing].
As liquor was with them, and having met them with it,
[the Indians] were now habitual drinkers.

---

15. A Story of Kamehameha I

Mary Kawena Pakui, from whose book this story is taken, was born just after the overthrow of the last Hawaiian monarch and was the daughter of a Hawaiian mother and a Massachusetts-born American father; she learned many stories from her Hawaiian grandmother. Kawena told her stories to her neighbor Laura Green, who sent them to New York to her cousin, folklorist Martha Warren Beckwith, who published them in several volumes. The battle referred to took place on Oʻahu, where the Kākuhihewa line of chiefs was the most celebrated, in 1795; the enemy were driven over a cliff and said to leap like mullets. Motifs J1250, J1280.

After the battle of Kamehameha against Kalanikupule, at the time of the leaping of the *'anae,* a certain soldier came before the attendants of the king and boasted, saying he was Kamehameha's own brother.

When the counselor heard this, he was very angry and said, "Insolence! Who told you, you braggart, that you were related to the divine one? This is excessive and vain."

"Yes, it is true," answered the man, "I am his younger brother, and he is the first-born."

When the counselor heard these words, he was filled with wrath. "Only one younger brother has the divine one, namely Keli'imaika'i—not you, impertinent one."

Here the conversation ended. The counselor went before the king and told him all that he had heard from the man.

Then the king commanded, "Go and fetch this mischievous person, and bring him before me."

When the man came, he crawled on his hands and knees before the king. The king arose and said in a loud voice, "Listen! Is it true, this thing that I have heard, that you, you boaster, have called me, the king, your elder brother?"

"Yes, O divine one, it is true."

"And who has told you that you are my younger brother?" asked the king.

"You, O my lord."

"Nonsense! When did I say that to you?"

"When we went to the battle on O'ahu of Kākuhihewa, you turned to us and said, 'Forward, my brothers, till you drink the bitter waters!' And hearing these gracious words, O king, has caused me to boast that I am your younger brother. Forward we went together and drank the bitter waters."

When the king heard this just reasoning, he laughed and ordered retainers to prepare a feast for his youngest brother.

16. Ke-lii-kuku

The Puna district is located on the "Big Island" of Hawaii. Pele is the volcano goddess. *Ohia* and *puhala* are types of trees. Motifs cf C450ff.

Another chief was the one who was called in Hawaiian Ke-lii-kuku (the Puna-chief-who-boasted). He was proud of Puna, celebrated as it was in song and legend. . . .

Ke-lii-kuku visited the island Oahu. He always boasted that nothing could be compared with Puna and its sweet-scented trees and vines.

He met a prophet of Pele, Kane-a-ka-lau, whose home was on the island Kauai. The prophet asked Ke-lii-kuku about his home land. The chief was glad of an opportunity to boast. . . . The chief said: "I am Ke-lii-kuku of Puna. My country is charming. Abundance is found there. Rich sandy plains are there, where everything grows wonderfully."

The prophet ridiculed him, saying: "Return to your beautiful country. You will find it desolate. Pele has made it a heap of ruins. The trees have descended from the mountains to the sea. The ohia and puhala are on the shore. The houses of your people are burned. Your land is unproductive. You have no people. You cannot live in your country any more."

The chief was angry and yet was frightened, so he told the prophet that he would go back to his own land and see if that word were true or false. If false, he would return and kill the prophet for speaking in contempt of his beautiful land. Swiftly the oarsman and the mat sails took the chief back to his island. As he came around the eastern side of Hawaii he landed and climbed to the highest point from which he could have a glimpse of his loved Puna. There in the distance it lay under heavy clouds of smoke covering all the land. When the winds lifted the clouds, rolling them away, he saw that all his fertile plain was black with lava, still burning and pouring out constantly volumes of dense smoke. The remnants of forest were also covered with clouds of smoke through which darted the flashing flames which climbed to the tops of the tallest trees.

Pele had heard the boasting chief and had shown that no land around her pit of fire was secure against her will.

Ke-lii-kuku caught a long vine, hurled it over a tree, and hung himself.

---

17. Pele and Kahawali

> The sleds referred to in this story were made of wood and used for sliding down grassy hillsides. Motifs A120, A120.1, A139.13, A182, A197; cf A194.2.

In the reign of Kealiikukii, an ancient king of Hawaii, Kahawali, chief of Puna, and one of his favorite companions went one day to amuse themselves with the *holua* (sled), on the sloping side of a hill, which is still called *ka holua ana o Kahawali* (Kahawali's sliding-place). Vast numbers of the people gathered at the bottom of the hill to witness the game, and a company of musicians and dancers repaired thither to add to the amusement of the spectators. The performers began their dance, and amidst the sound of drums and the songs of the musicians the sledding of Kahawali and his companion commenced. The hilarity of the occasion attracted the attention of Pele, the goddess of the volcano, who came down from Kilauea to witness the sport.

Standing on the summit of the hill in the form of a woman, she challenged Kahawali to slide with her. He accepted the offer, and they set off together down the hill. Pele, less acquainted with the art of balancing herself on the narrow sled than her rival, was beaten, and Kahawali was applauded by the spectators as he returned up the side of the hill.

Before starting again, Pele asked him to give her his *papa holua*, but he, supposing from her appearance that she was no more than a native woman, said: "*Aole!* (no!) Are you my wife, that you should obtain my sled?" And, as if impatient at being delayed, he adjusted his papa, ran a few yards to take a spring, and then, with this momentum and all his strength he threw himself upon it and shot down the hill.

Pele, incensed at his answer, stamped her foot on the ground and an earthquake followed, which rent the hill in sunder. She called, and fire and liquid lava arose, and, assuming her supernatural form, with these irresistible ministers of vengeance, she followed down the hill.

When Kahawali reached the bottom, he arose, and on looking behind saw Pele, accompanied by thunder and lightning, earthquake, and streams of burning lava, closely pursuing him. He took up his broad spear which he had stuck in the ground at the beginning of the game, and, accompanied by his friend, fled for his life. The musicians, dancers, and crowds of spectators were instantly overwhelmed by the fiery torrent, which, bearing on its foremost wave the enraged goddess, continued to pursue Kahawali and his companion. They ran till they came to an eminence called Puukea.

Here Kahawali threw off his cloak of netted ki leaves and proceeded toward his house, which stood near the shore. He met his favorite pig and saluted it by touching noses, then ran to the house of his mother, who lived at Kukii, saluted her by touching noses, and said: "Compassion great to you! Close here, perhaps, is your death; Pele comes devouring." Leaving her, he met his wife, Kanakawahine, and saluted her. The burning torrent approached, and she said: "Stay with me here, and let us die together." He said: "No; I go, I go." He then saluted his two children, Poupoulu and Kaohe, and said, "I grieve for you two."

The lava rolled near, and he ran till a deep chasm arrested his progress. He laid down his spear and walked over on it in safety. His friend called out for his help; he held out his spear over the chasm ; his companion took hold of it and he drew him securely over. By this time Pele was coming down the chasm with accelerated motion. He ran till he reached Kula. Here he met his sister, Koai, but had only time to say, "Alas for you!" and then ran on to the shore. His younger brother had just landed from his fishing canoe, and had hastened to his house to provide for the safety of his family, when Kahawali arrived. He and his friend leaped into the canoe, and with his broad spear paddled out to sea. Pele, perceiving his escape, ran to the shore and hurled after him, with prodigious force, great stones and fragments of rock, which fell thickly around but did not strike his canoe.

When he had paddled a short distance from the shore the *kumukahi* (east wind) sprung up. He fixed his broad spear upright in the canoe, that it might answer the double purpose of mast and sail, and by its aid he soon reached the island of Maui, where they rested one night and then proceeded to Lanai. The day following they moved on to Molokai, thence to Oahu, the abode of Kolonohailaau, his father, and Kanewahinekeaho, his sister, to whom he related his disastrous perils, and with whom he took up his permanent abode.

Folktales from a
Number of Traditions

Animal Tales

Stith Thompson, the great American authority on folktales, suggests that because, for our ancestors, the world of animals and the world of human beings were seen as close together and overlapping, we have many stories in which animal characters behave as human. Whatever the reasons for the worldwide popularity of such stories (which make up a sizeable portion of the Aarne-Thompson international index of folktales), they certainly have found a role in American tradition. "The Donkey, the Dog, the Cat and the Rooster" is a version of the tale well known in the Grimm collection as "The Bremen Town Musicians." "Lion, Fox and Cowboy," from African American tradition, includes a human as well as animal characters and, indeed, deals with what happens when animals encounter the more powerful beast, Man. And in "Mr. Snake and the Farmer," beast and human interact; here the narrator's pressing a moral for his story connects it to the animal fables familiar from the works of Jean de La Fontaine and the legendary Aesop as well as oral sources. Of course, animals appear in other tales in this volume; a number of animal trickster stories, popular particularly in African American tradition, are included in the "Tricks and Tricksters" section.

18. The Donkey, the Dog, the Cat and the Rooster

Folklorists refer to this story generically as "The Animals in Night Quarters," although it is well known from the Grimm collection, where it is called "The Bremen Town Musicians." It makes a point about how humans sometimes treat domestic animals. This version was written down by students at historically black Hampton Institute, where they were members of a folklore-collecting club. AT 130.

Once upon a time there was a man who owned a donkey, a dog, a cat and a rooster. They became discontented for some reason. The man was a cruel master, he worked the donkey very hard from before sunrise until long after sunset. The donkey got mad and very discontented and said that if this continued, he would leave. It was continued, and so one morning when the man got up the donkey had gone. This made the man mad and he kicked the dog and he ran away into the woods. The next morning the cat was sitting in front of the fire and the man told it to get out of his way, so the cat ran off and did not come back.

The man used to get up very early but the next morning he got up a little later than usual which made him mad and he said the rooster was to blame because he didn't crow at the right time, so he flogged the rooster and the rooster got mad and ran away.

After a while as the donkey was wandering about in the wood looking for something to eat he met the dog. "Hello, what are you doing here," he said.

"Oh I ran away," answered the dog. "Master kicked me, so I couldn't stand it."

"Well, let us go together," said the donkey.

After a while they met the cat. "What are you doing here?" said they to her.

"What are you both doing here?" she replied.

"Oh the old man flogged us and we left."

"Well, we will all three go together and get our living."

As they were searching about for something to eat they ran across the rooster. "Well! What are you doing here?" they exclaimed. The rooster told his story, and then they decided to live together. If they were going to live together they must first have a house. The rooster said he knew of an old deserted house he had seen as he was coming down the road. "Now we will go there and take possession of it."

When they got there they found the door fastened and a little smoke was coming out the chimney and they could smell something good to eat. There was no roof on the house. The rooster said "We must see what is inside. Now let the donkey stand close to the wall, the dog on his back, the cat on the dog's back and then I'll get on the cat's back and look over and tell you what I see."

When the rooster looked over he saw some gamblers sitting about the fire cooking their supper. This frightened the rooster and he fell in and scared the men so that they all ran off.

Then the donkey, the dog and the cat came inside. They said, "These men ran off but they will come back again, what shall we do?"

The rooster, who seemed to be wiser than the others, said "I'll tell you what to do. Let the donkey go down by the gate, the dog lie at the door, the cat at the hearth and I will go as usual to the roof. If the spy comes back he will come to the fire to make a light, then let the cat touch him; when he goes to the door the dog can touch him and as he leaves the gate the donkey can strike him and I will give the alarm."

By and by the spy did come, but soon ran back to his companions crying that the house was haunted! For he said, "When I went to take a light something slapped me on the face; then I ran out of the door and something cut me on the leg and when I got to the gate something gave me an awful blow on the back with a stick and then the ghost cried—'Hand him up here to touch! Hand him up here to touch!'"

19. Lion, Fox, and Cowboy

Narrated in 1952 by Walter Winfrey, originally from Arkansas, in Inkster, Michigan, to folklore collector Richard M. Dorson, this story posits humans as being the most dangerous animals. AT 157.

This fox was beat up by a lion. And he wanted to get even with the lion. He lay down side of the road, and he saw a cowboy riding a horse. He had a 45 on his right side, he had a 45 on the left side, and he had a 45 Winchester across his saddle. And the fox crawled off and met this lion. So he asked him had he ever seen a man. So the lion told him no. If he did see one he would roll his hair over his head and jump to him and tear him to pieces.

So the fox told him, "You come and go with me in the morning and I'll show you a man." So he placed this lion in the middle of the road, and he laid beside the bushes. The cowboy rode up the road and the lion saw the cowboy. He rolled his hair up over his head and made for the cowboy. So he takes his 45 from the left side and shot the lion in the left side. The lion grabbed a handful of leaves and stuck it in his left side. The cowboy drawed the gun from the right side, and hit the lion in the right side. That turned the lion—he wheeled and run. There was a hill he had to go up and over, and as he was going over the top, the cowboy shot him with the 45 Winchester.

He made it to his den. The fox went by his den, and he was laying grunting and aching with pain. The fox asked him, what was the matter. Did he see the man? He said, "Yes, he pulled out something and th'owed and bit me in the left side. And I grabbed some leaves and stuck it on my left side, and made it towards him. He th'owed something with his right hand and hit me on the right side." And he said, "I wheeled and run." And he says, "You know that little hill I have to go over? Just as I went over that hill he th'owed up something and it said *Sshow!* And my tail flew up (going over the hill) and he cut me a brand new ass."

20. Mr. Snake and the Farmer

This story was told by J. D. Suggs, a prolific narrator whose talents were made known to folklorists by Richard M. Dorson. It was recorded in Calvin, Michigan, c. 1952, by Dorson. Mississippi-born Suggs is discussed in the introduction, and Dorson's questions and comments are included here in the text. AT 155.

Richard M. Dorson: Maybe you'll tell me a story or two, that you were telling me the other night. How about the one concerning the farmer and the snake?

[Laughing] I tell you, that's a good one. It goes something like this. Well, you know, a snake, in the wintertime, he goes in the ground and he don't never wake up. When the cold weather gets bad, he never wakes up till the weather warms up.

So the farmer goes out, he's going to break his ground up at the end of February. So he plows up Mr. Snake. "Ain't that something? Here's Mr. Snake."

And Mr. Snake says, "Why I'm just so *cold,* I don't know what I'll do. I just practically froze this winter." He was so stiff, he couldn't move. Said, "Will you put me in your bosom, Mr. Farmer, and let me warm . . . up?"

The farmer says [laughing nervously], "No. Mr. Snake, you'll bite me." Said, "I know it."

"No, I wouldn't bite." Said, "Let me tell you, Mr. Farmer, I'm just *cold.* Don't you know I wouldn't bite you after you warmed me up?" . . .

Said, "No. . . . But you a *snake.*"

Said, "Mr. Farmer, I won't bite you. Just warm me up, please. . . ."

Farmer take him up and unbutton his shirt, put him in his bosom. Oh, he's a *great* big snake. I think he must have been a rattlesnake. . . . And so he plowed along until about nine o'clock. He stopped his mules and unbuttons his bosom, and he pulled it out, like this, you know, and he looks down in there, says, "How you feel, Mr. Snake?"

He says [in a feeble, high-pitched voice], "Well, I feel a little better. I'm kind of warming up."

"Good, good." Says, *"Gitty-up!"* So he goes around and he plows till about ten thirty. Then, "Whoa!" Mules stop. He opens his bosom, and he looked down (just like I'm looking in my bosom now), and he says, "How you feel, Mr. Snake?"

He says [slightly stronger voice], "Well, I'm feeling pretty good. I'm warming up good."

He says, "Good, good. *Gitty-up!*" Mules started on up, and he plowed and he plowed till about eleven thirty. And so he could feel the snake kind of twisting, you know, and he just stopped, you know. Pulled his . . . shirt out and looks in his bosom again.

"How you feel, Mr. Snake?"

Says [strong voice], "Oh, I'm feeling a whole lot better. I'm warming up. You feel me moving?"

Said, "Yeah! I *thought* you was doing better."

"Yes, I'm feeling a whole *lot* better."

"Well," farmer says, "Well, I'll be out plowing awhile longer, and I'll quit and go to dinner, then I'm going to get my dinner and put him out at the end."

So he plowed till about fifteen minutes till twelve. He pulled out his shirt and he looked down there again. He said, "Well how are you, Mr. Snake?"

Says, "Oh, I'm warm. I'm just feeling good."

He says, "Good." Says, "Well, I'll go a round or two, and then when I get ready to go to dinner, I'll put you out at the end." So he plowed around, and when he got near about back, Snake didn't wait for him to open his shirt. He done stuck his head out, twitching away out between the shirt buttons, and looking at him in his face and licking out his tongue. Well, a snake's angry. Every time he see you and go to licking out his tongue, he's mad. And the farmer *knew* he's going to bite then.

He said, "Now, Mr. Snake." Said, "Now you told me you wouldn't bite me after I warmed you."

"Yeah. But you knowed that I's a snake."

He said, "Yeah. [Laughing] But . . . don't do that, don't bite me. Please."

"You see, I'm a snake. I'm *supposed* to bite you."

He said, "Yeah. But you told me you wasn't going to bite me."

"Yeah, but you know I's a *snake* before. I'm supposed to bite you, and you know that." So he all went on [and bit] the farmer, right in the mouth. His face begin to swell, so he goes to the house, running. He didn't take time to take his mules out of there. Went in.

Wife says, "Well, what the matter?"

He said, "Well, Mr. Snake. I seen him out there in the field. I plowed him up, and he said he was so cold he was stiff. And if I would warm him up, he would not bite me." And said, "After I got him warm, he bit me in the face." And said, "Let me tell you one lesson. Don't care when you see a snake, don't never warm him, put him in your bosom, put him up, cause when he gets warm, he's sure going to bite you."

Then he laid down and died.

And that's why he left word with his wife, "Don't never fool with a snake."

Richard M. Dorson: There's a real lesson in that story, isn't there?

Real lesson there. That's correct. Well, you know we have people that way. Long as you got something he wants, he just gets right in your bosom, and soon as he get what he wants, then he's going to do you harm.

Richard M. Dorson: I see.

When you know that a fellow is a crook or a thief, a robber, don't care how he tell you how he done quit it, don't never put him in your bosom, for when he gets warm, first chance, he going to trip you.

Richard M. Dorson: So there's something really to be understood in that story.

Yes. Never put a snake in your bosom.

Jack and His Fellows: Classic Hero Tales

The classic fairytale hero is the young man who sets out into the world and manages to triumph over adversity and over adversaries (both human and supernatural) and who winds up a great success in his undertakings. By the eighteenth century in England, this hero was commonly named Jack, and that name carried over with English-language tales that came to America (though America would become the recipient of hero tales like "The Long-Tailed Shirt" from other languages and cultures). Success comes for the hero—whether he's called Jack or something else—through courage, perseverance, ambition, cleverness, bargaining, just luck, or usually some combination of these factors.

21. The Long-Tailed Shirt (El Cotón de Jerga)

This tale was originally told in Spanish, and its collector, Arthur L. Campa, provides the Spanish title "El Cotón de Jerga," though this story is popularly known as "Los Tres Consejos" ("The Three Wise Counsels"). Campa does not name an informant but says that the stories in his collection, taken from the Hispanic tradition of tale-telling in the Southwest, "might be told by a group of *rancheritos* [ranch hands] sitting under a cottonwood on a summer night in Texas, or retold by a *viejito* [old man] sitting under the walls of a neighborhood store." *Pesetas* are coins. AT 300 + 910.

Once upon a time there was a very poor woman and her son. One day the son said to her: "Mother, tomorrow I am going to go out in search of work; we are so poor that we can hardly eat any longer." The old lady protested, but seeing that her son was determined to go, she gave him her benediction and three pesetas, saying: "This is all I have; make good use of them."

The following morning the son left with a few pieces of dry bread in his pocket and the three pesetas his mother had given him. By nightfall he arrived at a farmhouse, and, since it was the custom in those days to give lodging to travelers, he knocked at the door, and they let him in. They invited him to supper later in the evening, and when they were through eating, he asked the man of the house if he would tell him a story before he went to bed. The man said he would, for a peseta, and the traveler consented, so he said: "*A donde fueres haz lo que vieres* [Wherever you go, do as you see others do]"; that is, "When in Rome, do as the Romans do." "Now give me my peseta."

The young man was very disappointed at such a short tale, but he finally paid his host for it. And after a while, he thought he would try again: "My friend, if you will tell me a story, I'll give you another peseta, but make it a long one this time." The man agreed and said: "A married man must be on guard." The young man protested, saying that it was too short a story, but he paid him a second peseta.

Later in the evening, thinking that he might get a real story, he promised another peseta to his host for a longer story. The host answered: "Give me a peseta first, and I'll tell you a story." The young man handed him his last peseta, and waited for the story. "*El pobre a la diligencia* [A poor man must work]," said the man. With that, the traveler lost the three pesetas his mother had given him. Early next morning he left the farmhouse and went into the city, where he asked for lodging at the home of a very old lady. "Good afternoon, grandmother" said the young man. "Can you give me a night's lodging?" The old lady answered him: "Yes, my grandson, come in."

After supper that night, the young man sat down to talk with the old lady. He asked her if she knew where he could find work, but the old lady said she did not know of a job anywhere. She told him about a new proclamation sent out by the king. His daughter, the princess, would not laugh and had never laughed, so the king promised to marry her to the first man that made her laugh. Many clowns and funny men had come from afar, but the princess just looked at them. No one could make her laugh.

The next morning the young man went to a tailor and asked him to make him a long-tailed shirt out of a couple of gunny sacks. Back at the old lady's house he picked up an old broomstick, put on his long-tailed shirt and went to the palace grounds, thinking to try his luck making the princess laugh. When he got there, he saw a platoon of soldiers drilling. Suddenly he remembered the first story his host had told him. *"A la tierra que fueres haz lo que vieres,"* that is, "When in Rome, do as the Romans do." So he shouldered his broomstick and joined the platoon of soldiers. They drilled with their rifles, and he drilled with his broomstick, dressed only in his long-tailed shirt. He was simply doing as the Romans did, but the princess, who had never seen anything so ridiculous, could not contain herself, and burst out laughing.

The king, pleased and surprised to hear his daughter laugh for the first time, asked her: "What are you laughing at?" She pointed to the young man in the long-tailed shirt, and said: "Don't you see that funny looking man drilling with the soldiers?" The king saw the young man and had him brought before his throne. "Young man," he said, "I promised my daughter's hand in marriage to the first man who made her laugh. You made her laugh, so you shall be married to her tomorrow."

"Your majesty," answered the young man, "I cannot marry your daughter, for I am a poor man." "That does not matter," said the king, "I never go back on my promise."

Preparations were immediately begun for the wedding; beautiful clothes were laid out for the young man, but on the night of the wedding he refused them saying: "the princess liked me in this long-tailed shirt, and it shall be my wedding suit." On the night of the wedding, the princess served a glass of drugged wine to her husband, hoping that it would put him to sleep immediately. At midnight, a seven-headed serpent would come and eat him. In this way she planned to remain single for the rest of her life. The young man with the long-tailed shirt remembered the second story his host had told him: *"El hombre casado el cuidado."* So as soon as he was married, he became cautious. "A married man must be on guard," he thought over and over. When the princess offered him the wine, he did not drink it, so he stayed awake all night. At midnight, he saw the head of a serpent coming through the window. He took his sword, and with one blow he sliced off the serpent's head.

One by one all the heads showed through the window, and he kept chopping them off. Then he cut the tongues from all the heads and put these in his handkerchief. The following morning, the servants found the dead serpent and told the king about it. They put it in a wagon and dumped it in the woods.

A charcoal maker, going through the woods, saw the serpent and put it in his wagon, then he went to the king to show him what he had killed. So the king called his son-in-law and said to him: "Didn't you tell us you had killed the serpent?" The young man asked them to show him the serpent's tongues. When they could not find them, he took his handkerchief and showed them the tongues he had cut out the night before. The king had the charcoal maker hanged on the spot.

After several days, the young man remembered the third story his host had told him: "A poor man must work," so he said to the princess: "I must go out and work, for I am a poor man." The princess insisted that he did not have to work any longer, now that he was a prince, but he insisted on going to look for work. He arrived at a large hacienda where they were hoeing corn; he asked the mayordomo for work, and he gave him a job. At noon all the men stopped working and went to lunch. "Come on, *amigo*, it is time to eat." But he only answered: "If I felt like eating, the princess would bring me food."

The men said to themselves: "What is this fool talking about?" Finally, they went and told the count, who owned the hacienda, about the fool who insisted that, if he was hungry, the princess would bring him food. The count came to talk to the young man, and invited him to eat, but he only answered: "If I felt like eating, the princess would bring me food." They all laughed at him, and the count said: "I'll bet you the princess would never bring you food no matter how much you wanted her to." The young man answered him: "I have nothing to bet, but I'll wager my neck against all your palace and riches that tomorrow, between eleven-thirty and twelve o'clock, the princess will bring my lunch to this cornfield." The count agreed, but the young man insisted that they put it in writing. They put it in writing and both signed it.

That evening, when he got back from work, he said to his wife: "Tomorrow I want you to go to the count's hacienda and bring my lunch to the cornfield where I am working, between eleven-thirty and twelve." The princess was very upset and went to tell her father, the king. "He is your husband, so you must do as he says," answered the king.

The following day the royal cooks prepared a fine dinner while the princess' husband hoed the cornfield. His friends teased him and threw pebbles at him. The young man warned the men not to throw rocks at "the prince." This seemed so ridiculous to the men, that they went and told the count. He told them to prepare the gallows for the hanging of "the prince." Along about eleven o'clock, the count went to the tower and looked toward the king's castle with his spyglass. He was greatly worried to see a cortege of several carriages coming toward his own palace. They came straight to where the young man with the long-tailed shirt was now making adobes. He came out of the mud and ordered the servants to set up the tables for his lunch. They unloaded a tent, chairs, tables, and food. When the table was set, he asked the princess to join him at lunch, and then called the count. After the lunch, he turned to the count and said: "Where is that paper we signed?" The count produced the paper and with it the keys to his castle. The young man took a horse from the stables and gave it to the count, who mounted it and rode away very sad.

Then the young man with the long-tailed shirt took his bride and showed her all that he had won. He picked out a fine suit for himself and took off his long-tailed shirt for the first time. He moved into the castle with his princess and invited his father-in-law to a big fiesta. He also brought his poor mother to live in the castle with him and they all lived happily for many years.

22. Old Bluebeard

This tale was told in the summer of 1923 by Jane Gentry of Hot Springs, North Carolina, to sociologist Isabel Gordon Carter and is part of Carter's historic early collection of Southern mountain folktales. Despite its title, this is not a version of the famous folktale widely known as "Bluebeard," a version of which does appear as story 29, "Old Foster." AT 301A.

One time they was an old man and woman had three sons, Jack, Will and Tom. Will was the oldest one, Tom he was next and Jack was the least one. The old woman and the old man died and left Jack, Will and Tom to look after the place. They was workin' away over in the field and each tuk his time goin' to git dinner. Tom, he was the oldest, was first and he tried to see what a good dinner he could git up. He hung the meat up afore the fire to boil and he fixed some turnips and some potatoes and fixed everything nice for his brothers and when hit was ready he went out to blow the horn—they didn't have no dinner bell in them days—and when he blowed the horn down in the holler he saw an old man comin' with his beard as blue as indigo, his teeth as long as pipe stems and his thumbs tucked behind him. And the man says, "Have ye anything to eat?" Will says, "No," cuz he didn't want the old man to come in and eat up the nice dinner he'd fixed up for his brothers.

Old Bluebeard says, "Well, I'll see about hit!" And he went in and eat up everything Will had cooked up.

And Will had to fly around and fix up something for his brothers. He fixed what he could, but he couldn't fix much cuz he didn't have time. Then he went out and blowed down the holler and when his brothers come in they says, "What in the world tuk you so long to fix up such a shabby dinner?"

And Will says, "Well, I fixed ye up a good dinner, but when I went out to blow for ye to come in an old man come up the holler with his beard as blue as indigo, his teeth as long as pipe stems and his thumbs tucked behind him and he walked in and ate up everything I'd fixed. So I had to fly around and fix you something else."

Tom says, "Well, I knowed he wouldn't have eat it all up if I'd been here."

Will says, "All right, tomorrow is your day and we'll see what he does to you."

So next morning Tom put him on some meat to boil in front of the fire and when he come in from the new ground he got him some turnips and potatoes and pumpkin and baked him some bread and fixed him up a good dinner. And when he went out to blow the horn he saw an old man comin' up the holler with his beard as blue as indigo, his teeth as long as pipe stems and his thumbs tucked behind him and he said, "Have ye anything to eat?" And Tom says, "No."

Old Bluebeard says, "Well, we'll see about that." And he went in and eat up everything Tom had fixed except jest a little bit of pumpkin. And Tom had to fly around and git up something for his brothers and when they come in Jack says, "Why didn't you keep him from eatin' hit up?"

Tom says, "Tomorrow is your time to git dinner and see if you can keep him from hit." And Jack says, "Bedad, I will."

So next day Jack put him some meat to boil in the fireplace and got some turnips and potatoes and fixed 'em and when he went out to blow the horn for his brothers to come in, old Bluebeard was a comin' up the holler with his beard as blue as indigo, his teeth as long as pipe stems and his thumbs tucked behind him. Jack says, "Now, you jest come in and have something to eat." Old Bluebeard says, "No, I don't want anything." Jack says, "Yes, but you must come and have dinner with us." Old Bluebeard says, "No, I don't want to," and he tuk around the house and tuk out down the holler. Jack tuk out down the holler after him and saw him git down a den—a hole in the ground—and when the brothers come home and Jack was gone they thought old Bluebeard had eat Jack up 'stead of his dinner.

After a while Jack come in and they says, "Jack, where you bin?" Jack says, "I bin watchin' old Bluebeard, watchin' where he went to, and I watched him go down a hole in the ground and I'm goin' to foller him." So Jack tuk a big old bushel basket out and put a strop on hit and him and his brothers went to old Bluebeard's hole. Will says he was agoin' down. Jack says, "We'll take turns. Will, go first."

So Will he climbed in the basket and they let him down in the hole and when he shuck the rope they pulled him up and asked him whast he found. Will says, "Well, I went until I saw a house and then I shuck the rope." "Oh shaw, Will, what ud you shuck the rope then fer? Why didn't you find out what was in the house?" Will says, "Well, you go in and find out." Tom says, "All right I will."

So he clumb in the basket and went down 'til he was on top of the house and then he shuck the rope and they pulled him up. When he told 'em he shuck the rope when he was on top of the house, Jack says, "You're nary one no account but me."

So he went down and looked in the room and there sat the prettiest woman he ever saw in his life. And Jack says, "Oh! you're the prettiest woman I ever saw in my life and you're goin' to be my wife." "No," she said, "Old Bluebeard ul git you. You better git out of here." "Oh no, he won't," says Jack. "He's a good friend of mine and I'm goin' to take you up and marry you." "No," she said, "you wait 'til you get down to the next house. You won't think nothin' of me when you see her."

So Jack put her in the basket and shuck the rope. And when she come out, Will says, "Oh! you're the prettiest woman I saw in my life!" and Tom said, "Oh! you're the prettiest woman I ever saw in my life."

Jack went on down to the next house and looked in and there was the prettiest woman he ever did see, the other wan't nothing along side this one. Jack says, "You're prettiest woman I ever saw and you're goin' to be my wife. My brothers can have the other one but I'm goin' to have you." She says, "Oh no, Jack, when you go down to the other house you won't think nothin' of me. "Yes, I will too," says Jack. "You jest come git in this basket."

So he put her in the basket and shuck the rope. Then he went down to the next house and there was the prettiest woman. Jack says, "Oh! you're jest the prettiest woman I ever did see and you're goin' to be my wife. My brother's kin have the other two but you're goin' to be my wife. Come git in this basket." But afore she was pulled up she give him a red ribbon and told him to plait it in her hair so he'd know her when she come out and she give him a wishin' ring. Jack put her in the basket and shuck the rope. When the brothers saw her they stopped talkin' to the other two and fell in love with her right away. Tom says, "You're goin' to be my wife," Will says, "No, she's goin' to be mine." And they started fightin'.

She says, "I won't have nary one. I'm goin' to marry Jack." They said, "No, you won't fer we'll leave Jack down there." So they pulled up the basket and they commencet to fight and left Jack down there.

Jack jest sit there and Old Bluebeard come in and walked around but he didn't give Jack nothin' to eat. Jack jest sit there and after a while he turned the ring on his finger seein' how he'd fell away and said, "I wish I was in my old corner beside the fire smokin' my old chunky pipe." And there he was and there was the woman with red ribbon plaited in her hair and she said, "Oh Jack!" And they was married and they uz rich when I left there.

23. Jack and His Dogs

This story was written out in the 1950s by Dewey Baker, about eighteen years old, of Leslie County, Kentucky, for local teacher and folklore collector Leonard Roberts. AT 303.

Once there was a boy by the name of Jack who lived with his mother. Jack and his mother owned a little farm. Jack helped his mother in the field and done the hard work.

One day Jack was playing with his dogs, when all at once he saw two old women coming down the road. Jack hollered at his mother, "I see two old women coming down the road and they are dressed in old rags."

His mother said, "That is the way all naughty people look."

The two old witches come to the house and asked for some bread, and Jack gave them some. Jack said to his mother, "Mother, they have hands like dogs."

Jack's mother said, "That is the way all naughty people look."

Then Jack said to his mother, "Mother, they ate that bread like a dog."

Jack's mother said, "That's the way all naughty people eat." Then the two old witches asked Jack to show them the way to another road. Jack didn't want to, but he finally did show them the way. But first he set a basin of water on the porch and stuck a willow switch in the basin and said to his mother, "When the water turns to blood and the limb shakes, turn my dogs loose."

Then Jack started out to show the women the way. When he had got about a quarter of a mile he looked back and saw they were down on their knees following him like a dog. Then he begin to run, and they come faster. Then he climbed a tree, and they turned their tails into axes and begin to chop. They nearly had the tree chopped down when Jack dropped an egg which he had found in a hen's nest before he had gone to show them the way. He dropped an egg and said, "Fill up!" and the tree became normal. Then they begin to chop harder. Then the tree was nearly down when he dropped another egg and said, "Fill up!" And they begin to chop harder, and Jack had one more egg in his pocket.

Jack's mother had went out on the porch where she saw the willow limb shaking and the water had turned to blood. Then she turned the dogs loose and they started after Jack's trail.

When the dogs had reached Jack the tree was nearly falling. Then Jack saw the dogs. Jack said to the dogs, "Drag them around and around for one mile!" Then he said, "Drag them around for three miles!"

Then the two old witches was dead and Jack was safe.

24. The Big Old Giant

Vance Randolph, Ozark Mountains resident and folklorist, heard this story, a version of the famous "Jack and the Beanstalk," from A. L. Cline, Joplin, Missouri, July 1922; Cline heard it as a child, circa 1895, in Benton County, Missouri. AT 328B.

One time there was a boy found a dead crow, and the crow had a funny looking grain of corn in his mouth. It was big as a walnut, and blue instead of yellow. So the boy planted it down by the big bluff and poured a hatful of stump water on it. Next time he come that way, the corn had growed up big as a tree, with regular bark on it, and blade-fodder hanging down forty foot long. The boy couldn't see no tassel, on account of the trees on top of the bluff, and he couldn't see no ears on the stalk, neither. He went home and told the folks, but they just laughed and didn't pay no attention. So finally he says to himself, "I'll go back and climb that there cornstalk, if I *never* see the back of my neck!"

Well, he clumb and he clumb and he kept on a-climbing, right on up past the top of the bluff, but there wasn't no ears on the stalk yet. He got so high up he couldn't see nothing but clouds. After while he come to a big pasture, so he got off the cornstalk to look around and stretch his legs. The grass in that pasture was ten foot high, and there was buckbrush in it bigger than apple trees. Pretty soon he seen some monstrous big sheep. There was one old sheep had a fine brass bell on it, about the size of a molasses barrel.

"The folks won't never believe this," says he to himself, "without I take something back to show 'em." So he out with his knife and started to cut the bell off'n the big sheep's neck. It took a long time to saw through the leather strap, pretty near a foot thick, but he finally done it. The bell was too heavy for him to lift, so he rolled it along on the ground, and it kept a-ringing. Just as he got to the edge of the big pasture, the boy heard a terrible loud hollering, and here come the big old giant that owned them sheep. He was maybe thirty foot high, and he was a-waving a club as big as a saw-log.

Well, when the boy seen this here giant a-coming, he just rolled the bell over the edge, and then he jumped onto the big cornstalk and slid down. The big old giant throwed the club, but it missed him. The boy was pretty near to the bottom, when the old giant jumped on the cornstalk and started down after him. Just as the boy lit on the ground the cornstalk broke off, and the big old giant come a-roaring down the mountain and busted open like a rotten apple. By the time the boy's folks got there the big old giant was dead, and that was the end of him.

The folks got the neighbors to help, and they went out and buried the big old giant in the night, and never did tell no outsiders, so as to keep down scandal. But next winter every family for miles around showed up with quilts and laprobes and saddle blankets made out of some mighty funny looking wool. Nobody in the country ever seen cloth like that before, and the old-timers all say them things was made out of the big old giant's pants.

Some berry pickers found the big sheep bell four miles up the creek. The boy's pappy wanted to put it in the new church-house, but the preacher says a bell like that was not made with human hands, and maybe it was the Devil's work. And he says good Christian people better not ring that bell, because who knows what might come a-running? So they just left the big sheep bell there in the brush where it fell. And it's still a-laying there to this day.

25. Jack and the Fox

Told in the summer of 1923 by Jane Gentry of Hot Springs, North Carolina, this is another of the stories written down by the pioneering collector of American folk narratives Isabel Gordon Carter. AT 402.

One time they was an old man and three sons, Jack, Will and Tom. He called 'em up and divided his fortune. Give 'em all their portion and started 'em out to see who could marry the richest. Jack says to his father, "I don't want but one thing you've got, that's the old pet fox."

Will and Tom got theyselves all dressed up and started out. They didn't want Jack to foller 'em, he looked like such a slab, so they made him go by hisself. So he tramped all day long. Finally along about dark he looked up the hill and saw a farm house and he thought he'd better go there and try to git lodgin' fer the night. Didn't have a penny, jest old pet fox. He went on up to the house and out in the yard he said, "Hello!" And here comes the prettiest little cat walkin' to the door.

"Who keeps house here?" says Jack. She says, "Cat and a mouse. I use to be a woman but the witches got mad at me and witched me into a cat, but," she says, "if you'll stay here three days and nights and not let a thing come into this house, not the least thing even down to a mouse, I'll be a pretty girl and I'll marry you." So he squeezed the old fox and it said, "Gold enough." "Yes, bedads, I will," says Jack.

So he put his old fox down and he cut him some clubs and fixed hisself at the door. Everything from a elephant to an ant tried to come in on him that night—all kinds of varmints. Next morning he went to the cat about hit and there's the prettiest baby he ever saw. So he got breakfast. The varmints weren't bad to try to come in of a day—always at night. And that night he got him some lamps and candles and he jest killed snakes and rats an other varmints all night long. Next mornin' he saw jest the prettiest little girl he ever did see. And he squeezed the fox and hit says, "Gold enough." So he fit [fought] all that night and she was a pretty woman and they uz married. So they hitched up the horses and carriage and started out fer his father's so as Jack cud show him his wife.

When they got near, they heard the banjo and the fiddle and music and all, and Will and Tom and their wives was there. So Jack jest pulled out on a turnpike and left his wife and put on his old clothes and tuk his pet fox under his arm and went in. So Will he pushed his wife behind one door, Tom, he pushed his behind the beds so they wouldn't see Jack he was so shabby. So Jack come on in and he squeezed his fox and hit says, "Gold enough." And then Jack, he went and got his wife and carriage and all and drove up. And Tom tuk his wife out one door and Will tuk his out the other—'cause they weren't rich. So Jack he come out the right end of the horn. He married plumb rich.

26. The Boy That Never Seen a Fraid

The classic "The Boy That Never Seen a Fraid" was told by Don Saylor, eighteen, of Leslie County, Kentucky, during a recording session organized at a school by Leonard Roberts. AT 326.

This boy one day decided he'd go out into the world to see if he would see anything to be afraid of. Well, he started out one day and walked all day. He was tired and hot. And that night he come and seen a big white house—purty too—up on the side of the bank. He hollered and said, "Hello." Nobody didn't answer. "Well," he said, "I think I'll just go up there and see if anybody lives up there."

He went up there and they wa'n't nobody in there. He opened the door and they's a little bed back in the corner. And he said, "I can't understand why nobody lives here. This is an awful purty house." Says, "I believe I'll just go on down the road."

He went on down about a half mile and saw a little hut on the side of a hill. It was getting dusty dark. He said, "Hello." And they's an old man come to the door. He said, "I'd like to get to stay all night here."

And the old man says, "O.K."

And he went up and eat supper and he says, "Why ain't they nobody lives up there in that big white house about a half a mile up the road?"

He said, "Oh, that place is hainted." Says, "Won't nobody live up there."

He said, "How much will you give me to go up there and stay in that house tonight?"

He said, "I'll give you twenty gold guineas."

And he says, "O.K."

And he went up there. They's a little bed in there and he had him a quilt. He laid down, and about the time he laid down in walked two big bears. And he said, "Whoops-ye-see, I wished I had me two big bulldogs."

About that time open flew the door and in they walked. They went to fighting. The bears were trying to get him and the dogs were pulling 'em back. They fought for about an hour, and then the door flew open and they all walked out.

Well, he laid down and went to sleep. The next morning the old man come up and said, "Hey, are you dead, are you dead?"

And the man run out on the porch and said, "Dead? Why, man, you should have come up here last night. Had the awfulest fight ever was."

"Gee! I wouldn't come up here for nothing. I heard it. I thought they were tearing the house down up here." The old man says, "Let's go down and eat breakfast."

He says, "O.K."

He went down and eat breakfast and fooled around that day. Then he asked the old man, says, "How much will you give me to stay up there again tonight?"

"Well," he said, "I'll give you ten gold guineas."

He said, "O.K."

He eat supper and went back up again that night. About the time he laid down they's two big bulls come in and he said, "Whoops-ye-see! I wish I had two big bulldogs." And about that time they come in and they fought for about an hour. Then the door flew open and they all walked out.

Well, the old man went up and hollered and said, "Are you dead, are you dead?"

And he jumped up and run to the door and said, "No! Man, I had the awfulest fight up here last night ever was. You ought to a-come up."

He said, "Gee! I wouldn't come up here for nothing."

Well, they went down and eat breakfast and fooled around that day. Along that evening he said, says, "How much will you give me to stay tonight up there?"

He said, "I'll give you five gold guineas."

He says, "O.K." He said, "I believe I'll just take me a skillet and stuff up there and fix my own supper."

He got him a skillet and took it up there, built him a far and got his supper, and he was setting down eating. And he was about half through and the doors flew open and in slid a big coffin. And he said, "Whoops-ye-see! Boy, I'll have me some good kindling wood." He jumped for his ax, and about that time the coffin lid flew open and out stepped a man with his head cut off. The man motioned to him and said, "Follow me."

And he said, "Wait till I eat." And it said, "O.K."

Well, he eat and started to the door and said, "Huh-oh, forgot my hat. And I have to go back and get it." Well, he got his hat and traveled through a big lot of barns, briars, and ever'thing, a long ways. Finally this man with his head cut off come to an old barn. They walked inside and he picked up an old mattock and he started digging. He dug and he dug, and finally he said, "Here, you dig a while. I'm tard [tired]."

This boy was a-thinking, "Boy, he's going to kill me or bury me or something, but I don't know what." But he still wasn't afraid though. He dug and he dug. Finally he handed it to this man with his head cut off and said, "Here, you dig a while. I'm tard."

Well, the man dug a long time and finally he hit something that went, "Clank!" He dug around it and said, "Come here and help me pull this out."

He said, "O.K."

He went over and helped him pull it out. He opened up the lid and set down beside it. It was a big chest full of gold. He said, "Now I was killed and robbed for this. They's going to kill me," he said, "and I wouldn't let them have it—I died before I would. I was buried here. I'm going to give it to you." Said, "You are the only person that has ever stayed down there in that white house of a night without being afraid." And he says, "I want you to give that old man that lives down there below you, I want you to give him a part of this money too."

And the boy said, "O.K."

He picked up this money, about all he could carry, and started down the road with it. And when he got down there he slid it under his bed and laid down and went to sleep.

The next morning the old man come up there and said, "Hey, are you dead, are you dead?"

And he jumped up and run to the door and said, "Dead! Man, you orght to come in here and look what I got."

He said, "Man, I wouldn't come in there for nothing."

"Well, I'll bring it out and show it to you." And he brought it out and showed him his chest full of gold. And he says, "That ghost told me to give you a part of this." Said, "Here, how much do you want?"

He says, "Gee! I wouldn't take none of that for nothing in this world."

He said, "Well, I'll take it."

He then took it and throwed it back under his bed, and went down and eat breakfast. Then he fooled around there and he was rich and everything. Finally he got married and lived happy ever after.

Brave, Resourceful, and Kindly Women

Although when we think of fairytales, we commonly think of male heroes, and although a great deal of attention has been paid to the American Jack tales, American oral tales are full of women who triumph through their bravery, resourcefulness, or other virtues. In the Italian American "The King and the Poor Man's Daughter," an up-from-poverty princess helps a peasant through her cleverness, while in the Appalachian tale "Old Foster," a young woman exposes a murderer of other women. In "Mutsmag," the protagonist is constantly ahead of her adversaries, and in "The Millman's Daughter," told by a Polish American narrator, a daughter not only pulls her father through danger but gains them great wealth in the bargain. In "Lady Featherflight," collected in the nineteenth century, hero Jack is saved by the giant's daughter and her knowledge of magical objects that aid their escape through the classic magic tale episode of the obstacle flight. Maria in the Mexican American "The Green Bird" makes an epic and dangerous journey to save her brothers, but kindliness also enables women to succeed in "Rose" and "The Talking Eggs."

27. The King and the Poor Man's Daughter

Folklorist Ruth Ann Musick collected this story from Italian American narrator Marietta Hervatin, Rivesville, West Virginia, in 1952; in turn she had the story from her mother. AT 875 + 1533.

The king's son went hunting, accompanied by a servant, and, when a storm came up, he stopped at a small house. A poor, old man lived there with his wife and daughter. Knowing that the man was the king's son, the family wanted to treat him to the best they had, so they killed their only chicken and had it for supper. The daughter divided the chicken, giving the neck to her father, the backbone to her mother, and the feet to the servant. She kept the wings and breast for herself and gave the two legs to the king's son.

After supper everyone went to bed and the old man and woman discussed their daughter and said, "What kind of a daughter do we have? See what part of the chicken she gave us?"

The king's son overheard them talking, so the next day he asked the daughter why she divided the chicken as she did.

She said, "I gave your servant the feet so he can walk well; I gave Mother the backbone because she is the head of the house and she needs the backbone; I gave Father the neck because one of these days he will have to stretch his neck to see me; and I gave you the legs because you are the king's son and I wanted to give you the best part; and I kept the wings and breast because one day I will fly away from this house."

The king's son thought that she was smart for doing this, and since he liked her very much, he asked her to marry him. She said she would if he didn't mind being married to a poor girl. He said he didn't, so they were married.

Soon after the wedding he told her that she was not to interfere in any of his business, and she said that she wouldn't.

Not long after this, a fair was held near the king's son's palace. One of her poor friends brought a cow to the fair, and, seeing an unused wagon in the field which belonged to the king's son, he tied his cow to it. While she was tied there, the cow had a calf. After the fair was over the poor man started to take his cow and new calf home, but the king's son stopped him and took the calf, saying the wagon had had the calf. The poor man was so afraid that he said nothing. The king's son's wife saw everything and felt sorry for her poor friend, but she remembered that her husband had said she wasn't to interfere in any of his business. She told her poor friend that she could tell him how to get his calf back, but that he was not to say anything to her husband about it.

He was to come back with a fishing hook the next day and go fishing in the field where there was no water, so he did. Her husband saw him and asked what he was doing. The poor man said he was fishing.

The king's son said, "How can you fish here where there is no water or fish?"

The poor man answered him, "How can your wagon have a calf?"

The king's son couldn't answer him and gave the poor man his calf. He knew that the poor man wasn't smart enough to think that out for himself, so he went to his wife. He told her that he'd said she wasn't to interfere in his business, but he knew that she'd thought of the trick, as the poor man wasn't smart enough.

She said, "Yes, I thought of it. Those poor people work hard to raise their cow and calf and they need the money they get from selling them."

Her husband then told her to take all that belonged to her and return home, but that she was to eat supper with him for the last time. While they were eating she added something to his wine, which put him to sleep. She then told the servant to carry him to her home, as she wanted to see her mother and, as her husband was drunk, she didn't want to leave him at home.

While they were in her mother's home, he came to his senses and found himself lying on the floor with his feet in the ashes near the fireplace. He looked around saying, "Where am I?"

She answered, "Right here with me."

He said, "Why did you bring me here?"

She replied, "You told me to take everything that belonged to me, and the only thing I really owned was you, so I brought you here with me."

He then got up and said, "I see you are very smart, so come back with me."

They both went back and lived happily from that time.

28. The Pretended Corpse

Although reprinted in the *Journal of American Folklore*, this story originally appeared in H. E. Taliaferro's 1859 volume, *Fisher's River (North Carolina) Scenes and Characters.* The stories in Taliaferro's book date from the 1820s, so this text represents an example of rather early American storytelling. AT 958C.

Once there was a man who had a wife an' child, an' he went to sell his tobacco, an' left them alone in the house. He lef' home about eight o'clock at night, so's to have his tobacco at market early in the mornin.' He lef' some money an' a pistol with his wife. Late that night a storm came up, an' a man came to the door an' knocked, and the wife went to the door with the baby in her arms. The man told her he was drivin' a hearse through, an' he'd like to leave his dead brother there for the night, sayin' he could find some place else to sleep. She told him she reckoned it'd be all right to leave the coffin in the hall. After the man lef,' she went out an' looked at the corpse, an' noticed its hand had moved. She went back in the room an' got the money an' pistol. She heard the corpse git up an' open the door for the other thief, so she went out on the back porch an' down the steps. At the bottom o' the steps was a well, a little deeper than a man's head. She walked around the well an' stood on the other side. One o' the men came out on the back porch. She told him to go back, but he kept on, so she shot him. The other one went down the steps in the dark after her, but he fell in the well. She put some boards over the well an' sat on them till her husband came home next day.

29. Old Foster

One of the stories collected in 1923 from Jane Gentry of Hot Springs, North Carolina, by Isabel Gordon Carter, this tale is a version of "Bluebeard," the story of the dangerous, predatory murderer of women (often his wives) finally thwarted by a clever woman. AT 955.

They use to be an old man, he lived way over in the forest by hisself, and all he lived on was he caught women and boiled 'em in front of the fire and eat 'em. Now the way my mother told me, he'd go into the villages and tell 'em this and that and get 'em to come out and catch 'em and jest boil they breasts. That's what she told me, and then I've heard hit that he jest eat 'em.

Well, they was a beautiful stout woman, he liked 'em the best (he'd a been right atter me un your mother) so every day he'd come over to this woman's house and he'd tell her to please come over to see his house.

"Why, Mr. Foster, I can't find the way."

"Yes, you can. I'll take a spool of red silk thread out of my pocket and I'll start windin' hit on the bushes and it'll carry ye straight to my home."

So she promised him one day she'd come. So she got her dinner over one day and she started. So she follered the red silk thread and went on over to his house. When she got there, there was a poor little old boy sittin' over the fire a boilin' meat.

And he says, "Laws, Aunt,"—she uz his aunt—"what er you doin' here? Foster kills every woman uz comes here. You leave here jest as quick as you can."

She started to jump out the door and she saw Foster a comin' with two young women, one under each arm. So she run back and says, "Jack, honey, what'll I do, I see him a comin'?"

"Jump in that old closet under the stair and I'll lock you in," says Jack.

So she jumped in and Jack locked her in. So Foster come in and he was jest talkin' and a laughin' with those two girls and tellin' the most tales, and he was goin' to taken 'em over to a corn shuckin' next day. Foster says, "Come on in and have supper with me."

So Jack put up some boiled meat and water. That's all they had. As soon as the girls stepped in and seed the circumstance and seed their time had come their countance fell.

Foster says, "You better come in and eat, maybe the last chanct you'll ever have."

Girls both jumped up and started to run, Foster jumps up and ketched 'em, and gets his tomihawk and starts up stairs with 'em. Stairs was shackly and rattly, and as they went up one of the girls wretched her hand back and caught hold of a step and Foster jest tuck his tomihawk and hacked her hand off. It drapped into whar she was. She laid on in there until next day atter Foster went out then Jack let her out.

She jest bird worked over to where the corn shuckin' was. When she got there Foster was there. She didn't know how to git Foster destroyed. The people thought these people got out in the forest and the wild animals ud ketch 'em.

So she says, "I dreamt an awful dream last night. I dreamed I lived close to Foster's house and he was always a wantin' me to come to his house."

Foster says, "Well, that ain't so, and it shan't be so, and God forbid it ever should be so."

She went right on, "And I dreamt he put out a red thread and I follered hit to his house and there uz Jack broilin' women's breasts in front the fire."

Foster says, "Well, that ain't so, and it shan't be so, and God forbid it ever should be so."

She went right on, "And he says, 'What er you doin' here? Foster kills every woman uz comes here.'"

Foster says, "Well, that ain't so, and it shan't be so, and God forbid it ever should be so."

She went right on, "And I seed Foster a comin' with two girls. And when they git thar, the girls their hearts failed 'em and Foster ketched 'em and gets his tomihawk and starts up stairs with 'em."

Foster says, "Well, that ain't so, and it shan't be so, and God forbid it ever should be so."

She went right on, "The stairs was shackly and rattly and as they went up, one of the girls wretched her hand back and caught hold of a step and Foster jest tuk his tomihawk and hacked her hand off."

Foster says, "Well, that ain't so, and it shan't be so, and God forbid it ever should be so."

She says, "Hit is so, and it shall be so and here I've got the hand to show."

And they knowed the two girls was missin' and they knowed it was so, so they lynched Foster and then they went and got Jack and bound him out.

30. The Millman's Daughter

Readers will recognize this tale as a version of "Ali Baba and the Forty Thieves." It was told by Joe Woods, who is discussed in the introduction, a Polish-born narrator recorded in Michigan by Richard M. Dorson. Woods began to hear traditional stories while a child in Poland and had spent a life that included wanderings around the United States. AT 954.

The millman was a poor man because he had no job. He was so poor he had to go to the woods to get some kindling. So when he had pick up all the limbs and bunch 'em up, he was sitting on a stump, load his pipe, and started smoking. It was happen he was sitting by a brook. The water was flowing from under the ground, the mountain, by a big crack. He sees a man coming to the wall, with a cane in his hand. Then he tap it the wall: "Isam, isam, open up." That was the magic password. Then the walls was open like artificial door, like magic door. Man walk in and door shut behind him, himself.

Man was awful scare. He cannot believe his eyes. So he run home and tell that story to his beautiful daughter, and she was a schoolteacher, and a darn smart woman.

And she says: "Wait, papa, and we try to get in tomorrow and do same thing what he do."

But millman say: "Gee, I can't wait for tomorrow. I like to find right away what is there."

"No father, you are wrong. If we go now they might be there and catch us red-handed."

So next day in the morning, father and daughter walk to the same place to the brook. She didn't have no cane, but she had a big wooden bread-mixture spoon. And she tap the wall and say, "Isam, isam, open up."

So they walk right in. But she was scare maybe the door close and lock them in, so she get locked in from inside. So she hold the door, and tell the father roll big boulder, put it against the door and the doorpost, so the door stay open.

So when they come in, they come to a big cavern. The light was coming from above, through the air shaft. And what they see, can't believe themselves. There was the barrels of golden money, silver money, and trunks of rings, bracelets, watches, diamonds. They think that must be bandit hide-out. And so the father say: "Let's get away from here. If they find us here they'll kill us to keep the secret,"

But daughter say: "No, father, so long as we stay here, we gonna take some of that money for ourselves, because we are poor all our lives, so we get little better now. And that money, anyhow, ain't come to them honestly, 'cause they are crook." So she send him home to get a couple empty sack. When he come back he load up so much he can so he can take home.

So they didn't show the money right away, but they buy some wheat and make flour and sell it. So they get rich slowly, and not show off at once.

One time there came a younger man to the tavern—because they had a tavern too (by the mill)—and he wanted some lunch and bottle a wine. So your waitress was a young and beautiful—that was the millman's daughter. So there was nobody there, just them two selves, so he started talk to her. He says, "Oh, you so beautiful I can't take my eyes off you." He asked her if she was single. He asked her if she have any boy friends.

"Oh, yes," she said. "I got lotsa boy friends now, because before, when we were poor, I have no friends at all. Now when we got a little bit richer, I have lotsa friends."

So he ask her: "Oh, well, how you gonna get rich so quick? Did some relation die and left you some money?"

"No," she says, "we have no relations. But that's my father's and my secret. I can't tell you that."

So the stranger says, "See you again some time." He went out.

And that stranger was the leader of the bandits from that underground cavern—like Janosek. So he went back to his cavern, call his band together. They had a meeting.

"Well," he says, "My dear comrades, when I told you somebody was in the cavern, you didn't believe me. You see, any time I put some more money, I put a mark on the top. So today I find it who was in here. There was the millman and his daughter."

But his partner asked him: "How you find out? How you sure the millman was here?"

"Well I tell you. I was in the tavern today and I had lunch and drink. And the millman's daughter serve me. She give me herself, and she told me before she was poor and now she was rich. Before I left I pay her for my meal. I give her big money and she give me some change." (Maybe he give her hundred dollar, you know.) "In that change was a coin on the top what was in our treasure" (mark money). "So tonight we gonna go there and kill them both if we find them there, and take back that money, and all the rest what they have."

So they hire couple team with the empty barrel on. The bandits hide themselves inside the barrel. And the leader was the driver. So he drives that team right under millman tavern's door. He tied the team to the post, hitching post, and he went in. But he was looking like different man, not like stranger before. He was old man, had gray whiskers and gray mustache and gray hair. Only he had it young stranger voice. He can't change that.

So he order food and drink. And she ask him what he got on the wagon load. "Oh," he says, "I got some fruit there, pears and peaches, and I take them early to the town."

So when he was eating, she went to the back door, run to the wagon. She was figuring take up the pears for herself, you know. (That was at night, you know.) And when she lift up the cover the barrel, she heard a voice from the barrel. "Ready, boss?" You know, the fellers wait for orders.

She was awful surprised. But she was quick thinker. She says, "Not yet." She run to the back yard, and to old millman father, send him to the police station, tell the police chief send a squad of strong men, so he can get bandit with his band— because he'd been looking for him long time, years and years.

So the police chief send twelve strong mans surround the house and the wagon. And chief police, and lieutenant, walk right in to the drinking room. And the chief says: "All my friend, put your hand up. We was looking for you long long time. But now we get you."

So he raise his hand, and they put the handcuff on him, take his false hair and false whisker out. And then that was a surprise, the biggest in the world. Because the chief bandit, at the daytime, was a rich landlord from the same village where they are living, and the best friend chief of police.

So they went outside, was everything quiet outside. Ten policeman was standing round the wagon. So he tell that leader, give his word now to them fellers. Because they wait for time (for orders).

But he says: "They find out, they find out. Fight, fight." But when the bandit jump out with the pistol in the hand and the sword, it was too late. So the bandit give up themselves.

Well they put him in jail, and after the trial they was hang up for robbery and murder. Then government agent, millman and his daughter went to the cavern underground. And the government take three-quarter, and the millman and his daughter take one-quarter.

And she was marry and live happy. That's all.

31. Mutsmag

This story is from one of Richard Chase's books; Chase, who is discussed in the introduction, played a major role in popularizing American folktales with the publication of his *The Jack Tales* in 1943. He created his own composite written versions based on oral versions he heard, a practice folklorists have criticized more recently; he gives his sources for this story as (from Wise County, Virginia) Elijah Rasnik, John Addington, Mag Roberts Hopkins, Web Hubbard, Nancy Shores, Homer Addington, James Taylor Arms, and (from Boone, North Carolina) Crastis D. Williams. A *riddel* is a sifter; a *shop-house* is a sort of blacksmith's shop; *journey cake* is an alternate name for johnny cake, that is, cornbread baked or fried into a flat cake. AT 327B + 1119.

One time there was an old woman had three girls, Poll and Betts and Mutsmag. Mutsmag she was the youngest, and Poll and Betts they treated her awful mean, made her do all the work while they'd lie in the bed of a mornin,' didn't give her nothin' to eat but left-overs.

Well, the old woman died and all she had was a cabbage patch and an old case-knife. She left the patch of cabbage to Poll and Betts, and she didn't leave Mutsmag nothin' but that old knife. Poll and Betts started in eatin' that cabbage, didn't let Mutsmag have a bite of it. And directly they eat it all up. So then Poll and Betts they decided they'd go a great journey and seek their fortune, so they borryed some meal to make journey cakes. Mutsmag begged and begged couldn't she please go too, and they told her no, she couldn't, but she begged and begged till fin'lly they told her, said, "All right, you crazy thing, but you'll have to fix your own journey cakes. Here, go get you some water in this."

And they handed her a riddel. So Mutsmag took the riddel and ran down to the spring. Tried to dip her up some water, it 'uld run out. Dip it up, it 'uld all run out. Then a little bluebird lit on a limb, tilted over and watched her; and directly it started in singin,' says:

"Stop it with moss and stick it with clay,
then you can pack your water away!
Stop it with moss and stick it with clay,
then you can pack your water away!"

"Much obliged," says Mutsmag. "I'll try that." So she smeared clay inside the riddel and pulled some moss and daubed hit over the clay and stopped ever' hole. Packed her riddel back to the house plumb full of water. So then her sisters *had* to let her go.

They got down the road a piece, and Poll and Betts started in whisperin'—turned around all at once, grabbed Mutsmag and tied her to a laurel grub. Snatched her journey cakes and off they run. Mutsmag pulled at the rope and pulled at it; and fin'lly she thought of her old knife and give the rope a rip and aloose it come. So she took out after Poll and Betts.

They looked back directly and there come Mutsmag. "Law! There's that crazy thing again! What'll we do with her this time?" Well, there was an old shop-house right there 'side the road. So they grabbed her and shoved her in that old shop-house. The door-latch was on the outside, so when Poll and Betts slammed the door on Mutsmag there wasn't no way for her to get out. She tried and tried but she couldn't. So finally she set in to hollerin'. Old fox heard her and come to the door.

"Who's in there?"

"Hit's me—Mutsmag."

"What ye want?"

"I want out."

"Unlatch the latch."

"Ain't none. Hit's out there. See can't you push it up."

"What'll ye give me?"

"I'll take ye to the fat of a goose's neck."

So the fox he reached for the latch and pushed it up, and Mutsmag took him where the fat goose was at, and then she put out and caught up with Poll and Betts again.

"Law! Yonder comes that crazy thing! What in the world will we do with her now?"

"Let's make out she's our servin' girl and make her do all the work when we stay the night somewhere."

So they let Mutsmag alone. And about dark they come to a house and hollered and an old woman come out. They asked her could they stay the night. Says, "We got us a servin' girl. She'll do up all the work for ye."

The old woman said yes, they could stay, so Poll and Betts went on in and sat by the fire and Mutsmag went to scourin' the pots.

Now the old woman had three girls about the size of Poll and Betts and Mutsmag, and she sent 'em all up in the loft to sleep. So they cloomb up the ladder and laid down in the straw, went right to sleep—all but Mutsmag. She stayed awake and listened. Heard somebody come in directly, stompin' around and fussin' at the old woman about supper not bein' ready. Mutsmag looked down quick through the cracks and knotholes, seen it was a giant.

"Hush! Hush!" the old woman told him. "You'll wake up them three fine fat pullets I got for ye up in the loft." Says, "You can get 'em down now and I'll cook 'em for ye."

"HOW'LL I KNOW 'EM FROM YOUR GIRLS?"

"My girls got nightcaps on."

Mutsmag reached right quick and jerked the nightcaps off them three girls, put 'em on her and Poll and Betts, laid back down and went to snorin.' The old giant reached up through the scuttlehole and felt around for the girls that didn't have no nightcaps on. Pulled 'em down out the loft, wrung their necks and throwed 'em over to the old woman. She went to put 'em in the cook-pot, and when she seen what the old giant had done she lit into him with the pot-ladle and nearly beat him to death.

"You ugly old coot!" she hollered at him. "You've gone and got the wrong ones!" And she hit him over the head again. Well, she went to battlin' the old giant with that ladle and the shovel and the poker and whatever she could grab up to beat him with and he went to dodgin' around; and while all that was goin' on, Mutsmag took her old knife and ripped the bedclothes and tied knots and made her a rope. Then she knocked a big hole in the shingles, tied the rope to a rafter and throwed it out, and Poll and Betts and her got away.

Well, they traveled on, and the next evenin' they come to the King's house, and he invited 'em in to stay the night. Poll and Betts went to braggin' about what'nall they done at the old giant's place, made like they was the ones done it. Mutsmag never said a word.

And directly the King said to Poll and Betts, says, "All right. You girls ought to be sharp enough to go back over there and get shet of both of 'em. That old woman's a witch and she's worse than her old man, even if he is a giant. Reckon you can do that for me?"

Of course Poll and Betts couldn't back out then, so they said sure, they could do that. Left there the next mornin,' but instead of goin' anywhere close to that giant's place they took out in another direction and that was the last anybody ever seen of 'em.

Well, Mutsmag she never said nothin.' Stayed on there and worked for the King. Then one evenin' she put out and went on down to the giant's house. Had a half-bushel poke of salt with her. So she cloomb up on the old giant's house, got up there next to the chimney, and everwhen the old woman raised the pot-lid Mutsmag sprinkled salt down in the pot of meat she had cookin.' So directly the old giant started in eatin.'

"OLD WOMAN, THE MEAT'S TOO SALTY!"

"Why, I never put in but one pinch!"

"YOU MUST A' PUT IN A HALF-BUSHEL, OLD WOMAN! FETCH ME SOME WATER HERE!"

"There hain't a bit of water up."

"GO TO THE SPRING AND GET SOME! HURRY NOW! I'M JEST ABOUT DEAD FOR WATER!"

"Hit's too dark."

"THROW OUT YOUR LIGHT-BALL!"

So the old woman throwed her light-ball out toward the spring, but Mutsmag was standin' there and caught it on the point of her old knife; and when the old woman came runnin' with the water bucket, Mutsmag squinched the light-ball in the spring and the old woman stumped her toe and fell and broke her neck. So Mutsmag cut off her head with that old knife, took it on back to the King.

He gave her a bushel of gold, says, "I declare, Mutsmag! You're pretty sharp." Says, "That old giant now, he's got a fine white horse he stole from me. Hit's a ten-mile-stepper, and I been tryin' ever' way in the world to get that horse back. You get it for me and I'll pay ye another bushel of gold."

So Mutsmag she went on back about the time it was gettin' dark. Had her apron pocket full of barley. Went in the stable and there was the fine white horse. Hit had bells on its halter, and the rope where it was tied was awful thick and had more knots in it than you could count. Well, Mutsmag, she took her old knife and went to cuttin' on them knots and the horse throwed up his head—

"Dingle! Dingle!"

The old giant come a-runnin' and Mutsmag hid under the trough. The giant he opened the stable door, looked around, went on back. So Mutsmag threw some barley in the trough. The horse went for it and them bells didn't dingle so loud. Mutsmag she started in on them knots again. But the horse eat up all that barley, throwed up his head

"Dingle! Dingle!"

And here come the old giant! Mutsmag hid by the door. The giant he shoved the door back on Mutsmag, came right on in the stable, looked around, looked around, went on back.

Mutsmag throwed a double-handful of barley in the trough and worked at them knots just as hard as she could tear, but the fine white horse got the barley eat up, throwed his head around—

"Dingle! Dingle!"

And the old giant come so fast Mutsmag just did have time to jump and hide under the bresh of the fine white horse's tail. Giant came on in, had a lantern with him, looked around, looked under the trough, jerked the door back and looked there, looked in all the corners, up in the rafters. Then he got to feelin' around under the horse's belly, stooped down, shined his lantern, looked, says, "HOLD ON NOW, MY FINE WHITE HORSE! YE GOT TOO MANY LEGS BACK HERE!"

And just about that time the fine white horse switched his tail and there was Mutsmag. She made for the door but the old giant grabbed her, says, "NOW I GOT YE!"

"What you goin' to do with me?"

"DON'T KNOW YET. HAIN'T MADE UP MY MIND!"

"Please don't feed me on honey and butter, I just can't stand the taste of honey and butter."

"THAT'S THE VERY THING I'M GOIN' TO DO! HONEY AND BUTTER IS ALL YOU'LL GIT!"

So he locked her up in the chicken house, gave her all the honey and butter she could hold. Mutsmag jest loved honey and butter. She got fat in a hurry. He come to get her fin'lly, reached in and grabbed her by the leg, toted her on to the house, says, "NOW I'M GOIN' TO KEEL YE!"

"How you gain' to kill me?" Mutsmag asked him.

"DON'T KNOW. HAIN'T MADE UP MY MIND!"

"Please don't put me in a sack and beat me to death, 'cause I'd howl like a dog, and I'd squall like cats, and my bones 'uld crack and pop like dishes breakin,' and my blood 'uld run and drip like honey."

"THAT'S THE VERY WAY I'M GOIN' TO KEEL YE!"

So he got a big sack and tied Mutsmag in it. Went on out to cut him a club. Time he got good and gone Mutsmag took her old knife and give that sack a rip and a-loose it come. Then she sewed it back right quick and put the giant's old dog in there and as many cats as she could catch and all the old giant's dishes, and she went and got the biggest pot of honey he had and put hit in, too. Then she went and hid.

The old giant come in directly with a big club—looked like he'd pulled him up a good-sized white oak. Drawed back and lammed into that sack. The dog howled and them cats set in to squallin.' The old giant went to grinnin.'

"O YES! I'LL MAKE YE HOWL LIKE DOGS AND SQUALL LIKE CATS!"

Hit it a few more licks and all them cups and saucers and plates and bowls and pitchers started crackin' and poppin.'

"O YES! I'LL MAKE YOUR BONES POP AND CRACK LIKE DISHES!"

Beat right on, and directly the honey started dribblin' out.

"O YES! I'LL MAKE YOUR BLOOD RUN AND DRIP LIKE HONEY!"

So he hit the sack several more licks and then he untied it and went to dump Mutsmag out, and there on the floor was his dog killed, and his cats; and ever' dish he had in the house all broke up, and honey jest runnin' all over everything. He was so mad he nearly busted wide open. Throwed down his club and broke and run. Headed right straight for the stable.

But while he was a flailin' that sack, Mutsmag she'd fin'lly got the rope cut, and had left there a-straddle of that fine white horse and him a-hittin' ten miles ever' step. So the old giant looked to see which-a-way they had headed, seen a streak of dust a way off, and he put out. Came to a deep wide river directly, looked across and there was Mutsmag sittin' on a millrock with a rope through the hole and one end tied around her neck.

"HOW'D YOU GIT OVER THAR?"

"I picked a hole in a rock and tied it around my neck and skeeted the rock across."

So the old giant hunted him up a great big flat rock, picked a hole in it and put a length of rope through, and tied it to his neck, and when he tried to skip the rock across hit jerked him in, and that was the last anybody ever saw of him.

So Mutsmag went and got back on the horse where she had him hid in the bresh, rode on back to the King and he paid her two more bushels of gold—one for gettin' his horse and one for gettin' shet of that old giant.

32. Lady Featherflight

First published in the *Journal of American Folklore* in 1893, this fairytale was told to Mrs. J. B. Warner of Cambridge, Massachusetts, by Elizabeth Hoar of Concord, Massachusetts. AT 313C.

A poor woman, living on the edge of a wood, came at last to where she found nothing in the cupboard of the next day's breakfast. She called her boy Jack, and said: "You must now go into the wide world; if you stay here, there will be two of us to starve. I have nothing for you but this piece of black bread. On the other side of the forest lies the world. Find your way to it, and gain your living honestly." With that she bade him good-by and he started. He knew the way some distance into the thickest of the forest, for he had often been there for fagots. But after walking all day, he saw no farm, path, or tree, and knew that he was lost. Still he traveled on and on, as long as the daylight lasted, and then lay down and slept.

The next morning he ate the black bread, and wandered on all day. At night he saw lights before him, and was guided by them to a large palace, where he knocked for a long time in vain. At last the door was opened, and a lovely lady appeared, who said as she saw him: "Go away as quickly as you can. My father will soon come home, and he will surely eat you." Jack said: "Can't you hide me, and give me something to eat, or I shall fall down dead at your door?"

At first she refused, but afterwards yielded to Jack's prayers, and told him to come in and hide behind the oven. Then she gave him food, and told him that her father was a giant, who ate men and women. Perhaps she could keep him overnight, as she had already supper prepared. After a while, the giant came banging at the door, shouting: "Featherflight, let me in; let me in!" As she opened the door he came in, saying: "Where have you stowed the man? I smelt him all the way through that wood." Featherflight said: "Oh father, he is nothing but a poor, little, thin boy! He would make but half a mouthful, and his bones would stick in your throat; and beside he wants to work for you; perhaps you can make him useful. But sit down to supper now, and after supper I will show him to you."

So she set before him half of a fat heifer, a sheep, and a turkey, which he swallowed so fast that his hair stood on end. When he had finished, Featherflight beckoned to Jack, who came trembling from behind the oven. The giant looked at him scornfully and said: "Indeed, as you say, he is but half a mouthful. But there is room for flesh there, and we must fatten him up for a few days; meanwhile he must earn his victuals. See here, my young snip, can you do a day's work in a day?" And Jack answered bravely: "I can do a day's work in a day as well as another." So the giant said: "Well, go to bed now. I will tell you in the morning your work." So Jack went to bed, and Lady Featherflight showed him; while the giant lay down on the floor with his head in Featherflight's lap, and she combed his hair and brushed his head till he went fast asleep.

The next morning Jack was called bright and early, and was taken out to the farmyard, where stood a large barn, unroofed by a late tempest. Here the giant stopped and said: "Behind this barn you will find a hill of feathers; thatch me this barn with them, and earn your supper, and, look you! if it be not done when I come back tonight, you shall be fried in meal, and swallowed whole for supper." Then he left, laughing to himself as he went down the road.

Jack went bravely to work and found a ladder and basket; he filled the basket, and ran up the ladder, and then tried hard to make a beginning on the thatch. As soon as he placed a handful of feathers, half would fly away as he wove them in. He tried for hours with no success, until at last half of the hill was scattered to the four winds, and he had not finished a hand-breadth of the roof. Then he sat down at the foot of the ladder and began to cry, when out came Lady Featherflight, with the basket on her arm, which she set down at his feet, saying: "Eat now, and cry after. Meantime I will try to think what I can do to help you." Jack felt cheered, and went to work, while Lady Featherflight walked round the barn, singing as she went—

"Birds of land and birds of sea,
Come and thatch this roof for me."

As she walked round the second time, the sky grew dark, and a heavy cloud hid the sun and came nearer and nearer to the earth, separating at last into hundreds and thousands of birds. Each, as it flew, dropped a feather on the roof, and tucked it neatly in; and when Jack's meal was finished the roof was finished, too.

Then Featherflight said: "Let us talk and enjoy ourselves till my father the giant comes home." So they wandered round the grounds and the stables, and Lady Featherflight told of the treasure in the strong room, till Jack wondered why he was born without a sixpence. Soon they went back to the house, and Jack helped, and Lady Featherflight prepared supper, which to-night was fourteen loaves of bread, two sheep, and a jack-pudding, by way of finish, which would almost have filled the little house where Jack was born.

Soon the giant came home, thundered at the door again, and shouted, "Let me in, let me in!" Featherflight served him with the supper already laid, and the giant ate it with great relish. As soon as he had finished, he called to Jack, and asked him about his work. Jack said: "I told you I could do a day's work in a day as well as another. You'll have no fault to find." The giant said nothing, and Jack went to bed. Then, as before, the giant lay down on the floor with his head in Featherflight's lap. She combed his hair and brushed his head till he fell fast asleep.

The next morning the giant called Jack into the yard, and looked at his day's work. All he said was: "This is not your doing," and he proceeded to a heap of seed, nearly as high as the barn, saying: "Here is your day's work. Separate the seeds, each into its own pile. Let it be done when I come home to-night, or you shall be fried in meal, and I shall swallow you, bones and all." Then the giant went off down the road, laughing as he went. Jack seated himself before the heap, took a handful of seeds, put corn in one pile, rye in another, oats in another, and had not begun to find an end of the different kinds when noon had come, and the sun was right over head. The heap was no smaller, and Jack was tired out, so he sat down, hugged his knees, and cried. Out came Featherflight, with a basket on her arm, which she put down before Jack, saying: "Eat now, and cry after." So Jack ate with a will, and Lady Featherflight walked round and round the heap, singing as she went—

"Birds of earth and birds of sea,
Come and sort this seed for me."

As she walked round the heap for the second time, still singing, the ground about her looked as if it was moving. From behind each grain of sand, each daisy stem, each blade of grass, there came some little insect, gray, black, brown, or green, and began to work at the seeds. Each chose some one kind, and made a heap by itself. When Jack had finished a hearty meal, the great heap was divided into countless others; and Jack and Lady Featherflight walked and talked to their hearts' content for the rest of the day. As the sun went down the giant came home, thundered at the door again, and shouted: "Let me in; let me in!"

Featherflight greeted him with his supper, already laid, and he sat down and ate, with a great appetite, four fat pigs, three fat pullets and an old gander. He finished off with a jack-pudding. Then he was so sleepy he could not keep his head up; all he said was, "Go to bed, youngster; I'll see your work tomorrow." Then, as before, the giant laid his head down on the floor with his head in Featherflight's lap. She combed his hair and brushed his head, and he fell fast asleep.

The next morning the giant called Jack into the farmyard earlier than before. "It is but fair to call you early, for I have work more than a strong man can well do." He showed him a heap of sand, saying: "Make me a rope to tether my herd of cows, that they may not leave the stalls before milking time." Then he turned on heel, and went down the road laughing.

Jack took some sand in his hands, gave a twist, threw it down, went to the door, and called out: "Featherflight! Featherflight! this is beyond you: I feel myself already rolled in meal, and swallowed, bones and all."

Out came Featherflight, saying with good cheer: "Not so bad as that. Sit down, and we will plan what to do." They talked and planned all the day. Just before the giant came home, they went up to the top of the stairs to Jack's room; then Featherflight pricked Jack's finger and dropped a drop of blood on each of the three stairs. Then she came down and prepared the supper, which to-night was a brace of turkeys, three fat geese, five fat hens, six fat pigs, seven fat woodcocks, and half a score of quail, with a jack-pudding.

When he had finished, the giant turned to Featherflight with a growl: "Why so sparing of food to-night? Is there no good meal in the larder? This boy whets my appetite. Well for you, young sir, if you have done your work. Is it done?" "No, sir," said Jack boldly. "I said I could do a day's work in a day as well as another, but no better." The giant said: "Featherflight, prick him for me with the larding needle, hang him in the chimney corner well wrapped in bacon, and give him to me for my early breakfast." Featherflight says: "Yes, father." Then, as before, the giant laid his head down on the floor with his head in Featherflight's lap. She combed his hair, and brushed his head, and he fell fast asleep.

Jack went to bed, his room at the top of the stairs. As soon as the giant was snoring in bed, Featherflight softly calls Jack and said: "I have the keys of the treasure house; come with me." They opened the treasure house, took out bags of gold and silver, and loosened the halter of the best horse in the best stall in the best stable. Jack mounted with Featherflight behind, and off they went. At three o'clock in the morning, not thinking of his order the night before, the giant woke and called, "Jack, get up." "Yes, sir," said the first drop of blood. At four o'clock the giant woke, turned over, and said, "Jack, get up." "Yes, sir," said the second drop of blood. At five o'clock the giant woke, turned over, and said, "Jack, get up." "Yes, sir," said the third drop of blood. At six o'clock the giant woke, turned over, and said, "Jack, get up," and there was no answer.

Then with great fury he said: "Featherflight has overslept herself; my breakfast won't be ready." He rushed to Featherflight's room; it was empty. He dashed downstairs to the chimney corner, to see if Jack was hanging there, and found neither Jack nor Featherflight.

Then he suspected they had run away, and rushed back for his seven-leagued boots, but could not find the key under his pillow. He rushed down, found the door wide open, caught up his boots and rushed to the stable. There he found that the best horse from the best stall from the best stable was gone. Jumping into his boots, he flew after them, swifter than the wind.

The runaways had been galloping for several hours, when Jack heard a sound behind him, and, turning, saw the giant in the distance. "O Featherflight! Featherflight! all is lost!" But Featherflight said: "Keep steady, Jack, look in the horse's right ear, and throw behind you over your right shoulder what you find." Jack looked and found a little stick of wood, threw it over his right shoulder, and then there grew up behind them a forest of hard wood. "We are saved," said Jack. "Not so certain," says Lady Featherflight, "but prick up the horse, for we have gained some time."

The giant went back for an axe, but soon hacked and hewed his way through the wood, and was on the trail again. Jack again heard a sound, turned and saw the giant, and said to Lady Featherflight, "All is lost." "Keep steady, Jack," said Featherflight; "look in the horse's left ear, and throw over your left shoulder what you find." Jack looked, found a drop of water, threw it over his left shoulder, and between them and the giant there arose a large lake, and the giant stopped on the other side, and shouted across, "How did you get over?" Featherflight called, "We drank, and our horses drank, and we drank our way through." The giant shouted scornfully back, "Surely I am good for what you can do," and he threw himself down and drank, and drank, and drank, and then he burst.

Now they went on quietly till they came near to a town. Here they stopped, and Jack said, "Climb this tree, and hide in the branches till I come with the parson to marry us. For I must buy me a suit of fine clothes before I am seen with a gay lady like yourself." So Featherflight climbed the tree with the thickest branches she could find, and waited there, looking between the leaves into a spring below. Now this spring was used by all the wives of the townspeople to draw water for breakfast. No water was so sweet anywhere else; and early in the morning they all came with pitchers and pails for a gossip, and to draw water for the kettle. The first who came was a carpenter's wife, and as she bent over the clear spring she saw, not herself, but Featherflight's lovely face reflected in the water. She looked at it with astonishment and cried, "What! I, a carpenter's wife, and I so handsome? No, that I won't," and down she threw the pitcher, and off she went.

The next who came was the potter's wife, and as she bent over the clear spring she saw, not herself, but Featherflight's lovely face reflected in the water. She looked at it with astonishment and cried "What! I, a potter's wife, and I so handsome? No, that I won't," and down she threw the pitcher, and off she went.

The next who came was the scrivener's wife and as she bent over the clear spring she saw, not herself, but Featherflight's lovely face reflected in the water. She looked at it with astonishment and cried "What! I, a scrivener's wife, and I so handsome? No, that I won't," and down she threw the pitcher, and off she went.

The next who came was the lace-maker's wife and as she bent over the clear spring she saw, not herself, but Featherflight's lovely face reflected in the water. She looked at it with astonishment and cried "What! I, a lace-maker's wife, and I so handsome? No, that I won't," and down she threw the pitcher, and off she went.

All the men in the town began to want their breakfast, and one after another went out into the market-place to ask if anyone by chance had seen his wife. Each came with the same question and all received the same answers. All had seen them going, but none had seen them returning. They all began to fear foul play, and all together walked out toward the spring. When they reached it, they found the broken pitchers all about the grass, and the pails bottom upwards floating on the water. One of them, looking over the edge, saw the face reflected, and, knowing that it was not his own, looked up. Seeing Lady Featherflight, he called to his comrades: "Here is the witch, here is the enchantress. She has bewitched our wives. Let us kill her"; and they began to drag her out of the tree, in spite of all she could say. Just at this moment Jack came up, galloping back on his horse, with the parson up behind. You would not know the gayly dressed cavalier to be the poor, ragged boy who passed over the road so short a time before. As he came near he saw the crowd and shouted, "What's the matter? What are you doing to my wife?" The men shouted, "We are hanging a witch; she has bewitched all our wives, and murdered them, for all we know." The parson bade them stop, and let the Lady Featherflight tell her own story. When she told them how their wives had mistaken her face for theirs, they were silent a moment, and then one and all cried, "If we have wedded such fools, they are well sped," and turning walked back to the town.

The parson married Jack and Lady Featherflight on the spot, and christened them from the water of the spring, and then went home with them to the great house that Jack had bought as he passed through the town. There the newly married pair lived happily for many months, until Jack began to wish for more of the giant's treasure, and proposed that they should go back for it. But they could not cross the water. Lady Featherflight said, "Why not build a bridge?" And the bridge was built. They went over with wagons and horses, and brought back so heavy a load that, as the last wagonful passed over the bridge, it broke, and the gold was lost. Jack lamented and said, "Now we can have nothing more from the giant's treasure-house." But Lady Featherflight said, "Why not mend the bridge?"

So the bridge was mended,
And my story's ended.

33. How Toodie Fixed Old Grunt

The informant (as folklorists call those who tell them folklore) for this story was R. H. Robertson, Joplin, Missouri, who learned it from "a girl" who had heard many stories in Benton, Arkansas, at the tail end of the nineteenth century; Robertson told it to folklorist Vance Randolph in January 1938. AT 312.

One time there was a farmer and his wife lived in a little old cabin, right at the edge of the big timber. They had three daughters that was the prettiest girls for miles around. But the folks was awful poor, because the old man couldn't work much, and it was mighty hard for them to keep their skillet greasy.

An old bachelor named Grunt lived down the road a piece. He says he was tired of living by himself, so he married the oldest girl. She didn't want to marry old Grunt, but the folks talked her into it. He had a good farm and a fine big house, and money in the bank besides.

Things went along all right for about a year, and then all of a sudden old Grunt was raising hell all over the neighborhood, because he says his wife has run off with a peddler from Missouri. So then he married the next-to-the-oldest girl. She didn't want to marry old Grunt, but the folks talked her into it. He had a good farm and a fine big house, and money in the bank besides.

Things went along all right for about a year, and then old Grunt's second wife showed up missing, and he says she has run off with a cowboy from Oklahoma. So then he married the youngest girl. She didn't want to marry old Grunt, but the folks talked her into it. He had a good farm and a fine house, and money in the bank besides.

The youngest girl was named Toodie, and she had a boy friend name of Jack. When old Grunt and Toodie went uptown to get married, Jack searched Grunt's house, and he found where the two sisters was killed and throwed in a old cistern. So Jack hid in the bushes, and when Toodie come back he told her, "Old Grunt killed your sisters, look out he don't kill you."

Pretty soon Toodie and old Grunt had words about something, and he says, "You're my wife now, an' you got to mind whatever I say." Toodie she sassed him right back, and old Grunt says, "You better look out, or I will do you the same as I done them other fool girls," and he pulled out his big old knife. "I'm goin' to kill you right now," he says, "an' put you down the cistern!"

Toodie was fixed for him with both hands full of pepper, and all of a sudden she throwed it right in old Grunt's eyes. Old Grunt begun to beller and slash around, but he couldn't see nothing because his eyes was blinded with pepper. Jack come out from where he was a-hiding, and hit old Grunt with a stick of wood. And then him and Toodie wrastled old Grunt down and cut his head plumb off. It served him right, too. So they throwed him down the cistern, and worked pretty near all night a-filling the whole thing up with rocks. And then they put dirt on top, and Toodie planted flowers, so you couldn't tell if there had ever been a cistern on the place.

About three weeks after that Toodie told everybody her husband has run off and left her. She says she can't stay in a big house like that all by herself, and she got the old folks to move in with her. Then after awhile they needed a hired man to help with the work, and so Jack he moved in too.

Things went along all right for a while, and then the old folks died off. Toodie had a good farm and a fine big house now, and money in the bank besides. So her and Jack got married, and raised a big family, and they all lived happy ever after.

34. The Green Bird (El Pájero Verde)

"The Green Bird," from the American Southwest, was originally told in Spanish; for information on the informants, see the headnote for story 21. AT 550.

In a far away city there once lived a king and queen who had had two sons and a daughter. Each time that a child was born, the servants, who were very jealous, told them that it had been born dead, and threatened to kill the queen if she denied it.

When a child was born they paid a male servant to take it out and throw it in the river. The servant felt sorry for the children and did not throw them in; he took them, instead, to an old, old lady who lived on the edge of a forest. The old lady raised all three of the babies and named them Jesús, Maria, and José. The children loved one another a great deal, and they all thought that the old lady was their mother.

Many years later, when the old lady was on her deathbed, she called the children to her and said: "My children, I have already done my duty, and am ready to die, but before I go, I am going to tell you about something that may be found on top of the mountain in the City of Trina. This mountain reaches way up into the sky, and on top you'll find a green bird which talks, the singing tree, and the water of life. Whoever succeeds in getting all three of these will be happy all the days of his life. It is very hard to get there. No one has ever found the place. The stones along the road are people who have tried to reach the mountain top, but when they looked back they were turned to stone. Go to the City of Trina, climb the mountain, and bring back the bird, the water, and a branch from the tree."

The three children stayed by the old lady until she closed her eyes for the last time. They cried a great deal for her, but never forgot her counsel. Finally, José, the oldest, said: "My brother and sister, I'm going to bring back that bird. Whatever happens, don't worry about me; I'm not afraid. I am going to leave you a mirror, and when it becomes clouded you will know that I have died." The other two children were very sad and didn't want him to leave, but José left anyway. Every day Maria looked at the mirror, and it was always clear until one day, along in the afternoon, it became clouded, telling her that her brother had died.

Jesús turned to her and said: "I'm going to bring back our brother and the bird, so don't worry about me." Maria did not want her second brother to go away, but he finally convinced her and left early in the morning. Before leaving he too gave her a mirror, and told her to look into it, and when it became blurred she would know that he had died. Maria looked at the mirror every day, and one day, along toward evening, it began to cloud until it was completely blurred. Maria cried all night, and was so worried that she did not know what to do.

Finally, she said: "I am going to look for my two brothers." She put some lunch in a little basket, and started early in the morning toward the City of Trina. After walking all day long, she came to a little cabin at the foot of a very high mountain. She was very tired, so she knocked on the cabin door, hoping to find a place to sit down and rest. Nobody answered, so she knocked again, but finally opened the door and walked in. There, on an old bed in a corner of the room, was an old, old man with a beard that reached to his knees, and eyebrows and eyelashes that reached to his chin. He tried to speak, but the beard was so heavy that he could not speak. Noticing that the old man was trying to tell her something, Maria took a pair of scissors and cut his beard so he could talk. She asked him first if he had seen her two brothers, and the old man told her that they had passed by a few days before. Then he added: "They have turned to stone along the way. You, too, will turn to stone unless you follow my advice. I have lived here hundreds of years, and have never seen a single person climb to the top of the mountain. If you want to find your brothers, stop up your ears with cotton, and no matter what you hear, don't turn to look back."

Maria thanked the old man, ate her lunch, and did as he told her. She started up the mountain, and noticed the path lined with stones on both sides. Despite the cotton in her ears, she began to hear voices telling her to turn back, but she remembered what the old man had said. When she was nearing the top, she began to hear beautiful music, and almost turned around, when again she remembered the advice of the old man. She kept on climbing and noticed that there were fewer stones the higher she climbed. The voices began to threaten her, louder and louder: "Turn back or you shall die!" But she kept going, until she reached the top, and suddenly everything became quiet.

Straight ahead of her was a beautiful tree on the edge of a clear pool of water. A soft voice spoke and said: "You have finally come! You have suffered a great deal because of me, but I'll make it up to you." Maria was so taken by the beauty of the place, that she could neither move nor speak. She looked toward the tree, trying to find out who was speaking to her, and saw a beautiful green bird. He spoke again: "I am the speaking bird; this is the singing tree, and this is the water of life." Then she heard a beautiful voice singing a song she had never heard before. The bird hopped down from his perch and lighted on her shoulder, but she was not afraid. "Where are my brothers?" she asked. He told her that if she took a bucketful of the water in the pool and sprinkled it on the stones along the path on the way down she would eventually find them. The bird also insisted that she take a branch from the singing tree and water from the pool, because, without these two things, he could not live.

On the way down, Maria began to sprinkle the rocks with water, and they turned into all sorts of people. Some of them were dressed in clothes she had never seen, and they told her they had been turned to stone hundreds of years before. Finally, the last two stones turned into her two brothers, so they all started back together to their little cottage in the forest, bringing the bird, the branch, and the water.

Back at the palace, the king had gone on a long journey and had been away for a long time. When he got back, the servants told him that the queen had died while he was away. He also learned that three very poor children in his kingdom had found the speaking bird, the singing tree, and the water of life. He was very sad and wanted company, so he sent for them and gave them a banquet. The servants became very jealous, and decided to poison the bird and Maria when they sat down to eat at the king's table. The bird waited until the food had been served and then turned to Maria and said: "Do not touch your food, for yours and mine are poisoned." Then he turned to the king and told him what the servants had done. The king became so angry that he made the servants eat the food instead, and they died on the spot.

The bird kept on talking and said to the king: "You foolish king, don't you know that your wife is not dead? She is imprisoned in a dungeon of the palace." He immediately sent his soldiers to look for her, and they brought her to him. Then the bird said again: "You foolish king, don't you know that these are your own children?" The king said that it was impossible, for his children had died at birth. But the bird told him to look at their foreheads. He looked at the three children and saw the royal seal.

After the excitement at the table, they noticed that the green bird had fallen from his perch. It had died of a heart attack. Also, the water and the tree suddenly dried up. The king had a coffin made for the green bird, and placed it in the palace, where it may be seen today.

35. Rose

Mary Brown of Cambridge, Massachusetts, who "heard it . . . from a woman of Irish extraction," published this tale in a folklore journal in the late nineteenth century. AT 425C.

Once upon a time there was a widower with one daughter, and he married a widow with two daughters, each of whom was older than his own daughter Rose. The two elder daughters were all for balls and parties. Little Rose had to do all the work, and when they went to a party she was obliged to help them dress, brush, and comb their hair, and never was allowed to go herself. She never complained but was very kind to her father, and always prepared his meals.

Once it was necessary for him to go on a long journey. He asked each of his daughters what he should bring them for a present. The elder daughters wanted silk dresses, jewelry, and all that was rare. Little Rose stood by, not saying a word. Her father asked: "Little Rose, what can I bring for you?" "Nothing, father, but a rose." And she kissed her father, and bade him good-by. "Rose, I shall bring you a rose, the very prettiest I can get, if it should cost me my life."

After he got to his journey's end, he came to a splendid palace. The house was empty, but all in order. His breakfast was ready but he could see no one. He stayed all night, in the morning went into the garden, and oh, the beautiful rose! After he plucked the rose, and had gone a few steps, a great lion met him, frothing at the mouth, and told him, "For this rose you shall die." The father said that he had a very beautiful daughter at home, whose name was Rose, and that, as he was leaving, he promised to bring her a rose; and he pleaded, "If you will only let me go home to my little daughter to bid her farewell."

So the Lion let him go home, on condition that he was to return. And as he came home Rose was looking out of the window and saw her father coming, and ran to meet him. "Why," said she, "father, what makes you look so, sad?" "Nothing, my child except that I have plucked a rose, and for this rose I must die."

"No, father, you shall not go back and die for the rose, but I will go back and ask to have you pardoned."

So she went to the palace. As she entered it seemed to her that everything which her eyes fell on seemed to say, "Welcome, Beauty, here!" Even on her cup and saucer, and on every piece of furniture in her chamber were the words, "Welcome, Beauty, here!" She went out to find the Lion, and said that she had come to ask him to forgive her father, and that the rose was for her. But the Lion said he would not do it unless she would promise to be his wife. Her father was very dear to her, yet she did not like to marry a lion. The Lion gave her a beautiful gold ring, and told her that whenever she wanted to see her father she was to lay the ring on her table before going to sleep, and she would be at home in the morning. Her father was now getting old, and she grieved for him. At night she laid her ring on the table, at the same time making a wish that she would like to see her father. The next morning she found herself with her father, whom she found much changed. His hair had turned white from grief at the thought of losing his Rose, or having her marry the Lion.

That night she laid her ring on the table, and wished herself back at the palace. The palace was more beautiful than before, and the table all ready. On every plate were the words, "Welcome, Beauty, here!" On the first morning she went out into the garden. The poor Lion was lying very sick, and she looked at him. "Oh, I cannot bear to see my poor Lion die, what am I to do?" Finally, she said that she could not bear it any longer, and she called out, "I will be your wife." With this a beautiful young prince stood before her. So they were married, and he sent for her father, and the step-sisters who had been so cruel to her were made servants to stand at the post of the gate before the palace, and all the people were happy.

36. The Talking Eggs

Originally told in Louisiana Creole by an African American narrator, "The Talking Eggs" was among a group published in the late nineteenth century by the New Orleans scholar Alcée Fortier. AT 480.

There was once a lady who had two daughters; they were called Rose and Blanche. Rose was bad and Blanche was good; but the mother liked Rose better, although she was bad, because she was her very picture. She would compel Blanche to do all the work, while Rose was seated in her rocking-chair. One day she sent Blanche to the well to get some water in a bucket. When Blanche arrived at the well, she saw an old woman, who said to her: "Pray, my little one, give me some water; I am very thirsty." "Yes, aunt," said Blanche, "here is some water"; and Blanche raised her bucket, and gave her good fresh water to drink. "Thank you, my child, you are a good girl; God will bless you."

A few days after, the mother was so bad to Blanche that she ran away into the woods. She cried, and knew not where to go, because she was afraid to return home. She saw the same old woman, who was walking in front of her. "Ah! My child, why are you crying? What hurts you?" "Ah, aunt, mamma has beaten me, and I am afraid to return to the cabin." "Well, my child, come with me; I will give you supper and a bed; but you must promise me not to laugh at anything which you will see."

She took Blanche's hand, and they began to walk in the wood. As they advanced, the bushes of thorns opened before them, and closed behind their backs. A little further on, Blanche saw two axes, which were fighting; she found that very strange, but she said nothing. They walked further, and behold! it was two arms which were fighting; a little further, two legs; at last, she saw two heads which were fighting, and which said: "Blanche, good morning, my child; God will help you." At last they arrived at the cabin of the old woman, who said to Blanche: "Make some fire, my child, to cook the supper"; and she sat down near the fireplace, and took off her head. She placed it on her knees, and began to louse herself. Blanche found that very strange; she was afraid, but she said nothing. The old woman put back her head in its place and gave Blanche a large bone to put on the fire for their supper. Blanche put the bone in the pot. Lo! in a moment the pot was full of good meat.

She gave Blanche a grain of rice to pound with the pestle, and thereupon the mortar became full of rice. After they had taken their supper, the old woman said to Blanche: "Pray, my child, scratch my back." Blanche scratched her back, but her hand was all cut, because the old woman's back was covered with broken glass. When she saw that Blanche's hand was bleeding, she only blew on it, and the hand was cured.

When Blanche got up in the morning, the old woman said to her: "You must go home now, but as you are a good girl I want to make you a present of the talking eggs. Go to the chicken-house; all the eggs which say 'Take me,' you must take them; all those which will say 'Do not take me,' you must not take them. When you will be on the road, throw the eggs behind your back to break them."

As Blanche walked, she broke the eggs. Many pretty things came out of those eggs. It was now diamonds, now gold, a beautiful carriage, beautiful dresses. When she arrived at her mother's, she had so many fine things that the house was full of them. Therefore her mother was very glad to see her. The next day, she said to Rose: "You must go to the woods to look for this same old woman; you must have fine dresses like Blanche."

Rose went to the woods, and she met the old woman, who told her to come to her cabin; but when she saw the axes, the arms, the legs, the heads, fighting, and the old woman taking off her head to louse herself, she began to laugh and to ridicule everything she saw. Therefore the old woman said: "Ah! my child, you are not a good girl. God will punish you."

The next day she said to Rose: "I don't want to send you back with nothing; go to the chicken-house, and take the eggs which say 'Take me.'"

Rose went to the chicken-house. All the eggs began to say: "Take me," "Don't take me"; "Take me," "Don't take me." Rose was so bad that she said, "Ah, yes, you say 'Don't take me,' but you are precisely those I want." She took all the eggs which said "Don't take me," and she went away with them.

As she walked, she broke the eggs, and there came out a quantity of snakes, toads, frogs, which began to run after her. There were even a quantity of whips, which whipped her. Rose ran and shrieked. She arrived at her mother's so tired that she was not able to speak. When her mother saw the beasts and the whips which were chasing her, she was so angry that she sent her away like a dog, and told her to go live in the woods.

The Grateful Dead and Other Magic Helpers

Though brave and resourceful, folktale protagonists are often aided in their quests by helpers they meet along the way, helpers who commonly possess magical powers. The helper may just appear unbidden, like the old woman in "The Girl That Weren't Ashamed to Own Her Kin," or in response to some kindness done by the hero. Sometimes (as in "Old Shake-Your-Head") the helper is a dead person, one of the "grateful dead," the folklore motif whose name was borrowed by the famous American musical group. In the Disney version of the Cinderella story, it is of course a "fairy godmother" who helps, though in the story from the Cinderella cycle printed here ("One-Eye, Two-Eyes and Three-Eyes") help comes from rather a different source. Sometimes the helpers are multiple, as in "The Boat That Went on Land and Sea," in which specialized powers are called for. Helpers may provide the tale audience with the symbolic psychological assurance that help is often at hand in daily life. And that help often comes from those who are first helped suggests something about human reciprocity. Helpers appear in tales in other sections, but in the tales in this section, that help seems especially central to the story.

37. The Girl That Weren't Ashamed to Own Her Kin

Sam Caudill, who died in the early 1930s, told this story to folklorist Marie Campbell, who spent time in the Kentucky mountains collecting folktales and other local lore. AT 501.

I ain't got no sleight with tales for idle telling, but, iffen you would love to hear me tell an olden tale, then I'm a-bound to try what I can do.

A widow woman had a girl that couldn't do any kind of work. The widow woman never tried to train her girl how to spin and weave and sew. She just quarreled at the girl all the time till the girl never had the heart to even try to work.

One day the widow woman was quarreling and fussing at her girl, and the king came passing through. He stopped to find out what was the matter. The widow woman said she was quarreling at her girl to keep her from working herself to death. She said the girl wanted to spin and weave and sew all the time, day in and day out.

The king said that was the kind of girl he'd love to marry his boy to. So he took the girl with him to his castle, aiming to have the wedding the next day. But the queen said they better try out the girl's reputation for working.

The next day the queen put the girl in a room with a spinning wheel and big baskets of wool. She told the girl to spin all that into yarn by sundown. The girl sat there and cried, for she couldn't spin. An old woman with a big, wide thumb came, and said she would spin all the wool into yarn if the girl would ask her to the wedding. The girl said she would, and the old woman spun the yarn before sundown and vanished away.

The next day after that the queen took all the yarn and put it into a room with a loom. She told the girl to weave all the yarn into cloth before sundown. Same as the day before, an old woman came, only this time with a big, wide foot. She made the same kind of bargain and wove all the cloth before sundown and vanished away.

The last day of working, the queen took all the cloth and told the girl to sew it all into things to wear before sundown. The old woman that came that day had a big lip that hung way down. She made a bargain to get asked to the wedding, and sewed all the cloth before sundown and vanished away.

The queen said she was satisfied, and they had the wedding the next day. A whole big crowd came to the wedding and amongst them the three old women that helped the widow woman's girl.

The girl was proud to see them and made them welcome. She told the king and queen the old women were her aunts. The king's son asked them what happened to their thumb and their foot and their lip. They told him it was from spinning and weaving and sewing so much. The king's son looked at his pretty bride and said he wouldn't ever let her spin or weave or sew another time as long as she lived.

The ugly old women put it in his mind to think that-a-way and keep the girl from having to work. That way they paid the girl their thanks for her not being ashamed to own them for her kin.

38. Old Shake-Your-Head

Told by the storyteller identified as Big Nelt of Gander Community, Kentucky, this tale was collected by folklorist Marie Campbell. AT 507A.

It's purely a shame how jealous some folks get over their younguns at school and the foolish or mean things that being jealous will make them say and do. It puts me in mind of a tale about the King of Ireland's son that was in the same school with the sons of the King of Spain and the King of France and the King of Greece. These other three kings got jealous because the King of Ireland's son was smarter than theirs and stood higher in his books.

They figured their sons never could make a good show of being smart as long as the King of Ireland had his son in that same school. So they plotted mean things to do. Banded together, they had the power to tell the King of Ireland that he had to get rid of his boy or get him out of that school and out of the country somehow.

The King of Ireland couldn't fight the kings of three countries. So he took his boy out of school and let him go out in the world to seek his fortune. He gave the boy five pounds of cash money—I don't know how much that would be worth, for I never did see cash money weighed out that way.

The king's son put his cash money in his pocket and his clothes in a suit satchel and set out a-traveling—a foot, I reckon, for it don't make no mention of a horse.

He traveled past a graveyard way off from nowhere. The noise of a big tussle made him stop and look, though he was too scared to stand still. He saw four men fighting over a coffin with a dead man in it. Two men wanted to bury the man in the coffin; two men raised objections. The two men that objected said the dead man owed them five pounds in cash money, and they aimed to take his corpse and make soap grease out of it and sell his coffin to somebody that was poor and would trade for a second hand coffin.

The king's son listened to how things stood. Then he pulled his five pounds out of his pocket and paid the dead man's debt. The two men that had been fussing about what was owing set to work and helped the dead man's two brothers bury him.

With his pockets plumb empty, the king's son walked along. Pretty soon a red-haired man whose head doddled about when he walked or talked caught up with the king's son. He said to the King of Ireland's son, "Let me be your serving man and help you seek your fortune. You can call me Old Shake-Your-Head."

The King of Ireland's son took Old Shake-Your-Head for a serving man and let him carry the suit satchel. After a day's traveling, they came to a giant's castle. Old Shake-Your-Head told the giant about another giant that aimed to do him harm and showed him how to protect himself. The giant liked Old Shake-Your-Head for his kindness and offered him some gold from a big pile under his bed.

Old Shake-Your-Head said, "No, I'd a heap rather have that light black horse iffen you want to do me a favor." I don't know how black a light black horse would be, but color made no manner of difference to Old Shake-Your-Head. This was a magic horse that would carry out of all danger anybody that would throw a leg over his back, and that was what made Old Shake-Your-Head want the light black horse.

In the same manner Old Shake-Your-Head got a two-handed sword at another giant's castle and a cloak of darkness from the last giant's castle.

"Now, we're fixed to travel," Old Shake-Your-Head said to the King of Ireland's son. "How would you like to travel to the King in the Golden Castle and ask him for his daughter?" That suited the King of Ireland's son fine.

The King in the Golden Castle was willing to marry his daughter to the King of Ireland's son, but the girl had set her heart on a black-haired giant that lived in the next country. She thought up ways to get out of marrying the King of Ireland's son.

She gave him her thimble that he had to keep all night and give back to her in the morning. Her serving maid turned into a rat and got the thimble away while the King of Ireland's son was asleep. She gave it to the giant, and he flung it away in the high weeds. Old Shake-Your-Head didn't sleep, so he saw what went on. He crawled around in the high weeds and found the thimble and gave it to the King of Ireland's son, and he gave it to the king's daughter in the Golden Castle.

The girl tried the same trick with her comb. And in the same way it got back to her in the morning. Maybe she aimed to think up some more tricks, for she still wanted the blackhaired giant. But the King of the Golden Castle said to her, "Now stop your foolishness and marry the King of Ireland's son. He is a smart boy and he is our kind of folks." And he said to the King of Ireland's son, "I wish you would kill that big rascal, for he aims to make trouble after you get married."

The King of Ireland's son took his two-handed sword and chopped off the giant's head. Then he married the Princess of the Golden Castle. After the wedding he never did see the red-haired man that had been a help to him. Old Shake-Your-Head had gone back to his coffin in the graveyard and lay down to rest in peace till the Judgment Day.

"Old Shake-Your-Head" is one of Grandpap's tales. He favored tales with graveyards and ghosts and all manner of scary things. Tales to make people laugh he liked too.

39. One-Eye, Two-Eyes and Three-Eyes

Told by Conrado V. Garcia, Tolleson, Arizona, to Calvin Claudel (who was interested in American folklore with French and Spanish backgrounds), this story is one closely allied to the Cinderella cycle. AT 511.

Once there was an old woman who had three daughters whose names were One-Eye, Two-Eyes and Three-Eyes. The mother hated Two-Eyes and loved One-Eye and Three-Eyes. Two-Eyes had to do all the work around the house and serve her two sisters.

It happened that the king was to give three balls three nights in succession, to which all the girls were invited. The king wanted his son, the prince, to choose a wife from among the girls at the ball.

The old woman began to plan for One-Eye and Three-Eyes to attend the ball. Two-Eyes had to sew night and day to make their dresses.

"I want to go to the ball, too," said Two-Eyes to her mother.

"No," replied the mother. "You will have to stay here to watch and take care of the place while I take One-Eye and Three-Eyes to the party."

The day before the party the prince went hunting. As he was passing by the window, he saw Two-Eyes weeping while she was sewing.

"Why are you weeping?" asked the prince.

"I want to go to the ball, and must stay and watch the place while my mother and sisters are away."

"Why don't you slip out after they leave?"

"But I have no dress," explained Two-Eyes.

"Don't worry about that," spoke the prince. "I shall send you a dress."

That evening after the old woman had left with One-Eye and Three-Eyes to go to the ball, a coachman arrived with a pretty dress for Two-Eyes. She put on the dress, and the coach took her to the party. She was so beautiful when she arrived that her mothers and sisters did not recognize her. The prince danced with her all the time and did not dance once with the two ugly sisters. This made the old woman very angry.

Before the ball broke up, the coach took Two-Eyes back home. As the mother and daughters were going back home, she said to them:

"That girl with whom the prince danced all the time looked very much like Two-Eyes. Tomorrow night, One-Eye, you will stay to watch her."

So the following night the old woman and Three-Eyes went to the ball, and One-Eye stayed behind to watch Two-Eyes. Now One-Eye got very sleepy and lay down to rest. Soon she fell sound asleep. The coachman again returned to bring Two-Eyes another pretty dress and take her to the ball.

The prince danced only with Two-Eyes. This made the old woman very, very angry. When the ball was almost over, the coachman took Two-Eyes back home. Before Two-Eyes went to bed, she noticed that One-Eye was still fast asleep. Upon their arrival home, the old woman and Three-Eyes found Two-Eyes and One-Eye asleep.

"I could have sworn that it was Two-Eyes dancing with the prince at the ball again. Three-Eyes, tomorrow night you will watch," said the mother. "You have three eyes and can watch well."

The following night the old woman and One-Eye went to the ball. Three-Eyes remained at home to watch. Three-Eyes got sleepy and lay down to rest. In order to watch, she kept her middle eye open as she slept with the other two closed. When the old mother and One-Eye returned, they questioned Three-Eyes about Two-Eyes. Three-Eyes told her mother and One-Eye how with one eye she had seen Two-Eyes dress up and leave for the ball.

The old woman was so angry that she locked up Two-Eyes in a dark room upstairs without food and water.

The next day the prince came to the old woman's house.

"I am looking for the girl I wish to marry," said the prince.

Now the old woman was very glad and thought she would marry off one of her ugly-eyed daughters. She first presented One-Eye.

"No, that is not the girl," spoke up the prince.

Then the old woman brought out Three-Eyes.

"No, she is not the one," explained the prince. "The girl I am looking for has two eyes; and she lives here, I am sure."

The old woman had to let Two-Eyes out of the room upstairs.

"That's the girl!" exclaimed the prince, as soon as he laid eyes on Two-Eyes.

So Two-Eyes and the prince were married and lived happily ever after.

40. The Boat That Went on Land and Sea

This tale appeared in Louisiana Creole in a local French-language newspaper in St. John Parish, Louisiana, in 1878. Recent research, however, indicates that the tale probably is a translation into Creole from an English-language source. AT 513B.

Once there was a king; he and his queen had just one child, a girl, who was pretty—but pretty! Prettiness could go no further.

All the sons of the other kings in the neighborhood, as well as the generals, colonels and corporals all wanted to marry her. But this king didn't want that, no indeed! He didn't want to hear any arguments that would separate him from his daughter. But I'll tell you-all, I believe the daughter herself did want to leave home. There was a young carpenter who worked on the king's house, who was a much finer fellow than all those princes. He had already admired the princess, and she had looked him over too. Then they went to making sweet-eyes—no joking about it and then, you hear me, they got secretly engaged.

People were after the king and queen so much that he put a notice in the paper to say that he would give his daughter to the one that could make him a gift of a boat that would go on both land and sea. All the princes and their young companions got tool boxes, ran into the woods, and started chopping trees to build some boats.

When they were all working harder than horses, an old one-eyed black man came into the woods, asking for charity. He had nothing on but old rags, which stank worse than an alligator. Those princes held their noses and said, "Pooh! On your way, you old crocodile!"

The young carpenter had stopped work and was about to eat his dinner when the old man came up to him: "Hey, old grandpaw, you got here just in time. Sit down on my logs and we'll eat together." When they had finished, the old man took out a clay pipe from his pocket and started to smoke. He blew out a big cloud of smoke and it smelled of roses, jasmine and violets. A wind then started to blow and—Vroup! it drove away all the smoke. Then what do you think the carpenter saw? Instead of the old man, there was a pretty fairy seated in a gilt buggy drawn by pigeons. She had a diamond wand in her hand and she said to the young carpenter, "My son, you have a good heart, a better than any young man in this district, so you will get what you deserve."

She tapped the wood with her wand and it turned into a boat, a finer one you-all never saw, with a crew and all you need to sail off. Then she introduced the ship's officers to the young carpenter. "This one is a good marksman. He can fire anywhere and hit anything. This other one is 'Good Diver.' He can dive into the sea and bring up anything you want. The next is 'Good Runner,' who goes like the wind and can circle the world like a telegraph. This other one is 'Good Listener,' who puts his ear to the ground and hears all that's going on everywhere. The other members of the crew don't have to receive orders, they can guess whatever you want done and wherever you want to go. With these you will win the king's daughter."

The fairy went off into the air and the young carpenter got on board and blew the whistle the fairy had given him. They immediately set off to meet the king. Once arrived, everyone came on board to try out the ship. But the king was sad at the thought of giving up his daughter, and when they reached the sea he told his wife to throw her diamond ring into the water. Having thrown it, she began to cry and say she would never give up her daughter unless someone returned her ring. This made the young carpenter feel awful, but Good Diver came and told him he was able to recover the ring immediately. He jumped in, boudjoum! like a big bull-frog, and in five minutes returned the ring to the queen. Then they turned the ship about and the carpenter went to talk to the king. The king declared, "I have another thing to request before I give you my daughter. The queen wants the feathers of a bird of paradise, so go hunting and kill the bird, then bring it to me, and then you will have my daughter."

This saddened the young carpenter, but before he had a moment to think about it Good Marksman said, "That's just my kind of business." He called Good Runner and went outside. He aimed carefully toward the land of Paradise and fired. Boom! Then Good Runner left at a run to fetch the bird, but Paradise was so far off that Good Runner grew tired and lay down to sleep. Everybody waited, but Good Runner did not come. Good Listener put his ear to the ground and he heard Good Runner snoring a long way off.

He called Good Marksman, who put a little bomb into his gun and aimed it near Good Runner's ear. The bomb went, "Pralapaow!" and woke Good Runner and he galloped back with the bird of paradise.

The king had nothing left to say, so the young carpenter married that lovely girl, and they had a great wedding, with everything handsome. They would caress each other; they billed and cooed like pigeons going, "Roucoutoucou." Then they had many children, and lived as happy as fishes in the water. My friends, charity always pays, let me tell you!

Magical Powers and Magical Objects

Although the appellation *magic tale* refers broadly to a number of elements, certainly magical powers and magical objects play significant roles. A hero may receive the power to understand the language of animals, as in the Ozark tale "He Heard Animals Talking." Or he may obtain objects that have the power to help him achieve his objectives or otherwise succeed—whether a napkin that spreads out a wonderful meal ("Nor'west Wind and Jack") or a tiny walnut that holds enough water to ease a kingdom's drought ("The King's Well").

41. He Heard Animals Talking

Ozarks folklorist Vance Randolph heard this narrative from Mary Burke, Springfield, Missouri, May 1932. She had heard it circa 1895 from family members in Christian County, Missouri. AT 670.

One time there was a boy in the pasture, and he seen a big old spread-head just flopped over on its back and played possum. The boy was kind of chicken-hearted, so he let the old viper go. That's why the snake throwed a charm on him, so he could hear all kind of animals a-talking, and understand everything they said.

Like the day his folks was going to buy a spotted pony, and the pony says, "If them people knowed what I know they wouldn't buy me, because there's a rupture under my saddle-girth." The boy loosened the girth and seen the rupture, so they didn't buy the pony. There was a lot of talk about how smart he was, but the boy didn't tell nobody that he could hear the horses a-talking.

And then him and one of the neighbor girls was going to get married, but early in the morning he heard the cows say, "If that boy knowed what we know, he wouldn't marry Flossie, because she sneaks out of a night with the hired man." The boy watched careful and seen how things was, so he give Flossie the gate. There was a lot of talk about how smart he was, but the boy didn't tell nobody that he could hear the cows a-talking.

Another time he was coming home from town, and the squirrels kept a-chattering in the trees. One squirrel says, "If that boy knowed what I know, he wouldn't go no further, because the robbers is fixing to kill him." So the boy went back to town and told the sheriff there was outlaws on the Gander Mountain trail. Pretty soon the posse caught the robbers and locked them up. There was a lot of talk about how smart he was, but the boy didn't tell nobody that he could hear the squirrels a-talking.

The main thing is, when anybody has got a gift like that, you got to keep your mouth shut. But the boy didn't know much, so he told a grass widow about it. She says my goodness, that's wonderful, and we will get rich easy. Him and her laid awake pretty near all night planning how they would listen to dogs, and find out where people has buried their money. Maybe they could hear some race-horses a-talking, and then bet on the one that is going to win. Also the longhorns might talk about whether any steers has been stole, so they could collect rewards from the Cattlemen's Association.

When the boy went out to the barn next morning the horses began to nicker, but he couldn't make out what they was talking about. The cows didn't have nothing to say neither, and they just kind of grunted. The squirrels was a-chattering in the trees, but the boy couldn't understand a word of it. He seen that the charm was broke, but he didn't know what had went wrong.

The grass widow wouldn't have nothing to do with him after that, but he married Flossie and everything worked out pretty good after all. Flossie says the grass widow is a witch and ought to be run out of the country, but the folks never paid her any mind. The boy didn't know much about them things, and he never did find out that the old spread-head was mixed up in it.

42. Nor'west Wind and Jack

L. B. Russell sent a manuscript to the Texas Folklore Society containing this story. He had urged his mother, Emeline Brightman Russell (d. 1910), to write down the stories she had told her children in the 1850s, and she had done so, resulting in the manuscript. AT 563.

Once an old woman had a little home and had one apple tree. She had a son Jack. One night the Nor'west Wind blew down the old woman's apple tree. She bade her son Jack to go to the Nor'west Wind, and stick his hat in the hole from which the Nor'west Wind blew down her apple tree.

So Jack went and came to the Nor'west Wind, and said, "I am going to stop up the hole that you blow your breath out of."

The Nor'west Wind begged Jack not to do that, but he said his mother gave orders to him to be sure and stop up the hole for blowing down her apple tree. The Nor'west Wind says, "If you will not do it, I will give you a colt that will when you say, 'Shake, colt, shake,' shake down everything you want or wish for."

So Jack took the colt and started home. He had to stop at a tavern that night, and before going to bed he says to the innkeeper, "Don't you say, 'Shake, colt, shake,' to my colt tonight."

The innkeeper says, "No," and Jack went to bed.

In the morning Jack went on home to his mother and told her that the Nor'west

Wind had given him a colt that when she said, "Shake, colt, shake," would shake down everything in the world she would wish for. So the old woman tried him and said, "Shake, colt, shake," and he didn't do a thing. Then she was more mad than ever. She told Jack to go right straight back and stop up the hole of the Nor'west Wind with his hat.

So Jack went and came to the Nor'west Wind and said, "Your colt was no good and I'm going to stop up the hole that you blow your breath out of."

"Oh, please don't," says the Nor'west Wind. "If you won't do it, I'll give you a napkin and when you say, 'Spread, napkin, spread,' it will spread out with all the dainties you can imagine, everything good to eat."

Well, Jack took it and started on home, and he had to stop at the tavern he had stopped at before. So he says to the innkeeper, "Don't you say, 'Spread, napkin, spread,' to my napkin tonight."

The innkeeper says, "No, I won't."

So Jack went to bed, and in the morning he took his napkin and went home. He told his mother that all she had to do was to say, "Spread, napkin, spread," and it would be spread with everything nice to eat that she could imagine. So she says, "Spread, napkin, spread," and not a thing did the napkin do.

So this time she was very angry and told Jack the Nor'west Wind was just fooling them, and that he should go right straight back and stick his hat in the hole where the Nor'west Wind blew his breath out.

So the Nor'west Wind begged once more. He says, "I'll give you a pot which will fight all your battles if you will let me off just one more time. When anyone says, 'Thump, pot, thump,' it will jump up on to their head and thump them till you tell it to stop."

Well, Jack took the pot and started on home, and had to stop at the same tavern, and before going to bed, he says to the innkeeper, "Don't you say, 'Thump, pot, thump,' to my pot tonight."

The innkeeper says, "Oh, no, certainly not."

So in the dead hours of the night Jack was awakened from his sleep by a dreadful noise like some one being murdered. He hurried to see what it was, and found his pot thumping the innkeeper nearly to death. And he was calling Jack to take it off. Jack says, "You rascal, that's the way you have stolen my colt and put another colt in its place, and stolen my napkin and put another napkin in its place, and now I'll let the pot beat you to death if you don't deliver to me my colt and napkin."

So Jack made him have the colt and napkin brought before he would stop the pot from thumping him. In the morning he took his colt, his napkin, and his pot home to his mother. And all they had to do was to say, "Shake, colt, shake," or "Spread, napkin, spread," to get everything in the world they wanted or wished for. And Jack had his pot to fight his battles, and the poor old Nor'west Wind got rid of Jack's importunities and has the hole open to blow down apple trees to this day.

43. The King's Well

"The King's Well" was told by seventeen-year-old Jane Muncy, September 1955, Hyden, Kentucky, to folklorist Leonard Roberts. Jane Muncy (Fugate) has been considered one of the most talented American tellers of traditional stories, recognized by Roberts even in 1955 as an exceptional narrator and later recorded as an adult by folklorist Carl Lindahl. She is discussed in the introduction. AT 577 + 1050 + 1052 + 1088 + 1115 + 1640.

Once upon a time there was three boys that lived with their mom and dad way out in the woods. Their names were Jack, Bill, and Merrywise who was the youngest and they always thought him the foolishest and fancy free one of the bunch. So Jack and Bill started out one day to seek their fortune and of course Merrywise put up such a fuss because he wanted to go with them. So they took him along. They said, "Merrywise, you will have to mind us and you can't go off on no foolish rambles. You will have to stay right with us and act your age."

Merrywise said, "Well, I will." So they fixed their lunch and started out on their long walk to seek their fortune. They walked along and walked along for about three or four hours and they set down to eat some sandwiches out of their bag, and Merrywise said, "Hush, I hear something." And they heard a strange chopping sound and it was away off up in the woods up in the mountain. He said, "I believe I'll go up and see what that is."

They said, "Oh, no, Merrywise, we've got to hurry. We've got no time to fool around with you."

He said, "Well, I want to know what that is. I've got to go see what that is." So he follered the noise and he got way up in the woods and he saw an ax and it was chopping all by itself. Chop, chop, chopping all the trees down. So he got the ax and took the handle off and put the ax part in his hip pocket and went on back down the hill.

His brothers said, "Well, what was it, Merrywise?" He said, "Nothing, nothing, nothing at all."

They said, "See, we told you we got to hurry and we've wasted time fooling around with you and your funny ideas." So they walked on and walked on and set down again. Then they heard a stream like a waterfall and it kept a-running and a-running. They walked up there and found a stream and a beautiful pool of water and they got a drink.

So Merrywise said, "I wonder where all this water comes from."

"Oh, never mind where it comes from and come on. We've got to hurry, come on."

Merrywise said, "No, I want to go see where it comes from." So they said, "Go on but we're not going to wait long on you."

He took off up into the hills and when he got up there he follered the stream until he saw a little tiny walnut. There was a hole in the walnut and out of it was coming all this stream of pure water. So he took some moss off the root of a tree and stopped up the hole in it and stuck the walnut in his shirt pocket and went on back to his brothers.

They said, "Well, where did it come from?"

He said, "Oh, it comes out of a rock up there."

They said, "Now Merrywise, we're not going to wait on you any more. You'll have to come on 'cause we're not going to stop again."

He said, "Well, I won't stop any more." So they went on and they journeyed and journeyed for days and days and finally they come to what looked like the King's territory. And they saw a big sign and it said, "Any man that can dig and find water to run in the King's well I will give him the hand of the princess in marriage. Any man that tries and does not succeed will be laid down on the chopping block and his ears will be cut off."

So they went on for awhile and saw the sign again saying the same thing. They talked about it awhile and decided to try it. Bill said, "Well, I'm a strong man, everybody always said I was the strongest of the bunch. I think I could dig the longest and find the water for the King."

And Jack said, "All right, everybody says I have more perseverance and I think I could stay with the job longer and dig that well for the King and get the hand of the princess."

Merrywise spoke up and said, "Well, I think I'll try too." They said, "Merrywise, you can't do nothing and never could do anything."

So they went on to the King's place and Merrywise said, "I'm going up to the King and talk to him and see if he won't let me."

Bill said, "Oh, no, you don't. I'm the oldest and I'm going first." So he went in and talked to the King and said, "King, I want to enter this contest and try to win your daughter in marriage."

The King said, "All right, but you get your ears cut off if you don't do it." Said, "Our whole land is starving for water and somebody just has to find water purty soon."

So Bill dug and dug and dug as hard as he could but he never could find any water. So they laid him on the chopping block and chopped his ears off.

Next came Jack and he stepped up and said, "I have a lot of perseverance and I think I can do this job and win the hand of the princess."

The King said, "All right, but remember if you don't you get your ears chopped off."

So Jack dug and he dug and dug. He would get tired and rest a-while and start digging and digging again. He dug and dug all day and never did strike any water. Nothing but pure old dirt. And finally he said, "I just have to give up for I've dug as long as I can." So they laid him down on the chopping block and cut his ears off.

So Merrywise stepped up, saying, "I might as well get my ears chopped off as the rest of them." He said, "King, I want to dig your well."

The King said, "All right, Merrywise, go ahead, but remember if you don't strike water you get your ears cut off."

So Merrywise dug and dug and it wasn't long until he was out of sight. And he took the walnut out of his pocket, took the moss out of the hole, and throwed it down. Then he told them to throw down a rope and they throwed down one and he come up out of there with the water rolling up right behind him. And purty soon the whole well was full of pure clear water that come out of that walnut.

And the King said, "Well, how did you do it, Merrywise?" He said, "I just dug in the right place."

So the King, like many other fathers, didn't want to give up his youngest daughter if he could help it. And he said, "Now Merrywise, you are a country boy and have just come out of the woods and you wouldn't suit my daughter. Wouldn't you just as soon have half of my kingdom in money as to have my daughter's hand in marriage?"

He said, "Well, I guess I would just as soon have the money." So he took the money and he went back home and he built his parents a fine house. He stayed around with them awhile until he got tired and wanted to go on some more adventures. He said to them, "I believe I'll go back and see what my brothers are doing back there in the town with their ears cut off."

They let him go and he started out. He still had his hatchet in his back pocket. He come to the same place where the other sign was and there was another from the King. It said, "Any man that can rid the forest of the giants that are bothering the King can have his daughter's hand in marriage." Well, he thought a little about it and went on till he come to another sign saying the same thing. So he said, "I believe I'll look into this." He went on to the King and said, "King, what is this contest you have got on now about getting rid of giants?"

The King said, "Well, Merrywise, this giant has come into my forests and he has cut down all of my trees and is ruining the whole countryside." Said, "All my forest is gone and I've got to get somebody to get shet of him or I'll not have anything left in my country."

So Merrywise said, "Well, I think I'll enter this contest."

The King said, "You remember that if you don't you will get your head chopped off this time."

He said, "All right, I'll risk getting my head chopped off." So he went up into the woods and he heard all kinds of thrashing and racket, and he come to where the Giant was cutting down trees and rolling them in bundles and getting ready to march home with a load. Merrywise said, "Hey, Mister Giant."

The Giant said, "Well, what do you want?"

He said, "I heard you were taking all the King's forest. How many trees can you cut down in a day?"

The Giant said, "Oh, a few hundred. Why?"

He said, "Why, I can cut down more trees than that."

The Giant said, "Ho, ho, ho, you little old thing, I know you can't."

He says, "Yes, I can."

The Giant said, "Well, let's have a contest and find out." Said, "You start in over there and I'll start over here."

Merrywise said, "All right." So he went over on the other side of the forest and put his hatchet together and it started chopping down trees right and left, right and left. The old Giant was still on one tree. Purty soon he got tired and said, "I believe I'll go over and see how the little midget is doing with his chopping." So he went over there and there laid half the forest, and Merrywise standing there wiping the sweat.

The Giant said, "Well, how did you do it? You have already won. I've just got ten trees chopped down." Said, "Let's go to dinner."

Merrywise said, "That's a good thing to do." All this time the Giant was thinking, "Now I can't have this little creature going around chopping down a hundred trees to my one. I'm going to take him home and do away with him the best way I can." So he said, "Come on home with me."

Merrywise said, "Let me help you carry this big load of trees you have ready." He had a big steel band around the trees and had them in a big bundle.

The Giant said, "Well, all right." So the giant got the trunks on his shoulder and Merrywise set down on the limbs and the Giant drug the trees through the forest until he come to his big castle. Merrywise got off the branches and said, "Boy, I sure had a heavy load to lift."

The Giant said, "That was a big load for me. I'm tired."

They went into the house and Merrywise said, "Boy, I sure could stand something to eat, couldn't you?"

The Giant said, "Yeh, I think I'll fix about a hundred chickens and fix me a big tub full of cottage cheese and maybe a big tub full of milk and have a little bite."

Merrywise said, "Well, that sounds like a purty puny supper to me." Said, "I can eat more than that."

Giant said, "Come on and let's eat then." Merrywise was sitting beside the window and the Giant was on the other side of the table. The Giant kept setting things before Merrywise. He thought he would eat all he wanted and would soon go off to sleep so he could do away with him. But Merrywise eat some of the food before him and kept pitching the rest out the window.

The Giant said, "Boy, you sure can eat a lot to be such a little man."

Merrywise said, "Yeaw, I sure can eat when I'm hungry."

After supper the Giant said, "Are you ready to lay down?"

Said, "You sleep in this bed right here and I'll go in this other room."

Merrywise waited till the Giant went in and then he said to himself, "I'll play another trick on him. I'll just sleep under the bed." He put a great big piller under the covers and then got under the bed. In the night the Giant come in the room with a great big club with some long nails sticking out of it and he just beat and beat on that piller. And Merrywise was laying under the bed just laughing away. The Giant said, "Well, that fixed him," and walked out and went to his room and to sleep.

Well, next morning Merrywise come out of the bed and stretched and said to the Giant, "You sure have a lot of flies in your house, old feller." Said, "Last night they lit on me and just like to worried me to death. I could hardly sleep."

The Giant looked at him and said, "Well, shore enough?" He said, "Merrywise, you are too big a feller for me. I'm going to another part of the world where there is nobody like you. This place is not big enough for both of us." So the Giant picked up his little sack on his back and left.

So Merrywise went back to the King and said, "King, I've ridded the forest of the Giant and I dug your well for half of your kingdom. I'm not a poor country boy any more. I'm a rich man and I want your daughter's hand in marriage."

The King said, "I'm proud of you, Merrywise. You can have all my kingdom and my daughter."

So the King moved over to spend his old age in the Giant's castle, and Merrywise became the new King.

Lucky Accidents

For the heroes of American tales, luck may play as much of a role in gaining success as bravery or cleverness. "Old Stiff Dick" is a variant of the folktale well known in the Grimm collection as "The Brave Tailor," and here Jack gets rich through how things just fall out for him (though his bravado and talent for self-promotion help). In "Jack and the King's Girl," Jack gets the princess by following her instructions about a *previous* matter. In a widely told story from the African American John and Old Marster cycle ("The Old Man and the Coon"), the slave inadvertently says the right thing.

44. Old Stiff Dick

This was one of the stories that Jane Gentry told to sociologist Isabel Gordon Carter in the summer of 1923, part of the first extensive collection of American folktales. AT 1640.

They uz a little old boy long time ago, didn't have no mammy or poppy, jest growed up in the hog weeds, and he didn't even know his name, but everybody called him Jack. And he jest stayed here and yonder, wherever he could drop in at night. So one day he was a walkin' the road and he had him a belt around his waist and he had him a little old knife and he was a whitlin' and makin' him a paddle. So he come along past a mud hole and there was a lot of little old blue butterflies over hit. So he struck down with his paddle and he killed seven of the butterflies. So he goes on a little piece further and he comes to a blacksmith shop, and he gets the blacksmith to cut letters in his belt, "Stiff Dick killed seven at a lick." So he goes on a piece further and he passes the king's house. King runs out and says, "I see you're a very brave man; I see where you've killed seven at a lick."

"Yes, bedads, I'm a mighty brave man."

So the king says, "Stranger, I want to hire a brave man to kill some animals we have here in the woods. We have a wild municorn here killin' so many people, soon we'll all be kilt. If you'll kill that municorn, we'll pay you one thousand dollars, five hundred down, and five hundred when you bring the municorn in."

So Dick says, "All right."

So the king paid him five hundred dollars. Stiff Dick stuck that in his pocket and said to hisself, "Bedads, if they ever see me around here agin." And he tuk out. When he got way up in the mountains the municorn smelled him and here it come,

> Whippity cut,
> Whippity cut,
> Whippity cut.

Stiff Dick tuk to runnin' and the municorn after him. The municorn was jest clippin' Stiff Dick. They run up the mountains and down the ridges. So long late in the evening they started down a long ridge, the municorn jest a runnin' after Stiff Dick. And away down at the end of the ridge Stiff Dick saw a big oak and he made a beeline to see if he cud clumb hit. So the municorn was jest a gettin' so close that agin they got there the municorn was jest behin' him. Jack jest slipped around the oak right quick and the municorn stove his horn into hit and he just rared and plunged. As soon as Stiff Dick saw he was fastened for all time to come, he went on to the king's house.

King says, "Did you get the municorn?"

Dick says, "Municorn? Laws an massy, never was nothin' but little old bull calf come tearin' out there after me. I jest picked it up by one ear and tail and stove it agin a tree and if you all wanst hit, you'll have to go up thar and git hit."

So the king got him a great army and went up and killed the municorn, come back and paid Jack five hundred dollars more. King says, "Now, Stiff Dick, there's one more wild animal living up here, a wild bull-boar. I'll give five hundred dollars now and five hundred more when you ketch hit."

Jack tuk the five hundred dollars and says to hisself, "You'll never see me anymore."

But after he'd gone a little ways here come the wild boar after him,

> Whippity cut.
> Whippity cut,
> Whippity cut.

All day long around the mountains, across the mountains and down the ridges, all the day just a runnin'. So along late in the evenin' away down in the holler he saw an old house and when be got down there the door was open. So he run right in the door and up the wall and the wild boar run right after him and laid down right under him. Boar was tired and soon fell asleep. So Dick eased up the wall and over and down the outside and shut the wild boar up in there. So he went down to the king's house.

King says, "Did ye git the wild boar?"

Stiff Dick says, "Wild boar? Laws a massy, I never saw nothing but a little old boar pig come bristlin' up after me. I jest picked hit up by the tail and throwed hit in an old waste house. And if you all wanst hit, you'll have to go up thar and git hit."

So king got up an army of men and went up and killed the wild boar and went back down and paid Stiff Dick his other five hundred dollars.

King says, "Now, Stiff Dick, there's one more wild animal we want to git killed. That's a big brown bear. So he give Dick another five hundred dollars.

Stiff Dick says to hisself, "If I can jest get out of here no brown bear ul never see me."

So he got way up on the mountain; old brown bear smelled him and here he come,

> Whippity cut,
> Whippity cut,
> Whippity cut.

Across the hills, up the ridges, every way to dodge the bear. The bear uz right after him. So late in the evenin', way down at the end of a ridge he saw old pine tree that had been all burned over and was right black. Jack made a beeline fur that tree. The bear was jest a little ways behind when Jack run up the tree. Bear was down at the root of the tree and he was so mad he tried to gnaw the tree down. Hit gnawed and gnawed. Jack keep a easin' down on another old snag and another old snag and directly he got on a snag jest above the old bear and the old snag broke and Jack fell just a straddle the old bear and they jest burnt the wind. Stiff Dick was so tickled and so scared, too, that he was jest a hollerin' and screamin' and directly he run the bear right thru the town and the soldier boys heared him a screamin' and they run out and shot hit. Stiff Dick got off it when it fell, and he was jest a swearin' and a rarin'. He was swearin' he was breakin' hit for the king a riddy horse. And king come out and heard Stiff Dick a swearin' he was a breakin' the bear for the king a riddy horse and he got mad and made the soldier boys pay Dick five hundred dollars. And when I left there Stiff Dick was rich.

45. Jack and the King's Girl

Richard Chase, who included this tale in one of his influential books that popularized American folktales in the 1940s by retelling in writing and print the stories he heard in Virginia and North Carolina, gives R.M.W. (R. M. Ward) as his only source for this story. Ward's own title for it was "Lazy Jack." AT 571.

Jack had an uncle lived a right smart distance from where he and his mother lived at, and he decided one time he'd like to go up and see his uncle.

Jack had done got so he wasn't lazy no more—not so much as he used to be. So he worked hard all week, gettin' in wood and fixin' ever'thing up around the place, then he pulled out.

Had to go right by the King's house on the way to his uncle's. The King had a awful pretty girl, but all her life she never had laughed, and the King had put out a adver-tize-ment that anybody that would make her laugh could marry her.

Jack got down close to where the King lived and that girl was out on the porch, she saw Jack, says, "Where ye started, Jack?"

Jack told her and she says to him, "I hope ye have a good time."

So Jack went on. His uncle was awful pleased to see him. They'd work a little and ever' night somebody'd come there to play and make music. Jack had such a good time he plumb forgot about goin' back home.

So fin'ly his uncle says to him, "Jack, your mother'll be gettin' uneasy about you. She'll be needin' ye about gettin' up wood, too. Don't you reckon you better go on back home?"

Jack says, "Yes. I guess I had better go, pretty soon."

"You fix up and go back today, Jack, and I'll give ye a present. I'm goin' to give you a big darnin' needle. You can take that and learn how to sew your own overhalls when they get tore."

So he went and hunted up a big darnin' needle he had, put a long thread in it and gave it to Jack.

Jack pulled out, put the thread over his shoulder and let the needle swing down behind him.

Got down to the King's house; that girl was there, says, "You gettin' back, are ye, Jack?"

"Yes," says Jack. "Had a awful good time."

"What's that you got over your shoulder?"

"Hit's a big darnin' needle uncle gave me, to hire me to go back home."

"Needle?" she says. "Law me! I never did see a man tote a needle that-a-way. You ought to stick that in your shirt bosom."

"Well'm," says Jack.

Jack got in home, told his mother all about what a good time he'd had. Started in to workin' about the place, and he kept studyin' about gettin' back to his uncle's again.

So fin'ly Jack's mother says to him, says, "You've worked right good this week, Jack. You fix up your wood and all, and I'll let you go back to your uncle's again. But you mustn't stay so long this time."

Jack got ever'thing fixed up and pulled out.

Got to the King's house; that girl was there, says, "Hello, Jack. Where ye started this time?"

Jack told her. She says, "Hope ye have a good time, and get another good present."

Well, Jack and his uncle went several places that week, and Jack had such a good time a-hearin' fiddle music and banjo pickin' he never studied about goin' back home.

So one day his uncle says, "You better go on back home now, Jack. I'm goin' to give ye another premium. Hit's a swoard my grandpa gave me. Hit was used in the Revolutionary War."

He went and got the swoard and gave it to Jack. Jack started on home. He took that swoard and stuck it right through his shirt bosom and out the other side.

The King's girl was out in the yard, saw Jack comin', says, "Hello, Jack."

Then she saw that swoard stickin' out of Jack's shirt, says, "Law me, Jack! You've plumb ruined your shirt. Why you ought to have carried that on your shoulder."

"Well'm," says Jack, "next time I will."

Jack got back home, played around with that swoard till fin'ly he got a little tired of it. So he worked right on all week, got ever'thing shaped up, says to his mother, "How about me goin' back to uncle's again?"

His mother let him go. Jack saw the King's girl out at the gate and stopped and talked to her awhile. Got back to his uncle's and had a big time. A gang of young folks 'uld come up there to Jack's uncle's place and they'd get to makin' music and singin' old songs, stay till nearly daylight. Then him and his uncle 'uld go some other place the next night, till fin'ly his uncle says, "Hit's about time you went back home, Jack."

"Yes, I reckon it is," says Jack.

"I'm goin' to give ye a nice present today. Maybe hit'll keep you home a month this time. I got a young colt here. You can take it home with ye and break it to ride. Hit'll take ye some time to get it broke good."

So he got a halter and brought Jack the colt. Jack thanked him and started on home. Got down close to the King's place, Jack got right down under the colt and got it up on his shoulder.

The King's girl saw him comin' a-totin' that colt, she ran out to the fence, says, "Law me, Jack. You the awfulest fool man I ever did see. You ought to ride that."

"Well'm," says Jack, "I'll try to think of that next time."

When Jack got home, he went to foolin' around with his colt, never thought a thing about goin' back to his uncle's till nearly about a month. Then his colt began to get sort of old to him, and he commenced to talk about goin' back to see his uncle.

"Why, Jack," says his mother, "I 'lowed you wouldn't never leave your colt."

"Well," says Jack, "you can take care of it while I'm gone." So Jack got all his work done up and pulled out again.

That girl was out in the yard and her and Jack talked awhile, then Jack went on to his uncle's.

They worked around the place a little, went huntin' a time or two, and ever' night some young folks 'uld come up there and Jack 'uld get to frolickin' with 'em. They made music and got to playin' Weevily Wheat and Skip to My Lou and runnin' eight-handed reels and all. Jack never did have such a good time and his uncle was an awful good hand to call figures. Jack plumb forgot all about that colt and his mother bein' likely to run out of firewood, till pretty soon his uncle said he reckoned Jack better be gettin' on back.

"Yes," says Jack, "I guess I ought to have went 'fore this time."

"I got a nice little heifer up here, Jack, and I'm goin' to give it to you so you can have a good milk cow to go with your horse. You keep it fed up real well, and your mother can milk it for ye."

Got him a line and tied that heifer by the horns, gave it to Jack. Jack thanked him and started leadin' his heifer on back home.

Jack got down close to the King's house, he saw that girl was out at the washin' place where they were all a-workin' with the clothes. So Jack remembered and he went to jump on that heifer's back; somehow or other he landed on it hind side to, grabbed hold on its tail and started in hollerin.' That young heifer started bawlin' and jumpin' from one side the road to the other, and went a-gallopin' on down to where the King's folks was a-washin' at. The King's girl looked up and saw Jack gettin' shook up and down and a-slippin' first one side, then the other'n, on the heifer's back and him a-hold of its tail and a-hollerin' for help, and she raised up and laughed so loud they heard her all over town. She stood there and laughed and slapped her hands till the King came out. And when he saw Jack and that calf, he started in to laughin' too, laughed till he had to sit down.

Fin'ly some of 'em caught the heifer and holp Jack off.

The old King took Jack over in town and bought him a new suit of clothes. Then he hitched up two fine horses to a buggy and rode Jack and his girl over to a big church and had 'em married.

The girl she went on home with Jack, and the last time I was down there they were all gettin' on right well.

46. The Old Man and the Coon

This is a version of probably the best-known tale of the clever slave who tries to outwit his master; such tales were long popular in African American tradition. A *Buckra* is a white man. In addition to being short for raccoon, *coon* is a derogatory term for a black person. Motifs K1956, N400, N680.

One time a rich Buckra had a sensible old man servant who had come from Africa. This old negro knew everything about everything. Nobody could stump him with a question. The master tried a heap of times, and he always did make the right answer. His friends tried him too, and they never caught him in a miss. The Buckra bragged on the old man, and very often he'd win a bet about him. One day the Buckra man gave a big dinner, and he invited a heap of friends to his house. He laid a wager saying nobody could ask his old servant a question he couldn't answer, and he gave his friends leave to try the old man any way they wanted. The money was put up, and the friends called a boy who'd been working around the place, and they sent him into the woods to catch a coon. The boy went with a dog. When dinner was over, and the gentlemen were sitting on the piazza talking, the boy came back with the raccoon. They called for a barrel, and they took the coon and put him under it and hid him completely, so nobody could see what was inside.

Then they sent for the old African. He'd been hoeing cotton in the field, and nobody told him why they sent for him. He came, and then the massa said, "Old man, we sent for you to tell us what's in this barrel."

The old man looked at it, and walked around it, and looked at it closely, and listened to hear if anything moved. All the gentlemen watched him. When the old man made up his mind he couldn't find out what was in the barrel, he stopped, he studied, he scratched his head, and then he made his answer: "Massa, you've got the old coon this time."

He didn't know he was speaking a true word about what was in the barrel. He was talking about himself when he said they had the old coon this time, but the massa and the other gentlemen didn't know that, and they all gave the old man a round of applause. The massa won the bet, and he shared the silver money with the old man.

Riddles and Clever Words

In folktales, the ability to answer riddles or other questions or to use language cleverly often symbolizes intelligence or at least being able to strategize effectively. In "The Three Questions," an Irish tramp gains a kingdom by providing "smart" answers to a king's questions, and in "Under Gravel Do I Travel," a man saves his life by "spinning" a riddle no one can answer (called by folklorists a "neck riddle" because it saves someone's neck). In the Mexican American tale "The Three Shining Stones," the protagonist carefully constructs the riddles he can use to win the princess as he journeys toward her, building them from out of what he encounters along the way. In "She Always Answered No," Jack manages to win a woman's love by posing questions that turn her own language against her.

47. The Three Shining Stones

Eminent Mexican American folklorist Américo Paredes recorded this story from a teller identified as J.A., "a mestizo male in his late sixties," originally from Guanajuato, Mexico, in East Chicago, May 2, 1963. Despite the narrator's modesty about his "poor telling of it"—in fact a sort of ritual disclaimer—it is a particularly well structured narrative. AT 851 + 853A.

This is the way my story goes, for your good understanding and my poor telling of it, for this was a king who had an extremely beautiful daughter. She was besieged by many personages of high lineage—courtiers, counts, marquises, dukes, and I don't know what. But she disdained them all, perhaps because they weren't the type of men she longed for in her dreams or her imagination, and she always lived in despair, because she did not know what she wanted. Aside from this, it is told that the princess was gifted with second sight. Whenever suitors would arrive she would tell them what they were going to say before they could tell her what they thought or what messages they carried.

Her father lived in anguish because of his daughter's restlessness, because she was not happy, and he had the idea once of proclaiming an edict in which he sought some knight who would make a favorable impression on his daughter. And as a condition, he stated that they must bring three riddles. The king in his edict proclaimed, that is to say, that he was looking for a suitor who would favorably impress his daughter. No matter his rank, either nobleman or plebeian, if the aspirant to the hand of the princess came with three riddles, and she guessed them, he would be punished. But if she did not have the wit to guess the riddles, he would be the chosen one, the future husband of the princess, but first he must make the princess say, "That cannot be!"

Well then, way out in the country a *ranchero* [ranch hand] got ready, a poor devil. He wanted to go, too, and see if it was his fortune to become the princess's husband. So he said to his mother, "Mother," he says, "make me some tortillas, because I'm going on a journey."

"Now, where are you going, son?" the little old woman asked him.

He says, "Don't you know the king has passed a law asking for suitors to make matrimony with the princess?" He says, "I'm going to see if I can marry the princess."

Knowing how poor they were, the mother of the *ranchero* told him he would only be going to get himself executed, you know. Cut his neck off, decapitate him. But he kept on asking her to prepare him some provisions for the journey. He saddled his little burro, mounted it, and left.

He traveled, and he traveled, and he traveled, until he began to feel hungry. It was late in the afternoon, and then it began to get dark. Then he saw a light way off in the distance. He says, "When I get to that bonfire, I'll get off my burro and warm over my tortillas." So the closer he got to the fire, the brighter was the light that came from it, more and more brilliant. But no sir, it was not a fire but a precious stone that was shining there.

Hmm! He didn't know just what it was, but he picked it up and put it in his *morral* [saddlebag]. He kept on going, he kept on going, and farther on he saw another light in the distance. He says, "This time I will be able to stop and have my supper at that fire, because I am very tired and very hungry." It turned out to be the same thing; it was another stone, but more beautiful than the first. He picked it up and put it in his *morral* and kept on going, looking for a place where he could warm over his tortillas.

What happened was that later he saw another light, farther away. He says, "This is the right one. It is much brighter, so it must be a real fire." But the same thing happened; when he got there, it was another stone, even bigger and more beautiful. In short, the day dawned on him, and he had not found a fire, so he kept on going. With the first light, he saw something in the fields; it was an ox. It happened that the ox had got into a wheat field. He says, "I don't think it is right for that animal to eat the wheat. I'm going to drive it out." He says, "*Caray!* This is where I make up a riddle for my princess. Yes. I'll say to her, 'I drove the good out of the better.' Hmm!"

He went on. Later he ran out of water; he had used up all the water in the gourd he carried, the way *rancheros* do, you know, and he was very thirsty. The little burro was sweating and sweating from the fatigue of the journey. And in his torment he went and put his lips against the little burro, to wet them. He says: "*Caray!* This is where I make another riddle for the princess. I will tell her, 'I drank water not rained from the skies or gushed out of the earth.' Let's see if she can riddle that." In the end he may have quenched his thirst or he may have not, but he made up his riddle.

Toward the end of the journey, he ran out of provisions and didn't have anything to eat. And as always happens, you get hungrier than ever when there's nothing to eat. He passed by a place where a sow was giving birth to some piglets, but the piglets could not get born. So he stared at the sow and he says, "I'm going to help that sow have those creatures." And he cut the piglets out of the sow. "*Caray!*" he says. "I must roast one of these, let me see how I'm going to do it. It may be very young, very tender, but my hunger is great."

But he couldn't find firewood or anything; all he found was a lot of paper, leaves from a book perhaps, or newspapers. He made his fire with them and roasted his meat. "Ah," he says, "here is where I make up another riddle for the princess. This will be the third," he says. "I'm going to say to her, 'I ate meat that was never born, roasted on words.' Hmm, *caray!*"

He finally came to the imperial city. He came to the door of the royal palace, and the sentinels asked him what he wanted. Why, it just happened that the royal edict had echoed to the very limits of the kingdom, where he lived, and he also was a suitor for the princess's hand. Well, those fellows didn't turn him away, because it was the law, you know, an imperial or royal order. They went and told the king that there was a beggar out there who wanted to take part in the contest too, among those chosen to talk to the princess. The king ordered them to let him in. So he came in, and the servants laughed, all those charged with taking care of the guests, for the most select nobility was there, the richest of the rich, you know, hoping to be favored by fortune. So they ordered this beggar to be put in the stables, over among the chicken coops. And it was ordered that they take him what was left from the banquets they were celebrating, and a tallow candle. He was content to be over there in the chicken coops, but that night he didn't use the tallow candle they gave him. They say he took out the first stone he found.

When the stone was uncovered, it shed such a brilliant ray of light that it awoke a certain curiosity in the palace, to the point that the princess sent to find out what was the reason for that shining light. So her maids of honor came, and they told her the beggar had something never seen before. Something large and marvelous. So then the princess says, "Go tell that beggar to sell it to me, cost what it may. But he must not say no."

So the maids of honor, or the servants, of the princess went and told the beggar that the princess said he must sell her that stone or that light, cost what it might. But he must not say no. So then he says, "Tell the princess I will not sell it to her; I am giving it to her as a gift. But she must let me sleep by the door of her bedroom."

So they went and told the princess the condition set by the beggar, for that was what they called him. The princess was alarmed, you know; she was full of scruples. She said, "No. Not that."

But her ladies-in-waiting said, "Young mistress, what does it matter, princess?" Or your highness. "You will be inside, and he outside. What harm is there in that?"

"Well. Tell him it is all right, to give me the stone."

The next night he did the same thing. By this time, they were treating him better, you know. They gave him better lodging, better treatment, more courtesy. The next night he took out the next stone. The same thing happened; it alarmed the palace people because of the strong light, the brilliant light it gave off. Again the princess inquires through her servants, and they tell her it is another stone, even more precious, that the beggar has. She sends them to tell him to sell it to her, and he must not say no. So when he is told what the princess says, he tells them once more he will not sell it; he will give it to her as a gift if she will let him sleep at the foot of her bed.

And they come and tell her, and she is alarmed, so the ladies say to her, "But what does it matter, highness? The beggar can go no farther than he is allowed, and he will be content with that. Furthermore," they say, "we will be close by."

"Very well." She accepted then.

The third night the same thing was repeated, you know, with the prettiest and biggest stone, the most valuable. The princess herself considered the stone was worth more than all of the palace where she lived. She sent word to him in the same manner, that she wanted the stone, but he must not say no. So he told them, "Go tell the princess I will give it to her as a gift. But she must say no to everything I say to her."

So the ladies went and told the princess what the beggar said. "Oh, no," she said, "not that."

"But what does it matter?" they said. "If he says anything to you, all you have to do is say no. Suppose he tries to go too far, all you have to do is say no."

"Oh, well. Tell him it's all right."

Now the beggar already had the privilege of sleeping at the door and of sleeping at the foot of her bed. So once he was there, he says, "Princess, you won't be offended if I sit on the edge of your bed?"

"Well, no."

"Princess, you won't be offended if I take this stone?"

"Well, no." Because she had agreed to say no to everything he said and not a word more. So he took the smallest stone and put it in his *morral*.

"Princess, you won't be offended if I take this other stone?"

"Well, no." So he put the middle-sized stone into his *morral*.

"Princess, you won't be offended if I take the other stone?"

"No, no." So he put the biggest stone into his *morral*.

"Princess, you won't be angry if I ask you for your nightgown?"

"Well, no." So he took her nightgown and put it in his *morral*.

"Princess, you won't be angry if I get in bed with you?" "No." And that was the way the thing ended.

Next morning he left with all those things in his *morral*, you know. And this was the day he was to be judged on his riddles. But the princess was provoked because of all the things he had done, so during the night she lulled him to sleep and asked him the answers to his riddles. And he told her. So he appeared before the king's audience that day, and he was no longer the ragged beggar but was dressed in a fine suit and couldn't be told from the rest of the courtiers who were there as suitors. So he went in and said his riddles to the princess before the king. And the princess answered all three of them. So then the king told his lackeys to punish the beggar by giving him fifty blows with a stick. It would kill him, more or less.

So then the beggar says, "Your majesty, give me a boon."

The king allows it. "What do you wish?"

"Permission to go out in the hall and sell these fifty blows they are going to give me."

"Sell them! How?"

"Well," he says, "I'll take care of that."

So the king said yes. When he went out of the audience chamber, all the rest of them were there—marquises, counts, and I don't know what—full of curiosity and laughing at the man, you know, because they didn't take him seriously. He was the funniest thing they had ever seen in all their lives. They asked him what had come of his audience with the king. Would he marry the princess?

"No," he says, "but the king has made me a gift. Fifty of them."

"Fifty what?"

"The finest wood that grows in the realm. But I don't want them. I can't take them away with me; they're no use to me."

The nobles thought it was fifty acres of woodland, so they said, "We'll buy them. How much do you want for them?"

"Oh, fifty pesos. A peso apiece."

So one of them bought them, and the beggar goes back to the king and says, "Majesty, I have sold the blows you were going to give me, at a peso apiece."

"You don't say! Who bought them?"

"I'll bring you the buyer right now."

So the king says to the buyer, "Is it true that you bought what I promised to give this gentleman?"

"Yes, Majesty. All fifty of them."

Then the king ordered the blows given to the buyer, and the princess said, "Father, that cannot be!"

And the beggar says, "The prize is mine."

So then the king says, "How can you be so daring as to aspire to reach a star?" Because he was nothing down here below, and who can reach the stars?

But then he says, "Well, look, Majesty. All things are easy if you know how to do them. And the hand of the princess belongs to me for reasons I will explain. But first let me tell you a little story. On the way to your palace a hare ran suddenly in front of me, and I barely had time to pick up this stone and throw it at her. I almost hit her."

"Ah!" says the king. "What a beautiful stone! It's a treasure, a great treasure!"

"Well then," he says, "I resumed my journey, and a little farther on the same hare ran across the road again. I tried to catch her," he says, "so I bent down and picked up this other stone and threw it at her. And I hit her in the hind legs," he says. "She almost stopped," he says. And he put down the second stone before the king.

"Good Heavens!" says the king. "This is an even greater treasure!"

"So I resumed my journey," he says, "and the same hare crossed my path again, so I picked up this other stone and threw it at her. And this time I did get her." And he put down the third stone before the king.

He says, "Look. As proof of what I said, I brought along her hide." And then he took out the princess's nightgown.

Well then, with those proofs, you know, the king had to consider that, well, he had already gone pretty far. And so it is that after having lived in complete wretchedness, and having slept in a chicken-coop, he is now sleeping in the richest and most comfortable beds, covered with silken coverlets, and with one of the most desirable of women. And us over here, living this sad life of ours.

48. She Always Answered No

Folklorist Vance Randolph, who intensively investigated the Ozarks region, collected "She Always Answered No" from Marie Wilbur, Pineville, Missouri, June 1930. Randolph asked his informant if she knew what the unspoken third question was, but she said no. Part of the pleasure of the tale perhaps lies in the audience's wondering or guessing. AT 853A.

One time there was a pretty girl with red hair, and she kept house for her daddy because her mother had run off with a peddler. And there was a boy named Jack that wanted to go with her, but the old man told her to say "No" every time a boy asked her a question. So when Jack says, "Can I come to see you Sunday night?" the pretty girl answered "No." And when he says, "Will you go buggy riding with me?" she says "No." So then he says, "Well, do you want to get married?" but the pretty girl says "No" again. Jack seen he was not getting nowheres, but he didn't know what to do about it.

Jack thought about this awhile, and then he went to see old Gram French and give her two boxes of snuff. Gram listened while Jack told all about his troubles, and then she says, "Well, you better go marry one of them girls at Gizzard Springs, and let the redhead go." But Jack says to hell with Gizzard Springs, and if he can't get the pretty girl with the red hair he don't want no woman at all. And then he begun to talk like he is going to hang himself in the barn, or else maybe he will run off and join the army. Gram just set there until Jack quietened down, and then she told him to go and ask the redhead three questions. She made him say the questions over till he learned all three of them by heart, to make sure there wouldn't be no mistake.

When Jack got to the house he seen the old man was not at home, and the pretty girl was out in the barn looking for eggs. So he says, "Do you want to live single all your life?" and the pretty girl with the red hair says "No." Then Jack spoke up again and he says, "Do you want to marry anybody else except me?" The pretty girl looked kind of funny when she heard this one, but finally she says "No." When it come to the third question, Jack took a big breath and then he whispered in the pretty girl's ear. She jumped like she was shot, and hollered "No!" at the top of her voice. Then she looked at Jack, and they both busted out laughing. So Jack just grabbed the pretty girl with the red hair and throwed her right down in the hay. They was as good as married right then and there.

When the girl's daddy come home, she told him all about what happened and how she answered "No" every time, but Jack had got the best of her just the same. The old man grumbled considerable, but after while he says, "Well, if a boy is smart enough to figure out them three questions, he ought to make a fair-to-middling husband anyhow." And so Jack and the pretty girl with the red hair went to town and got married, and they lived happy ever after.

49. The Three Questions

"Pappy" Jackson, a railroad porter originally from St. James Parish, Louisiana, told this tale in New Orleans to Arthur Huff Fauset, a folklore collector, who published it in the 1920s. AT 922.

'Twas an Irishman goin' along an' there was two men that the king said if this man could answer three questions he could have the kingdom. So the king had this colored man tied. He was to cut his head off. This ol' Irishman passed an' the colored man was cryin' worried. The Irishman said, "Faith an' bejedders, what are you cryin' about?"

The colored man said, "My head is to be cut off Friday if I don't answer three questions for the king."

So the Irishman said, "I'll take your place." So he taken the colored man's place an' that Friday he walked roun' to de king's th'one. The king asked the Irishman what he wanted.

The Irishman said, "Well, I came to take the colored man's place. He said if he answered your questions he could be king, so if I answer them I be the king."

So the king asked him, "How big is that mountain set out there in front of the th'one? How many baskets to fill up the dirt?"

The Irishman said, "Accordin' to the size of de basket. If the basket is big as the mountain then only one basket."

The king rubbed his hair. He said, "How much do you think I worth, me being the king?"

The Irishman said, "Well, faith n' jedders, you not worth as much as the Lord an' they sold him for thirty pieces of silver." The king got worried. He roached his hair. He said, "What am I studyin' about?"

The Irishman said, "What a damn fool you are." He got to be king.

50. Under Gravel Do I Travel

This riddle tale was told by Bob Wyrick, Eureka Springs, Arkansas, June 1948, to Vance Randolph; Wyrick originally heard it circa 1910 in Green Forest, Arkansas. AT 927.

One time there was a fellow got into trouble about something, and it looked like a gang of men was going to hang him. But the people was all great riddlers in them days, and they got to talking about riddles on the way to the hanging ground. So finally they told this fellow that if he could spin a riddle that nobody in the crowd couldn't answer, they would turn him loose. He says he wanted to think it over. So the boss of the gang says, "Well, we will ride slow, and you can think all you want. But when we get to the hanging ground your time is up."

After while the whole bunch come to the place where they was fixing to hang him, and the fellow set on his horse right under the gallows. He told them he could think better on horseback. When they started to put the rope around his neck he says, "Hold on, boys. I have thought up a riddle." So then he sung it out like this:

Under gravel I do travel,
On oak leaves I do stand,
I ride my pony and never fear,
I hold my bridle in my hand.

They made him sing the riddle over three times, and everybody thought about it awhile. But there wasn't nobody that knowed the right answer, so finally they all give up. Then the fellow pulled off his hat and showed them where he had stuck some gravel in it, and he pulled his boot out of the stirrup and showed some oak leaves he had put in. And he says I'm a-riding my pony, and I ain't scared of nothing, and I have got my bridle in my hand this minute.

The folks kind of grumbled about it, but they seen the fellow had got the best of them, and so they turned him loose. And that's all there is to the story.

51. The Bride of the Evil One

Elizabeth Johnston Cooke, one of a number of occasional contributors to the *Journal of American Folklore* in the late nineteenth century, said that she had been told this story by "Old William," her African American gardener in New Orleans. The Devil does not usually appear in such a role in American folktales as he does here, and Hell as a destination for the protagonists as well as two of the riddles proposed give the story the veneer of a Christian orientation. AT 812A*.

In former times there lived, on a great plantation far out in the country, the richest and most beautiful lady in the world. Her name was Maritta, and she was beloved by all who knew her, especially so by her parents, with whom she dwelt.

She was so rich that one could not count her wealth in many days; and her home was a palace, filled with rare things from all quarters of the globe. Rich hangings of damask and tapestry adorned the walls, and massive and wonderfully carved furniture filled the rooms. Instead of gilt, as is usual in splendid mansions, the mirrors and pictures were framed in gold, silver, and even precious stones. Then, the dining-table was a wonder to behold—glittering with costly glass and golden service. The lady Maritta always ate from a jewelled platter with a golden spoon; and her rooms were filled with wondrous vases, containing delicious spices and rare perfumes of many kinds.

Half the brave and daring fine gentlemen of her country had sought her hand in marriage; but her parents always declared that each was not rich enough. So loath were her parents to give her up, that they finally said she should never marry unless she could view her suitor ten thousand miles down the road.

Now, as roads in general are not straight for so great a distance—to say nothing of one's eyesight—the poor lady was quite in despair, and had almost decided to remain a spinster.

At last the Evil One, seeing the covetousness of this old couple, procured for himself an equipage of great magnificence, and went a-wooing. His coach was made of beaten gold, so ablaze with precious stones that the sun seemed mean in comparison with it. Maritta beheld it thirty thousand miles off, and all the household were called out to view it; for such a wonder had never been seen in that part of the world. But so great was the Evil One's power for conjuring that he was a very short time in arriving. He drove up to the door with so grand a dash and clatter and style that Maritta thought she had never beheld as princely a personage. When he had alighted most gracefully, uncovering and bowing to the mother and father, he knelt at the feet of Maritta, kissed her hand, and turning to her astonished parents, asked the hand of their daughter in marriage. So pleased were they all with his appearance that the wedding was hastened that very day. After the marriage compact was completed Maritta bade adieu to her proud parents; and tripping lightly into his coach, they drove away with great effect.

Then they journeyed and journeyed, and every fine house or plantation which they approached, Maritta would exclaim "Is that *your* home, my dear?" "No, darling," he would reply with a knowing smile, "my house is another cut to that." Still they journeyed, and just as Maritta was beginning to feel *very* weary they approached a great hill, from which was issuing a cloud of black smoke, and she could perceive an enormous hole in the side of the hill, which appeared like the entrance to a tunnel. The horses were now prancing and chafing at the bits in a most terrifying manner; and Maritta thought she saw flames coming from out their nostrils. Just as she was catching her breath to ask the meaning of it all, the coach and party plunged suddenly into the mouth of the yawning crater, and they sank down, down into that place which is called Torment.

The poor trembling lady went into a swoon, and knew nothing more until she awoke in the House of Satan. But she did not yet know that it was the Evil One whom she had married, nor that, worse still, he was already a married man when she had made his acquaintance. Neither did she know that the frightful old crone was his other wife. Satan's manner had also undergone a decided change; and he, who had been so charming a lover, was now a blustering, insolent master. Lifting his voice until it shook the house, as when it thunders, he stormed around, beating the old hag, killing her uncanny black cat, and raising a tumult generally. Then, ordering the hag to cook him some buckwheat cakes for breakfast, he stamped out of the house, towards his blacksmith shop, to see how his hands were doing their work. While the wretched young wife sat in her parlor, looking very mournful and lovely, wiping her eyes and feeling greatly mystified, the old hag was turning her cakes on the griddle and growing more and more jealous of this beautiful new wife who was to take her place. Finally she left the cakes and came and stood by Maritta. "My child," quoth she, "my dear daughter, have *you* married that man?"

"Yes, dame," replied the pretty Maritta.

"Well, my child," said she, "you have married nothing but the Devil."

At this the wretched young wife uttered a scream and would have swooned again, except that the hag grasped her by the arm, and putting a rough horny hand over Maritta's mouth, said in a low and surly voice, near her ear: "Hist! Should he hear you, he will kill us both! Only do my bidding, and keep a quiet tongue, and I will show you how to make your escape."

At this Maritta sat up quite straight, and said in trembling tones: "Good dame, prithee tell me, and I will obey, and when I am free, I will send you five millions of dollars." But the forlorn hag only shook her head, replying: "Money I ask not, for it is of no use to such as I; but listen well." Then seating herself on the floor at the feet of Maritta, her black hair hanging in tangles about her sharp ugly face, like so many serpents, she continued in this wise: "He has two roosters who are his spies; and you must give them a bushel of corn to pacify them but I shall steal the corn for you. He also has two oxen; one is as swift of foot as the wind can blow; the other can only travel half as fast. You will have to choose the last, as the swift one is too well guarded for us to reach him. The slower one is tethered just outside the door. Come!" she cried to Maritta, who would have held back, "a faint heart will only dwell in Torment."

At this thought the poor Maritta roused herself, and summoned all her strength. Her hair had now fallen loose and she was all in tears. But she mounted quickly, looking over her shoulder, to see if he was coming even then. "But dame," cried she, "will he not overtake me, if his ox is so much more fleet of foot than mine?"

"Hold your slippery tongue," replied the hag, "and mark my words. Here is a reticule to hang at your side; this is a brickbat which I put in the bottom, and on that I place a turkey egg and a goose egg. When you feel the hot steam coming near you, drop the brickbat for he will soon return, and missing you, will start on your chase, mounted on the ox. As he approaches near, you will feel the heat of his breath like hot steam. When you drop the brickbat a wall will spring up from the earth to the sky; and the Devil cannot pass it until he tears down every brick, and throws it out of sight. When you feel the hot steam again, drop the turkey egg, and there will come a river; and when he reaches this river he cannot cross over until his ox drinks all the water. Do the same with the goose egg, and a river will again flow behind you, thus giving you more time in which to reach home. Now off with you, and Devil take you, if you don't hold on tight and keep up your spirits. But, hark ye, if he catches you, I will poison you when you come back."

At this terrible threat the lovely Maritta was so frightened that she forgot to thank the old hag or say good-by. In the twinkling of an eye the weird-looking creature had raised her mighty arm, and gurgling out a frightful laugh, she lashed the ox with a huge whip. Away he sped, verily as fleet as the wind, with the beautiful lady clinging on, her arms wound around his neck, and her soft face buried in his shaggy hair. Onward they floated, above the earth, it seemed to Maritta, over hills and plains, through brake and swamp. Just as the lady began to rejoice at being set free—for it seemed a kind ox, and, after all, it was not so very hard to hold on, as she glided along—she heard a piercing shriek behind her; and suddenly a burning hot steam seemed to envelop her. Thinking of the brickbat, in an instant she snatched it from the reticule—almost breaking the eggs in her haste—and flung it behind her, nearly suffocated with the heat. Then she turned to look: and lo! a great dark wall shut the awful sight from her gaze.

Onward, onward they sped, as she urged the ox by kind words, stroking his great neck with her delicate white hands. After they had traversed a great distance, Maritta began to think of home and the loved ones, when her reveries were broken by a gaunt black hand clutching at her hair over the back of the ox; and again she felt the intense heat. Too terrified to put her hand in the reticule, she gave it a shake, and the turkey egg fell to the ground. On the instant water was flowing all about her, cooling the air and quite reviving her. Then a harsh voice fell upon her ear, crying: "Drink, drink, I tell you; mighty hard on you, but you must drink!"

Soon the river was left far behind, and again Maritta aroused herself as she began to notice many familiar landmarks, which told that she was nearing home. After urging the ox on at a great rate for many more miles, she dropped the goose egg, in order to give herself ample time, although as yet she had not again felt the approach of her fiendish husband. At length the welcome sight of her own broad fields greeted her anxious and weary eyes; and soon her dear home arose upon the horizon. With a few more strides the wonderful ox halted at her own very door, and she fell from his back more dead than alive.

For some moments she was unable to rise and embrace her alarmed parents, who had seen her approach. They had only had time to retire into the house, when Satan rode up to the steps. Throwing himself from the ox, he banged for admittance, in a vastly different manner from that of his first visit. But the father confronted him, and he had to content himself with talking to Maritta over her father's shoulders, while the poor lady was cowering in a corner of the room clinging to her mother. However, the touch of loving parental arms reassured her, and she demanded of Satan what he wished further. "I have," replied his Satanic majesty, "three questions to propound to you and if not properly answered, I shall take you by force again to my realms." Then placing his feet wide apart, with head thrown back, one arm akimbo on his hip, and snapping the fingers of his other hand, he sang in an impudent, swaggering manner:

What is whiter than any snow?
What is whiter than any snow?
Who fell in the colley well?

The gentle Maritta lifted her soft eyes, and, raising her sweet voice sang in a pure and tender strain:

Heaven is whiter than any snow,
Heaven is whiter than any snow,
Who fell in the colley well?

"Yes, ma'am," replied Satan, rather taken aback. "That's right." Then he continued:

What is deeper than any well?
What is deeper than any well?
Who fell in the colley well?

Maritta replied in the same strain:

Hell is deeper than any well,
Hell is deeper than any well,
Who fell in the colley well?

Again the Evil One took up his strain:

What is greener than any grass?
What is greener than any grass?
Who fell in the colley well?

Maritta lifted her voice a third time:

Poison is greener than any grass,
Poison is greener than any grass,
Who fell in the colley well?

Greatly confounded at her answers, the Evil One stamped his feet in such a manner that smoke and sparks flew upward, and an odor of sulphur filled the room. Then turning on his heels he cried to the mother that he had left a note under the doorsteps with the Devil's own riddle on it.

A thousand or more acres of green corn grew about the house; and the Devil, pulling it all up by the roots, carried it in his hands, tore the roof off the mansion, and raising a fearful storm, disappeared in it. When the storm had abated, the mountains around about were all leveled to the ground. After the panic caused by his wonderful conjuring had subsided, the mother bethought herself of the note, and when found it read as follows:

Nine little white blocks into a pen,
One little red block rolled over them.

None could guess it save Maritta, who said it meant the teeth and tongue.

52. A Bark Peeler's Life

Mike Todd, who was born in New York state's Catskill Mountains in 1877, "one of the few old-time bear hunters left" in New York, was the teller of this story. A retired fire lookout, in the 1950s he was engaged to tell stories at a children's summer camp. AT 1567G.

They peeled a lot of bark for the tanneries in the old days.

That was hard work. Men worked fifteen to sixteen hours a day in the bark woods—from sun to sun was the rule. The men got covered from head to foot with the sticky sap from the hemlock trees. I see 'em just as sticky you'd take off a pair of overalls and let 'em dry and they'd stand up by themselves. It was the spring of the year and another thing they had a lot of trouble with in the bark woods was the gnats—the no-see-ums. They'd just kill you in warm and cloudy weather. You'd daub your face with kerosene and tar. In the shanties they'd use smoke—a house full of smoke to drive out the gnats.

Contractors would hire a gang of men to peel bark, and there was a man down around Shandaken that had about a dozen working for him and living in a shanty. His name was Conrad. He didn't feed 'em too good and they had a lot of bad butter. It didn't smell too good and it didn't taste too good. So they made it up that Judd Todd—he was one of twelve sons—would ask the blessing at the dinner table. He got down to the table and he says:

Oh Lord of Love
Look down from above
And give us something better;
We're crammed and jammed and daily damned
With Conrad's stinking butter.

Tricks and Tricksters

In American tales, there is often a delight taken in the use of tricks, perhaps because of a cultural belief that the underdog can triumph if clever enough or because getting ahead is itself so important a value that tricks become emblematic of cleverness toward that end. In Jack tales, the hero's abilities as a trickster may be important to his prowess; in African American tales, the trickster—whether Brer Rabbit or the slave John—shows how to win by the use of wits in the face of greater power. Trickery may get a wife ("Aunt Kate's Goomer-Dust," "How Brer Rabbit Brought Dust Out of the Rock"), the best crops ("Bouqui and Lapin: The Farm"), or free room and board ("The Tricky Yankee"). Or it may save your own skin from harm ("The Tar Baby," "The One-Eyed Giant," "John, His Boss-Man, and the Catfish"). But trickery is, well, tricky, and it does not always succeed. The young woman in "'All of These Are Mine'" stalks on home when her new husband's attempt to trick her fails, Brer Rabbit's trick leads to his destruction in "When Brer Frog Gave a Dinner," and sometimes Old Marster outwits his would-be trickster slave in "Talking Turtle."

53. Aunt Kate's Goomer-Dust

This trickster story was told by someone named J. H. Story, Pineville, Missouri, July 1922, to folklorist Vance Randolph. Story traced the tale back to having heard it in Arkansas in the 1870s or 1880s. Related to AT 593.

One time there was a farm boy named Jack and he wanted to marry a rich girl that lived in town, but her pappy was against it. "Listen, Minnie," says the old man, "this feller ain't house-broke, scarcely! He's got cowdung on his boots! He cain't even write his own name!" Minnie didn't return no answer, but she knowed what Jack could do, and it suited her fine. Book learning is all right, but it ain't got nothing to do with picking out a good husband. Minnie had done made up her mind to marry Jack, no matter what anybody said.

Jack wanted to run off and get married regardless, but Minnie says no, because she don't figure on being poor all her life. She says we got to make Pappy give us a big farm with a good house on it. Jack he just laughed, and they didn't do no more talking for awhile. Finally he says well, I'll go out on Honey Mountain tomorrow, and see what Aunt Kate thinks.

Aunt Kate knowed a lot of things that most folks never heard tell of. Jack told her what a fix him and Minnie was in, but Aunt Kate says she can't do nothing without silver. So Jack give her two dollars, and it was all the money he had. Then she fetched him a little box like a pepper-duster, with some yellow powder in it. "That's goomer-dust," she says. "Don't get it on you, and be careful not to get none on Minnie. But you tell her to sprinkle a little on her pappy's pants."

Late that night Minnie dusted some powder on the old man's britches, where he had hung 'em on the bedpost. Next morning he broke wind right at breakfast, so loud it rattled the pictures on the wall and scared the cat plumb out of the kitchen.

The old man thought it must be something he et. But pretty soon he ripped out another one, and it wasn't no time at all till he was making so much noise that Minnie shut the windows for fear the neighbors would hear it. "Ain't you goin' down to the office, Pappy?" says she. But just then the old man turned loose the awfullest blow-out a body ever heard, and he says, "No, Minnie. I'm goin' to bed. And I want you should fetch Doc Holton right away."

When Doc got there Pappy was feeling better, but pretty white and shaky. "Soon as I got in bed the wind died down," he says, "but it was terrible while it lasted," and he told Doc all about what happened. Doc examined Pappy a long time and give him some medicine to make him sleep. Minnie follered Doc out on the porch, and Doc says, "Did you hear them loud noises he keeps talkin' about, like somebody breakin' wind?" Minnie says no, she didn't hear nothing like that. "Just as I thought," says Doc. "He just imagined the whole thing. There ain't nothing wrong with your pappy only his nerves."

Pappy slept pretty good, on account of the medicine Doc give him. But next morning, soon as he got up and put his clothes on, he begun to break wind worse than ever. Finally he fired off a blast that sounded like a ten-bore shotgun, so Minnie helped him back in bed and sent for the doctor. Doc give him a shot in the arm this time. "Keep that man in bed," says he, "till I get Doctor Culberson to come over and look at him." Both of them doctors examined Pappy from head to foot, but they couldn't find nothing wrong with him. They just shuck their heads, and give him some more sleeping medicine.

Things went along like that for three days a-running, and finally Doc says Pappy better stay in bed all the time for awhile, and take medicine every four hours, and maybe he would be happier in a institution. "Put me in the asylum, just because I got wind on the guts?" yelled Pappy. And with that he begun to raise such a row the doctor had to give him another shot in the arm.

Next morning Pappy set up in bed a-hollering how the doctors are all damn fools, and Minnie says she knows a fellow that can cure him in five minutes. Pretty soon Jack come a-walking in. "Yes, I can cure you easy," he says, "but you got to let me and Minnie get married, and give us one of them big farms." Pappy wouldn't even speak to Jack. "If this halfwit cures me," he says to Minnie, "you can have any goddam thing you want." Minnie walked over and stirred up the coals in the fireplace. Soon as it got to burning good, Jack took the tongs and throwed Pappy's britches right in the fire.

When Pappy seen them pants a-burning he was plumb speechless. He just laid there weak as a cat, and Jack marched out like a regular doctor. But after while the old man got up and put on his Sunday clothes. He never broke wind, neither. Minnie fixed him a fine breakfast, and he et every bite of it and never even belched. Then he walked round the house three times, without feeling no gas on his innards. "Well, by God," he says, "I believe to my soul that damn fool did cure me!" On the way down town he stopped in to see Doc Holton. "I finally got well, without no thanks to you," says he. "If you had your way, I'd be in the crazy-house this minute!"

Soon as he got Doc told, Pappy went over to the bank and deeded his best farm to Minnie. He give her some money to buy horses and cows and machinery. And so her and Jack got married, and they done all right. Some folks say they lived happy ever after.

54. "All of These Are Mine"

Zora Neale Hurston, the noted African American novelist, studied anthropology and folklore at Columbia University and set out to collect African American folklore in her native Florida and in Louisiana in the early 1930s. Although she published scholarly work in the *Journal of American Folklore,* she published her book *Mules and Men,* from which this tale comes, for a broader audience, setting a number of folktales, including this one, in the context of a novelistic account of her fieldwork. This story came from a narrator whom Hurston identifies as Mack C. Ford during a tale-telling session in a community of phosphate miners in Pierce, Florida. The story ends with a rhyming closing formula such as are common in African American tales. AT 859D.

Well, the startin' of it is, a farmer was courtin' a girl and after he decided to marry her, they married and started home. So when he passed a nice farm he said to the girl: "You see dat nice farm over yonder?" She said, "Yes." He said: "Well, all of these are mine." (Strokes his whiskers.)

Well, they traveled on further and they saw a herd of cattle and he said, "See dat nice herd of cattle?" She said, "Yes." "Well, all of these are mine." He smoothed his whiskers again.

So he traveled on a piece further and come to a big plantation with a big nice house on it, and he said: "All of these are mine."

So he traveled on further. He said, "See dat nice bunch of sheep?" She said "Yes." "Well, all of these are mine."

Traveled on further. Come across a nice bunch of hogs and he said: "See dat nice bunch of hogs?" "Yes." "Well, all of these are mine."

So the last go 'round he got home and drove up to a dirty l'il shack and told her to get out and come in.

She says, "You got all those nice houses and want me to come in there? I couldn't afford to come here. *Why you told me a story.* I'm going back home!"

He says, "Why no, I didn't tell you a story. Every time I showed you those things I said 'all of these were mine' and Ah wuz talkin' 'bout my whiskers." So the girl jumped out of the wagon and out for home she went.

Goat fell down and skint his chin
Great God A'mighty how de goat did grin.

55. The Tar Baby

"The Tar Baby" is probably the best-known African American trickster story because of its inclusion in Joel Chandler Harris's Uncle Remus books and because of an animated version produced by Walt Disney. This version was recorded by folklorist Richard M. Dorson from storyteller E. L. Smith, Calvin, Michigan, in the 1950s; Smith was originally from Georgia. Here the Tar Baby story itself is preceded by the incorporation of another story, sometimes told separately, about the theft of milk, which provides an explanation for the placing of the tar figure to capture Rabbit. AT 15 + 175.

There was a Rabbit and a Fox. So they was having what they call a house-raisin'. An' the Rabbit was s'posed to be a doctor. And they had milk in the spring. An' this here Rabbit, every once in a while, he'd work a little bit and he'd holler "Whoooooooooo." Fox said, "Who is that?"

"Somebody callin' me."

Says, "What they want?"

"Oh I don't know, I ain't goin' to see."

"Oh yes," says, "Youse a doctor, you'd better go and see."

So he went on down to the spring, and got in this milk, and drink some of it, come on back. And when he got back the Fox says, "Who is it, what was it?"

Says, "Just Started."

All right, went on, worked a little bit, and directly he says, "Whoooooooooo."

"Who is it, who is that now?"

"Somebody else callin' me. I ain't goin' this time."

Fox says, "Yeah you go ahead," says, "you got to go, youse a doctor." He went on, down the spring, and drink up this milk, part of it, 'bout half of it, come back. Fox says, *"What his name?"*

"Half Gone."

He went on back and worked a little bit, directly he said, "Whoooooooooo." Says, "What is that now?"

"Somebody else calling me."

"Well, better go see."

"No, I ain't going."

"Yeah, you go ahead." So he went on down the spring and drink it all up, filled the jug with water. Kept on doing that till the Fox 'cided he would see what, who it was. He put him a tar baby down there.

So, Rabbit he come down there an' seed him sitting there, say, "What you doing here?" Tar baby didn't say nothin' to him. "Speak du'n ye, I'll knock you over." Tar baby just sit there, didn't say a word. He hauled off and slapped him with one foot. When he slapped him that foot stuck to him. He says, "Better turn me loose, I got another un here," says, "I'll kick you with this, I'll kick you over." So he kicked him with that foot and that un stuck. He says, "You better turn me loose," says, "I got another one here," says, "I'll hit ye, kick ye with hit," says, "I'll kick ye clear over." He kicked him with that un, and that un stuck. He says, "Better turn me loose," says, "I got a head here, if I'll butt ye, I'll butt ye to pieces." So he butted him, and his head stuck. There he was, couldn't get loose.

Fox he come down the spring, "Mhm, I knowed I'd get ye, I knowed you was the one drinking up my milk." He took him loose, started to the house with him. Says, "I don't know what hardly to do with you," says, "I'm going take ye to the house." Got up the road pretty good piece toward the house, an' there was a big thick briar patch there. He says, "I'm a good mind to throw you out there in them briars."

Rabbit says, "Ohh Mr. Fox, please don't throw me out there in them briars." Says, "I'll get all scratched up and all tore up with them briars," says, "don't throw me out there."

"Yes I is, you *shut* up. Throw you right out there in the middle of 'em." After a while he took the Rabbit you know, and th'owed him over in the briar patch, and the old Rabbit kicked up his heels, said, "Ohh ho, here's where I want to be, here's where I was bred and bo'n anyhow."

56. Bouqui and Lapin: The Farm

Folklore scholar Calvin Claudel collected this story from his mother, Leota Edwards Claudel, Avoyelles Parish, Louisiana. Bouqui and Lapin figure in a number of Louisiana French tales. *Lapin* is French for rabbit, and the character is the same trickster figure found also in English-language stories, such as stories 55 and 63. *Bouqui* is the Wolof word for hyena, and the name is thus an interesting American retention from an African language; Bouqui generally is the dupe in these stories in which he appears as a character. AT 1030.

One year Bouqui and Lapin decided to farm together. Bouqui cut the weeds and grass away and plowed the ground, while Lapin did the planting. He planted turnip seeds, carrot seeds, beet seeds, garlic seeds, and onion seeds. He then sliced off the sprouting eyes of Irish potatoes and planted them. Next with a pole he stuffed into the fresh soil the green vines of sweet-potato plants. He also planted some gourd seeds. After he had finished all the planting Lapin said:

"Bouqui, I'll tell you how we'll divide our crop. You take the top part that grows over the ground, and I'll take the bottom part that grows under the ground."

"All right," answered Bouqui, "just so I get my share. . . . But look here! I've done all the hard work of plowing; you'll do the harvesting."

"That suits me," replied Lapin with a cunning smile on his face.

The harvest time came. Lapin went into the field, dug the turnips, carrots, beets, garlic and onions. He then gathered the sweet potatoes and the Irish potatoes. Next he picked and piled up the gourds, saying to Bouqui:

"Bouqui, here is your share, the gourds. You can make vegetable soup with the onion tops and turnip greens. If you have too much of the others, you can feed them to your cow."

Bouqui knew he had been tricked; so he said:

"Lapin, I get only tough turnip greens, which will be dried up soon. You get all the good turnips, carrots and juicy potatoes. . . . It will be different next year; I'll take the part that grows under the ground."

"Fair enough," replied Lapin. Then, as he was leaving, he added to Bouqui: "You can make dippers to drink from with the gourds."

Next year Lapin came to Bouqui and asked:

"Now, Bouqui, what do you want to do this year? You complained last year that you were cheated. This year do you want me to do the plowing and planting, and you'll do the harvesting?"

Bouqui was glad for an opportunity not to do the plowing, but wanted to be sure not to be tricked this season. So he replied:

"Yes, but remember, I get the part of the crop that grows under ground this year."

"Oh, of course," answered Lapin, "that's the bargain."

Lapin worked the ground and planted a large crop. He planted beans, cabbage, lettuce, celery, tomatoes, corn, spinach, pumpkins, melons, thyme, parsley, eggplants, okra, peas and even peanuts. The crop grew and grew. When it came time to gather the harvest, Bouqui did not show up; so Lapin went to get him and said:

"Remember our bargain, Bouqui. You either harvest the crop this year, or we'll starve."

When Bouqui got into the field, he knew he had been more badly cheated than ever. He gathered the beans, cabbage and lettuce and had nothing but roots for himself. Next he harvested the celery, tomatoes and corn; he had nothing but roots. At last he took in the spinach, pumpkins and melons; everything went to Lapin. He gathered squashes, thyme, eggplants, okra, peas and parsley, and there was not even one thing for him to eat or live on. He did not even have feed for his cow. At last he came to the peanuts. He had to have food for the winter; so he harvested the peanuts, and that was his part of the crop.

57. The Hare and the Porcupine

Lithuanian American Marcella Papevis of Benld, Illinois, told this story, published by folklorist J. Russell Reaver, June 1949. Readers will recognize it as a version of a famous story from the Aesopic fables. AT 1074.

There were two neighbors, a hare and a porcupine, who did not get along very well. Unknown to the hare, the porcupine had three children.

One day the porcupine suggested they run a race, the winner to get both their homes since they had not been able to get along together. When the porcupine suggested this race, the hare thought, "My, what a silly fool this porcupine is. He can barely crawl around, and here he wants to run a race with me." The hare was very confident he could win.

The porcupine said, "Let's not run today. Let's run tomorrow so that we can rest up before running the race."

He suggested they run the race in the forest because it would be safer there. If they ran on the road, he said, someone might catch them and kill them. That day they agreed to run in a square, at each corner of which they were to stop to rest before going on to the next lap.

That night the porcupine took his three children and put one at the end of each of the first three laps.

The next morning they began the race. At the start the hare shot out like a bolt of fire, but the porcupine went back to his hole to sleep. When the hare arrived at the end of the first lap, he found standing there the porcupine, who said, "I've been waiting for you. Where have you been?"

The hare then spit on his legs so that he could run faster, but at the end of the second lap the porcupine beat him again. The hare began to be frightened because he was beginning to feel worn out, and here he found the porcupine ahead of him again!

But the hare spit on his legs once more and ran on. At the end of the third lap, the same thing happened.

When the hare reached the end of the race, the porcupine was there waiting for him. Then the hare said to his legs, "Legs, legs, what good are you to me?"

The legs answered, "We tried to win the race, but we couldn't because our front legs are short and our back legs are long. Since the porcupine's legs are all long, he won the race."

Then the hare asked, "Ears, ears, what good are you to me?"

"We were listening so that we could beat the porcupine."

"Eyes, eyes, what good are you to me?"

"We were looking just so that we could beat the porcupine."

Then the hare said, "Tail, tail, what good are you to me?"

At that time the hare had a long tail. The tail said, "I was just trying to get in the way so that you'd get caught and we wouldn't have to run any race."

The hare became very angry at his tail; he put his tail in a narrow crack in a tree and pulled and pulled until he pulled it off.

When he returned home very tired and without a tail, the porcupine made fun of him and laughed and laughed.

The hare said, "Brother, you can have this place," and went out to the woods and died.

58. The One-Eyed Giant

Leonard Roberts collected this narrative in the course of fieldwork he did between 1951 and 1955 with a Kentucky family, the Couches of Harlan and Leslie Counties, who had a large store of folklore in their traditions. It is extraordinary in that it mixes a story seemingly drawn from Homer's *Odyssey* with several widely told tall tales (see the "Lies and Other Tall Tales" section of this book). AT 1137 + 1881 + 1889C + 1890A + 1895.

Back in 1901 I was down in Mississippi, at Camp Shelby. I had me two companions down there and we took a notion we would go on a fishin' trip down the Mississippi River. It was an awful wilderness down there where we went, and time we got down to where we wanted to go we was lost. We looked away acrost the river and saw a little blue smoke boiling up out of a little shack. We got to callin' and hollerin' for help. Well, we called and called and after while they was an ol' one-eyed giant lived over there—after while he got his boat and come over and got us.

He took us over to his shack or cave where he lived. Now on the trip down the river we three men had to climb trees to get away from the snakes of a night and other varmints, and I had a skinned place on my belly. Purty bad sore. The old giant took us in to his cave and welcomed us. He started feedin' and fattenin' us up mighty good. I didn't know what it was for and they didn't neither. But it looked like he was fattenin' us up like a farmer a-fattenin' his hogs. He was goin' to eat us.

Well, it come a time, one of my buddies was good and fat. The old giant come and took him out. We never heard a thing of him again. And in a few days he come and took the other'n out and left me alone in his cave. Next time he come back I asked him, said, "Why, where's my buddies?"

He laughed and said, "Hawr, hawr, hawr. You needn't mind your buddies." Said, "They make good steak," and said, "when that sore's cured on your belly you'll make good steak, too!"

Now he'd go out of a day and he'd herd his goats. He had an awful good herd of goats. And he'd come back in of a night and herd his goats in the cave and then lay down out front and sleep. I knowed my time was short when I saw that sore on my belly healin' up purty good. I had a notion one day that I would ex-cape. But when he'd come in to the cave and get ready to sleep he'd set a big rock up in the cave door, after he'd herd his goats in. And they weren't no way for me to ex-cape out through it.

He went to sleep one evenin' in the front of the cave and I took my chance. They was a big bunch of arn [iron] a-layin' around there, like pokin' sticks for his far. They was kindly sharp on one end. I took and chunked up the far and helt them arns in that far till they got good and red. You know, he was a one-eyed giant. His eye was right in the middle of his forehead. I het them arns good and hot and I slipped up to him and I rammed about four of them right down that big eye. He raised from there a-buttin' them walls and a-carryin' on. He got right in the entrance of the cave and he roared out, "YOU WON'T GET AWAY WITH THIS!"

I managed to stay out of his way till he hushed and then he moved the rock from over the cave door. And he set right in it. Well, he had one old goat there he called his pet. I picked that very old goat because he was the biggest and got right up between that goat's legs, right under the bottom of his belly and got a-hold of his wool. I tried to stampede that goat herd out of there, but he stopped 'em and let 'em out one at a time. They kept a-goin' out of the cave, and this very old particular goat that I was on—or under, I mean—when he come up to the old giant he stopped. That old giant rubbed him over. He said, "I knowed you'd never fail me." Said, "You're my pet and I love ye." Was I scared! But it happened that he didn't find me, and the old goat passed on through.

When all of them passed on through and got out he knowed that I'd somehow ex-caped. When I got out from there I made for the river, and he come out of there a-squallin.' And when I looked around and down the river I saw seven other big giants a-comin.' I made my getaway and got to the boat in the river and hopped in it. I felt awful anxious by the time I hit the water. And by the time they all got up there why I was two-thirds of the way acrost. Now there was some great big high mountains standin' on that side of the river bank, clifts [cliffs] there that weighed tons. Well, they grabbed one of them clifts and throwed *it* at me. In the place of sinkin' me they just shoved me on all the way acrost.

When I come out of that danger I had an old hog rifle-gun, but I just had one bullet. I took up the river bank and had to climb trees at night from the snakes and wild varmints. One day about noon I was settin' on the bank of the river, and of course I was lost. There come along a great big flock of wild geese and flew up in a waterbirch right over where I was a-settin' and lit on a limb. I managed and studied how I would get that flock with one bullet. Well, I finally thought of a way to get all them geese at one shot. I shot right up through the middle of that limb and split it and it clamped back and caught all them geese's toes. I clomb up the tree, took my old galluses and tied all them geese together and tied myself to them. I thought I'd jump off with 'em to the ground. But instid, them geese flew off with me.

They flew on and on with me, and when they got to goin' further than I wanted to go I just ripped out my knife and cut the old strings that I had tied to 'em and myself. That dropped me, and the luck was I fell right down in an old holler snag. I felt something under my feet and rubbin' against my britches legs. Felt awful soft but I couldn't find out for awhile what it was. I soon found out it was some cub bears. I heard a racket all at once comin' down the holler of that tree, just rip, rip, rip. I reached up with my hand—I couldn't see and just happened to clinch an old bear right by the tail. Well, I had that old rusty Barlow knife with the blade about half broke off. I tuck that knife and I commenced jobbin' that bear, and she tuck right back up that holler tree and carried me out the top.

I clomb down and started on. I didn't have any bullets left in my old hog rifle-gun, but you know we always carried a wiper-an-ramrod. As I was goin' along I loaded my old rifle with powder and with that wiper. Putty soon I come upon one of these old Russian wild boars and a bear a-fightin.' I taken aim with that wiper and killed that bear. And then me and the boar had it around a few trees. I took around a little sugar maple, about six, eight inches at the stump, and that boar made a lunge at me and hit that tree. His tush [tusk] went plumb through it; and come out on the other side. I grabbed me up a rock and bradded that tush on the other side and there I had that old boar, too.

Well, I went on home for a horse to come and get my meat. When I started to go across an old field by the river I got tangled up in some old sawbriars and down I come. I fell on a whole flock of pateridges and killed 'em. Gathered up my pateridges and went on; till I come to the river. I had to wade it and I was so dirty and ragged I just left on my huntin' shirt. I waded that river and when I come out I'd caught a whole shirttail full of fish. I just rolled up my shirt like a poke and took 'em on.

I moved on in home. Well, the old horse I had he was awful pore, and he had a putty sore back from a saddle scald. But I got that old horse ready and started back with him to get my bear and boar. Got over in the woods putty close to where my wild meat was at and that old horse slidded up and fell and hurt hisself, and he wasn't able to carry no bear in. I just stripped him and turned him loose in the woods, live or die.

You know, in about fifteen years after that I was back in that same place again a-huntin.' I saw a tree a-shake, shake, shakin' up toward the top of the mountains. I decided to investigate and see what it was. I went up there and saw what it was. A acorn had fallen in the horse's back and made an acorn tree. A big gang o' wild hogs was follerin' that old horse around, bitin' his heels, making him kick up and shake off them acorns for 'em.

---

59. The Three Little Pigs

This tale was told by Mrs. A. C. Ford, 82, of New Hampshire, and published early in the twentieth century by collector Mary A. Owen; Mrs. Ford heard it from her grandmother, who had heard it from *her* grandmother. AT 1150 + 124.

Once, an old sow had three little pigs.

The first little pig said, "Mother, may I go out and seek my fortune?"

"No, no; the Old Fox'll eat you ALL up."

"No, he won't if you build me a house of straw."

So she posted off and built him a house of straw.

Then along came the Old Fox, and said,

"Piggy, Piggy, *please* let me in."

But Piggy would not.

"If you don't, I'll go up on top of your house, and blow and blow and knock it down, and eat you ALL up."

Piggy would not.

So he went up on top of the house, and blew and blew and knocked it down, and ate Piggy ALL up.

Then the second little pig said, "Mother, may I go out and seek my fortune?"

"No, no, the Old Fox'll eat you ALL up, as he did your little brother."

"No, he won't if you build me a house of wood."

So she posted off and built him a house of wood.

Then along came the Old Fox, and said,

"Piggy, Piggy, *please* let me in."

But Piggy would not.

"If you don't, I'll go up on top of your house, and blow and blow and knock it down, and eat you ALL up."

Piggy would not.

Then he went up on top of the house, and blew and blew and knocked it down, and ate poor Piggy ALL up.

Then the third little pig said, "Mother, may I go out and seek my fortune?"

"No, no; the Old Fox'll eat you ALL up, as he did your little brothers."

"No, he won't if you build me a house of stone."

So she posted off and built him a house of stone.

Then along came the Old Fox, and said,

"Piggy, Piggy, *please* let me in."

But Piggy would not.

"If you don't, I'll go up on top of your house; and blow and blow and knock it down, and eat you ALL up."

Piggy would not.

So he went up on top of the house, and blew and blew till he blew his whistle off, but he *couldn't* blow it down, so he came down, and said,

"Piggy, Piggy, don't you want some nice apples?"

Piggy said, "Yes, I do."

"Well! come over to my house in the morning, and I'll give you ALL you can pack home."

So Piggy went over in the morning, before he was up, and stole ALL he had, and took 'em home, and peeled 'em, and threw the peelings out the door, and turned the key just as Old Fox came along.

"Piggy, Piggy, where did you get such nice apples?"

"I went over to your house before you were up, and stole ALL you had."

"Piggy, Piggy, don't you want some nice potatoes?"

"Well! Come over to my house in the morning, and I'll give you ALL you can pack home."

So Piggy went over in the morning, before he was up, and stole ALL he had, and took 'em home, and peeled 'em, and threw the peelings out the door, and turned the key just as Old Fox came along.

"Piggy, Piggy, where did you get such nice potatoes?"

"I went over to your house before you were up, and stole ALL you had."

"Piggy, Piggy, don't you want some nice fish?"

Piggy said, "Yes, I do."

"Well! come over to my house in the morning, and I'll give you ALL you can pack home."

So Piggy went over in the morning, before he was up, and stole ALL he had, and took 'em home, and scaled 'em, and threw the scales out the door, and turned the key just as Old Fox came along.

"Piggy, Piggy, where did you get such nice fish?"

"Why, I went down to the river, and held my tail in all night, and when they nibbled, I jerked."

"Do you think I could catch any?"

"Yes, you could."

So he went down to the river, and held his tail in ALL night, and in the morning it was frozen fast, and he *couldn't* get it out.

By and by Piggy came down with her tea-kettle to get water to make her coffee, and there he was frozen in, tight and fast.

"Piggy, Piggy, *please* chop me out."

"No, no, you'd eat me ALL up."

"No, no, Piggy. I wouldn't disturb you any more."

So, at last, she went back to the house, and got her hatchet, and chopped and chopped till she got him out.

"Now, I've-got-you! Now, I'll eat you ALL up."

But Piggy ran and ran, and banged the door, and put her back against it just as Old Fox came up.

"Piggy, Piggy, *please* let my nose in, it's so cold," he kept saying.

So, at last, she let his nose in.

"Oh, Piggy! it smells so nice in here, *please* let my eyes in."

So she let his eyes in.

"Oh, Piggy! it looks so beautiful in here, *please* let my ears in."

So she let his ears in.

"Oh, Piggy! the kettle sounds so nice, *please* let my whole head in."

So she let his whole head in.

"Oh, Piggy! my head's so good and warm, *please* let my fore legs in."

So she let his fore legs in.

"Oh, Piggy! my fore legs are so good and warm, *please* let my body in."

So she let his body in.

Then he jumped, and his hind legs and tail came in.

"NOW I've got you, NOW I'll eat you ALL up!"

(Accompanied by a jump.)

"Oh! what's that I hear coming? A pack of hounds!"

"Oh, Piggy! where'll I hide? Where'll I hide?"

"Just jump into my churn."

So he jumped into her churn, and she took the kettle of boiling water, and poured it over him, and then she churned and she churned till he went ALL to butter.

60. Pat O'Grady

"Pat O'Grady" was told by Genevieve Richmond of Harrisburg, Illinois, in Harrisburg, December 31, 1950, at a gathering of teachers. She had the story from her grandfather, who was named Pat O'Grady; the story begins with the main character's having that name, though his name quickly changes to Willy the Wisp. AT 330A + 332.

Pat O'Grady was a blacksmith and he worked hard at this business, and he had a wife, and a son. He was working, and slaving away, trying to make a honest dollar. He threw his tools down. He was disgusted for that one day, and he started home. He climbed the hill, and he had all his tools on his back. When he got to the hill he stumped his toe on something, and fell back down the hill. When he got to the bottom of the hill he said "I hope death takes me if I ever come down this hill again." He walked on home and had forgotten all about what he had said, and the next day he was tired as usual, and he came along with his knapsack down the hill. He did fall that time, and when he got to the bottom of the hill, there was Death. They called him Willy the Wisp. Death said, "Willy the Wisp, did you forget what you said yesterday evening?"

He said, "Well yes, who are you?"

He said, "Well I'm Death; you said that if you ever came down this hill again you hoped that Death would take you, and I'm here to take you."

Willy said, "I have just a young son, I haven't lived long, give me a few years."

And Death said, "All right, you can have a few years."

Willy said, "And I don't have a very good profession. I'd like to live those few years in style, and be able to take care of my family."

And Death said, "Just what profession would you like to follow?"

He said, "I'd like to be a doctor, and be dignified, and have kind of a nice home."

Death said, "And another, you may have that wish," and he said, "you may have two more."

And Willy the Wisp said, "Well, there's a cherry tree in our yard, and I never get to eat any of the cherries off the tree. When spring comes they're gone before I can get any of them." He said, "I'd just wish to have these cherries for my own."

Death said, "Well that's your wish," and he said, "Anyone you find eating those cherries will stick to that tree till you've told them they can leave," and then he said, "The third wish; I have a rocking chair on my porch, and when I get through the day's work, and want to rest, my wife's always in the chair, or some of the neighbor's children, or some of the visitors, and I'd like to have that chair for myself."

Death said, "You may have all three of those wishes," but he said, "in ten years I'll come back for you, and another thing Willy, I want you to remember that if you see me standing at the foot of the bed, you give the patient up, for that patient shall die; but if you see me standing at the head of the bed, then the patient will get well."

So Willy the Wisp prospered for ten years. They passed quickly. He came home one spring from a trip out into the country, and there standing on the porch was Death, and he remembered that his ten years were up. And he said, "Oh no Death, I'm not ready to go yet."

And Death said, "You said ten years, and your ten years are up."

He said, "Well, just have a seat, and I'll tell the wife and son good-bye, so Death sat down in the rocking chair. And the minute he sat down in the rocking chair he knew Willy had him. He said, "All right, Willy, you have ten more years, but the next time you won't catch me sleeping." So he was gone for ten more years, and Willy prospered, and was very happy. The ten years passed quickly, and it was spring, and the cherries were ripe, and he came home one day, and there stood Death in the yard, while the cherry tree framed the back ground, and Willy said, "Death I'm not ready yet, I haven't tasted a cherry yet off that tree."

And Death said, "Well, gather you a little basket or box, and take them along with you."

And he said, "You gather me a box while I tell the folks good-bye." And of course the same thing happened; when Death reached up to get the cherries, Willy had him again. So ten more years went by, and Willy prospered. The Dukes, Lords, and Ladies all called him to come, and nurse them through their illnesses. One day he walked into the room of a famous Duke, and there he saw Death standing at the foot of the bed. The doctors had been called from far and wide, but no one could cure the Duke. Willy said, "Everyone step out of the room please. I want to be alone with the patient." And all of the family left the room, and quickly Willy took the Duke, and turned him head around, and Death was standing of course, at his head. Death was aggravated. He said, "You'll not do this again. When your ten years are up this time you've played all of your tricks."

And Willy had an enjoyable ten years, and oh he was too happy. His ten years were up shortly, and Death came back, and Willy prepared to go with him. He told all his friends good-bye, and his wife, and they departed across the Irish Sea. As they were on the ship, going across, Willy was looking out over the waters, and he said, "Death, you're really a wonderful person." He said, "You can do such wonderful things, even just that small bottle on the deck there," he said, "I just know you could make yourself invisible and get in there."

Death said, "That would be the simplest of tricks."

And Willy said, "As the last thing you can do for me, I'd just like to see it."

So swish swish and Death was in the bottle, and Willy corked it up and threw it into the Irish Sea. And that was during the time Methuselah lived so long. That was during that time.

61. Roclore and the King

Roquelaure (or "Roclore"), who traces back to the historical Duc de Roquelaure (1614–1683), is a comic figure in French and Louisiana French folklore. This particular story of his doings was recollected by Ethel LaBorde Smith from the telling of her grandmother, Eva Brouillette LaBorde of Marksville, Louisiana. AT 1590.

Once upon a time, many, many years ago, there was a very, very poor farmer whose name was Roclore. Roclore was so poor that all he owned was one poor old horse and a small piece of land. Roclore's land was divided into two parts by the king's land and, because of this, Roclore had to cross the king's land twice a day, in the morning on his way to his field and in the evening on his way home. Roclore had to work very hard to grow enough food for himself and his skinny horse to eat because the soil in his field was so poor. Roclore and his horse spent many long hours working in the field and, for this reason, Roclore loved his poor, ugly, skinny horse—and, my child, Roclore's horse was the skinniest horse you have ever seen; he had bones that stuck out all over!

Now, the king's lands were beautiful and green, and stretched for as far as the eye could see—and further. He lived in a magnificent palace and he was surrounded by everything his heart desired. The king had servants to do everything for him and these servants were careful to take *special* care of the king's most prized possessions—three solid white horses. These horses were very beautiful and very valuable, since only a wealthy man could afford such horses. But, my child, they were also very vain and selfish—they knew how fat and beautiful they were. The king's three horses were especially mean and hateful to Roclore's poor, ugly, old, skinny horse. Each morning, as Roclore and his working horse crossed the king's land on the way to their field, the three white horses would come running out of the stable to laugh at Roclore's horse. Late in the evening, when Roclore and his horse returned from their day of working in the field, the three lazy horses would be waiting in front of their stable to laugh at Roclore's horse again. When they saw Roclore's skinny horse coming, the king's three fat horses would begin to laugh, and my dear, they would laugh, and laugh, and laugh. They would laugh the hardest and the longest at the many bones that stuck out from Roclore's horse. It was a disgrace the way the king's horses would laugh at Roclore's poor horse! They would laugh so hard that the king would come out of his house and yell at Roclore, "Roclore, you get off my property and don't you cross it no more; your horse is so ugly and so skinny that he makes my horses laugh too hard and I am afraid they will all get sick."

Now, my child, Roclore and his horse listened to these insults for many years, until one night Roclore decided he had heard enough; he thought of something he could do to stop the king's horses from laughing at his poor horse. He slipped out of his tiny house and ran to the king's stable. At the king's stable, he found the three white horses asleep. So Roclore took out his pocketknife and slit the king's horses' mouths from ear to ear. He then returned home and went to bed.

The next morning, Roclore hitched his horse to the wagon and made his way to the king's palace. When he reached the king's door, the king ran out to chase Roclore and his horse away—but, he noticed that his horses had not come out to make fun of Roclore's horse. He ran to the stable to see what was wrong and he discovered that his three horses' mouths were split from ear to ear.

"What has happened to my beautiful horses?" cried the king.

"Well," replied Roclore, "they have laughed so hard and so long at my poor horse that it seems they have finally split their mouths."

But, the king did not believe Roclore and he was *most* sure that Roclore had done it. So the king told Roclore to get off of his land and to never, never set foot on it again.

Roclore left the king's land, but that night he had another plan. He went out to his barn and he shoveled dirt from his own land into the bed of his wagon. The next morning, Roclore arose early and took extra pains in dressing himself and in grooming his horse. He then hitched his horse to the wagon and went to the king's palace.

When he reached the king's front door, the king ran out to chase Roclore away, shouting, "Roclore, didn't I tell you not to ever set foot on my land again!"

Very calmly, Roclore climbed from his wagon seat and stood on the dirt he had placed in the back; he stood very straight and very tall and said, "Yes, you said not to ever set foot on your land again, but I am not on your land, I am on my *own* land." To this the king had no reply because Roclore had again outsmarted him, and from this day on, Roclore was never bothered by the king.

62. The Tricky Yankee

The stereotype of the Yankee trader or peddler was an enduring one in the American South, where in the nineteenth century traveling tradesmen, especially from New England, were a feature of life; the stereotype endured into the twentieth century, when this story was collected in 1930s North Carolina by folklorist Ralph Steele Boggs. AT 1525D.

A Yankee stopped at a Southern hotel. The hotelkeeper had heard that Yankees were tricky, so he asked the Yankee to show him a trick. The Yankee promised to show him before he left. After a few days the Yankee said he was going to leave, so he'd show him that trick. He asked the hotelkeeper for a brace and bit. Then he asked him to show him his best barrel of wine. The hotelkeeper brought the brace and bit, and showed him his best barrel of wine in the cellar. The Yankee bored a hole in one side of the barrel and asked the hotelkeeper to plug it up with his left thumb. Then he laid the brace and bit up on the shelf and walked off without paying his board bill. The hotelkeeper was afraid to take out his thumb and run after the Yankee, because it would mean the loss of his best wine.

63. How Brer Rabbit Brought Dust Out of the Rock

Particularly familiar from the popular Uncle Remus books written by Joel Chandler Harris, the African American trickster figure Brer (Brother) Rabbit, sometimes just called Rabbit or Mr. Rabbit, peoples many folk stories with his cunning tricks. Here he outsmarts those more powerful than he in the art of courting. Motifs K62, K1889, K1950.

Mr. Fox, he had a mighty handsome daughter, and all the chaps were flying around her to beat all.

Brer Coon, Brer Wolf, Brer Rabbit, and Brer Possum were courting her all the time, and they all asked Brer Fox for his daughter.

Now the gal, she favored Brer Rabbit in her mind, but she didn't let on who her favorite was but just snapped her eyes on all of them.

Now old Brer Rabbit, he wasn't so handsome, and he wasn't proud, that's for sure, but it appears that somehow he did have a mighty glib way with the gals.

Well, when they'd all asked Brer Fox for his daughter, he asked the gal, did she want Brer Wolf? And she tossed her head and allowed that Brer Wolf was too bodaciously selfish. She said, "Brer Wolf's wife wouldn't get even a bite of chicken breast as long as she lived."

Then the old man, he asked how she liked Brer Possum. She just giggled and allowed that "Brer Possum is a mighty ornery, little old man, and he belongs to a low-class family anyhow."

Old man Fox, he allowed, "That's so, for a fact," and sounded out her affections for Brer Coon, but she made out that Brer Coon was beyond all endurance. Then the old man told her Brer Rabbit had asked for her too, and she made out that she was mighty taken aback and didn't want any of that lot.

Then old Brer Fox, he said that the gal was too much for him, but he told the suitors to bring up the big stone hammer. They could all try their strength on the big step rock that they used for a horse block, and the one that could pound dust out of the rock could have the girl.

Then Brer Rabbit, he felt mighty set down on, because he knew all the other chaps could swing the stone hammer to beat him, and he went off sorrowful like and sat on the sand bank. He sat for a while and looked east, and then he turned and sat a while and looked west, but maybe you don't know that Brer Rabbit never came to himself except when he looked north.

When it came to him what he was going to do, he jumped up and clipped on home, and he hunted up his slippers, and he filled them with ashes, and Lord bless your soul, the old chap knew just what those slippers would do about getting dust out of the rock.

Well, the next morning they were all there early. Old Brer Rabbit, the last one, came limping up like he was mighty lame, so he would be the last one.

Now Brer Wolf, he took the big hammer and he fetched it down hard, and Brer Wolf was a mighty strong man in those days, but he didn't raise any dust. Then Brer Coon and Brer Possum, they tried, but old man Fox said he didn't see any dust, and Miss Fox stayed behind the window curtain and giggled, and old man Fox curled his lip and said, "Brer Rabbit, it's your turn now."

Brer Wolf looked mighty scornful, and Brer Rabbit had all he could do just to lift up the big hammer. It was so hard he had to stand on tiptoe in his slippers, and when the hammer came down, his heels came down, shish, and the dust flew so they couldn't see him for the cloud it made.

Old Brer Rabbit didn't count that as much; it was just one of his courting tricks.

---

64. John, His Boss-Man, and the Catfish

One of a number of stories about a clever black man's encounters with his more powerful boss (in many tales he's a slave, often called John, and the boss is his master, often called Ole Mahster or Marster), this tale was collected 1937–38 by the noted African American folklorist J. Mason Brewer. Here John does the outwitting, though sometimes Ole Mahster, known as the Colonel in this tale, gets the better of the situation. Motifs J1500, K330.

The Colonel would not allow John and the other hands to fish in the river, but occasionally after the crops were planted and the cotton had been chopped, he would let them fish in the slough on the plantation. And this was only under one condition—that they catch perch only. If a hand caught a catfish he was to throw it back in the water. If the Colonel caught a hand carrying a catfish home, he would take his black-snake whip and give him a good whipping. The Colonel said that catfish were too good for black people.

Most of the hands had stopped fishing, because the perch were so small that they were hardly worth the grease it took to fry them; and then, too, the children were always getting choked on the bones.

John was the only one who kept on fishing down in the slough. He caught catfish all right, but was clever enough to get them home and have Mariah cook them without getting caught. He would always wait until he saw the Colonel and his family leave for a visit to some neighboring plantation or to the little town down on the river before he went fishing.

One Saturday afternoon when the Colonel left the plantation and started towards town, John told Joseph and David to get his fishing pole from under the cabin. He put it on his shoulder and went down to his regular fishing place. He had been there about two hours when he heard something in the grass behind him. Looking back, he saw the Colonel walking toward the spot where he was fishing. He had caught a seven-pound mud-cat and had tied it on a string to a stob [stake] in the ground on the bank of the slough and he was terribly frightened. Before he could get over his scare the Colonel came up to where he was sitting and said, "John, how is your luck today?" He was looking straight at the catfish.

John pulled up the stob, took the string off, and began working with it.

"You know, boss," said John, "I've been having an awful hard time with this catfish; I've been fishing for perch and this catfish has been stealing my bait all day, so I just tied him up here on the bank to keep him off of my bait so I could catch some perches—but I'm through fishing now, so I might as well turn him loose."

And before Colonel Clemons could answer, the catfish was swimming down the slough. John then went on over to where he had the perch tied, took them out of the water, shouldered his pail, and went on home.

65. When Brer Frog Gave a Big Dinner

Although most stories in which Brer Rabbit is the protagonist feature the triumph of his tricky cleverness, in this one (from Georgia and published around the turn of the twentieth century) he is outwitted and meets a dreadful end; the tale has a darker vision than many African American animal trickster tales. Motif K1000.

Brer Frog he thought he'd give a big dinner to all his friends, so he sent out invitations to all his friends to come down and eat fried fish with him.

Brer Frog he invited Brer Fox and his wife, and Brer Wolf and his wife, and Brer Coon and his wife, but he didn't invite Brer Rabbit. Brer Frog didn't, because there were hard feelings between Brer Frog and Brer Rabbit from way back.

When the animals all went past Brer Rabbit's house on their way to the dinner, they asked Brer Rabbit why he wasn't going to Brer Frog's dinner. Brer Rabbit said he wasn't invited and he allowed that he wasn't powerfully fond of fried fish anyway.

So they passed on and when they came to the branch, they found Brer Frog frying fish over twenty little fires. Brer Frog hopped around from one frying-pan to the other, like a spry little old man like he is.

Directly Brer Rabbit he smelled the fish frying where he sat on the porch. It smelled so powerfully good, Brer Rabbit he just couldn't stand it. He took his way down to the branch, and he saw Brer Frog taking off the fish from his twenty little fires and set it on the table. Brer Rabbit he slipped into the swamp and made a big noise. The animals they said, "What's that?!" Brer Rabbit he made a big noise. Once more Brer Fox he said, "Where we going to run to?" Brer Frog he said, "I know the best place for me to get to." He just gave one jump over the animals' heads and went plunk into the water. Brer Terrapin he went slipping and sliding one side, then the other, and he went splash onto the water. They other animals, they just struck out for home.

Brer Rabbit he went up to the table and he ate his fill of fried fish.

Now Brer Frog is a mighty cold-blooded kind of man. Nobody ever sees Brer Frog in a passion. Brer Frog's eyes are on the top of his head. All the time while Brer Rabbit was eating that fried fish, Brer Frog he sat down in the water looking straight up at Brer Rabbit, and Brer Frog he was studying; but Brer Rabbit he didn't know that.

Brer Frog he took it mighty hard, because Brer Rabbit he broke up his dinner, and he thought to himself how he was going to punish Brer Rabbit.

Sure enough, that day week, Brer Frog he sent out invitations to all the other animals to another dinner.

So the animals all set out, and as they went past Brer Rabbit's house, they stopped and asked Brer Rabbit why he wasn't going to Brer Frog's dinner. Brer Rabbit he said his mouth wasn't set fir fried fish, and he allowed how he was power-fully busy anyhow and couldn't leave home.

The animals they made haste, and when they got to the branch they saw the bank all covered with little fires, and a pan of fish frying on every fire, and Brer Frog hopping from one frying-pan to the other and turning the fish. And Brer Frog he hopped up and whispered in the ear of each one of his guests. Then Brer Frog he set the table.

Brer Rabbit he sat upon his porch smoking his pipe, and the smell of the fish fry-ing came up on the wind, and Brer Rabbit he just couldn't stand it. He said he was bound to set a tooth into that fish. So Brer Rabbit he went clipity clipity down to the branch, and he found the table set, and it certainly looked powerfully tempting.

Brer Rabbit he went in the edge of the swamp and made a big noise. They animals they just struck out and headed for home. Brer Frog he said, "I know the nighest place for me to get," and he jumped plum over the table and went into the water kerplash.

Then Brer Rabbit he jumped on the table. Now that was just what Brer Frog knew Brer Rabbit was going to do, so Brer Frog had set the table on a plank, on the edge of the water, and he put leaves and brush all around the plank, so Brer Rabbit didn't see how it sat over the water. And when Brer Rabbit jumped on the plank, over it went, and Brer Rabbit and all the fish went kerplash down to the bottom.

Brer Frog he was right down there, and Brer Frog he said, "Oho, Brer Rabbit, you are mighty kind to fetch my dinner down to me," and Brer Frog he said, "You are my master many a day on land, Brer Rabbit, but I am your master in the water." And Brer Frog he killed Brer Rabbit and ate him up.

66. Mr. Deer's My Riding Horse

Mrs. William Preston Johnson, who was active in the 1890s in a New Orleans branch of the American Folklore Society that was busily collecting African American folklore, published this story, which she recollected from the telling of her "young nurse" as a child on Avery Island, Louisiana. Motifs J1706, K713.2.

Well, once upon a time, when Mr. Rabbit was young and frisky, he went courting Miss Fox, who lived way far back in the thick woods. Mr. Fox and his family were very nervous, and they very seldom came out of the woods except for a little walk in the clearing near the big house, sometimes when the moon shone bright. So they didn't know many people besides Mr. Rabbit and Mr. Deer. Mr. Deer he had his eyes set on Miss Fox, too. But he didn't suspect that Mr. Rabbit was looking that way but kept on being as friendly with Mr. Rabbit as he ever had been. One day Mr. Rabbit called on Miss Fox, and while they were talking, Miss Fox she told him what a fine gentleman she thought Mr. Deer was. Mr. Rabbit just threw back his head and he laughed and he laughed.

"What are you laughing about?" Miss Fox said.

And Mr. Rabbit he just laughed on and wouldn't tell her, and Miss Fox she just kept on pestering Mr. Rabbit to tell her what he was laughing about and at last Mr. Rabbit stopped laughing and said, "Miss Fox, bear me witness that I didn't want to tell you, but you just made me. Miss Fox, you call Mr. Deer a fine gentleman. Miss Fox, Mr. Deer is my riding horse."

Miss Fox she nearly threw over in a fainting fit, and she said she didn't believe it, and she would not till Mr. Rabbit gave her the proof.

And Mr. Rabbit he said, "Will you believe it if you see me riding past your door?"

And Miss Fox said she would, and she wouldn't have anything to do with Mr. Deer if the story was true.

Now Mr. Rabbit had been fixing a plan for some time to get Mr. Deer out of his way. So he said good evening to Miss Fox and clipped off to Mr. Deer's house, and Mr. Rabbit he was so friendly with Mr. Deer he didn't suspect anything.

Presently Mr. Rabbit just fell over double in his chair and groaned and moaned, and Mr. Deer he said, "What's the matter, Mr. Rabbit? Are you sick?"

But Mr. Rabbit he just groaned; then Mr. Rabbit fell off the chair and rolled on the floor, and Mr. Deer said, "What ails you, Mr. Rabbit? Are you sick?"

And Mr. Rabbit he just groaned out, "Oh, Mr. Deer, I'm dying. Take me home, take me home."

And Mr. Deer he's mighty kindhearted, and he said, "Get up on my back, and I'll tote you home."

But Mr. Rabbit said, "Oh, Mr. Deer, I'm so sick, I can't sit on your back unless you put a saddle on."

So Mr. Deer put on a saddle.

Mr. Rabbit said, "I can't steady myself unless you put my feet in the stirrups."

So he put his feet in the stirrups.

"Oh, Mr. Deer, I can't hold on unless you put on a bridle."

So he put on a bridle.

"Oh, Mr. Deer, I don't feel all right unless I have a whip in my hand."

So Mr. Deer puts his whip in his hand.

"Now I'm ready, Mr. Deer," said Mr. Rabbit, "but go mighty easy, for I'm likely to die any minute. Please take the short cut through the wood, Mr. Deer, so I can get home soon."

So Mr. Deer took the short cut and forgot that it took him past Miss Fox's house. Just as he remembered it and was about to turn back, Mr. Rabbit, who had slipped a pair of spurs on unbeknownst to him, stuck them into his sides and at the same time laid the whip on so that poor Mr. Deer was crazy with the pain and ran as fast as his legs could carry him right by where Miss Fox was standing on the gallery, and Mr. Rabbit was standing up in his stirrups and hollering, "Didn't I tell you Mr. Deer was my riding horse!" But after a while Miss Fox she found out about Mr. Rabbit's trick on Mr. Deer, and she wouldn't have anything more to do with him.

67. Abe and Dinah

"Abe and Dinah" was recorded in Richmond, Virginia, January 16, 1975, by Daryl Cumber Dance, who investigated the vitality of African American storytelling traditions in the 1970s. Motifs K1810, K1835.

During the days of slavery there was a couple, Abe and Dinah. Dinah was very devoted to the mistress and master; so was Abe, but Abe liked a little fun. So every so often the master would go to New York, to some of the big cities, to attend to business. And he had a lot of confidence in Abe, and he would say to him, "Now, Abe, I'm going away and I want you to take care of the household; I want you to look after everything for me. Look after my wine (I've got plenty wine down in the cellar), and I want you to take charge. I'm gon' give you the keys, 'cause I can trust you, Abe, you never bother anything. All those things, my clothes upstairs, I want you to have 'em cleaned up 'n' want you to shine up everything. And, Dinah, you take care a the household, too; I want all the silver and brass and all the crystal shined up. You watch it because I can trust you two with this household."

And Dinah was so humble. She was so proud of this trust, and she would say, "OH! Massa, I'm gonna look after things while you gone, not a thing will be outta place; I'm gon' take care of everything for ya."

And Abe, he would come up, "Yep, Massa, you kin depend on me. Everything will be in place when you get back. I'm gon' look after all o' your wine, all of your clothes, and everything—the silver in this household—I'm gon' see that everything's in place." And Ole Massa then would get ready, you know, and go off on a big trip, he and his wife and the household . . .

SOON as he would get out of sight good, Ole Abe would start to kickin' up: "SO GLAD he gone! SO GLAD he gone! I'm gon' have me a big time now!"

And poor Dinah would say to 'im, "Abe please don't do like you did last time; you know this thing is going too far. One of these days you gonna get caught. Ole Massa is not going to New York; he may come back!"

"Oh, he's not comin' back. He won't come back until his business trip is over, and I'm gon' have some life, Dinah. You kin sit back in the corner and be faithful, but I'm gon' enjoy myself." And soon as Ole Massa—they'd get out of sight and be gone maybe for three or four hours, Ole Abe would start a callin' up all his friends, tellin' 'em, "Ole Massa gone! Ole Massa gone! We gon' have a good time!" Ole Abe would go upstairs and put on Ole Massa's coat, pants, dress up in his clothes and strut around and look. He say, "Ah! Don't I look good!"

Poor Ole Dinah would sit there and just shake her head. "Abe, you ought not to do that. Abe, please don't do that, don't put on Massa's pants! Don't put on his coat, please don't do that."

"SHUT UP, Woman, I know what I'm doing." Then he would go way down on the plantation and get 'em to kill up two or three pigs, and get the hands down there to roast 'em, you know, and OH! then he would go down in the wine cellar, get Massa's best wine, all of the silver, make Dinah set the table: "Dinah, I say set that table, SET IT up!" And then he would invite all-1-1-1 of the slaves in. They would come in their rough clod clothes and looking all shabby and bad. He the man a' the house, all dressed up in Marster's long-tail coat, and poor Dinah—head all tied up still—so sad, oh, she was so worried. And then the guys would bring in the banjos and the home-made instruments, you know, and they would set up their own li'l band, you know, and they would play, and then they would all get out (he would put a covering on the flo' so they wouldn't tear it up, you know) and then they would get out and do a ole-fashion jig dance, you know. Then he—*he* would do it, and clap his hands and—Ole Dinah wouldn't take no part in it. She'd just sit there—she was so sad.

So on this occasion, this party, there was a man who was one of 'em—Abe would be at the door, "Well, come on in, boys." (He didn't even know their names.) "Come on in, boys!"

In came this man. He was all shabbily dressed . . . Dinah looked at 'im; she say, "I never seen that face 'round here befo.'" Say, "That man certainly got broad shoulders and strict lookin.'" Say, "He certainly turn like Ole Massa."

Abe came on in, "Yeah, boys, how yawl feel? Sho glad to greet ya, so glad to greet ya. I'm gon' have a good time tonight . . ." Dinah watched, and Dinah thought, "'Tis somethin' familiar 'bout the turn of that man." Of course, he had soot all over his face, had his hair all matted down to his head, you know, and had on old run-down shoes, ragged pants, old dirty-looking shirt. "You can't fool me. That man don't look right." So they started dancing. Well, that's what gave it away to Dinah, because HIS STEPS—were just a li'l bit too polished. They weren't like those other steps. She come, she say, "ABE, come here, come here. You see that man there. That man, I believe, is Ole Massa. He doesn't turn like the other folk."

By that time Ole Abe had plenty of wine in him, you know, he couldn't see. He say, "WOMAN, haven't I tol' ya to stop meddlin' wid me. I know dat ole nigger. He come from 'round dere on dat other plantation. I know 'im. Now don't come here worryin' me, I know exactly who he is."

Dinah went around, she say, "Lawd have mercy, I know sumpin' gon' happen 'round here because I feel it, I feel it. That's NOT one a' us. That gotta be Ole Massa and I believe it." So she got in the corner and start worrying . . . and they were dancing. So finally, 'bout break a' day, everything was over, everybody left, and Ole Dinah, Dinah started cleanin' up the house. She say, "I hate to do this." She say, "I just hate to do this, Abe, because I feel like something is gon' happen 'round here."

"SHUT UP, woman, let me git dis stuff straight here! I'm gon' have another one 'fo' Massa get back. I just want to get things back in order."

And just-t-t about daybreak good she looked around. Somebody knocked at the door, started coming in. She say, "Lord have mercy, Abe, I believe it's Ole Massa coming in; I believe it's Ole Massa! OH my goodness!"

And he walked in. There's Abe, had all a' the glasses on the table, had just washed some of 'em. He saw the wine bottles, everything all tore up. He said, "Well, ABE! what's going on here, what's the matter with the house? What's wrong?"

"Uh, uh, uh, uh, M-M-M-M-Massa, I-I-I was just givin' it a jun-jun-juneral cleanin' up. I just cleanin' up good. I just cleanin' up around here."

He say, "Well, what is all my wine bottles and all those empty bottles doin' on the table?"

"Uh, uh, I just went down in the cellar an-an-and was pouring wine from one bottle to the other, uh, uh, that's what I was doin.'"

He say, "Well, wait a minute, Abe, come here, let me see your clothes. That's my pants you got on and my coat. What's been going on in my house?"

"Uh, uh, uh—"

Dinah, say, "Oh, Lord, ABE, I tol' ya what's gon' happen, I tol' ya."

He say, "Dinah, I'm not gon' touch ya. I was here las' night, and I witnessed all of it. Dinah, you had no part in it, but ABE, take off those things, and let me call the help down from the field there, who is in charge of the field help, and I'm gonna tell him to give you as many lashes as your body can stand. I'm gon' try to kill you! My most trusted slave, and you turned on me like this!"

She say, "OH, please don't kill 'im, Massa, please don't kill 'im, don't kill 'im, DON'T kill 'im!"

He say, "Dinah, if it wasn't for you I'd kill 'im, but because you've been so faithful I'm gon' spare his life."

Husbands and Wives

As is also the case with modern jokes, older traditional stories about husbands and wives usually dwell on the pitfalls of the marriage bond. In the following tales, spousal inflexibility and the temptations of adultery underlie the humor.

68. The Stubborn Wife

Although Ralph Steele Boggs, who collected this story in North Carolina in the 1930s, does not say so, stories like this—in which a physical action on the part of a character figures prominently—often give the narrator the opportunity to mime the action in the course of the telling. AT 1365B.

Once a wife broke her scissors and asked her husband to buy her a new pair. He said he couldn't afford to buy any new scissors just then. She kept askin' an' askin' for the scissors, till he told her if she mentioned the word "scissors" again, he'd drown her. She answered back that she'd say "scissors" as long as she lived, and kept on talkin' about them. So he carried her to the river and threw her in. She kept saying "scissors" till her head went under the water. Then she stuck her hand up out of the water and made the sign of scissors with her fingers.

69. Singing Her Warning

This is a cante-fable, that is, a folktale that includes parts that are sung. It was recorded from Charles "Dixie" Archer, Cranberry Hall, near Cookstown, New Jersey, March 8, 1940, by Herbert Halpert, who very actively collected folk narratives over many years. AT 1419H.

I remember somethin' about it. I'll tell you how it was. There was a man married one time and there was another feller runnin' with his wife. And uh—so—he kinda judged it, but he didn't know it for sure. So uh—then one night—he was a sailor, follered the water. And uh—so one time he come home and he told his wife, "Now," he says, "I won't be home till such a night again."

So then, by Jim, this feller he come there and *he* [the husband] come before that man come. He come that same night this other feller [was going to come]. Well the signal was, this feller he'd come and knock on the blinds. So she says—she sung it:

"There's no use your knockin' on the blinds,
Yes, there's no use your knockin' on the blinds;
For the old man's at home,
And I am not alone,
And there's no use your knockin' on the blinds."

Then the old man commenced—says:

"There's no use your knockin' on the blinds,
There's no use your knockin' on the blinds;
For the baby is a-suckin',
And I'll do my own _____,
So there's no use your knockin' on the blinds!"

He was a-givin' him a hint to get away.

70. Rover in College (Rover au collège)

This story was told in French by Évélia Boudreaux, Carencro, Louisiana. AT 1750A.

The child left, and went to college far away, in another state. The child returned. His father said to him, "How's school?"

He said, "Papa, school is magnificent!" He said, "You should see, Papa, what they do with dogs." He said, "they teach dogs to talk. They teach dogs to read." And he said, "You like Rover so much, why don't you send Rover to college? But," he said, "Papa, this costs lots of money. You can afford it." And he said, "Since you love Rover so much, I would be happy to take him along."

"Well," he said, "my son, we'll do just that." He said, "Take Rover. Put him in school." He said, "I would be so happy to hear him speak. It would be such good company for me."

So the week went by. The holidays ended. The son and the dog left to go to college. When he was down the road, he did something with the dog; he had it destroyed. Always when he wrote to his father, he said to his father, "Papa, you should see how well Rover is learning. But," he said, "Papa, it'll take more money." He said, "I don't have enough money. It costs a lot for Rover's education."

So the father sent him some money. When he would write, he would say, "My son, how's Rover doing?"

"Papa, Rover is doing so well! He has started talking."

So the time arrived for the son to go home for the holidays. And the father was eager to see what progress the dog had made. When the child arrived, he said, "My son, and Rover, where's Rover?"

He said, "Papa, don't say anything!" He said, "I'll tell you a little secret." He said, "Rover was getting too smart. Rover was talking about what you used to do behind Mama's back!" He said, "I had to do away with him, with Rover. I didn't want him to ruin your marriage!"

"Well," he said, "my son, you did well!" He said, "It wouldn't have been good for your mother to know what I did behind her back!"

Priests, Preachers, and Other Professions

In American humorous tales, men of the cloth are often the butt of humor, held up as being hypocritical sinners: thieves ("The Stolen Hog"), drunkards ("What Did Paul Say?"), womanizers ("Bunkim"), or just greedy ("A Death Bed Scene"). But other professions may come in for a share of satire too—lawyers, for example, having fun poked at their doings and their pretensions.

71. The Stolen Hog

Scholar Thomas B. Stroup heard this tale in 1931 at a gathering of his own family in Fletcher, North Carolina, and later published it because it parallels a narrative from medieval literature, the similar Mak story told in the medieval English "Second Shepherd's Play." AT 1525M.

Once a certain preacher, when he ran shy of meat, went out in the thicket near his house and killed one of his neighbor's hogs (hogs at that time ran at large). And he and his wife dragged it to their yard to clean it. But just as they were getting through with the gutting, they looked up and saw two old women coming over the hill, their staves in their hands, on their way to meeting. And they were coming right to the preacher's own house, for he had appointed meeting at his house for that day. On seeing the old women (who were getting to meeting ahead of time), the preacher and his wife carried the hog into the house and, for lack of a better place to put it, pushed it under the bed.

The people gathered, and the meeting went along fine till all of a sudden the preacher in the middle of his sermon spied one of the hog's legs a-sticking out from under the bed curtains. He then bided his time till they "heisted" a hymn. And, when he could catch his wife's eye, he would put into the hymn, where the congregation wouldn't notice, some lines for only his wife to hear. They went like this:

"Oh, Glory, Hallelulia!
Oh, push that sow's leg under the bed.
Oh, Mattie, don't you hear me?"

While the song was still going on, a couple of hound sluts came in and started nosing around the bed; so the preacher put in something like this:

"Git out o' here, you flop-eared houn',
Glory, Allelulia.
For if you don't, I'll knock you down,
Glory, Allelulia."

72. What Did Paul Say?

This tale was narrated by Thomas W. Newell of Perry County, Mississippi, while stationed at an airbase in Canada during World War II. There it was written down by folklorist Herbert Halpert, who was serving as an Army officer but who continued to pursue his interests in folklore during the war. AT 1833A.

This guy couldn't preach unless he was full o' booze, so he had a boy—a little guy who he knew—to git him a pint of whiskey. And uh—this guy's name was Paul. So the little boy come back an' this preacher was up preachin'—about the apostle Paul. An' about the time this little boy walked in he says, "And what did Paul say?"

An' this little boy took it for granted that he was talkin' to him and he answered him, "He said if you didn't pay him for what you'd already got, he wouldn't let you have another damn drop!"

That's all.

73. Too Strong a Penance

This story was told by A. J. Smith, a well-known Cajun humorist, November 14, 1992, and was taped by Pat Mire and Maida Owens for the video documentary *Swapping Stories*. The story was told backstage between performances at the popular Cajun radio show *Rendez-vous des Cajuns* at the Liberty Theater in Eunice, Louisiana, to a stage crew and performers. The original publication also includes a story told by the show's emcee, Barry Ancelet, in response to Smith's story, suggesting the dynamic by which one tale sometimes evokes others, especially when stories are told in groups of people. Cf AT 1800–09.

The woman in confession confessed she hadn't been to church like she should have. And the priest asked her how come, and she said she worked with the circus. Always with the circus, she's on the road. She can't go to church like she should, you know. And the priest said, "Well, what is it you do with the circus?"

And she said, "I'm a contortionist."

"Ah," he said, "a contortionist." He said, "I haven't seen that since I was a young man. My daddy would bring me at the circus, you know. I wonder—after church—would you mind, [giving] me a demonstration of that?"

She said, "No problem." So, after church, she get out on the side lot, sit down on the ground, take one foot and put that behind her head. Take the other foot, put that behind the head too. So, one hand go up on top of her head like this. The other hand on top of her head. She turned her head about halfway around.

About that time, Miss Hebert and Miss Thibodeaux coming up the road like that. "Look at that, Miss Thibodeaux." She say, "I don't think I'm going to church. That priest give too strong a penance!"

74. The Man Who Stole Lumber

This tale was recorded from Évélia Boudreaux of Carencro, Louisiana, at the Festivals Acadiens in Lafayette, Louisiana, September 16, 1990; it was published as part of a statewide project in Louisiana that included special recording sessions for storytellers at local festivals. Cf AT 1800–09.

This man went to confession. And when he went to confession, he said, "Father, I stole some lumber!"

"Oh," he said, "Well, how much lumber have you stolen?"

He says, "Well, Father, I made a dog house."

"Oh," he said. "For your penance, you'll say two or three Hail Marys and two or three Our Fathers."

He said, "Father, that's not all."

"Well," he said, "What else?"

He said, "I built one of those little outdoor houses."

He said, "Yes? Well," he said, "for that you'll say a whole decade, ten Hail Marys and two Our Fathers."

He said, "Father, that's not all."

"Well," he said. "What else did you build?"

He said, "I built a house."

He said, "How big was your house?"

"It was a very big house," he said.

"Well," he says, "then I think you'll have to say the whole rosary."

He said, "Father, that's not all." He said, "I built a barn!"

"My God!" the priest said. "Well, you'll have to say two rosaries."

He said, "Father, that's not all." He said, "There's still some lumber left."

"Well," he said, "then in that case, I think you'll have to make a novena."

He says, "Father, I'm all excited." He said, "If you have the blueprint, I think I have enough lumber to make it."

75. A Death Bed Scene

"A Death Bed Scene" comes from one of George Korson's pioneering accounts of occupational folklore, the folklore of the coal mining industry; its main character is a wealthy mine contractor, though mining is not the focus of the story. AT 1860B.

Patrick O'Neill became wealthy as a mine contractor, and being a bachelor believed in spending his money during his lifetime. His unconventional manner of living and his neglect of the Church of his fathers over a long period of years brought him a reputation as a libertine. He was quite an old man when he had a stroke. His faithful housekeeper called a doctor. It took the doctor but a minute to tell Patrick that he was in a very bad condition.

"I belave I am," muttered Pat.

"Yes, you are, Pat," said the doctor, "and it will cost you a pretty penny before we of the medical profession have anything to do with you."

"What will it cost?" asked Pat, blinking his eyes.

"It will cost at least a thousand dollars," replied the doctor.

"Well, dochtor, don't ye think that's very excessive?"

"Not at all, Pat. You see, never before did we have an opportunity to make a dollar out of you, so it will cost you a thousand dollars before we do anything for you now."

"Very well," says Pat. "I'll give ye the thousand dollars on one condition."

"And what is that?"

"That ye won't let me die without the priest."

"Oh, that will be all right. We can arrange that."

The doctor knew very well that there was NO hope for Pat, yet he left him with the feeling that there might be a chance. Several days later, however, he told him the truth. "Well, Pat," says he, "you may call in the priest, for you're not going to get well."

The patient nodded his head in resignation and the priest was sent for.

The priest was an old man himself. When he entered the sick room he took one look at the dying man and said, "Well, you old reprobate, you've sent for me at last. Little you thought of me during the past forty years, running around carousing with nary a thought for the Church of your fathers. And now, Pat, don't you know that after the life you've led it will take a great deal of money for masses, prayers and offices to be read for you, if your soul's to be saved?"

"What will it cost, fa-ather?"

"It will cost at least a thousand dollars."

"Very well, fa-ather, I'll give ye the thousand dollars on one condition."

"And what may that be?"

"Both ye and the dochtor must be here when I'm dying."

"Oh! very well," said the priest. "I suppose that can be arranged."

So the room was cleared and Pat was given the last rites of the Church. Both the priest and the doctor were there. The doctor leaned over the bed to tell Pat that if he had any last request to make, to make it then.

"You have only a few minutes to live," he said.

"You're there yet, fa-ather?" muttered the patient.

"Yes; yes; I'm here," replied the priest.

"Are ye still there, dochtor?" asked Pat.

And the doctor assured him that he was.

"Well, dochtor," said Pat, "ye come around to the other side of the bed."

The priest hereupon leaned over to Pat and in a kindly but firm voice said, "Tut, tut, now it's your rosary you should be saying?"

"Well, fa-ather," said Pat as he breathed his last. "As a young man I went to your Church and many's the time I heard ye say from the pulpit that our Savior died between two thieves. I'd like to die the same way."

76. Bunkim

This story, from the field research conducted by Daryl Cumber Dance into contemporary African American tale-telling traditions in the 1970s, was recorded in Richmond, Virginia, February 24, 1975. AT 1781.

This Minister and this Deacon were bragging about the different women that they had had relationships with in the church. So they made a bet. The Minister bet the Deacon, "I can point out more women than you can."

And the Deacon say, "Well, I can point out just as many as you can."

He say, "Well, all right, next Sunday morning before I start my sermon, and every time a woman come in, and if I've had something to do with her, I'll say, 'Bunkim,' and if you've had something to do with 'em, you say, 'Bunkim.'"

And so every time a woman would come in the church that Sunday morning, the Preacher would look over at the Deacon and say, "Bunkim." The Deacon would look at the woman and say, "Bunkim." So they kept on; that kept up: "Bunkim!"

"Bunkim."

So finally, the Deacon's wife came in the church, and the Preacher looked at the Deacon's wife, and he said, "Bunkim!" And the Deacon looked at the Preacher and say, "Oh, naw you don't. You gon' unbunk that one!"

77. The Smart Indian Lawyer

"The Smart Indian Lawyer" was told by Antonio Lorenz, the village blacksmith in Hot Springs, New Mexico, and heard by Helen Zunser, who was conducting a folklore study of the village in the 1930s. Motif J1160.

A man was running for election, but he was very poor. He went to an old woman and said, "Give me half a dozen eggs on credit. When I get rich I'll pay you."

Now this old woman had boiled eggs, and she gave him half a dozen boiled eggs on credit. Long time passed and he got elected, but he was still too poor, and he didn't pay that old woman for her eggs. So after a while she started thinking, "Suppose I have those eggs, maybe they'd hatch and I have little chickens. By now I'd have lots and lots of hens." So she went and sued him.

Now the man was very worried. He sat and thought all day, "I lose the case, go to the penitentiary." He very worried. One day a friend of his came up, an Indian.

"Hello."

"Hello."

"Why you so worried?"

"O I'm worried because my case come to court and I surely go to the penitentiary."

So the Indian said, "You let me be your lawyer," and the man say, "All right."

Next day he came to court. Everyone was there, judge and everybody, but the Indian was not there. Other man was awfully worried.

The judge said, "Where's your lawyer? I put you in the penitentiary if he don't come pretty soon."

The man said, "My lawyer's not here yet, give me ten minutes."

The judge gave him ten minutes. They waited, but the Indian didn't come. So he said, maybe he got sick; to give him ten minutes more. So they gave him ten minutes more, but the Indian didn't come. But he begged and begged, and they gave him ten minutes more. Then just as they were ready to start, the Indian came in.

"Where you been?" said the judge "Why you so late when we're all waiting?"

"O," said the Indian, "I was just toasting hava beans to plant."

"What do you mean, toasting havas to plant? You can't grow from toasted havas."

"O sure. I can grow them the same as the old woman can raise chickens from boiled eggs."

So when they heard that, they laughed, and they threw the case out of court.

78. Closest to the Fire

This story that pokes fun at lawyers was told by Mike Todd, who also narrated story 52, a Catskills region woodsman who in the 1950s was employed to tell stories at a summer camp for children in New York state. AT 1860A.

This ain't no tale—it's a true story. Very near as old as I am, but not quite. It happened in Delhi. An agent named Lyons traveled around on horseback taking orders for everything; orders for hardware, groceries, clothing stores. He even took orders for fruit trees.

Well, this fall Lyons came to a hotel in Delhi during court week. Delhi is the county seat of Delaware County. He was wet and cold and he came into the main room and found a gang of lawyers seated around the fireplace. They wouldn't give Lyons a seat near the fire, so he sat off to one side.

The lawyers started asking questions of one thing or the other. They said, "You travel all over the State, what's the customs in Unadilla?" Another asked, "What's the custom in Roxbury, Hobart?" They were making fun of him. One feller thought he'd be a little smarter than the rest. He said, "You've been all over the State. What's the customs in Hell?"

Lyons said, "They're just about the same as here—all the lawyers closest to the fire."

Fools and Mishaps

Pleasure taken in the actions of fools is an element found throughout the world's folklore, and many American tales find their enjoyment in foolish, sometimes stupendously foolish, actions, or in the mishaps that overcome us, whether from our foolishness or not. There may be an element of trickery as fools have something put over on them ("Mule Eggs"), but often fools are just fools, ready to perform stupidly ("The Irishman and the Moon"), or are merely ignorant ("The Hot Dogs"). Foolish acts may come also from linguistic misunderstandings ("She's Got One Spoiled Tit," "I Run My Hand Up Missis' Dress"). Although foolish actions usually lead to laughter, in "The Girl Who Died of Fright," they are more destructive, and the point is a more somber one.

79. Mule Eggs

Ray Hicks, traditional narrator who played an influential role in spreading wide interest in tale-telling, told this story at the National Storytelling Festival, Jonesboro, Tennessee, October 3, 1998. His performance was recorded and was archived in the Library of Congress. The transcribed text includes audience reactions to his performance. AT 1319.

Hi, to all!

[Audience yells back, "Hi."]

. . . I've been sick several days. And I ain't a-feeling that good now, and I didn't think I was going to get to be with you all. And so, I told it in the other tent, but probably there's some here that didn't hear it. And I'm going to tell it over again—of a *mule egg*.

Now back, way back in Model T time (Model T Ford, Henry Ford), my father, Nathan Talbert Hicks, bought a used, used twenty-three model. Now, I was born in nineteen and twenty-two. August the twenty-nine. And so he bought the car used, . . . later on up, where I was . . . some older, you know.

And so they cleared—my grandfather cleared a lot of new ground, at that time. Of all the community people. And that's the way they lived. The people lived then about in a *lot* of places, Tennessee, all the states, lived different with their food, a-raising it, [not] as it is in the years later now, with the food shipped in.

And so all of them baked pumpkins. They was a yellow pumpkin, the biggest, that growed about that big. And in the wintertime, if you could keep em from spoiling, . . . and not break that stem off, in the wintertime, when there's a big snow on the ground, you could bake them and put just a little sugar on it before you baked it in the oven of a . . . wood cookstove. And you talk about a flavor. *Gree.* . . . It's a little more watery than a tater pumpkin, but you could boil em down and make pumpkin butter, and it'd give a biscuit a college education when you eat it. [Laughter and applause; Ray laughs too.]

You'd give it a college education, a good baked biscuit. *Goll.* And so, [my father] and Mama, my mother, went to Boone and the other kids, just left me there, it was on a Saturday, . . . to sell them pumpkins. And so, he told me to sell em at a quarter apiece.

And so, there's a little old wagon road come down in to home (and the road that's there now's been fixed, a gravel road, with the state, or Watauga County). And I was there with the pumpkins, and I heared a motor, the way they run pretty rough, vibrating: a Model T Ford did that, and they haven't gotten em fixed too good yet [laughter].

And it's a-going *bum-bum-bum-bum-bum-bum-bum,* coming down that rough, rough road. It come on down, there's a Model T Ford car. A fellow got out of it, and he come down, and he says, "I've heared it advertised in this country somewhere, that they is somebody in this country sells *mule eggs.*"

Said I: "You hit the right place; [laughter] now this is where you get em at. That yellow, yellow mule egg. Yellow, whole mule eggs."

"Well," he said, "what's the price of em . . . ?"

"They's twenty-five cents apiece."

He says, "I've always wanted to raise me a team of mules. To farm with. But, but," he says, "I ain't never lucked out to get a hold of none yet."

"Well, . . . you can get em *now,* if it works out. You can buy you two."

So he bought two, and I asked him, "Now it's hard, you'll have to sit on 'em anyway, four or five weeks." [Laughter] "To hatch em. And are you married?"

He said, "Yeah, I'm married, to a loving wife."

"Well, you and her can take turn-about a-keeping em warm." [Laughter]

And he took two and went off and cranked his motor up, *bum-bum-bum-bum*, and left. And them weeks come up, and I was a-selling em again, if I could sell any, and here come that same car, making the racket of a motor down the little old road, and he got out, and it was *him*. And he come down, and I could see he maybe wasn't mad, but he wasn't a-feeling good. [Laughter]

And he said, "Son, them mule eggs wasn't no good." [Laughter] He said, he said, "They spoiled on us."

"Well, . . . did you'uns forget and go to sleep and forget and let em get cold?" [Laughter]

Said, "No. We thought we kept 'em warm, . . . and they *spoiled* on us." Said, "God, they stunk when I cracked 'em open."

"Oh, you hit two bad ones. [Laughter] But I'll sell you two more for half price. [Laughter] I'll sell you two more for a quarter, twelve cents and a half apiece."

And he took two, went out toward the road. And Mama . . . kept a blackberry briar patch out just from the house there, in a rich holler out from the house, near the apple trees we had, and plum trees, and pear trees, and some grapevines. And he got out there with them two—one under one arm, one under the other'n—and he dropped the right one out, and it rolled (it was a little steep) and it rolled. And the other'n went out from under his left arm. And there happened to be two bunny-rabbits sitting in there in their nest. And [the pumpkins] jumped both of em. Two bunny rabbits was a-setting in that thicket of a briar patch, amid all the grapevines and the apple tree. And here he went at em. And they look a little like a mule, baby mule. [Laughter]

And here he took after one, and the other one'd run out, and he'd take after it. And then maybe they run in the same way, and he run till his breath is gone, and come through with his tongue a-hanging out, kind of panting, *ah-ah-ah-ah*, that way, and he said, "Son," he said, "you can keep them mule eggs." He said, "If they run that dang fast that little," [laughter] said, "I'll never do nothing with em when they get grown, no how."

[Laughter and applause]

80. The Hot Dogs (Les hot dogs)

The narrator of this tale, told in French, was Elizabeth Landreneau, Mamou, Louisiana. AT 1339; cf AT 1339A.

There were two nuns who came from Europe. They wanted to come to America because they had never come. They were curious to see it and they had never seen hamburgers. They wanted to eat hamburgers. They arrived at a hamburger stand, and they were out. They said, "We only have hot dogs left."

So they looked at one another. Well, they decided to get some hot dogs. And one, of course, was served before the other. And she raised her bun. As soon as she raised it, she quickly put it back down.

So the other one came, the second one came. She said, "What's the matter? You're not eating your hot dog?"

She said, "I was waiting to see what part of the dog you would get!"

81. Big Fraid and Little Fraid

One of Vance Randolph's many tales, collected during his years of folklore research in the Ozarks region, this narrative was told to him by Betrenia Bowker, Kansas City, Missouri, September 1951. She heard Johnny Statler tell it in the 1930s in Pierce City, Missouri. AT 1676A.

One time there was an old man, and he didn't like the young fellow that was coming to see his daughter. So he figured a way to scare the young fellow plumb out of the country. The old man dressed up in a sheet to look like a ghost, and then he went out in the woods. He set down on a log to wait till the young fellow come along.

Maybe the scheme would have worked, only they had a pet monkey that used to be with a medicine-show. The monkey dressed up in a pillow slip and followed right along behind the old man. The moon was shining bright, and pretty soon the young fellow come a-whistling down the path. The old man flopped his sheet, and give a couple of loud groans. So then the monkey flopped his pillow slip, and he give a couple of screeches. The old man turned around and seen the monkey, and it looked like a sure enough ghost. He give a yell and took out for the house, with the monkey right close behind him. The monkey squalled like it was scared, too.

The young fellow just stood there beside the path. He seen the whole thing, and it tickled him pretty near to death. "Run, big Fraid, or little Fraid will ketch you!" he hollered. And then the young fellow laughed so loud you could hear him plumb to the house.

The old man kind of give up trying to scare folks after that, and says he don't want to hear no more about it. So then the young fellow and the girl went right ahead with their sparking, same as always. After while they got married, and lived happy ever after.

82. She's Got One Spoiled Tit

Ethel Barnes told "She's Got One Spoiled Tit" to Vance Randolph, the noted collector of and writer on Ozarks region folklore, Hot Springs, Arkansas, April 1938; she thought she had heard it as far back as 1885. AT 1698G.

One time there was an old farmer that said he was a little hard of hearing. The truth is, he was so deef he couldn't hear it thunder. His cow had strayed off somewheres, and the old man walked all around the country asking folks if they had seen her, but they all shook their heads. Finally he met up with a preacher, and he says to the preacher, "Will you tell all the church folks about my cow being lost?" The preacher nodded his head to mean yes. So that night the old man went to church. He figured that when the people heard about the cow, he could maybe find out where she was saw last.

The sermon was pretty long, but the deef man set quiet till it was over. Then the preacher begun to tell the folks about a young couple that was going to get married. The fellow was a fine young man, he says. The girl was a teacher in the Sunday School, so the preacher laid it on pretty thick. He says this young lady is the cream of the crop and the flower of the flock and the pride of Durgenville, and then he says she is a fine sample of Christian womanhood and a inspiration to young people all over the country.

The old man couldn't hear a word, but he figured the preacher was telling the people about his cow. So pretty soon he got up and hollered, "Her rump's caved in, folks, and she's got one spoiled tit."

The preacher just stood there with his mouth open, as he had forgot all about the old cow. Some of the young folks pretty near died laughing. The girl begun to bawl, and the young fellow says he will kill that old bastard if it's the last thing he ever done. The meeting busted up in a terrible fight, and the sheriff grabbed the deef man and run for the jail-house. The sheriff was in the church and heard the whole thing, so he figured the old man better be locked up for his own good.

It was away late in the night before things quietened down. Then the preacher and some other folks come to the jail and told the sheriff how it was. So they turned the old man loose, and a fellow that worked in the bank took him home in a buggy. Some folks say that the deef man never did get it through his head what all the trouble was about. The poor old fellow didn't come to town very often after that. He says everybody in the settlement is plumb crazy, and it ain't safe for a respectable citizen to go there nowadays.

83. I Run My Hand Up Missis' Dress

Although recorded by Daryl Cumber Dance in the 1970s, as part of her collecting African American tales told at that time, this tale harks back to slavery days for its setting. AT 1698G.

During slavery days there were house hands and field hands. Well, this man was a house hand, but he had a friend who was in the fields; and every time he got a chance he would go out and talk with him. Well, the field hands very rarely got an occasion to come in the house, but every time he would talk to his friend that worked in the field, he would tell him how wonderful he was living in the house. He say, "OH, man, Ah tell ya, Ah have a good time up in that house." Say, "It's wonderful up there. They treat me good. Give me all kinds of good food and just let me have the whole use of the house. I just have a good time." Say, "I tell ya, every time I go upstairs," say, "you know what I do? I run my hand up Missis' dress."

He say, "Man, do you do that?"

He say, "I certainly do."

"If I could get in that house one time. Don't they ever need extra help?"

He say, "Well, I tell ya what I'm gon' do." He say, "Next time it's time to do a lot of cleanin' I'm gon' tell 'em I need some help, and I'm gonna ask them to let you come up there to do some of the heavy lifting and," say, "then you can see."

OH, he went back to work so happy! Every time he'd see him, he'd say, "Hey, man, when they gon' start the cleanin'?" Say, "I'm ready!"

He say, "It won't be long now."

Finally, it was almost time for spring cleaning, so he suggested to the mistress, he said, "I have a friend who is real strong and he kin do a lotta work 'round here. Kin he come up here and help me when you start moving things around?"

She says, "Oh, I would be happy to have him. That's all right. Just tell him to come on and help."

So next day he went down there and said, "Man, the chance is here. We're gon' start today, and she said you could come."

He came on in and helped around, you know, and finally he say, "I'm going upstairs now to do some work," and there the mistress was in the room, and ALL of a sudden, such a SCREAMING, "HELP!"

He ran up the stairs; he say, "What's the matter, what's the matter?" And there she was, screaming. OH, she was just out! Everybody was around, and they was holdin' him. He said, "What happened? What happened?"

So he saw 'em carry him out. He didn't even know—and he heard all this hollering, "Kill 'im, kill 'im, kill 'im!"

So he say, "What happened, what happened? He just said he was gonna help me." So he got near him and whispered, "Man, what happened? What happened? What happened up there?"

He say, "I ran my hand up Ole Missis' dress."

He say, "Man, didn't you have better sense 'n that? You fool!"

He say, "Well, you said you ran your hand up her dress."

He say, "Yeah, man, but those dresses were hanging behind the door!"

84. The Irishman and the Moon

In older humorous tales, Irishmen often are stereotyped as fools; here, in what are sometimes told as two separate tales, they blunder in more than one way. AT 1287 + 1336.

Once upon a time there were ten Irishmen who were always on the lookout for something to eat. One bright moonlight night they took a walk by the side of a river, and the greediest one of all espied the reflection of the moon in the water and he thought it was cheese. So he said to his companions, "Faith, boys, there's green cheese! Let's get it."

The others answered, "Sure an' we will, if you kin find some way for us to reach it."

No sooner said than done. He made a leap into the air and caught hold of the bough of a tree which stood near by, and bade the rest of them make a long line by swinging one on to the other's feet until the man at the end could reach what they thought was cheese. The weight was more than the first man could stand, so he thought he would lighten up by letting go his hold long enough to rest his hands, being perfectly ignorant of what would happen if he did so. Of course they all fell pell-mell into the river and stirred up the water so much that when they did manage to crawl out they could not see the reflection of the moon. Then they all declared that the last fellow had stolen the cheese and gone.

To see whether they were all there, after everyone denied taking the cheese, they thought that they should be counted, so the very cleverest one of all stood the rest in a row and began to count. Instead of counting from one to ten and including himself either as first or last, he only said, "Me myself, one, two, three, etc.," and the consequence was that he only counted nine. He repeated this for sometime, and getting tired of it and calling it a slow way to find out the thief, they all got little twigs, and forming themselves in a row, each one stuck a hole in the ground with his twig. After this was done, they took turns to count the holes and at last really saw that all ten were still there. As to where the cheese went they never could tell, and they lamented for weeks afterward over the lost piece of green cheese.

85. The Girl Who Died of Fright

More chilling than other tales in the section, where humor is more the intent, this Illinois story uses irony to build toward pathos and perhaps pity. AT 1676B.

One time there was a girl who said she didn't believe in haints. She said she wouldn't be afraid to go to a graveyard at night by herself. They told her she'd better not, but she claimed she wasn't afraid. Some one dared her to go. One evening about dark she started.

As the girl got close to the graveyard, she began to have a creepy feelin.' By the time she got to the cemetery she was about scared to death, but she went on in. She decided that she'd stick a stick in a grave to prove to them that she'd been to the graveyard.

She hunted around and found a stick and went up to a grave for to put it in as proof. But when she went to job [jab] it in the ground, she got her apron underneath the point of the stick. It jerked her down, and she thought a ghost had reached up out of the grave and was pullin' her in. It scared her so bad that she just dropped over dead right there.

Next morning her folks got uneasy about her not comin' home, and they got out to lookin' for her, and they found her lyin' across a grave with her apron pinned under a stick that she'd stuck in the ground.

I guess maybe the sudden scare caused her to have heart-failure. Anyhow she was scared of ghosts.

---

86. Talking Turtle

Julia Courtney, Pine Bluff, Arkansas, told this story in June 1953 to folklorist Richard M. Dorson. Motif B210.2.

Every day John had to tote water from the bayou, and every time he'd go to the bayou he would start fussin'. "I'm tired of toting water every day." The next day he went to the bayou and he repeated the same thing (you know just like you repeat the same thing). So last one day John went to the bayou, the turtle was sitting on a log.

Turtle raised up and looked at him, and told John, "Black man, you talk too much."

So John didn't want to think the turtle was talking. He went back to the bayou, got another bucketful of water. The turtle told him the same thing. John threw the buckets down, took and run to the house, and called Old Marster, and told him the turtle was down there talking. And so Old Marster didn't want to go because he didn't believe it. But John kept telling him the turtle was talking. So finally Old Boss 'cided he could go. But he told John if the turtle didn't talk he was going to give him a good beating. So they all went on down to the bayou, and when they got down to the bayou the turtle was sitting on a log with his head halfway in his shell.

And so John told the turtle, "Tell Old Marster what you told me." So John begged the turtle to talk. So the turtle still didn't say anything. So Old Marster taken him on back to the house, and give him a good beating, and made him git his buckets, and keep totin' water.

When John got back down to the bayou, the turtle had his head sticking up. John dipped up his water, and the turtle raised up and told him, says, "Black man, didn't I tell you you talked too much."

"Trick" Tales and Parodies

By their very nature folktales are highly stylized and formulaic, and their conventions are very recognizable. Hence they are easily parodied; they have been parodied in jokes, in cartoons, and recently in children's books. But parody is not lacking in the repertoires of oral tale-tellers themselves, and "The Toadfrog" and "Three Wishes" are indeed parodies of popular magic tale motifs. Such stories play with the expectations of listeners and then trick them. But other folktales work with other kinds of "tricks." "Between a Mountain Lion and a Grizzly" is a kind of practical joke perpetrated on the listener, and so is "The Lonely Old Man," a story that would scare a listener in more ways than one because the teller lunges toward the listener at the climax. Cumulative tales like "Johnny-Cake" engage in the linguistic trick of repeating the same phrases to advance the plot; telling such a story requires a certain agility of memory.

87. The Lonely Old Man

A *wampus,* who figures here, is a fearsome, fictitious creature. AT 366.

Once there was an old man who lived alone. He was roasting potatoes in the fireplace, and when he went to roll them out of the ashes, he noticed that one of them looked like a human toe. He ate the others first, but he was still hungry, so finally he ate the one that looked like a toe. When he'd finished eating it, he heard a voice outside saying, "Where's my big toe? Where's my big toe?" He went outside, but he didn' see anything, so he come on back in the house, and again he heard a voice saying, "Where's my big toe? Where's my big toe?" He went out again and saw a wampus sitting on the chimney top, with shiny eyes, sharp claws and teeth, and a long tail. The old man asked the wampus, "What are those shiny eyes for?"

"To look you through," replied the wampus.

"And what are those sharp claws for?"

"To scratch your grave."

"What is that long tail for?"

"To sweep your grave."

"And what are those sharp teeth for?"

"To chomp your bones!" said the wampus as he jumped on the poor old man. [The teller jumps at the listener to scare him as he utters these last words.]

88. Johnny-Cake

Fanny D. Bergen, who made a number of contributions to the *Journal of American Folklore* in the late nineteenth century, recollected this story from her childhood in Ohio. A johnny-cake is made on a griddle out of corn meal. AT 2025.

Once upon a time, there was an old man, and an old woman, and a little boy. One morning the old woman made a Johnny-cake and put it in the oven to bake. And she said to the little boy, "You watch the Johnny-cake while your father and I go out to work in the garden." So the old man and old woman went out and began to hoe potatoes and left the little boy to tend the oven. But he didn't watch it all the time, and all of a sudden he heard a noise and he looked up and the oven-door popped open, and out of the oven jumped Johnny-cake and went rolling along, end over end, towards the open door of the house. The little boy ran to shut the door, but Johnny-cake was too quick for him and rolled through the door, down the steps, and out into the road, long before the little boy could catch him. The little boy ran after him as fast as he could clip it, crying out to his father and mother, who heard the uproar and threw down their hoes and gave chase too. But Johnny-cake outran all three a long way and soon was out of sight, while they had to sit down, all out of breath, on a bank to rest.

On went Johnny-cake, and by and by he came to two well-diggers, who looked up from their work and called out: "Where ye going, Johnny-cake?"

He said: "I've outrun an old man, and an old woman, and a little boy, and I can outrun you too-o-o!"

"Ye can, can ye? We'll see about that!" said they, and they threw down their picks and ran after him, but they couldn't catch up with him, and soon they had to sit down by the roadside to rest.

On ran Johnny-cake, and by and by he came to two ditch-diggers, who were digging a ditch. "Where ye going, Johnny-cake?" said they.

He said: "I've outrun an old man, and an old woman, and a little boy, and two well-diggers, and I can outrun you too-o-o!"

"Ye can, can ye? We'll see about that!" said they, and they threw down their spades, and ran after him too. But Johnny-cake soon outstripped them also, and seeing they could never catch him they gave up the chase and sat down to rest.

On went Johnny-cake, and by and by he came to a bear. The bear said: "Where ye going, Johnny-cake?"

He said: "I've outrun an old man, and an old woman, and a little boy, and two well-diggers, and two ditch-diggers, and I can outrun you too-o-o!"

"Ye can, can ye?" growled the bear; "we'll see about that!" and trotted as fast as his legs could carry him after Johnny-cake, who never stopped to look behind him. Before long the bear was left so far behind that he saw he might as well give up the hunt first as last, so he stretched himself out by the roadside to rest.

On went Johnny-cake, and by and by he came to a wolf. The wolf said: "Where ye going, Johnny-cake?"

He said: "I've outrun an old man, and an old woman, and a little boy, and two well-diggers, and two ditch-diggers, and a bear, and I can outrun you too-o-o!

"Ye can, can ye?" snarled the wolf; "we'll see about that!" and he set into a gallop after Johnny-cake, who went on and on so fast that the wolf, too, saw there was no hope of catching him and lay down to rest.

On went Johnny-cake, and by and by he came to a fox that lay quietly in a corner of the fence. The fox called out in a sharp voice, but without getting up: "Where ye going, Johnny-cake?"

He said: "I've outrun an old man, and an old woman, and a little boy, and two well-diggers, and two ditch-diggers, and a bear, and a wolf, and I can outrun you too-o-o!"

The fox said: "I can't quite hear you, Johnny-cake, won't you come a leetle closer?" turning his head a little to one side.

Johnny-cake stopped his race, for the first time, and went a little closer and called out in a very loud voice: "*I've outrun an old man, and an old woman, and a little boy, and two well-diggers, and two ditch-diggers, and a bear, and a wolf, and I can outrun you too-o-o!*"

"Can't quite hear you; won't you come a *leetle* closer?" said the fox in a feeble voice, and he stretched out his neck towards Johnny-cake and put one paw behind his ear.

Johnny-cake came up close, and leaning towards the fox screamed louder than before: "I'VE OUTRUN AN OLD MAN, AND AN OLD WOMAN, AND A LITTLE BOY, AND TWO WELL-DIGGERS, AND TWO DITCH-DIGGERS, AND A BEAR, AND A WOLF, AND I CAN OUTRUN YOU TOO-O-O!"

"You can, can you?" yelped the fox, and he snapped up Mr. Johnny-cake in his sharp teeth in the twinkling of an eye.

89. Fido Is Dead (Fido est mort)

Revon Reed, Mamou, Louisiana, who was a noted student of Louisiana French folklore and culture, told this tale of Jean Sot, the foolish hero of Cajun French stories. AT 2040.

And then, the tale which makes me feel like laughing—He had gone to work for a man who had a big plantation, a big planter, a rancher. He left to go on vacation. He put Jean Sot in charge of the farm, with the servants, the blacks, and the others, and his wife and his wife's mother, his mother-in-law in other words, and he went on a vacation.

And after a week, he decided to call Jean Sot on the telephone. He called him. He said, "Uh, Jean Sot, how is everything over there?"

"Oh, sir! Everything is going very well, sir," he said. "All is well."

"Are you sure that everything is okay?"

"Well, there's just Fido," he said, "Fido is dead. The little dog."

He said, "Fido is dead?! How did he die?"

"Well, sir," he said, "he died while eating some burnt, uh, mule meat."

"Oh, no!" he said. "What happened, Jean Sot? How did this happen?"

"Well, sir," he said, "your barn caught fire. The mules couldn't get out of their stalls. They burned." He said, "Then, the little dog went and ate some of that burnt mule meat. It gave him a stomach ache, and he died."

Then, the other fellow grabbed his head on the other end of the telephone. He said, "How did the barn catch fire, imbecile? Tell me quickly!"

"Well," he said, "the barn caught fire because of the house that had caught fire before."

He said, "How did this happen, Jean Sot?"

"Well," he said, "you see, sir, your mother-in-law had a heart attack and she died suddenly and she was enshrouded with candles all around and," he said, "one of the candles ignited the curtains and, before we knew it, the house was on fire and the barn caught fire and the mule burned and Fido ate some of the burnt meat and he died. Otherwise, everything's fine."

"And what killed the poor old woman?"

He said, "Well, it's her daughter, your wife." He said, "When she found out that she had secretly run off with one of the workers on your plantation, that she had eloped with one of the servants, it killed the poor mother."

And with this, the other fellow fell into a fit. He did not know what was going on anymore. It all started with Fido who had eaten some burnt meat, but Jean Sot did not want to say too much all at once.

90. Between a Mountain Lion and a Grizzly

Mody C. Boatright wrote extensively about the folklore of Texas and the West and, in the book from which this story is drawn, created a fictional tale-telling context into which he situates the actual story as though it's being told by the cowboy character Joe to other cowboys, including one called Lanky. AT 2202.

"That puts me in mind," said he, "of a hunt I went on once in the Guadalupe Mountains. You see, we was out after big-horn sheep—used to be lots of 'em up there, but they are 'bout all gone now. Few up in the mountains where the tin-horn hunters never go.

"I was follerin' some of them critters around a ledge, and presently I looked around and seen where I was. The ledge was jest about a foot wide; and I looked down, and there was a bluff right straight down for five hundred feet, and I looked up, and there was a wall five hundred feet straight up. There wasn't no way to git off that ledge but to go on or to turn back like I come, and in some places the footin' was mighty ticklish, mighty ticklish.

"Well, I walked along till I come to a slick place, and my foot slipped, and I had to let go my gun to keep from fallin.' I shore hated to lose that thirty-thirty, too, for we had been friends for years, and many a deer and antelope I had fetched down with it. But I jest naturally lost my balance and had to let her go to save my neck.

"Well, not havin' any gun, I thought I had jest as well go back to the camp; so I started back like I come. I goes around a little bend, and there comes a mountain lion, a-creepin' along towards me, jest like a cat tryin' to slip up on a snow-bird.

"Says I, 'Joe, this ain't no place for you. I expect you'd better go on the way you first started.'

"So I turns around and goes back around the bend. When I gets about a hundred yards, there I sees a big grizzly bear comin' to meet me! And when he sees me, he sets up and shows his teeth and growls.

"Says I, 'Joe, maybe you'd better go back the other way, after all.' I thought maybe the cougar would be gone. But as soon as I gits turned around—and I had to be mighty careful in turnin', for the ledge was powerfully narrow—when I turns around, I sees the big cat sneakin' along toward me. And when I look the other way, there comes the bear. And they are both gittin' closer and closer, and there I am, and it's five hundred feet straight down, and it's five hundred feet straight up."

"How did you get off?" asked Lanky.

"How did I git off? Why, I couldn't git off. They got me, but whether it was the bear or the cougar, I never did know."

91. Three Wishes

"Three Wishes" was told by African American narrator Walter Winfrey, a retired auto worker, Inkster, Michigan, to folklorist Richard M. Dorson, who was interested in investigating black folk traditions outside the South, in the 1950s. AT 750A.

This was a cowboy, and he wanted to be a strong man. So he saddled his horse and went down the street riding along. A snake crossed the path before him, and he taken his gun out to shoot it. So the snake says, "Mr. Cowboy, don't shoot me, and I'll make you any deal that you want me to." So the cowboy says: "All right. Make me three wishes." The snake tells him, "Go ahead and wish." So the cowboy says: "I wisht I had muscles like Joe Louis. And I'd like to have features like Clark Gable." And he says, "I'd like to be as strong as this stud I'm riding."

So the snake says, "Okay, you go home, go to bed early, get up in the morning and see if you've got your wishes."

So the cowboy got up the next morning; he throwed his bathrobe back; he says, "I got the muscles like Joe Louis." He looked in the mirror, and he says, "I got the features like Clark Gable." Then he pulled his bathrobe back again and looks down. He says, "Well, I'll be durned; I forgot I was riding a mare."

92. The Toadfrog

Mary C. Parler, wife of folklore collector Vance Randolph, heard this story from a University of Arkansas student and told it to Randolph, May 1951. AT 440 (parody).

One time there was a pretty girl walking down the street, and she heard somebody say, "Hi, Toots!" But when she looked around there was nobody in sight, just a little old toadfrog setting on the sidewalk.

So then the pretty girl started to walk on down the street, and she heard somebody say, "Hello, Beautiful!" But when she looked around there was nobody in sight, just this little old toadfrog.

So then the pretty girl started to walk on down the street, and she heard somebody say, "You got anything on tonight, Baby?" But when she looked around there was nobody in sight, just this little old toadfrog setting on the sidewalk.

The pretty girl looked down at the little old toadfrog. "I know it ain't you a-talking," she says.

"It's me, all right," says the toadfrog. "I'm a handsome young man, by rights. But I'm turned into a toadfrog now, because an old witch put a spell on me."

The pretty girl studied awhile, and then she says, "Ain't there anything you can do to break the spell?"

The toadfrog says there is only one way, and that is for a pretty girl to let him sleep on her pillow all night. The pretty girl thought it was the least she could do, to help this poor fellow out. So she took the little old toadfrog home and put him on her pillow when she went to bed.

Next morning the pretty girl's father come to wake her up, and he seen a handsome young man in the bed with her. She told her father about the little old toadfrog, and the witch that put a spell on him, and how it all happened. But the old man didn't believe the story, any more than you do!

Lies and Other Tall Tales

Tall tales—sometimes called "windies" or just "lies"—are stories in which fantastic elements virtually pile on top of each other, though tellers of such tales tell them in a deadpan manner suggesting that the events are true. Thus part of the pleasure of them may lie in seeing if something can be put over on the audience of listeners. Or a listener may gravely pay attention only to come back with fantastic "lies" of his own. Although such stories were told by and about the celebrated German Baron Munchhausen and have even been found in ancient Roman writings, they have found particularly fertile soil in the United States and have been extremely popular among Americans, especially frontier and rural Americans. The fictional re-creation of storytelling found in "Carried by Buzzards" suggests something of the context of tall-tale telling, and such selections as "The Two Big Hunters" and "You Take Off Ten Pounds" indicate internally some awareness of the "lying" dynamic.

As an American folk hero, Paul Bunyan ("Paul Bunyan's Cooking Arrangements," "Paul Bunyan's Big Cow") comes out of the tall tales of the logging camps (though his considerable fame stems from mass media exploitation of his slender thread of oral tradition). And in many cases, cycles of tall tales about other protagonists stem not from fictional characters like Paul but from real people like Abraham "Oregon" Smith (who is discussed in the introduction) and Gib Morgan ("A Night in the Jungle"), who began spinning fantastic yarns about themselves that passed into more general circulation. In tall tales, human speech freezes ("Thawing Words"), mosquitoes drill through metal ("A Night in the Jungle"), and reptiles become alcoholic ("The Snake, the Frog, and the Liquor"), stretching our imaginations with the truth.

93. Carried by Buzzards

As with story 90, Texas folklorist Mody C. Boatright has created here a fictional context in which cowboys are telling each other tales, tales drawn from actual folk tradition; at this point, Red is telling one to Lanky. AT 1881.

"You see, I was ridin' back to the headquarters on a dark night. I was about half asleep, for I knowed that old Frijole—that was his name—would find the way. He always could. Well, I was ridin' along that way, when all of a sudden I finds us both fallin' down through empty space. Seemed like we never would hit the ground, and before we got bottom, I figgered out what had happened.

"Out in the edge of the Glass Mountains there was a big sink-hole right out on the mesa. It was as big across as a house, and six lariats deep right straight down—we afterwards measured it—and Frijole had loped off into that dang hole with me, and there we was makin' for the bottom.

"I thinks to myself, 'This is where you pass in your checks, Red. Some gits it early and some gits it late, but they all gits it.' Then we hits bottom.

"I guess I was shook up purty bad, for I woke up after while, and there I was settin' on a dead hoss. You see, Frijole had broke his neck landin', pore feller. I always will wonder what was a eatin' on him to make him lope off into a hole like that. Must of been somethin'.

"Well, I seen there wasn't nothin' I could do but wait for daylight and then try to figure out some way to git out; so I jist laid down and took a nap till mornin'.

"When daylight come, I got up and looked around, but the walls was straight up and down, and there wasn't nothin' I could git a-holt of to climb out. Then I took the rope off my saddle and begun to look for somethin' twenty feet or so up that I could rope, thinkin' I could pull myself up that far, and then maybe rope somethin' else a little higher up, and pull myself up again, and so on till I was out.

"But there wasn't a thing, Lanky, not a bush nor a rock, nor nothin' stickin' out I could git a loop on. Everything as slick as glass. 'Well, maybe the boys will come and hunt me.' I thinks, 'but how in the hell will they know to look down in here?'

"I waited all day, and not a soul come; and I waited all the next day, and still nobody come. The third day I was still there and no better off than I was in the beginnin.'

"By that time I was wishin' I was dead, for I had drunk all the water in my saddle canteen, and I was gittin' hungry, too."

"Couldn't you have eaten some of the horse meat?" asked Lanky.

"Yes, I guess I could of," said Red, "but at first I wouldn't out of friendship for the brute—for even if he did git me in there, I always figgered there was somethin' wrong; he went out of his head or somethin'—and after I got hungry enough to of et him, anyway, his carcass had spoiled and was stinkin' somethin' terrible. That's principally what made it so bad. Every breath I drawed was misery.

"Finally I says, 'Red, you can't stand this no longer. You'd shoot a pore dumb brute if you saw him in torment like this.' And so I cocks my six-shooter and holds it to my head, but somehow I can't pull the trigger. 'Stand it a little while longer,' I says to myself, 'and if help don't come, shoot.' I done that three or four times, I guess.

"After a while buzzards begun flyin' over the hole—dozens of 'em sailin' round and round. They knowed there was somethin' dead somewheres around, but they was havin' trouble locatin' it. They kept comin' lower and lower, till directly one comes down into the sinkhole. Then some more come, and they would fly right down close to me. 'I reckon you come after Frijole,' I says, 'but jist wait a little while and you can have me too.'

"And jist then I had an idear. I picks up my lariat right quiet-like and begins unravelin' it into little strands. In each little strand I tied a noose. Then I takes my seat by the side of the carcass and jist waits. Directly a big turkey buzzard comes right down close, and I throws a loop over his head and fetches him down. Then I stakes him to my belt, givin' him about six foot of rope. After a while I gits another one. I keeps on until I gits twenty of the vultures staked to my belt; then I fires off my six-shooter, scarin' 'em all at once.

"Well, sir, them birds jist naturally lifted me right out of that sink-hole."

"You were lucky," said Lanky.

"Lucky! Lad, that wasn't luck; that was head work. You ain't heard about my luck yet. Them buzzards begun flyin' away with me, but I seen what direction they was goin', and I jist let 'em alone and watched the lay of the land. And when they had me right over a big hay-stack at the headquarters of my own outfit, I reached down and unbuckled my belt, and damn me, if I didn't land right on the hay without any hurtin' a-tall.

"I walked up to the house and had a square meal and I et, too, I'll tell you—and then I felt as fresh and pert as ever."

"That was a lucky landing," said Lanky.

"It shore was," said Red. "I got off light. The worst thing about it was that them vultures carried off my belt; and a crackerjack it was, too, trimmed with rattlesnake hide and gold studs. Twenty-eight dollars and fifty cents it cost me over the counter at K. C., Misourey."

94. Paul Bunyan's Cooking Arrangements

This story is from a collection made by K. Bernice Stewart, who with Homer A. Watt published in 1916 the first group of stories about Paul Bunyan; she heard such stories in the lumber camps of Wisconsin and Michigan. These tales were usually told in the evening around a fire, and older narrators told them in a "French-Canadian dialect." A *forty* is a section of forest. Motifs X1031.1, X1031.4, X1031.7(i).

Bunyan's crew was so large that he was obliged to divide the men into three gangs; of these one was always going to work, one was always at work, and the third was always coming home from work. The cooking arrangements for so many men were naturally on an immense scale. Seven men with seven wheel-barrows were kept busy wheeling the prune stones away from camp. The cook-stove was so extensive that three forties had to be cleared each week to keep up a fire, and an entire cord of wood was needed to start a blaze. One day as soon as the cook had put a loaf of bread in the oven he started to walk around the stove in order to remove the loaf from the other side, but long before he reached his destination the bread was burned to a crisp. Such loaves were, of course, gigantic—so big, in fact, that after the crew had eaten the insides out of them, the hollow crusts were used for bunk-houses.

95. Paul Bunyan's Big Cow

This Bunyan tale was recorded from the narration of Perry Allen by Alan Lomax, perhaps the most famous of all American folklorists, though he is best known for his collections of folksong and folk music. Here Allen has just told about Bunyan's having acquired his great blue ox, Babe, and now goes on to tell of another huge beast who plays a role in the Bunyan cycle. Motifs B871.1.1(d), X1203(b), X1235(e).

Well, he heard tell of a big cow down in Vermont that measured that ox for size, the ox bein' six ax-handles between the eyes, the cow was recommended to be equally as large. So he got in touch with 'em down there, and he made a deal for the cow. . . .

Well, she'd a proved to be a great record milker, but he turned her out on evergreens, chestnuts, evergreen boughs and balsam boughs, and the milk got so strong, they couldn't use it for the table . . . so he started to get to makin' butter—uh—he had no storehouse. They tell about makin' a ton of butter a day, piled it up, near camp. And the boys wondered what he was going to do with so much of that butter piled up outdoors there. You know he was askin' the men a question gettin' no decided answer, they just kept pilin' that butter. Finally—uh—finally the ice and snow went off, and, he used that butter for to grease his loggin' roads and it enabled him to run his loggin' sleighs all summer.

96. The Peach Tree Deer

Emma Robinson heard this story told by her grandfather, David Beswick, and it comes from a manuscript written by her but traces back in oral tradition to locally renowned tall-tale teller Abraham "Oregon" Smith, who is discussed in the introduction. AT 1889C.

One day while out walking, I saw a deer standing looking at me from the edge of a clearing. I happened to have my gun with me; and when I put my hands in me pocket for a bullet, there warn't none. All I could find was a peach seed—small one at that. Well I pulled up and shot at that deer, but it wheeled and ran away.

About a year later I was on my way back to the states and thought I'd pass through that same clearing in hopes of finding my deer again. I was just about through the opening, and I saw the nicest peach tree just loaded with peaches. Well, now, I climbed up in the tree and started eating as all I had in me pack was cold corn bread and salt pork. Right in the middle of a bite I'll be gum if that peach tree didn't get up and run off in the forest with me. I looked down and there was the peach tree growing out of the head of the deer I had shot a year ago.

97. Thawing Words

This story is told about Bill Greenfield, the hero of a cycle of tall tales in upstate New York; it was narrated by Peleg W. Andrew of Corinth, New York, and published by Harold Thompson, who collected much New York state folklore. AT 1889F.

Everything that Bill experienced was remarkable, especially the weather. One time when he was hunting it got so cold that every morning he had to pound up the air so he could breathe it. Outside the camp he had a saw with twenty-one teeth to the inch—and that should have been fine enough to escape destruction—but the wintry wind blew all the teeth out of the saw. One day Bill froze his feet and hastened to plunge them into a bucket of water to thaw them out. This should have been effective, but he hadn't realized how far the frost had gone. "Well, sir," said Bill, "my feet was so cold, a inch of ice come on top of that water quicker'n you could count two." But Bill recovered in time to go hunting soon after with Abner, his father. They didn't want any more frozen feet; so they set a stump afire to warm themselves, but the cold was still so intense that the blaze, forty feet high, froze in a column. Abner went into a cave to get warm. He tried to talk, but no words came; so, after a pull at a bottle, he and Bill went home. On the next Fourth of July, Bill happened to go into that same cave again, when he was startled to hear Abner's words, just thawing out of the air, saying, "Here, Bill, have a drink."

98. Leading Blind Hogs

"Leading Blind Hogs" was included by Sue Gates in her 1938 collection of tall tales from Texas. AT 1889A.

Once back in the days when hogs were hogs and ran wild, a sort of disease came through the country and blinded nearly all the hogs. That fall the acorn crop was good and the hogs got rolling fat. One old grandma sow, who could see, figured out a system for leading the hogs to water. She had them form in a line, each hog taking the tail of the hog in front of him. The first hog took hold of Grandma's tail, and she led the whole lot to water and to the places where the acorns were.

Now there was a young fellow living about who was just itching to steal a hog. One day he saw the old sow leading the string of hogs through the woods. He cut off her tail and held it in his hand. Well, the hogs followed him, and he led the whole bunch off and sold them for ten dollars apiece.

99. The Two Big Hunters

"Chatoui" Wiltz Gutierrez, Delacroix, Louisiana, who told this story, was a member of the community of Isleños, Spanish-speaking descendants of Canary Islanders who settled in Louisiana's St. Bernard Parish, but he told this tale in French to folklorist Calvin Claudel in 1935. AT 1890 + 1890A + 1890E.

Two hunters once met in the woods while they were out hunting with their guns.

"Good day," greeted the first hunter to the second hunter, while he sat down on a log. "How has luck been with you today?"

"Oh, not so good," answered the second hunter. "And what have you killed?"

Now the second hunter knew that the first hunter was well known for his tales about how great a hunter he was and about how much game he had killed.

"Yesterday you should have seen what I killed," began the first hunter. "I had only one shell left. I saw a turtle on a log in the bayou. Well, I shot at the turtle's head, killed her and the shot glanced off her head, hitting and killing her, likewise a rabbit that was hopping by on the opposite bank. So I had turtle and rabbit meat, all I could eat."

"That's nothing," added the second hunter. "Last week I was walking in the marsh, out duck hunting. I came upon a pond where there were thousands of ducks. There were so many ducks on this pond that I could not see the water at all. I wanted to kill as many ducks as I could in one shot; because I knew when I'd shoot, the rest would fly away. I'd aim this way and that way, but I could not sight all the ducks at once. So this is what I did: I broke my gun into a circle on my knee." At this point the hunter showed how he broke his gun by breaking it across his knee, so that the mouth of the gun was pointing back at him. "This way," continued the second hunter, "I was able to aim all around the pond. I shot and killed every single duck."

"Well that was pretty good," spoke up the first hunter, "but I am sure I did better than that the week before. I was walking through the back part of the woods. . . . You know, the part right back there. Well suddenly I came upon a tree, a limb of which was covered with a row of birds. I aimed at them, just below the feet. The shot split the limb as it passed through. This happened so fast, that the birds were unable to move and fly away. All of them, about fifty, got caught by the feet into the crack of the limb as it sprang open and closed again. I went up and caught the birds, putting them into my bag one by one.

"Now I noticed that this was a red oak tree. I looked up and saw a coon sitting on a limb. As soon as I saw him, he ran inside the hollow of the tree through a hole right by me. Then I noticed the tree was swelling out, back and forth, just as when one breathes. It went like this: 'Huh, hum; huh, hum.' 'This can't be possible that a tree is breathing,' said I to myself. I looked more closely, and I saw coon fur sticking out through a crack. Then I saw thousands of other coons inside. I tapped the tree, and they began to breathe all the harder and all at the same time. The crack would open several inches and close again. The red oak must have had sides about four feet thick, with about a twenty-foot hollow across and so tall I couldn't see the top. Then the coons started to come out through the hole one at a time, and I'd kill each one as he came out. I killed so many that I had to go get my mules and wagon to haul them home. Besides the furs, you can imagine how much coon meat I had."

100. The Stretching Harness

Although reprinted in a folklore journal, this story—in a journalistic style of the day—originally appeared in 1833 in a Boston newspaper. AT 1917.

An elderly gentleman of unimpeached veracity, though, by the way, somewhat addicted to story telling, relates the following. During the early days of this town, before carts came into vogue, he was accustomed to haul his wood by the aid of an old black mare, kept in his service. Now the old mare's harness consisted of a breast plate, and traces, made of the untanned hide of an ox. At the close of a rainy day, he went to his wood lot, situated some forty or fifty rods from his dwelling, for the purpose of procuring a load of wood. After having cut a log which he judged might be a smart load for his beast, he fastened her to one end, set her head toward home, and gave her the rein. The old mare continued her course until she arrived at his door, when, to his surprise, he discovered that owing to the great extensibility of the traces, they had stretched the whole distance, without breaking or moving the load an inch. Throwing down his axe, he went to his beast, and removing the harness from her, threw the breast plate over a post that stood near the door, and went to bed. Upon rising the next morning, he found the heat of the morning sun had so operated on the contractibility of the traces, as to bring his wood up to the door, ready fir hewing and splitting.

101. Liars' Contest: Speed

Folklorist Herbert Halpert, in uniform during World War II but researching folk-lore at military bases in Alaska, Canada, and a U.S. Army school in Virginia, collected this story from a young warrant officer, Harry K. Young. AT 1920C*.

Well, there were two men arguing about how fast they were and to prove his point one of them said he went out to the well to draw a bucket of water. And as he started away from the well, the bottom of the bucket dropped out. He ran to his house, got another bucket and caught the water before it hit the ground.

And the other one said that he'd been out hunting. He shot a deer and skinned and dressed it and had it hanging up in his meat house at home before the bullet left the end of the gun.

102. The Snake, the Frog and the Liquor

"Slick" MacQuoid, Wilton, Maine, in his early forties at the time Richard M. Dorson collected this story from him, was employed to tell tales at a summer camp for girls. Motif X1321.4.4.2*.

Earl Sawyer here can tell you about a real surprising thing that happened to us on a fishing trip. It was up at Lake Mooselockmeguntic, and the general law had been taken off bait so we could use anything—worms, smelt or anything. But we only had flies, so we looked around for a frog, and saw a black snake swimming carrying one half-devoured in his mouth. We netted the snake, and pried the frog out of its jaws, and cut it up for bait. The snake kept following us with its jaws open the way they had been when carrying the frog; Earl felt sorry for it and poured a little liquor down its throat. Well, we had pretty good luck with the frog bait and in about an hour it was all gone. Earl said, "Lord, I wish we had another frog," and began looking around for one, when he felt a tugging at his trouser leg—and there was that snake back with another frog.

103. A Fish Story

Although sometimes associated with Anglo-Celtic rural America, tall tales are an international genre and are told by the members of various ethnic groups. This story was collected by Ruth Ann Musick, who recorded oral narratives from the members of a number of American ethnic groups in West Virginia (where many of them were involved in coal mining). It comes from Hungarian American narrator John Tokay of Carolina, West Virginia, who told it in 1959; he had heard it in Hungarian from his grandmother. AT 1960B.

Oto was a big, strapping man, who was said to be the strongest man in the land. There was nothing that the mighty Oto could not conquer.

One day a traveling man came by Oto's village and told of a great fish in his own country—a fish that no one could catch.

On hearing this, Oto saw a new challenge, and started out for the traveler's country. When he reached the land where the great fish was, he went to the blacksmith's shop and told the blacksmith to get a ship's anchor and sharpen the edges of it. He then went out and bought a cable an inch thick. He returned to the blacksmith's shop and tied the cable to the anchor. For bait, he used two twenty-pound turkeys and placed them on the giant hook.

Oto went to the river where the fish lived. The river was a mile across at this place, and, according to reports, the fish was so large that he needed a mile to turn around in.

Oto grabbed his hook and, with a mighty heave, threw it into the river; not realizing his strength, however, he threw too hard, and it landed on the far bank in a pigpen. Two large pigs saw the turkeys and tried to eat them, but they too were caught on the hook. Oto began pulling in the line for another toss, but while he was pulling the hook across the river, the giant fish grabbed the hook, and the battle was on.

Oto fought the fish for a week without either of them weakening. Finally, waiting until it leaped out of the water, he jumped on its back and began riding it like a horse. The fish bucked like a wild stallion, but it couldn't shake Oto.

The fish, now desperate, gave a mighty leap, and went so high that both it and Oto froze to death. When they landed, the people of the village, with the help of a number of trains, hauled the fish to the north country, so it wouldn't spoil. They put Oto up as a statue in the middle of the square of the new town they built.

The people then took out all the hooks with which unsuccessful fishermen had tried to catch the fish, and there were over a ton of them. Afterward, they removed the scales and sold them for sailboats. On the inside of the fish they built a cannery, and to this day they are canning the meat, and still have more than half of it left.

104. A Night in the Jungle

Gib Morgan (sometimes called Gid or Gil Morgan) is the hero of a cycle of tall tales connected to the oil industry. He was a real person (1842–1909) in the pioneer days of oil drilling and, as with other Munchhausen figures, the tales originated in his own yarn-spinning about his fantastic exploits. AT 1960M.

Gib had hardly got back to the United States from the Fiji Islands when Standard Oil of New Jersey hired him to go down to South America and put down some wells. It was wildcat territory down there, and they didn't know what was under the ground, but they said they were in the oil business and if he struck anything else like bay rum or Hoyt's Eau de Cologne, he was to case it off and go on after the oil.

Gib disobeyed his orders just a little bit, but if he hadn't, he never would have got down to the oil.

When he got to the first location, he found that they had driven the green stake right out in the middle of a jungle. They had put up a bunkhouse, but they hadn't screened it, and as it turned out screens would have done no good anyway. The first night the mosquitoes were so bad that Gib and his crew couldn't sleep. They built a smudge and tried to smoke the critters out, but it did more harm than good. For they saw the smoke and came from miles away just to see what it was, and when they got there they went to work on Gib and his crew. All the men were grumbling and threatening to leave, and Gib felt like throwing up the job himself. But he never had quit a job and he didn't want to start it now.

He began looking around for an idea. Then he thought of the two thirty-thousand-barrel oil tanks they had brought along for storage. He got the crew together and went to work setting one of them up. They didn't bother about the bottom. They just riveted the walls together and put the roof on. Then they got in it. Presently they began to hear something that sounded like musket balls glancing off the steel walls of the tank.

"Storms come up mighty quick down here," said the tool dresser on the grave-yard tour. "Listen to that hail."

"Not so fast, brother," said Gib. "Look at those walls and tell me what you see."

"Mosquito bills," said the tool dresser on the graveyard tour.

Then they all knew what was happening. The big mosquitoes were backing off and diving against the oil tank and ramming their bills right through it.

"Every man grab a hammer," yelled Gib, and picked up one himself and began bradding bills. Every time a mosquito bill came through, somebody was sure to clinch it.

This went on for an hour and a half until the walls of the tank were so thick with bradded mosquito bills that you couldn't put your hand on it without touching one. The critters on the outside were beating their wings and buzzing till they sounded like a hurricane in the Caribbean Sea. Presently they just naturally lifted that oil tank right up in the air and flew off with it.

105. "Jeez, the Mosquitoes Was Thick"

Folklorist Robert Bethke studied the folklore of the Adirondacks region of upstate New York, recording this story. AT 1960M.

I went fishin' up on the Jordan once. We went up there and we pitched a tent. We was goin' to stay overnight. Got in the tent, and I think all the mosquitoes that was up there was in the tent. So I got out and laid right out on the knoll, out there in the woods. And it got daylight, and I started down for the brook. Well, I'll tell ya—of all the black flies and all the times I've ever been in the woods, that was the worst. It was just so thick that when you walked through you'd leave a path. And you just couldn't see. I said, "This is the end of this thing." We quit fishin' right there!

Well, I was down at the camp one night. Jeez, the mosquitoes was thick. And I opened the camp door and I heard this commotion out there. It was two mosquitoes out there talkin'. One mosquito said to the other, "Shall we eat him here or take him down to the swamp?"

The other one said, "Jeez, we'd better eat him here. If we take him down to the swamp all the big ones will take him away from us!"

106. Turnip and Kettle

"Turnip and Kettle" was told by Fred Hunter, Bloomington, Indiana, June 26, 1948, and was included by folklorist William Hugh Jansen in his doctoral dissertation on Abraham "Oregon" Smith, the tall-tale teller and the protagonist of a cycle of tales told in Indiana and Illinois. These stories are often about Smith's doings in Oregon (where the historical Smith spent time in the nineteenth century). For a discussion of Smith, see the introduction; see also story 96. AT 1920.

One day he was telling a drummer about Oregon, how they grew turnips out there. He'd gone out one spring and planted his turnip seed, one to a field. One seed right in the middle of the field. He built a rail fence around each field. Three days later, he thought he'd go out and see how his turnips was coming. They'd growed so big they'd pushed the rail fence down. The drummer didn't say anything, just said he'd been down to Jeffersonville prison and they was making a big kittle there, biggest kittle he'd ever seen. Said the worker on the other side was so far away he couldn't hear his hammer. Abe said, "What in hell they want with such a big kittle?" Drummer said, "To cook your turnips in."

107. "You Take Off Ten Pounds . . ."

Folklorist Richard M. Dorson had this story from Maine storyteller "Slick" MacQuoid, who also told story 102; Dorson considered MacQuoid a "master narrator." AT 1920H*.

Two fishermen met at the Parker House in Boston and started to talk about their luck. One said he had caught a twenty pound salmon in Mooselookmeguntic [Lake]. The other said that the year before he had been out night fishing and the lantern fell out of the boat. A couple of months later he was trolling and felt a heavy tug at the line, and pulled up the lantern—still lit.

"Come now, you don't expect me to believe that," said the first fisherman.

"You take off ten pounds and I'll put out the light."

Some Other Humorous Tales

Americans of course have no monopoly on telling humorous stories, but humorous stories are certainly central to the American corpus of oral narratives. Today the short modern joke with its quick punchline is a staple. But there is also a wide variety of older humorous stories, as can be seen in many other sections of this book. A miscellany of more such tales is given here. "The Yank Reunion," from the Ozarks, takes a somewhat cynically humorous look at North–South relations after the Civil War. "The Coon-Monkey" is an almost epic Georgia tale of hunting gone wrong. In the African American "Saying Grace," a novice hunter gets into trouble while the story also—like the preacher stories given elsewhere—gently pokes fun at religion too. "What Madeline Done" is ever so slightly off-color and lampoons both sex and spiritualism. "The Longest Tale" laughs at storytelling itself.

108. The Yank Reunion

This story was narrated by Farwell Gould, Pittsburgh, Kansas, to Ozarks region folklorist Vance Randolph, June 1929; he had heard the story in the Ozarks around 1880. The G.A.R., the Grand Army of the Republic, was the organization of Civil War veterans who had served in the Union armies. Motifs J1250, J1350, J1440.

One time the G.A.R. boys had a big reunion in our town, and there was old soldiers come from all over the country. Most of them was getting along in years, and there was lots of white whiskers a-blowing around. But every man had a little copper badge in his buttonhole, and lots of 'em wore blue coats with brass buttons. And every once in a while you would see a black hat with crossed sabers on the front, like they used to wear in the Yankee cavalry.

There was a few old soldiers had money to spend, but lots of them was busted. The folks that run the saloons and sporting houses would be glad to kick their ass right out in the street, but they was afraid to do it. Them old soldiers claimed if it wasn't for the Federal Army the whole country would have been ruined, so the people would be living in caves to this day, without nothing to eat only wild onions. It was as much as a man's life is worth to lay a finger on a veteran. He would just holler "Hog up! Hog up!" and more old soldiers would come a-running, to bust everything in the place. They wrecked the Red Onion Saloon, and smashed them big mirrors that cost seven hundred dollars. When some old fool lost his wallet at Blanche Tucker's whorehouse they swarmed in like hornets, and set the beds afire, and run the girls right out in their shirttail. They'd have burnt the house plumb down, if the firemen hadn't got there just in the nick of time.

Things looked so bad that lots of the businessmen just boarded up their store windows. The best people in town was mostly Southerners, and they just stayed in their houses. They locked the doors, and kept the children home from school. The only good thing about the reunion was that it only lasted three days. By that time the old soldiers was mostly sick and wore out, so pretty near all of 'em had went home.

On the fourth morning there was just one left, and he was a cripple. He'd got one leg shot off in the war, and his left arm was gone. His face was all scarred up, with a black patch over one eye. He set on the sidewalk in front of the First State Bank, and held out his big black hat with the crossed sabers on it. People was putting nickels and dimes in the hat, so the old soldier could get back to Iowa or wherever it was he come from.

Pretty soon old Colonel Fordyce walked out of the bank. He pulled out his wallet, and put a five-dollar bill in the hat. "Thank you, Comrade," says the old soldier. "Seems to me I seen you somewheres. Wasn't you a sergeant in the Ioway First?" Old Fordyce threw his shoulders back and turned red in the face. "No, sir!" says he. "I rode with Forrest's cavalry."

The crippled man looked at him kind of funny. "Mister," says he, "my own people give me nickels and dimes, or sometimes a quarter. But this is the first help I ever got from a Confederate. Would you mind telling me how-come you throwed in that five-dollar bill?" Colonel Fordyce grinned. "Not at all, sir. The sight of you does my old heart good. You're the only Yank in this town that's trimmed up to suit me." And with that Colonel Fordyce walked down the street.

The old soldier just set there awhile, but he didn't say nothing. And pretty soon he got onto the northbound train, and that is the end of the story.

109. What Madeline Done

J. E. Dunwoody, Clinton, Iowa, heard this story around 1900 in McDonald County, Missouri, and relayed it to folklorist Vance Randolph in 1951. Randolph published many volumes of tales from the Ozarks but saved stories he thought would be found obscene or at least off-color, like this one, for a single volume he did not publish until 1976, in culturally more liberal times. Motif X700.

One time there was a woman named Madeline that showed up missing, and nobody knowed what become of her. Somebody seen her in the Antlers Hotel, and maybe she run off with old Colonel Baker, because the colonel is pretty well fixed. But when Madeline's sister heard about it, she begun to holler that somebody must have murdered Madeline, and hid the corpse. She wanted the sheriff to arrest Colonel Baker, but the sheriff won't do it because they haven't got no evidence. And nobody knowed where the colonel is at, anyhow.

Madeline's sister believed in spirits, and she says they are always a-rapping on tables. Sometimes a table will raise right up off'n the floor, even if a fellow that weighed two hundred pounds is trying to hold it down. So Madeline's sister rented a room at the same hotel, and there was a writing table in it. She got some other people that believe in spirits, and the whole bunch set down with their hands on the table. They kept asking the spirits what has become of Madeline, but there wasn't no answer for a long time.

Finally they could feel the table move a little. Somebody says, "Is Madeline dead?" and the table give a loud rap that means "No." Then Madeline's sister says, "Was she in this hotel?" and the table give two loud raps which means "Yes."

Pretty soon Madeline's sister says, "Was she here with Colonel Baker?" The table jumped a foot high, and give two raps the loudest you ever heard. So then she says, "What did Madeline do?" The table just flopped plumb over so its legs was sticking up, and the drawers flew open!

The fellow that works on the newspaper laughed like a fool. The rest of them people just set there goggle-eyed for a minute, and then they got up and went home. The story don't say what happened after that.

110. The Coon-Monkey

"The Coon-Monkey" was told by Allan Womble, August 17, 1972, to Georgia folklorist Mariella Glenn Hartsfield. Motifs X1124, X1232, X1232(b)*; cf X1211(bb), X1215.b(a)*.

This fellow had a coon-monkey. What he done, he was down here in Florida and he'd trained monkeys to work with the coonhounds. He was up here in north Georgia delivering, and he had the coon-monkey in the cab of the truck with him. He stopped to get gas at this station, and the owner said, "Hey, what you got there?"

Said, "That's a coon-monkey."

"Coon-monkey!?"

"Yeah, he works with the coonhounds and they are good. I mean all coon hunters should have one."

The owner said, "Hey fellow, what does the monkey do?"

"Well, he helps the dog get the coon out of the tree. Where you got a lot of Spanish moss, oh, you just don't beat them now. They're it. You couldn't hardly do without them."

"Well, look, I got a couple of dogs, and I'm interested."

He said, "Are you?"

"Yeah, I'll train them and sell them. Look, if you ain't in no big hurry, I'd love for you to stay over for a couple hours. We got plenty of coons, and we have trouble about getting them out of the tree. I'd like to see them work."

The coon-monkey's owner said, "Well, okay, I could put on a demonstration."

He said, "Well, come on, let's go to the house and eat supper, and we'll go down to the river there and see them work."

So they went and had supper and took off to the river; sure 'nuff, they turned the dogs loose and in a few minutes they'd treed a coon. This fellow unleashed his monkey, reached in his pocket, and give him a .38; he said, "Go git him." Right up that tree the coon-monkey went and—"pow!"—the coon hit the ground. The monkey come down. The man said, "That's his job."

Fellow said, "Good! Now, doggone, this is something. I'm telling you this is something. But I got a neighbor that's got some dogs." And he said, "You got the monkey sold?"

He said, "Yeah."

"Well, look, did you tell him when you was gonna bring the monkey?"

He said, "No."

"Well, let me have this one. I really want him. Sell this one to me and bring him another one. I got a neighbor over there that's got some dogs, and I want him to see this monkey work."

"All right. I hate to do the man that-a-way, though. I get $100 for the monkey."

The other man said, "I'll give you $150 and you just leave him with me and go and bring him another one."

"Well, in that case I might just do that." So he did. He said, "Now one thing. I was about to forget that. I'm selling them so fast and training them so fast, but there's nothing perfect; if anything, anything at all goes wrong, here's my phone number—you call me. I'll correct it."

"Okay, that's good enough, good enough."

So he left the monkey and went on back to Florida. Training more monkeys, you know.

The other man's neighbor come down the next day, and the man said, "Hey, I got a coon-monkey, boy. Now this here is out of this world."

"Now what's he do?" the neighbor asked.

"He climbs the tree and gets us the coon. Just like that. Now if you want to, we'll get your dogs and go try them out tonight."

The neighbor said, "Good, I want to see that."

So he said, "Now my boy is going to be using my dogs. We'll take your dogs, and I'll carry the monkey. We'll go over there where the Spanish moss is. I really want you to see how this baby here works."

That night, they went a way up the river where the Spanish moss was; they turned the dogs out, and they run, barking and a-running, barking and a-running, and barking and a-running for about thirty or forty minutes, until they'd settled on one tree. The man took the leash off the monkey, reached in his back pocket, and handed him the .38. Up the tree he went. He stayed up in the tree about five minutes. They shined the light up there a little bit, and they seen the monkey pass out of that tree into another one. The man said, "Well, that's unusual." Stayed up there about three or four minutes, and he'd pass out of that tree into another one. He went into three or four or five trees around there and come back down. Walked up to the neighbor's best coon dog and—"pow!"—shot him and killed him! He said, "Oh, my God! What has gone wrong with that fool monkey! My goodness, nothing like this, nothing like this. But he give me the phone number to call him. Let's run back to the station; I'll call him now. Man, he's done killed your best dog."

He got on long distance, and he called the man that was training the monkey. He said, "Hey, something done gone wrong up here."

"What's that?"

"I'm the guy that you sold the monkey to."

He said, "Yeah?"

"We took him out tonight, and he went up a tree and stayed fifteen or twenty minutes, passing around from one tree to another one up there, and come down and shot my neighbor's best dog."

"Oh, by heck," he said, "I forgot to tell you that. Now if there's anything that that monkey hates worse than a coon, it's a lying dog! There wasn't no coon up there."

---

111. Saying Grace

From the African American stories Daryl Cumber Dance recorded, this one was told by a narrator in Charles City, Virginia, March 18, 1975. Motifs X584, X1221, X1221(bb), X1221(bc); cf X434.2.

This fellow wanted to learn how to hunt, see. He heard about the hunting out in the country. He wanted to learn how to hunt, and he wanted to learn how to hunt bears. And they gave him a book, see, and he went to every class, and he learned how to handle the gun, and how to do everything else—how to hunt bears. And he finished the twelve lessons that he was supposed to have, and then he went on out bear hunting.

And he went on out in the woods and—he had his gun, you know, and everything, and after a while, he walked and walked and walked. And after a while he ran up on this big . . . black . . . grizzly bear. So he did what the instructions said. He thought back in his mind just what he had learned in school. The instructions say, "When you see a bear, get down on your knees"—you know!—"and put your arms on your shoulder, and raise the gun up like this [illustrating the manner of putting the gun in position to take aim and to shoot] and take aim, and then shoot." So he got down on his knees and put the elbow on his knee, and put the gun up there and pulled the trigger . . . and the gun just *clicked*. Didn't nothing happen. The gun just clicked. So he pulled the trigger again, and the gun just clicked. He had forgot to put the bullets in the gun. So the bear came on up closer—the bear got right up to him. And he didn't have nothing else in the book to go by, so he just, in his own mind, he decided to get down on his knees and pray.

And he prayed. He said, "Oh, Lord. There's the old bear. I know he must be a Christian bear. Lord, take care o' me. I know this must be a Christian bear. Brother Christian bear, I *know* you just wouldn't eat me." His eyes closed, down there on his knees praying. He got up and looked up, and the bear was on his knees praying. And he looked. And after a while, when the Bear got up off his knees, he looked at him. He say, "Brother Bear, what you doing?"

The bear say, "What *you* doing?"

He say, "I was praying."

The bear say, "You mighta been praying, but I was just saying my grace."

---

112. The Longest Tale

James Taylor Arms collected "The Longest Tale" from John Edwards, St. Paul, Virginia, December 23, 1941; Edwards heard his grandfather, also named John Edwards, tell it around 1890. AT 2301.

One time there was a king who offered his daughter to the man that would tell him the longest tale. The girl was very beautiful and would be the queen [when] her father died. So a lot of young men tried making up long tales. Dozens and dozens of them went in and told the king a tale. At last there came in a boy from the backwoods country and he started in telling his tale. Said that there once was a rich landlord and he built a big granary to horde his rents in wheat in. He had it full and to overflowing, but a locust gnawed through and got a grain, then it went in and got another grain and another grain and another grain and another grain and another grain. "Stop," said the king, "is that all you are going to tell?" "Sure," said the boy. "That's all the locust done. Just one grain after another. Won't you let me go on and finish the tale. He's only got out a few grains now, and the granary has thousands of bushels you know?" "No," said the king. "I've heard a plenty. Go ahead and take my daughter."

Religious Tales

Sometimes close to legends in their aspect, religious tales evoke reverence and sometimes awe at the power of the divine. Those included here come ultimately from Mediterranean Catholic tradition.

113. The Family That Had Lost the Little Girl (La famille qu'avait perdu la petite fille)

This story was told in French by Évélia Boudreaux, Carencro, Louisiana. AT 769.

There was a family that lost a little girl. And the family couldn't get over the loss of the child. And they wept. Almost every day, they wept.

One day, the mother had a vision. She saw lots of little children marching, and they were all dressed in white, and they all had candles. And she saw her own daughter with a candle, but her candle was not lit. And all the others' candles were lit.

So she asked her daughter, she said, "Dear, why is your candle not lit?"

She said, "Mother," she said, "you all weep for me." She said, "The Good Lord does not like for you to weep for me." She said, "You must accept that the Good Lord has taken me." And she said, "When you weep, you put out my candle." And she said, "The others' parents have accepted their death." And she said, "They don't weep. Their candles stay lit. So," she said, "you must not continue to weep for me like this." And she said, "You must accept that the Good Lord has taken me." And she said, "He wanted me." She said, "I belong to the Good Lord." And she said, "He took me when He was ready. So," she said, "you must accept your cross," she said.

114. The Horse with Wings (El Caballo con Alas)

West Virginia folklorist Ruth Ann Musick collected this tale from Sally Alvarez, Spelter, West Virginia, who had the story from her mother. Musick collected many stories from "ethnic" West Virginians and identifies this story as Spanish but does not indicate her informant's background in any particular national Hispanic tradition. AT 813 + 817*.

Alberto Rodriguez had a close friend named Gabriel Fernandez. Gabriel had received word that his mother, who lived in the neighboring village of Molina, was quite ill, and he wanted to go and see her. His wife was expecting their first child at any moment, however, and he felt he should be with her. Finally, at his wife's insistence, he decided to see his mother, but promised he would be home by late afternoon.

In order to reach the village of Molina, Gabriel, like all others before him, had to cross a narrow stream. There were large flat rocks, which the villagers used as stepping-stones, from one edge of the stream to the other. No one could recall a time when the water was so high that it was impossible to cross.

Gabriel reached the home of his parents and was informed that his mother was somewhat improved. He ate dinner with his father, and then helped him with the farmwork. About noon, when it had started to rain quite heavily, his mother thought he should start for home. She was afraid the stream would overflow and be impossible to cross, but the two men assured her there was no danger, since they had had many rains much heavier than this one, and the streams had never become impossible to cross by foot.

By late afternoon, Gabriel saw that his mother was feeling better and was in no danger, so he bade them goodby. His mother wanted him to stay overnight, but he insisted on leaving because he had promised his wife he would return home that day. When he reached the stream, he saw it was so swollen and the current so swift that crossing would be impossible. He stood at the edge of the stream, not knowing what to do. In desperation, he said loudly, "I would give my soul for some way to cross this stream."

At that moment he heard a noise behind him and, on turning around, saw a black horse. Thinking that it was a horse from a neighboring farm, he decided to ride it across the stream and leave it on the other side, where its owner would surely see it.

Gabriel got on the horse's back, but instead of walking across the stream, the creature seemed to sprout wings, and was *flying*. Gabriel was shocked. Then he remembered the words he had uttered, "I would give my soul for some way to cross this stream."

He felt sure that the horse was a messenger from the devil or even the devil himself. Making the sign of the cross he said, "My God, what did I say? Forgive me, I did not mean it." As he did so, the horse dropped him from its back.

In the meantime, Gabriel's wife was greatly concerned about him, for it was already nightfall. She asked Alberto's wife, who had been staying with her that day, to ask her husband if he would go and try to find him. Alberto and two other villagers took their lanterns and walked to the stream. There they found Gabriel unconscious. They carried him home and called a doctor, who found he had several broken ribs, a fractured ankle, and severe back injuries, all of which would necessitate many weeks in bed.

When he woke up, and Alberto asked what had happened, Gabriel told him the story about the black horse with wings. He could see by the expression on his friend's face that he did not believe him, and said, "You must believe me, Alberto. We have known each other since childhood. Have you ever known me to be one given to telling fancy tales or lies?"

Alberto admitted that he knew him to be a sincere and sensible man.

Gabriel said, "When the horse dropped me, I was still conscious. When I landed on the edge of the stream, the lower part of my body was in the water, and I was in such great pain that I could not move. I prayed to God to give me strength to pull myself up on the ground so that I would not drown. God must have heard my prayers, for I managed to crawl away from the water. That is all I remember until I woke up in this bed."

Alberto still found the story hard to believe, but he knew that Gabriel could not have walked across the swollen stream, and he also knew that the current was too swift for him to have swum across. Besides, he knew that his friend could not swim. So he came to the conclusion that he must believe the story. However, he said, "Gabriel, I believe you, but I advise you not to repeat this story to anyone, for they would surely think you had lost your senses. We must tell only the members of your family." The following day, Gabriel's wife gave birth to a son, and on his right hip was a birthmark in the shape of a horse's hoof.

Since that time at least one male member in the Fernandez family in each generation has had the same birthmark in exactly the same spot.

115. The Story of Arigo

This story was collected from Antoinette Scarlata, an Italian-born narrator who ran a grocery store in Granville, New York. Although the narrator has given the story a religious cast by insisting that what happens to the protagonist makes him a saint, the collector of the story, Sylvia Trop, saw it as bearing a relationship to Washington Irving's literary character Rip Van Winkle, a figure well known in upstate New York. AT 766.

In a small town in Italy there used to be a farmer, his wife, and son. Oh, I should say the town was about the size of Granville. I can't remember the name of the town. Anyway, this family was very religious and good people. They used to give away a lot of food. You know, every year when they harvest the crops they give most of it away to poor people. The son Arigo was a very good boy too, and when he grow up, the mother and father want him to marry a nice girl—one who is like the son—good, and one who'll give to the poor.

The son wasn't very interested in girls and he didn't care whether he marry or not. But the mother and father go to a neighboring village to visit some friends—

oh, the town is about as far as Middle Granville from Granville—and there was a cemetery on the way with a gate, near the road. I don't think you know what the old-country cemeteries look like—they've got a big wall around it and a gate with iron openwork, and a big lock, but with big walls around it. So they go to the friends' home, and they meet a very nice girl about their son's age, and they think she'll be a good wife for the son. They go home and tell Arigo about the girl, and they tell him to go meet her.

Arigo is mad at his parents for bothering him, but to make them feel good he tells them he go and see the girl. So he go to visit the girl, and he likes her and makes a date to come back on the next Sunday. On the way back he came near the cemetery, and out in the middle of the road he saw a skull. He felt badly and knelt down and prayed for the poor skull, then he lifted it gentle and put it near the gate so that the watchman could take care of it. He went home, told his family about the girl but didn't say anything about the skull.

The next Sunday he went to visit the girl, and on the way back he saw the skull out in the middle of the road in front of the cemetery. He knew the skull wasn't there when he was going to the girl's house, and he didn't know what was going on, but he prayed for the skull again and picked it up gently and put it near the iron gate. Meanwhile he was courting the girl, and every time on the way back he see the skull. He never told anyone about it. He got engaged and then they set the date for the wedding.

One night on his way back from his girl friend's house—he was getting married the next Sunday; they had everything planned.

Anyway, he came to the cemetery and he saw a big man standing in the road. He got kind of scared 'cause he thought he might be a robber, and so he curled up and stopped.

"Come on, Arigo," said the man. "Don't be afraid. I'm a friend of yours."

Arigo took a few steps forward and said to himself that it must be someone he knows. As he came toward the man, he said, "I don't know you."

The man said, "You're the man that's going to get married, aren't you?"

"Why, yes," answered Arigo. "How you know?"

"Well, I'm an old friend of your father, and I know everything that's going on."

"Well, if that's the case, then my father probably invited you to my wedding, eh?"

"No, you see, I haven't been here for quite a few years. Your father probably forgot all about me."

"Then if that's the case," said Arigo, "I'll invite you to the wedding. You will come?"

"I'll come," said the man, "if you'll save the first chair by the door because I might be late."

They said their good-bys, and each went away.

The next Sunday Arigo was married. They had a big, nice wedding, and afterwards they had a dinner in the house. Arigo was sure to save the first chair near the door—Oh, yes, and when they were on the road talking, Arigo and Trachon—that was the man's name—Trachon had said he wanted to take Arigo some place and Arigo said that he'd go. Anyway, Trachon sat down and ate a little or pretended to eat, and then he asked Arigo to go with him for only an hour. Arigo told his wife not to worry, that he'd be back in an hour and he knew that no one would miss him 'cause there were a lot of people and they were beginning to dance. So Arigo and Trachon went out, and Trachon brought him to the cemetery. Then Trachon unlocked the gate and took Arigo inside. They came to a tunnel and it was all lighted up. They walked through the tunnel, and then they came to an open space where they saw beautiful pasture and grazing land and some thin sheep.

"What's the matter with those sheep?" said Arigo. "Why are they so thin? They've got good grass to eat."

"I'll tell you later," said Trachon. Then they went a little further, and they came to land with burned grass and on this land were some fat sheep.

"Say," says Arigo, "how come those sheep are fat and they have nothing to eat?"

"I'll tell you later," said Trachon.

Then they went on a little way and they came to a big, tall, beautiful building. All around the building was flying little pigeons. They seemed to be trying to get into the building, but they couldn't get in.

"Why can't those little pigeons get into the building?" asked Arigo.

"I'll tell you later," says Trachon.

And then they went on and they came to a big, beautiful hall, and inside a table was set for a big feast.

"Why, this is ten times nicer than my wedding feast," thought Arigo.

Trachon took Arigo in and they sat down, and Arigo thought he saw his wife sitting at the table. Trachon told him that it must be someone that looks like his wife. They sat for awhile, and Arigo kept asking the time. Trachon says that just about twenty minutes are gone by, or just a half hour at the most. Arigo keep telling him, that he has to be back in an hour. So pretty soon Trachon starts to take Arigo to the gate. When they came to the building with the pigeons flying around, Trachon told him that the pigeons represent little children, who died and who have to go through trials and hardships before they can get into the beauty of life.

Then they came to the fat sheep on the scanty pasture land. Trachon said that the fat sheep stand for the poor people and that here they could be fat without food and money. When they came to the lean sheep on the good pasture land, Trachon said that these thin, skinny sheep stand for the rich people—that they had everything when they were living but now they can't get anything, that even though they eat all day, they can't get fat. And then Trachon told Arigo about the skull in the middle of the road.

He said, "I was that skull and your good prayers helped to get me inside this cemetery. It's your goodness in praying for me that helped me."

Arigo said he had to go and Trachon said, "Go ahead. You'll be back soon. I'll see you again."

And so Arigo went back to the town. But when he got back, everything was changed and he didn't recognize any of the people. He asked someone where he could find his house and family, and that person said, "Why, they used to live here years ago, but the house and family are gone now." Arigo didn't know what to think, and he realized that although Trachon said that minutes were passing, by the town time it was years, and probably one hundred years had passed since his wedding day.

Arigo went to a priest and told him the story, and the priest after talking to him knew that this great man was a saint. Arigo was old and bent and had a long white beard. That night he stayed at the priest's house and the next day he died. When he died all the church bells began to ring 'cause this man was a true saint.

Legends from a Number of Traditions

Ghosts and Wraiths

Legends, almost by definition, tell of *unusual* events that challenge our conceptions of normalcy and of life's expected rhythms. Ghost stories, tales of encounters with the spirits of the dead—certainly not fixtures of our everyday reality, though many people believe that ghosts are real—are thus a staple of legendry, taking us across boundaries of everyday life to sudden encounters with something else.

Ghosts are often place-specific revenants who haunt a particular locality, whether a house ("The Haunted House," "The White Lady of the Van Rensselaer Mansion"), a mine ("A Haunted Mine," "The Ghost Miner"), or part of a south Texas ranch ("The Gate That Would Not Stay Shut"). They are usually human but may be animal in form ("A Ghost Dog").

Legends often tell about a particular ghost's reason for being here. It may be a dead priest trying to find a living one to say a last mass ("The Ghost Priest"), a farmhand warning people about the presence of robbers ("The Good Ghost at Wheeler"), a presence trying to lead people to hidden treasure ("A Ghostly Baby Snatcher"), a spouse keeping tabs on a living husband or wife ("Ghost Haunts Her Re-Married Husband," "Ghost Appears in a Photo"), or simply neighbors carrying on an old property dispute after death ("Conflict Over a Boundary Line"). La Llorona, the often-seen woman of Mexican American folklore, looks for her dead children, while the Vanishing Hitchhiker is just trying to get home. But a ghost may not have a particular rationale at all. No one says why the ghost nun ("The Vanishing Nun") gets on a bus. And the ghost of the worker trapped in cement ("The Negro in the Concrete") seems to scream solely out of his own anguish.

Although legends may simply recount a ghost's history, we generally become aware of ghosts because some living person encounters one, and oral narratives often tell of such meetings. Sometimes we even seek out such encounters, as when the young men in "The White Lady of the Van Rensselaer Mansion" go at midnight to see about the ghostly lady's existence. And "Calling Mary Worth" consists of a transcript of an account of a teenage ritual for actually trying to summon a ghost.

Ghost legends speak of our attitudes toward death and the dead and of our beliefs and doubts about other realities. They also reflect other cultural proclivities. In our mobile American society, for example, we seem to have a wealth of traveling ghosts.

Ghosts may point the way to hidden treasure; for another legend in which they perform that function, see story 236. Other ghost legends in other sections include stories 238, 239, 246, 252, and 253.

116. The Haunted House

This story was written down in 1938 by Emma Phillips, who came from a part of New York state once noted for occult practitioners; she recorded it when she was a student at Wayne State University in Detroit. Motifs E281, E380, E402.1.8, E422.1.11.4; cf E231.4.

A story which was often told when I was a child was an experience of my maternal grandmother. It happened when she was a young mother with three small babies, a boy about a year and a half old and twin baby daughters. My mother was one of the twins in this story.

Grandfather was away from home attending a lodge meeting when grandmother was frightened by hearing heavy footsteps in the basement and a dull sound as if someone were throwing potatoes about in the potato bin. The noise and tramping of feet continued until grandmother, completely terrified, gathered all three babies up into her arms and ran across the street to a neighbor's house.

The next day grandfather went to see his father-in-law who was a spiritualist, and accused him of sending his spooks down to frighten his daughter who he knew would be alone that night. His father-in-law denied any such trick and offered to hold a séance in the basement of the home in an attempt to discover what was causing the noise.

As soon as it could be arranged the séance was held. During the course of the meeting blood dripped from under great-grandfather's finger nails. This indicated that there had been a murder committed in this house. The basement was dug up and the skeleton of a child was found buried there.

117. Ghost of a Mistreated Slave

This Maryland legend was recorded from "a woman who lived in the house . . . haunted" by Aunt Betsy, the ghost who is its subject, Sandy Springs, Maryland. Motifs E230, E279, E281.0.3*.

Aunt Betsy has been in this house for a long time. I don't know how long it's been exactly, but I'll tell you this: in the cellar there's a whipping post. Many years ago, during the days of slavery, this farm was part of a very large tract owned by the first John Thomas to settle the area. Many things went on in those days that we can't hardly imagine now. I mean they went on right in this very house.

Aunt Betsy was an old slave who was chained and beaten until she died right in the basement here. And ever since that time, her spirit has haunted this house. You can hear her dragging her chains behind her as she walks down the front steps. I'll never forget one particular incident when Mr. T was still alive. We were having a very large dinner party one evening when Aunt Betsy began her tricks. Before the guests came in and sat down in the dining room, Aunt Betsy came in and blew out all the candles on the table and went through the entire house slamming doors. It was just dreadful. But on the whole, she's never done us any real harm; just little mischievous things, you know.

118. The White Lady of the Van Rensselaer Mansion

This story was collected from Florence Wojtal by Cornelius J. Laskowski, who was gathering folklore from Polish Americans in Albany, New York. The Van Rensselaer family was prominent in New York from Dutch colonial days. Their mansion in Albany underwent various developments over the years and in the 1890s was partially dismantled and moved to Williams College in Massachusetts, where it was finally demolished in 1973. Motifs E338(b), E338(e), E425.1.1.

Once when my father was a young man, he and several other boys decided to discover for themselves whether the legend about the beautiful white lady who was supposed to haunt the Van Rensselaer mansion was true. And so stiffening their courage with a little whiskey, they set out, timing themselves so that they would arrive at the deserted mansion about midnight. However, their calculation was a bit faulty, for they arrived there sooner than they had expected. So they sat down in the long grass nearby and waited for midnight. Suddenly, my father felt a sharp tap on his shoulder. He turned about; and lo, there stood a dwarf with a long white beard and a red cocked hat. His face was so ominously cruel in the moonlight that my father and the others ran away as fast as their legs would carry them. After running for some time, my father and the other boys stopped to see what had become of the mysterious little figure. It had not followed them, and so they concluded that perhaps the little devil was afraid of them. They returned, ready to fight the long white beard if necessary.

But the dwarf was nowhere to be seen. Just then one of the boys read his watch in the clear moonlight. It was practically midnight. My father and one of the boys took their stand at one window, while the others clustered about another. For a long time they peered into the inner darkness of the house. Nothing moved. A long shaft of moonlight played directly into the hall and lit up the ancient staircase. They waited tensely. Then suddenly one of the boys gasped. There at the head of the stairs stood a woman in white. Her arms were heavy with chains, chains that were long and dragged after her. Slowly, majestically the white figure descended the stairs. Midway, the figure stopped and appeared to be aware of someone else in the house. Then it resumed its descent more quickly. As it reached the foot of the stairs, it suddenly vanished. And so did my father and the others!

119. A Haunted Mine

This legend is from a collection of folklore from the Central City, Colorado, area made by Caroline Bancroft. Central City, Bancroft notes, is "Colorado's most famous and oldest lived mining camp," a focal point for the Pike's Peak gold rush of 1859. Its population was multicultural, though the folklore of the Cornish population (nicknamed the "Cousin Jacks") was particularly rich. The Prize and Seuderberg are mines; a *tribute-patch* was a mining area leased from its actual owner. Motifs E231, E275.1.

Back in 1868 a man by the name of Connelly who was a great go-getter had a quarrel with a Cousin Jack by the name of Gleason over the end line. Gleason had a "tribute-patch" on the Prize and Connelly was leasing the Seuderberg. In those days they hadn't yet holed through to make them connecting. One night when Gleason was climbing the shaft after the day's work, Connelly leaned over the collar and shot him. Connelly never paid for his crime as these mines were in the Irish end of town and all of Connelly's compatriots refused to testify against him. Gleason's body fell to the bottom of the shaft, was shattered to bits, and his spirit roams the Prize mine to this day demanding that justice be done. No Cousin Jack who understands the language will work there because they can't bear his beseeching them to do something about his case.

120. The Ghost Miner

Also from Caroline Bancroft's Colorado folklore collection (see story 119), this legend continues on the theme of mine ghosts and hauntings. Motif E336.

Former Nevadaville residents remember that the older Cousin Jacks disliked working in the LaCrosse tunnel because of a ghost who didn't look like a ghost but exactly like a man. He would be seen riding on ore cars and then hop off and disappear with a friendly gesture into the sidewalls of the tunnel. He was dressed like a miner and at first they used to think he was trying to lead them to some rich body of ore.

But he beckoned at so many different places, that they finally ended by distrusting him and feeling nervous.

121. The Negro in the Concrete

This legend was narrated by James T. Andrews, Indianapolis, 1966. The idea of ritually sacrificing a person into a building foundation is found in many cultures; though here the "sacrifice" results from an accident, not a deliberate act, this legend provides an oblique connection to the ancient idea of foundation sacrifice. Motif E266.2(a).

Traveling west on highway U.S. 36 coming from Indianapolis one can find a haunted bridge. The bridge itself is south of the highway down a gravel dirt road situated near the border of Marion County and Hendricks County. The bridge, as told to me, was built in the early 1900s or the tail end of the 1890s. It's built of concrete and is very tall and wide.

The story behind the bridge was born before the bridge was even completed. It seems that a Negro worker was sawing a wooden beam which was too long. He was on a wooden framework above the center support. The worker had already started to pour the cement into the support. While sawing, the Negro workman lost his balance and fell directly into the freshly poured cement below. Unfortunately, the other workers could not retrieve the man. The only thing that tells of this misfortune is the end of the workman's saw still protruding from the center support of the bridge and the screaming that occurs every time a train passes over the bridge.

122. The Gate That Would Not Stay Shut

This story is set on the vast and famous King Ranch, many of whose ranch hands are Mexican American; the ranch stretches along land near the Gulf of Mexico north of the Rio Grande River in south Texas. Motifs E272(a).

Down closer to the Animas Well, there is a wire gap in the fence. It was once a gate. It would never stay shut. The Mexicans thought maybe the hinges were wrong; so they took the gate away and put a wire gap in its place. The gap will not stay shut either. A person may shut it and tie it with a wire. The next morning it will be open. Some time during the night it becomes open. No one knows how. It has been locked with a Yale lock and chain. Next morning the lock would be unlocked, the chain hanging on the wire of the fence, and the wire gap wide open, letting cattle through by the dozens.

Some have said that the opener must be a ghost of some kind that has a habit of passing every night through the gap. No one has the courage to guard the gap all night.

123. Conflict Over a Boundary Line

Drawn from Pennsylvania German folk tradition, this legend was published in the late nineteenth century; it certainly comments on relations between neighbors and on attachment to property. Motif E467.

Many years ago there lived in that portion of Northampton County—known as the Settlement, *In'sha land* (Indian land)—two men of selfish nature, and whose farms unfortunately joined. Strife was kept up on account of one of them attempting to remove the corner stones which had been placed to mark the limits of the farms as well as the dividing line. Matters grew worse and worse, and the decisions of the courts failed to produce either harmony or a satisfactory adjustment of affairs, when it was announced by the gossips that the farmers had decided to fight out their differences with "fire and brimstone in the hereafter."

Death put an end to their earthly dissensions, but the report spread that at certain times during the night could be heard the clanking of chains and the swift passage of fiery balls to and fro along the dividing line of the farms. Occasionally the balls of fire would come in contact, when there would be heard hissing sounds, and innumerable sparks of fire would dart out in all directions while the balls ascended, as if in conflict, and finally returned toward the ground to continue their course up and down the old line of dispute.

124. Ghost Haunts Her Re-Married Husband

This story from a late nineteenth-century collection of folklore from the Allegheny Mountains refers to the folk belief that a person born on Christmas will have the power to see ghosts. Motif E221.

Miss F-, who was not born on Christmas week, and therefore had no natural power of seeing spirits, related the apparition of her brother's first wife. This lady was devotedly attached to her husband, and when in the last stage of consumption could not die until he made oath to remain single for the remainder of his life. Not long after he perjured himself [that is, remarried], but the peace of that household was gone. Ever after there was "a sense of something moving to and fro" upon them all. His sister, in common with the rest, heard the sighs and sobs of the disconsolate ghost, she saw her dim figure floating through the dusk, and was chilled to the heart by its icy atmosphere as the spirit went by in passages or upon the stairs.

125. The Dead Lover's Light

Widow Mary, whose house figures in this New York state legend, was the widow of the prominent Henry W. Livingston. He died in Europe in the nineteenth century, and after a period of sorrow, she turned the grand house they had built in Columbia County, New York, into a great social center; neither Livingston haunts the house, however, though the ghosts of others do. Motif E310.

When the Widow Mary lived there, she was never alone. There were temporary guests, and there were permanent guests. One of the latter was a young girl who was there with her guardian. She had a suitor of whom the guardian did not approve. Every night he would ride near the house, and the girl, watching from her window, would signal with a lamp whether it was safe for him to come to the house.

The affair dragged on and on. She would not give up her love, and her guardian would not relinquish her disapproval. Then the young girl died, perhaps of that inexplicable thing that doctors then called a "decline."

Shortly after the girl's death the Widow Mary closed up the house and went off on a trip. One night while she was away, a villager, returning home late at night, saw the light flashing in the girl's window.

He went home and in awed whispers told his wife. She cautioned him not to mention it. People would think he was crazy. But others saw the light. The story of the girl's sad plight was common knowledge, and it did not take long for someone to say it was her unhappy ghost still trying desperately to signal her lover.

The light has continued until this day and has been seen by many people. There is no natural explanation for it. There is never anyone in the room—at least no living person.

126. A Handshake

Folklorist Frank C. Brown collected great quantities of folk materials in North Carolina, though these were not published until after his death in several volumes. This legend was narrated by Nilla Lancaster, Wayne County, 1923. Motif E211.

A long time before the Civil War a young man, George Deans, was engaged to a beautiful young girl, Rachel Vincent. The girl was very deeply in love, and when she became aware of her lover's infatuation for another girl, she began to pine and droop. Day by day she grew weaker and soon she was near to death. She had her friend send for her lover. She told him that he had proved untrue to her in this world but she would claim him in the next.

A few days later she was buried in the family graveyard.

One night this lover went to call on the other girl and made love to her. He had to return home by the graveyard where his first love was buried.

When he passed by, the ghost of his dead love appeared and clasped his right hand in a strong grasp.

He went on home white as cotton, his hand in an agony of pain. The next morning his hand was shriveled up. They sent for the doctor, but it was no use. He was dead in three days.

127. Ghost Appears in a Photo

Emelyn Gardner collected folklore intensively in remote Schoharie County in upstate New York, just north of the Catskill Mountains. She identifies her informant for this narrative only as A.H. Motifs E532(c), F855.

Mrs. George Roe, who lived just above here, was a witch when she was living, and now that she is dead is a ghost. Jack Wayman and his wife were at the Roe place sometime before she died and heard her tell Mr. Roe that she would haunt him after she was dead, in everything he did. She said she would be in every picture that he would have taken. She meant if she was dead or alive.

She died a year ago last March, and the next September Pearl Roe, Rose Roe, Golda Bradley, and I went down to George Roe's to take some pictures. George and his son were grinding a scythe, and I wanted their picture while they were working. There was no one in front of the camera when I took the picture except the two men working at the grindstone. But as you will see from the picture, there is a tall figure in back of the men. This picture is a good likeness of Mrs. George Roe, and it has been on exhibition some time for others to examine. They all say it is Mrs. George Roe.

128. A Miser's Ghost

J. Hampden Porter collected this legend from Allegheny Mountains informants in the late nineteenth century. Motifs E293, E422.1.

A miser, whose ruined house still stands, disappeared and was never seen again. Two single women, living in a poor way in the neighborhood, suddenly came into possession of money, concerning which they gave an improbable account. Inquiry was made, but it came to naught. The dead man's ghost, however, headless and bleeding, walked upon the hill where their cottage stood. It passed along the garden fence between sunset and dark, and the elder of these murderesses was soon literally frightened to death. Her companion lived longer and suffered more. She wasted away, said one of the many persons from whom I heard this tale, "till nothing of her was left but a little pile of bones." Then death came, and it took four strong men to lift the coffin in which her body was enclosed. The hidden money was there.

129. Wyoming's Headless Horseman

Headless horsemen may be particularly associated with Washington Irving's famous story set in the fictitious Sleepy Hollow, but headless ghosts are a staple of ghost legendry. This one was collected by Robert Morris from Joe Walsh, who heard it in Wyoming, the setting for the story. Motifs E422.1.1.3.1, E422.1.1.5*.

Many years ago one of the ranchers of the surrounding area of Cattle Creek was sending his complete herd of cattle to the railroad in Cheyenne, which was then hardly more than a stop on the main line.

It was a hot, sultry day in August when the cowboys started the herd rolling. After several hours' travel they decided to pull up for a short rest. The trail boss was scanning the horizon with his field glass when he picked up a sight he could scarcely believe. There in the glass, as big as you please, was what appeared to be a headless horseman.

Not trusting himself, the trail boss called his sidekick forward and asked him to take a look in that general direction. The young cowboy looked through the glass, and his face immediately mirrored a look of horror and disbelief. The two men realized they must investigate this strange phenomenon.

Leaving the herd in charge of the next in command, they rode off in the direction of the horseman. Riding over a rise and into a washout, they could find no indication of a horse or rider and could find no trace of either being anywhere near. Were they both seeing things?

With both relief and disappointment, they headed back toward the herd. When they arrived back where they had left the herd, another surprise awaited them. The herd was gone, and again there were no tracks or anything to contribute to their disappearance.

Both of these men died several years later, still unable to explain this strange happening, but people of Wyoming say that even today on a hot summer night, you can see the headless horseman leading the mystery herd across the Wyoming hills.

130. A Ghost Dog

Although especially well known for his books of Ozark folktales, Vance Randolph also gathered much material on the supernatural beliefs and legends of that region. In this story, the ghost is not human but animal in nature. Motif E521.2.

Around the town of Bunker, in Reynolds County, Missouri, they still tell of the ghost dog that Dr. J. Gordon encountered years ago. Crossing a little stream on horseback, near the Bay Cemetery about nine miles west of Bunker, late at night, he saw a figure like a dog, but very much larger. The thing apparently walked on the water without a sound or a ripple. Dr. Gordon saw it many times, once in bright moonlight. Sometimes it crossed ahead of him. Once it jumped on the horse behind the doctor. The animal plunged wildly, and the doctor fired his derringer into the ghost dog twice, but it was not dislodged. He struck at the beast with his fist, the gun still in his hand, but could feel nothing, and his arm slashed right through the figure as if there was nothing there.

131. Reforming a Thief

"Reforming a Thief" was recorded circa 1910 as part of the activities of the student folklore association at historically black Hampton Institute. A. M. Bacon, who was associated with Hampton, recorded this legend and worked with the eminent folklorist Elsie Clews Parsons, who visited Hampton in 1920, to publish these materials. Motif E293.1.

Once upon a time was a family of people who were different from all the people around them. They had very nice stock around them, a large orchard, all kinds of poultry, and a beautiful flower-yard. When one of the family died, they that remained buried the one that was dead. When all of them died but one, he became very lonely and died very soon. There was not anyone to bury him, so he lay on his bed and decayed. After his death the house was said to be haunted, and no one could go inside of it. The next year after the last one of the family died, the fruit-trees bore a tremendous quantity of fruit, but no one came to get it.

When people rode along the road which was near the house, they were often tempted to take some of the fruit that hung over the road; but when they put their hands to get the fruit, someone would speak to them and frighten them, so that they would forget the fruit. One day an old man who was a thief came by the house, and saw all the fruit and the poultry, and a large number of eggs lying under the flowers. He asked the people around why they did not get some of those things that were wasting there. The people answered by telling him if he could get any of them, he might have them. "Very well," replied the old man, "I will have some of those things before I sleep to-night." So he laid his coat that had his arms down just a little ways from the house, and stopped there until night came. As soon as it was a little dark, the man arose and went inside of the orchard, and tied eight hens which were up a large apple-tree to roost. When he had tied the eight, he discovered a light somewhere, he did not know where. He looked down on the ground, and there were two large dogs with lamps on their heads, which were giving him a good light. When he saw this, he became so frightened that he turned the hens loose and fell backwards out of the tree. The dogs jumped after him just as soon as he got to the ground. The man jumped up and began to run as fast as he could, with the dogs right behind him. His home was about four miles, and he ran every step of it. When he got to his house, he fell in the door speechless, and lay speechless for a long time. When he came to his senses, he told his wife and family about what had happened to him. After that there was not a man in the community that was any more honest than he was. He had been a rogue all of his life up to this time. After this happened he always worked for what he got.

132. Guarding His Own Body

Folklorist S. P. Bayard recorded folk traditions having to do with magic and the supernatural in the Pennsylvania–West Virginia border counties, including this narrative "from an old man." See the headnote to story 157 for more information on this area. Motifs E300, E425.

He was going after dark to the house of a neighbor—an old bachelor who had just died—to take his turn at "setting up with" the body—a custom that has now died out in the region. As he rode up to the house, he saw a man sitting on the fence that ran between the road and the front yard. He called to the man, supposing him to be the watcher he was to relieve in the duty of guarding the corpse; but without replying, the other fell suddenly back off the fence into the yard and disappeared. At the same moment my friend's horse "scared" and ran past the house. After coaxing the horse back with some difficulty, he examined the yard, but could see no tracks, nor any imprint at the spot where the strange man had fallen to the ground. When he entered the house, he found that the other watcher had evidently been gone for some time, since the fire had been allowed to go out; and after making up the fire again, and thinking the matter over, he suddenly recalled that the person on the fence had had a long white beard, just like that worn by the old man who lay dead inside. He is therefore convinced that the man on the fence was the ghost of the departed, who had come back to guard the body after its appointed watcher had deserted.

133. The Ghost Priest

W. Stuart Rogers gathered folklore from Irish Americans in Schenectady, New York, including this legend from Irish-born Beatrice Timoney Kennedy; the setting appears to be Ireland. Motif E415.3.

There was once a farmer who went into the village to sell some cattle. He became tired and sought a place to rest. He went into a church nearby and started to say his prayers. He was so tired that he fell asleep and the sexton locked the door on him. At twelve o'clock that night the farmer awoke to hear a bell ringing, and a priest came out to the altar and asked if there was anyone in the church who could say Mass. The farmer said nothing, but the next day he went to the village priest and told him what had happened. That night the priest accompanied the farmer to the church. When the other priest came out to the altar again at the stroke of twelve, he asked if there was anyone in the church who could say Mass.

The village priest said, "Yes, I can." The first priest replied: "God bless you! I was paid to say a Mass twenty-five years ago, and I died before I could give it. I've returned here every night since, waiting for someone to say it for me. Now I can rest in peace."

134. The Good Ghost at Wheeler

The Wheeler in this legend is in Steuben County, New York, where Doret Meeker recorded the story from Mary Neff and Susan Saunders. Motif E363.3(g).

Up above Wheeler in Mutton Hollow, there lived a crew of men who kept their mouths tight as to their own business. The neighbors began to whisper among themselves that these men were rustlers, and soon their suspicions proved true.

One summer the hired man at Mutton Hollow was severely burned. The rustlers refused to call a doctor, preferring to let the man die slowly. After this, no one passing through Mutton Hollow ever lingered! Should he linger, he inevitably heard the hoofbeats of a headless horse galloping after him. So far, no one knew why the headless-horse ghost was fated to haunt Mutton Hollow.

Then, one evening, a farmer starting his rig up the Hollow road saw the apparition of the hired man emerging from the woods, riding a headless horse! The farmer turned his own horses around in the field and whipped them back to Prattsburg.

There was no need to verify the farmer's story; no one cared to experience his adventure, especially after dark. It was decided by the people that night that the rider of the headless horse appeared in order to protect law-abiding citizens passing through the Hollow and to warn them of danger. He also had the duty of haunting the rustlers until they were forced to leave their hideout.

Thereafter, after dusk, the Good Ghost appeared every few nights.

135. The Blue Light

As with story 116, this legend was written down by Emma Phillips, of upstate New York, while a student at Wayne State University in Detroit. Motifs E530.1.3, N271.

My father tells this story as a true experience that happened to his great-grandfather who was a stage coach driver in Pennsylvania just after the Revolutionary War.

Times were rough and some inns had very bad reputations. Innkeepers were an evil lot who were apt to murder a guest for his money. Great-great-grandfather was a crack shot and could protect his patrons from highway robbery. He was also an expert driver and managed his horses very well.

There was a Jewish peddler who often rode on the stage coach and had become very good friends with my ancestor. There grew up about this peddler a belief that he had amassed a great fortune which he carried upon his person.

On one trip which the peddler took with my ancestor it was necessary to stop over night at an inn. The next morning the peddler did not show up to continue his journey. The innkeeper said that the peddler had gotten up early and crossed the hills on foot to go to some farms which were off the main road. This explanation was satisfactory and the stage coach continued on its way but my ancestor never saw his friend, the peddler, again.

About a year later my ancestor was again making the same journey. In the stage coach were only men passengers. Suddenly a terrific storm came up. The thunder roared, the lightning flashed, and the rain came down in torrents. As suddenly as the storm arose it subsided. But the storm had delayed the trip somewhat and the horses seemed nervous.

When the stage coach was about a mile or more from the inn at a particularly lonely part of the road, the horses suddenly stopped and refused to go another step in spite of repeated urging. Moreover they showed great excitement, rearing and snorting. The driver finally got down to investigate. Nothing seemed amiss and my ancestor attempted to lead the horses forward. Still they refused to go forward, rearing and snorting and evidently much afraid.

Suddenly my ancestor observed a strange blue light flickering about the heads of the lead horses. He called the attention of the passengers to the light and they all watched it flickering about the heads of the horses inspiring them with the greatest terror.

Presently the blue light sailed away from the horses and floated into the field alongside the road. The farther away it went the brighter it appeared until the men distinctly saw it disappear at the foot of a large oak tree.

The next day a group of men took picks and shovels and went to the oak tree where they began to dig. It wasn't long before they discovered the bones of a man.

Bits of clothing and the empty knapsack clearly proved that this was the burial place of the Jewish peddler. It was concluded that the peddler had been murdered for the money which he carried upon his person.

---

136. A Ghostly Baby Snatcher

Folklorist C. L. Sonnichsen does not name a narrator for this story, but it comes from a collection of ghost stories he made in El Paso, Texas, and he says that he got most of his material from Pauline Polser and Josefina Escajeda. Motifs E280, E371, E451.4.1.

When Señor Zartuche was a baby, he was the victim of a malicious ghost who came every night at midnight and took him out of the house into the yard. There they would stay a few minutes; then the ghost would bring him back. Nobody knew why a spirit should behave in this eccentric manner, and nobody was able to do anything about it. The members of the family, of course, were completely terrorized, as who would not be, to see a sight like this? But in spite of the cries and entreaties of the family and in spite of the kicks and squalls of the boy himself, the gloomy spectre carried out his nightly schedule.

Yes, it was hard on everybody, but particularly on the little boy. Every night he waited for the ghost, his little body shaking with terror. Day by day he grew thinner and paler, and it was quite obvious that soon there would not be any little boy for the ghost to carry out.

At last his mother was reminded of something she had once heard—that if one made himself into the shape of a cross on his bed, with arms flung out wide and face to heaven, he would be safe from witches. Perhaps the same treatment would make a ghost think twice about what he was doing. As a last resort, therefore, the mother got into bed with her child, and, as soon as she heard the ghost coming, assumed the required position.

The thing drew near, its fiery eyes fixed on the child, its claw-like hands extended to seize him. Then it saw the mother and drew back. "Now," she thought, "is the time to speak to it," for, as all Christian people know, a ghost cannot speak to a living person unless the person speaks first. She got out the right words with some difficulty:

"En el nombre de Dios, diga lo que quiere?"—In the name of God, what do you want?

The ghost began to talk. It told the woman of a buried treasure in that very house. She must dig in a particular spot and she would find first of all a saddle. Under the saddle were two earthen pots, one full of gold and the other of silver. Finally, pointing with a skinny forefinger, the ghost showed her where to dig.

By this time the *señora* was so frightened that she fainted away with a groan that would have wrung your heart. When she came to herself, the ghost was gone to return no more.

Of course she wanted to find the treasure. She thought of starting to dig at once; but unfortunately, when she awoke from her fainting fit, she had forgotten in which corner the treasure was buried. She began to dig, nevertheless, since a Mexican house has only a limited number of corners and Mexican people have plenty of time. Her family helped her, but none of them found either the saddle or the gold under it. At last they gave up in despair.

Some time later, a man who had heard the story decided to try his luck. He dug a little deeper than anybody else, and there was the saddle. He pulled the rotted relic out, and beneath it were the two earthenware pots. But do not suppose there was any gold or silver in them! Of course not! Everybody knows that the person to whom the ghost points out the location of buried treasure is the only one who can find it. In this case the two earthenware pots were full of charcoal.

137. Two Manifestations of La Llorona

La Llorona, or the Weeping Woman, is the ghost most sighted by Mexican Americans. She is commonly found by bodies of water, because she is said to be searching for her children who drowned and she weeps and wails for them. In other versions of her story, however, she is seen as a figure who appears to men to tempt them to their destruction. Folklorist Rosan A. Jordan recorded this La Llorona narrative from a Mexican American woman to whom Jordan has given the pseudonym Betty. Motifs E225, E323.1, E323.5, E361, E425.1.1; cf E381, E412.2.2.

There's two stories about La Llorona. According to one, this woman was married and everything, but every time she had a baby she would kill it. She would feed it to the hogs or something, until finally they caught her and punished her. They sent her to prison or something. After she died she would come back and haunt people. She goes where she hears a baby crying. She tries to get near crying babies—you know, whenever a child is neglected or anything. And she's supposed to always be dressed in white, and she has long black hair, and people say when they see her she just stands and looks at crying babies with real sad eyes.

According to the other story her baby was always crying and she didn't like it. And then one time it rained and rained and she threw it in the river and drowned it. And her punishment was that she had to find that baby. So every time it rains a lot she appears around rivers and ponds looking for her baby. This is the creepy one.

138. La Llorona

This account of La Llorona is from New Mexican Hispanic folk materials assembled by R. D. Jameson, though collected by someone else (noted only as C.S., who got it from R. M., Dawson, New Mexico). Here the ghost assumes a skeletal form that may be related to the *calavera* figures of Mexican folk art. The fact that she here appears to men and that her "bastard" child is mentioned may suggest her manifestation as ghostly sexual temptress, though she does not actually tempt these particular men. See also the headnote to story 137. Motifs E412.2.2, E422.1.11.4, E422.4.4.

One night two men were walking home from work. The morning dawn was just beginning to break through. Just as they approached the Catholic church they saw a woman standing in front of it. Suddenly her cape blew open and they saw her body. It was a skeleton. Some people say it was la llorona coming back to get a priest to baptize her baby who was born a bastard and never baptized. She is supposed to appear there every so often until a priest will go with her and she will never rest until the baby has been blessed.

139. The Vanishing Hitchhiker

Legends about a hitchhiking ghost have been widely told in the United States, and "The Vanishing Hitchhiker" has been called "*the* classic automobile legend." Jan Harold Brunvand, *The Vanishing Hitchhiker: American Urban Legends and Their Meanings* (New York: W.W. Norton, 1981), pp. 24–40, gives a number of versions of the story, including one collected possibly as early as 1935; however, the story may derive from older narratives about a ghost seeking help for a dying person or a ghost jumping on a mounted horse. The man who narrated this version of the legend (recorded in Riverside, Illinois, in 1939) claimed that he actually knew the boys in the story. Although in some versions the ghost is literally a hitchhiker, often, as here, the ghost is simply offered a ride. Motif E332.3.3.1.

These boys went to a public dance. It was in a small town and they knew most of the people there. They saw a very attractive girl in a white dress, and one of the boys asked her to dance with him. Her hands were so cold that he thought she was ill. However, after the dance was over they offered to take the girl home and she consented. They got into the car and she gave them her address. But when they got to the Oak Ridge Cemetery the girl said, "I forgot. I promised I'd get out here."

They boys saw her go through a hedge. They waited, but she didn't come back. They went into the cemetery and looked around but found nothing. They saw a man and a woman leaving, but couldn't find the girl. Worried, they went to the address she had given them. The people there said, "Are you sure she gave you this address?" They showed the boys some pictures and the boys recognized the girl at the dance. "That's even the dress she was wearing," they said. Then the people told them that the girl was their daughter and that she had died two years ago. This happening preyed so on one of the boy's minds that he went to the Elgin hospital for the insane and died about six months later.

140. The Vanishing Bride

"The Vanishing Bride" was included in a published collection of Louisiana folklore that had been collected in the 1930s as part of the Federal Writers' Project, a government project meant to employ writers and others during the Great Depression. Because of the high water table in New Orleans, the dead are "buried" in above-ground tombs, and the cemeteries are a particularly prominent feature of the city's cultural landscape. Three Catholic cemeteries are called St. Louis, numbered 1, 2, and 3. Motif E332.3.3.

New Orleans taxicabs still avoid one of the St. Louis cemeteries whenever possible. At least they never stop to pick up a young woman dressed in white who might hail them from the entrance. One driver answered her signal late one night and drove her to the address she gave him. There, she asked him to go up on a gallery [porch], ring the bell and inquire for a man who lived there. The man came out, but when the driver told him of the girl waiting in the cab, he asked for her description. And when this was given, he said that was his wife, but she had been dead and buried for some time, that she had been interred in her bridal dress. Then the taxi driver realized that it had been a wedding gown the girl was wearing. The men raced down to the cab and jerked open the door. The phantom was gone. Husband and driver fainted. From then on the bride at the entrance of that cemetery hails taxis in vain.

141. The Vanishing Nun

Ruth Dodson published this legend in a Texas Folklore Society publication in 1943. Dodson notes that "a Mexican woman in Corpus Christi told [this story] to my sister." Motifs E332.3.3.1(h), E581.4.

A friend of hers who lives in Laredo wrote her that she was returning home on a bus. When the bus passed through Goliad a nun got on. There were also a good many soldiers coming from Houston to Laredo. The nun talked to the soldiers and told them that the war would end in 1942. After traveling for some time, a soldier noticed that the nun was no longer on the bus. He called this fact to the attention of the driver, who stopped to investigate. No one had seen the nun fall from the bus, which had not stopped since she was last seen. Strange to say, her baggage was gone, too.

When the driver reached Laredo, he went at once to the convent to see if a nun was expected and to report the case. The Sisters told him that they were expecting no one. Finally they placed pictures before him to see if he could identify anyone of them. He selected one as the picture of the missing passenger. But this was the picture of a nun who had been dead for several years.

142. The Traveling Spirit

Grace Partridge Smith, who was an active folklore collector for a number of years, recorded this story from "Egypt." Egypt has long been a nickname for southern Illinois, though the origin of that designation has been debated. Motif E581.4.

At the side of a highway, a woman stopped a bus and asked for a ride. The motorman stopped and let her get on. She would not sit in a seat, but insisted on standing in the aisle. The motorman talked to her and so did the passengers. She told them where she had come from and where she lived. By and by they came to a bridge, and a little later the driver of the bus noticed that the woman was gone! No one had seen her go either. Everyone was surprised and a little confused. Most of them had talked with the woman and they had all seen her get on and they all knew that she had been in the bus. When they reached the town—a little further on—where she said she lived, the bus driver decided to investigate. So he went to her house. Those who came to the door said she had died about that time, that is, the time she got on the bus.

143. Ghost Cannot Pass Flowing Water

Collected in the Allegheny Mountains in the late nineteenth century, this narrative includes the idea that the actions of ghosts are limited by various factors; here the spirit cannot cross over water. Motif E434.3.

Mr. C-, riding on the same road one dark autumnal evening, suddenly found his mare attacked by an invisible adversary. Blows were struck at her head, but the animal, though snorting, plunging, and rearing in terror, could not stir from the place; something met it at every turn. The rider tried to pray, but in vain. He was able to think the words, yet not to utter them. In his extremity the name of God at last burst from his lips. At once the horse sprang forward, and clasping its neck the pair dashed down hill into a brook. Whatever it was that beset them could not follow across.

144. Draga's Return

The mines of West Virginia attracted workers from many countries so that the narrative lore of the state is very varied. This story was related by Yugoslav American Homer Delovich of Monongah. Though a ghost story, elements of it are suggestive of the vampire traditions of eastern Europe in that the ghost is "laid" when a stake is driven into the mortal remains of the haunting figure. Motifs E422.1.3, E422.1.4, E436.2, E442, E471.

There is an old saying in Yugoslavia that if a cat crosses the body of a dead person, the spirit of that person will reappear as a ghost. Such a fantastic thing happened to the body of Draga Vellich. The family had been careful that a cat did not come near the body, but a window was left open near the coffin. A hungry cat jumped to the window sill and then across the body.

The first night after Draga was buried, his spirit returned to haunt his family. His wife was awakened by his cold arms about her and his cold lips kissing her. A strange noise was heard by all—a roaring, rolling noise—so penetrating that the whole house seemed to shake. Draga's wife and the surrounding neighbors were terribly frightened. But it all stopped in the early morning when the cock began to crow.

After repeated visits of the ghost, Draga's wife went to the priest and told him of the strange happenings. He told her, when the ghost returned, to tie some thread from a spool to the spirit as it caressed her, and in the morning they would follow the thread to see where it might lead.

The following night the ghost returned, and Draga's wife followed exactly the instructions of the priest. The next morning the priest and some men followed the thread to the grave of Draga. The priest told the men to get a long, sharp stake. They ran the stake through the grave, the coffin, and the body of Draga. This stake held the spirit down in the grave, and no longer was Draga's wife haunted by it.

145. Calling Mary Worth

This text from the Indiana University Folklore Archives provides not only a legend narrative but also an interesting example of how people, often teenagers, visit the scene of a legend or undertake other actions influenced by a legend, a phenomenon known as legend ostention. This text was collected in Salem, Wisconsin, from Heather Morton by Lynne Grams. Motif E380.

A long time ago, there lived an incredibly ugly woman named Mary Worth. Some say she was born that way, and others say she was in a bad accident when she was young. Whichever it was, her face was horribly marred. She was bitter, too, and as time went on she became more and more evil. People stayed away from her for fear of what might happen to them if they went near her. One day, as she looked in a mirror, she could stand her ugliness no more. In a fit of rage and insanity, she put a curse upon the mirror, and shattered it, fatally cutting herself in the process. From that time on, if anyone stares straight into a mirror (providing the room is completely dark), concentrates and says, "Mary Worth, Mary Worth, come to me; come to me!" she will appear. She will come as a distant shadowy figure at first, that gets more distinct as she comes closer. If you continue to watch and look upon her completely, she will shatter the mirror, trying to mar your face as hers was. From then on you will never be able to look into a mirror without her image appearing and coming for you again.

I first heard the Mary Worth legend at a typical girls' pajama party, about three years ago, when I was a junior in high school. It was told by a new friend of mine, who had recently moved to southeastern Wisconsin from Baton Rouge, Louisiana. She was accepted into our group for a number of reasons. She was smart, cute, and could tell some of the best ghost stories ever. Most of what she told us was "positively true," including her tales of various séances she said she had participated in. "Mary Worth" was one of the better ones. Heather vowed that anyone who disbelieved could see Mary's grave anytime, for she was buried in an ancient cemetery down south. To verify her story further, she gave us examples of friends of hers in Baton Rouge who had called into the mirror. One girl tried it and was found by her mother in a state of shock, in a pile of shattered mirror glass, with cuts all over her face, none serious however.

The events leading up to the telling were commonplace to anyone who has ever been to a "P.J." party. Around eleven o'clock or so a few of the girls will retire from the usual topics of school and boys and go off to a quiet corner to discuss the supernatural, or possibly to work a ouija board. The group gets larger until the entire party is either participating or observing in these "mood-setting" events. This is exactly what happened at this party, which, incidently was at Heather's house. Her house must have had a conducive atmosphere for spirits or visitations of the dead if ever there was one. It was an old 19th century model, dark and austere. And we had the whole upstairs to ourselves.

Finally, the inevitable happened—someone suggested a séance, which was also typical of the high school pajama parties I attended. We had one, but nothing really happened. A couple girls started crying, and another almost fainted, but the only "signs" we got from Joan of Arc or Marilyn Monroe were some scratching noises on the roof and the wind rustling the tree branches against the window.

The séance unsuccessful, and the mood for haunting still unsatiated, Heather told us about Mary Worth. A few girls wanted to try it and since the bathroom was the easiest to get completely dark, the bathroom mirror was the one decided upon. It was tried only once. The feeling standing there in the dark calling the dead was uncanny, even with the other girls. The silence and complete darkness created a sensation of total fright that was unbelievable. We could not have stood there more than a few minutes, though it seemed much longer. Suddenly with one consolidated shriek, everyone headed for the door. It was an unorganized and urgent push on everyone's part to get out as soon as possible. With that, the supernatural was put aside for the night, at least on the surface. Underneath, we were uneasy for the rest of the night.

146. Man Sees Own Ghost

The "ghost" of a living person is known as a wraith. This story was collected in southern Illinois where it "has been told in White County for many years." Motif E723.1.

A few years ago I was told a curious tale about an old fellow who one night saw his own ghost. The incident happened in White County. The main character was an old hunter, a firm believer in ghosts. It is related that the old man had been out hunting 'possums, and was on his way home by way of an isolated country school. It was a crisp night, made almost as light as day by the bright moonlight. And, as the old man neared the school yard, he was thinking of accounts he had heard of the ghost of a murdered Negro that was supposed to haunt that particular spot. He was walking in the middle of the road in front of the old school house when he saw a man approaching from the opposite direction. As the stranger came closer, the old man saw that he too was a hunter, that he was dressed in a costume exactly like his own, and that he carried his gun in exactly the same way. The old man halted in his tracks; the approaching figure also halted. When the old hunter started forward again, the stranger moved forward with the same motions. As they came closer, the old man suddenly realized that the figure he was meeting there in the bright moonlight was his own self—as if he were looking into a huge mirror. Without stopping to investigate, he got away from there as fast as he could run. He always insisted that this was an authentic experience, and some of those who tell the story think it may be true somehow.

Witchcraft, Magic, and Healing

Belief in human ability to affect our environment through supernatural or supernormal means (magic) is widespread. Even everyday superstitions reflect such a belief. We can confer good luck upon ourselves through a horseshoe or four-leaf clover, and a broken mirror at least warns us to watch out.

In legends, anyone may know how to summon some form of magical assistance, and in "Bewitching a Dog," one boy in a party of young peach thieves happens to know how to stop the guardian dog that tries to run them off. More commonly, however, magical powers are possessed by particularly potent individuals, whether they are referred to as witches, wizards, or hoodoo doctors, or whether they are simply recognized as having certain gifts, such as the ability to stop the flow of blood. Some such actual individuals, like Dr. Daniel Roberts and Jesse Bayles, who appear in legends in this section, may be remembered by name long after they are dead.

Although we sometimes speak of "good witches," in traditional belief, witches generally use magical powers maliciously. Indeed, anthropologists explain witchcraft beliefs and narratives as a social means of accounting for difficult-to-understand evils that afflict individuals or groups: these evils must have been sent magically by malicious persons who are witches and wish us harm (sometimes for specific reasons, sometimes out of pure malice). In American legends, witches may steal from locked stores ("The Six Witches"), cause a gun to misfire ("A Bewitched Gun") or churned butter to fail to come ("The Butter Witch"), disturb sleep and shake people's houses ("Uncovering a Witch"), or kill livestock ("Bewitched Cattle"). And they may have amazing powers: to fly ("The Six Witches"); to turn themselves into animals, especially cats ("Death of a Witch Cat," "The Brothers Who Married Witches"); to leave their bodies by shedding their own skin ("Out of Her Skin"). Fortunately, there are ways to counteract witchcraft, and many witchcraft legends may in fact function to reassure people that evil can be successfully combated and witches defeated. Shooting at a tree named after a supposed witch may fix a bewitched rifle ("A Bewitched Gun"), and a red-hot spindle dropped into a churn injures the witch who has prevented butter from forming and throws off her magic ("The Butter Witch"). In European and Euro-American Christian contexts, witches were commonly seen by ecclesiastical and other authorities as being in close league with the Devil. In American folk legends, however, that connection is not necessarily made. Christina Goldberg, "Traditional American Legends: A Catalog," *Indiana Folklore* 7 (1974): 77–108, provides a useful survey of American witch legends.

African American hoodoo (the term is related to *voodoo,* though the derivation of one from the other is unclear) is a highly developed system of magical belief and practice also called *conjure.* Although hoodoo may involve types of folk medicine and the use of herbs, hoodoo "doctors" may be potent users of a variety of magical powers ("Rival Hoodoo 'Doctors,'" "Punishing a Wealthy Planter") for good or ill.

There is certainly a rich body of American folk medical lore, derived from Native American, European, and African sources, but in legends, healing comes about as a result of supernormal forces, perhaps divine or magical or both. The ability to stop bleeding, though limited to those who have the power, is widespread ("Blood Stopping"), but other practitioners may have other powers, such as being able to blow the pain and heat from burns ("Blowing the Fire Out of a Burned Arm").

218

147. The Six Witches

This witch narrative from African American tradition was written out by W. S. Burrell as part of the work of a student folklore society at Hampton Institute, the historically black college, in 1903. Motifs G242.7, G266.

Once upon a time there was a house which was scarcely noticed, that stood just outside of a very famous little village. In this house, lived an old lady and her five daughters. The house looked terribly bad outside; but if anyone had gone inside of it, they would have found it very different from the outside. The old lady and her daughters were witches, and it is said that they got all they wanted from the village stores.

One afternoon two travellers happened by this house just about sunset, and asked if they might stay all night. The old lady told them they could if they would be satisfied with the place she would give them, as she was not a rich person. The men told her it was all right, just so they were not out of doors. She asked them to come and sit down, she would have them something to eat in a few minutes. So she did. And the two men ate, and then went to bed very soon, for they were very tired from walking so hard. One of them went to sleep very soon after he got into bed; but the other one would not go to sleep, because he thought the old lady and her daughters were up to something.

Just as soon as the old lady thought the men were asleep, they reached up the chimney and (each) got an old greasy horn and put it to their mouths, then said a few words and was gone. The man that was not asleep grew very much frightened for a while, but soon got over it. As soon as he got over his fright, he got up and put on his clothes, and looked for the horns that the old lady and the five daughters used. He succeeded in finding the horns up the chimney. And as soon as he got them, he put one of them in his mouth and said a few words, and out he went. When he stopped, he was in a man's store in the village, where he found, to his surprise, the old lady and her daughters.

He did not know how he got in the store: so he went up to the old lady and began to talk with her, but she gave him no answer. The old lady looked at her daughters and said a few words which the man could not understand; and out they went, and left the man alone in the store. The man said as near as he could the same things the old lady said, but could not get out. He would rise up as far as the ceiling of the store and strike his head, but could not get out. When day came, the poor man was so afraid, that he did not know what to do. The clerk of the store came down very soon and unlocked the door.

"I have been missing things out of my store for a long time," replied the clerk, thinking that the man had hidden himself in the store before he closed it the night before.

"Oh, no!" replied the man. "If you will allow me a chance, I will tell you just how I happened to be here."

So he told the clerk all about it, and also took the clerk to the old lady's house, where his partner was. When the clerk entered the old lady's house, he saw several things that he knew he had in his store and had missed them. So he went back to the village, and sent the sheriff after the old lady and her daughters, and let the man go free. When the old lady and her daughters were brought to trial, they were guarded; and when they got ready to pass the sentence on them, they began to sing a little song, which everyone wanted to hear. They sang for about fifteen minutes; and as they sang, they began to move directly upwards until they got so far up in the air that a person could hardly see them, and then disappeared. Those that were guards began to quarrel with each other because one did not shoot and the other did not shoot. So they got mad, and began shooting each other.

148. Witches and a Blessing

Published by Clifton Johnson, a popular writer at the end of the nineteenth century whose books include one about New England folklore, this story is a semi-humorous account of how witches can be thwarted in their evil intentions. Motifs G248.1(a), G271.2.4.

This clergyman's name was Hooker. He was travelling on horseback when, one evening, night overtook him at Springfield, Mass., and he sought an inn. Other travellers were before him; and the landlord informed Rev. Mr. Hooker that he had only a single vacant room left, and, unfortunately, that room was haunted. The clergyman said he did not mind that, and took the room.

He had retired, and everything was still when twelve o'clock came, and with it the witches. In they flocked through keyholes and cracks, until they filled the room. The visitors brought with them many shining dishes of gold and silver, and prepared for a feast.

When everything was ready they invited the clergyman to partake. Although he knew very well that if he ate with witches he would become one, he accepted the invitation.

"But," he said, "it is my habit to ask a blessing before eating;" and at once began it.

The witches couldn't stand blessings, and fled helter-skelter, leaving feast and plate in possession of the preacher.

149. Casting Spells Over Animals

Wheaton Webb, who published this story in a state folklore journal, heard it some time between 1937 and 1942 while living in Worcester, New York, from Gene Fancher. Motifs G265.6.4.1, G265.7.

Another witch who used to cast spells over animals was William Spellman, who was a bachelor witch up on South Hill in my boyhood. He had long black hair, and never shaved, and scarcely ever washed. He was a tall, slim, dark-featured man with high cheekbones like an Indian. He could imitate any sound you ever heard. He lived all alone, and hardly anybody ever visited him. He lived in the next house beyond the Mud-Lake Schoolhouse.

The South Hill folks believed he was full of witches. Get anywhere he was, you'd think there was a quail, or a dog, or a guinea hen or suthin' in the room.

I've seen him rub his dog back and forth a few minutes, and all of a sudden the dog would go into all shapes. He'd keel over and start to dance on his hind feet. In a few minutes you'd see fire raise up all over the dog. He'd grab the dog, and that dog would dance all over on his hind legs. The dog had long pointed ears, and somehow he looked possessed. Some said Spellman could put a spell on a cow or a horse by rubbing him. When he was around, the South Hill cows would get dozy. Some, I've heard say, claimed he'd been to their barn and witched their horses in the night.

150. A Bewitched Gun

"A Bewitched Gun" was collected in Tennessee from William T. Howard, who traveled as a representative for a sewing machine company (thus coming into contact with many people), who in turn had heard it from a Mr. Massengale in Scott County. Motifs G265.8.3.1.1, G271.4.2(bd).

For many years I made my living by hunting, and many deer, bear, turkeys, and all sorts of varmints to be found in these mountings, have I killed.

I was considered a powerful good shot with a rifle, and that I certainly was.

One morning, howsom'ever, I went out, and the first thing I knew I had a fine shot at a big deer, which was standing stockstill, broadside toward me. I raised my gun, took good aim, and expected of course to drop him dead in his tracks. But I missed him, point blank. He made a few jumps and then stood stockstill until I had wasted three shots on him, and hadn't cut a hair. Then he ran off.

This sort of thing went on for several days. I had lots of powerful fine close shots, but couldn't hit a thing.

I told my wife that there was something awful wrong, either with me or with the gun. She told me I had better go to the witch-doctor, as it was likely my gun was bewitched.

I went to the witch-doctor, who told me to go into the woods near a certain house, pick out a tree, and name it after the woman who lived there. He said she was a witch, and had bewitched my gun. He said after I had named the tree as he directed I must shoot at it, and listen to see if there was any noise made at the house—for if I hit the tree the witch would be hurt, and then my gun would be all right.

I did as he said, and at the first crack of the gun I heard the woman cry out, as if she had been hit instead of the tree. I went to the tree and found that it was hit. From that time on my gun was as good as ever, and my shooting was as reliable as it had ever been.

151. The Brothers Who Married Witches

Active folklore collector Fanny Bergen was told this story by a young African American girl, Chesterton, Maryland, at the end of the nineteenth century. Motifs D702.1.1, G266.

Once there was a man who kept a store, and his wife was a witch, but he didn't know it. They kept having things stolen from the store, and couldn't find out who took them. It was really the clerk that stole them, and the storekeeper's wife always helped him to get away, for after he'd stolen anything she'd say, "Over the woods and over the water, follow me." And then he'd fly off with her to some safe place, where he could hide the things, and then fly back to the edge of the town, and from there he'd walk to the store, so he couldn't never be caught. At last the storekeeper watched one night, and caught the clerk stealing, and they was going to hang him for it. But when he was on the gallows, the witch came along and said, "Off the gallows, and over the water, follow me." And so he got off clear.

The storekeeper had a brother that had a wife that was a witch, too. This brother was a miller, and he had a heap of trouble about getting any one to tend the mill nights, because the men he'd get would either get scared away, or else if they stayed they surely got killed. Anyhow, the miller got one man that said he wasn't afraid to stay and watch, if they'd give him a sword and a butcher-knife. So they gave them to him, and he lighted a row of lights, and took his sword and his knife and laid down to watch. Pretty soon in came a lot of black cats—miaou, miaou—and one of them began to go around and spat out the lights with her paw. The man, he got up and cut at her with the sword, and cut off her paw, and then they all ran out and left him. He found a hand lying there and picked it up, and it had a gold ring on it, like one the miller's wife wore. In the morning the miller's wife was sick, and they sent the man that watched for the doctor. When the doctor came, he found her in bed in a great deal of misery, and he asked her to let him feel her pulse. She put out her left hand to him, and kept her right hand all the time under the bed-clothes. The doctor, he asked her to put out her right hand, and when he got hold of it he found it was cut off. And that week she died.

152. Broom-Charm

Written out in 1899 by Nannie Williams as part of the Hampton Institute folklore collecting project, it offers information on how to deal with a witch (here in the form of a cat). Several other stories, including 131 and 147, stem from this project, which involved a student folklore society on campus. Motif G256*(b).

Once an old colored man was harassed several nights by what he said was an old witch riding him, so he planned to catch her. She came every night in the form of a yellow cat. This night, as the old man lay down before the open fire-arch, which had in it a big hot fire, he saw the same yellow cat come in the door and take her seat right before the big fire in front of him. He immediately got up, and took his broom and put it across the door; and then he went back, stirred the fire up, put on several more logs, and made it as hot as possible. The yellow cat, which was the old witch, could not move out of her place, but simply turned from one side to the other. She could not move as long as the broom lay across the door. After the old man had burned almost all the fur and skin off the cat, he removed the broom and told her to go. No sooner was the broom removed than the cat flew.

The old man said that he knew who she was: so the next day he went to this neighbor's house to see how she was; and before he got there, the woman's husband met him, and asked why he burned his wife so badly last night. He said she was in bed with the skin burnt off of her.

153. Out of Her Skin

Another story from the Hampton Institute Student Folklore Society (see, for example, the previous story and its headnote), this one develops the idea that a witch can leave her skin and return to it (but be thwarted if the skin is found while temporarily abandoned). Motif G229.1.1.

Once there was a woman who could turn into a witch. When the husband would go to bed, she would slip out, and go off into the woods and turn into a bear. Once she went off and turned into a bear, and a man shot her in the shoulder. When she went home, her husband asked what had happened. She said that she got hurt through an accident. The next time she turned into a panther, and wandered off in a very thick woods and ran the women and children. One night she was off, and a man saw her and shot her in the hip.

While she was gone, the husband missed her and got up. He saw her skin lying by the fire. He got some red pepper and put it inside of the skin. Then he locked the door to keep her from coming into the house that night. When she came back, she slipped through the keyhole and went to get into her skin. Every time she went to get in it, the pepper would burn her. She would say, "Skinny, skinny, don't you know me?" Then she would try again: it would burn her still. She would say, "Skinny, skinny, don't you know me?" The husband woke up. She got into it, but could not stay. Then she was tarred, and burnt to death.

154. The Butter Witch

From the Indiana University Folklore Archives, this story was collected by Peggy Saunders from Dr. C. R. Bogardus, Austin, Indiana, December 20, 1959. Witches commonly interfere in the butter-churning process, which would have been a common household task at one time. Motif D2084.2; cf D2084.2(dd).

There was a time, following the Civil War, when Aunt Peggy Lewis couldn't make butter, no matter how much she churned. Finally one day an old, old woman from up on the head of Lockhouse called on her and hearing about the strange state of affairs, told Aunt Peggy that her milk was being bewitched. She explained to her that to break the witch's spell she should take the spindle from her spinning wheel and heat it red hot in the fire and drop it exactly in the center of the churnful of milk, and after this she would no longer have trouble making butter and would also find out who cast the spell.

The next day when the butter wouldn't come, she heated the spindle, but as she attempted to drop it in the churn, it burned her fingers, causing it to fall slightly off center. She removed it, resumed churning, and immediately the milk made butter.

Shortly afterwards a neighbor rushed in saying that Old Jane had surely died. Aunt Peggy said she thought all along that Jane had bewitched the milk.

At the same time Aunt Peggy was heating the spindle, an aged negress, old Jane McIntosh, who was locally suspected of being a witch, and her husband, old Henry, a former slave of Roderick McIntosh, were coming over the mountain between the head of Ellis Branch, where they lived, and Owl's Nest Branch, on their way to Hyden. Just as they passed the gap, Old Jane screamed and fell to the ground as though dead. Henry picked her up and carried her to the house where she eventually revived. However, those who knew about such things said that had Aunt Peggy's spindle fallen in the exact center of the churn, the breaking of the spell would certainly have killed Old Jane.

155. A Wizard Protests Being Overcharged

The "doctor" in this story (collected in upstate New York) is Dr. Daniel Roberts, who emigrated from Wales and died in New York in 1820; he was locally reputed to have magical powers and that reputation lived on in local folklore after his death. Motif D1415.

Another story related of the doctor is that, having occasion to visit a town in one of the counties north of us, he stopped for a night at a tavern where the accommodation afforded was decidedly bad and the price demanded in settlement excessively good. He paid without protest and, returning to the dining room then deserted, wrote with a piece of chalk a sentence upon the chimney above the mantel, and started on his journey, which was being made on foot. Presently, one of the maids entered the room, and seeing the chalked characters upon the chimney attempted to read them, when she immediately began involuntarily to dance. Her mistress soon appeared, and reading the sentence, likewise began to dance. At this stage the landlord, hearing the unusual racket and the wild ejaculations of the dancing pair, stepped into the room, and casting his eyes upon the mysterious marks, his heels also instantly began to clatter upon the bare sanded floor, in unison with those of his wife and servant. Being of a plethoric temperament, his breath soon showed signs of failing; so, while a little of it yet remained, he made use of it to call his stableman, whom he besought as he valued his legs not to read the sentence upon the wall but to go with all possible speed after the man who had lodged with them and beg of him to return. The stableman, mounting a horse, started in pursuit of the doctor, whom he soon overtook, and to whom he related how the devil had taken possession of his master's household, stating that he had been sent to beg him to come back and release them from the power of his Satanic Majesty. The doctor quietly told him to return and simply erase the characters chalked upon the wall and all would be well; but to tell his master never again to charge so exorbitant a price for such poor accommodation as he had furnished him.

156. Death of a Witch Cat

Folklorist Ruth Ann Musick, best known for her West Virginia collections, took this story from recollections set down in 1929 by John S. Williams, a retired schoolteacher in Mount Vernon, Indiana. He attributed it to his great-grandmother, so that it "would probably date back to the latter part of the eighteenth century." Motifs G211.1.7, G262.

Well, Granny said one time when my pap was a little boy, they was killin' hogs, an' several of the neighbors was helpin' 'em. They had two hogs hangin' up and was scrapin' the hair offen another one, when all at once they heerd a cat squall down in the woods. They lived in the woods them days in ole Virginny, jist like we do now here in Indianny. Directly they heerd a thrashin' noise down in the woods an' out bounced a big yaller cat. There was a little boy about six years old, belongin' to a neighbor's family, standin' by a big iron kittle whicht was full of scaldin' water. That ar' big yaller cat, with hits fur all turned the wrong way, ran between the little boy's legs, bowed up its back, an' tumbled him into that kittle of bilein' water where he scalded to death before you could say "Jack Robinson"!

The big yaller cat run off into the woods, laughin' jist like a woman. The poor little boy was fished out of the kittle, stone-dead. Of course the butcherin' went on, but they didn't have a big dance that night as was the custom. Next day the poor little boy was buried down on a hillside, in the woods.

A few days after the funeral, one of the neighbors, whose name I have forgotten, missed his wife, an' the whole neighborhood turned out to find her. On the same morning my grandpap missed his butcherin' knife, the one they had used on butcherin' day. They scoured the woods for miles in every direction, visited all the cabins far and near, but no trace of the missin' wife could be found. But on the evening of the second day, two of the searchers comin' up outen the woods, passed the grave of the poor little dead boy, an' there beside it lay the dead body of the neighbor's wife with her throat cut from ear to ear, an' Grandpap's butcher knife on the ground near her. After the dead woman was buried, some of the neighbor women held a quiltin' party, an' my granny was there. At this party they all agreed that the dead woman was a witch, an' that she had turned herself into a big yaller cat an' had scalded the little boy to death, an' that remorse had caused her to commit suicide after she had turned herself back into a woman again. But Grandpap was happy because he got back his butcher knife.

157. Uncovering a Witch

The published source of this story includes material collected in Monongalia, Wetzel, and Marshall Counties in West Virginia and Greene County, Pennsylvania, a region that folklorist S. P. Bayard describes as a place of narrow valleys and steep hills originally populated by English and German settlers. His informants in the area were Mary Pierson Rogers and Hannah Bayles Sayre. The latter's father and grandfather had reputations as great "wizards" or "witch doctors" (both terms she used). Her father, a tenant farmer and the protagonist of this story, kept a book of magic that no one else dared open. Another story about Bayles follows this one. Motif G265.

While living in one of their various log-cabin residences along the Pennsylvania-West Virginia border, the Bayles family discovered that certain hardships which they were experiencing were due to the witchcraft of a neighbor. She troubled them at first by causing their rest to be disturbed by a number of cats, who would suddenly appear in the room, frolic over the beds, and then disappear just as mysteriously as they had come—since the house was shut up for the night and there was no opening through which animals of their size could enter or leave.

Following this, the Bayleses were visited by a sudden shaking of the whole house, which was repeated night after night, sometimes throwing them out of their beds. To his wife's questions about these doings, Bayles would make no reply except that "the devil was about; but he knew who was doing it; he'd fix them."

His opportunity apparently came when the witch paid them a visit, during which Bayles kept a close watch on her, and finally thought he had detected her in an effort to burn the house down by inserting a live coal between the log wall and the inner board wall of the cabin. He immediately accused her. She, of course, appeared shocked by the charge, but he persisted in it; told her that he knew of her evil doings: that she had come at first "with cats," then "with trying to shake the house down;" and finally, heaping invectives on her, he ordered her to go and never return. She fled hastily, and they neither saw her nor were troubled by her magic again.

158. Bewitched Cattle

For information on Bayles, the protagonist of this story, see the headnote to story 157. Motifs G265.4.2.1*, G270.

On another occasion, Bayles spared the life of a *malefica* in like manner after first giving her a severe punishment as a lesson of his power. This time it was a question of the molesting of cattle: "running" them unmercifully, and causing them to fall and break their legs, or sink exhausted into a stream and drown. A witch in Greene County had killed a great deal of stock for one farmer against whom she had a grudge, and in an evil hour for her she commenced to harass Bayles's herd. One afternoon, the Bayles cattle suddenly went wild, and ran down one hillside, across a stream, and through a meadow on the opposite slope—all but one old cow, who fell before she had reached the stream. Jesse Bayles seized a butcher knife, ran to the cow, and quickly cut a piece from one of its ears. In the flurry of the moment he dropped the piece—and here evil magic was clearly seen to be at work; for although the beast had fallen on a clear, sandy spot "where you could have picked up a pin," the bit of flesh could not be found anywhere. There was nothing to do but cut off another piece of the ear. A man who was with Bayles at the moment asked him if he intended to cut the whole ear off—evidently speaking at an unpropitious moment, for Bayles cursed him, and told him to mind his own business or he would get a knife driven into him. The piece of the cow's ear was taken to the house and flung into the fire.

Shortly after, a boy from the witch's home came running at full speed, and begged them to go up to help the woman: she was dying. No one in the wizard's house moved or spoke until after the third call for help had come. Then, saying that "he guessed she'd got about enough," Bayles sent two of his family to the rescue. As they approached across the fields, they could hear the woman groaning and "catching her breath," and carrying on in a dreadful manner. The groans lessened as they drew nearer, and when they reached the house, the woman was sitting up, apparentlyfully recovered; but she confessed that they had almost killed her. Bayles later saw her, and warned her that if ever she harmed any of his cattle again, it would indeed be her last act.

159. Rival Hoodoo "Doctors"

In the world of African American hoodoo practice, there are specialized practitioners ("hoodoo doctors") knowledgeable in the applications of magic (and who also may be adept in the use of herbs in folk medicine). This story, collected in Eatonville, Florida, features the rivalry between two such practitioners. The term *hoodoo,* related to the term voodoo and also called conjure, covers a wide variety of African American magical practices. For discussion of voodoo and hoodoo, see Carolyn Morrow Long, *Spiritual Merchants: Religion, Magic, and Commerce* (Knoxville: University of Tennessee Press, 2001), pp. xvi, 74–75, 82–83, 17ff. This story was collected by Zora Neale Hurston, the noted novelist who was also an enthusiastic fieldworker in folklore and anthropology. Hurston writes of her experiences in collecting folklore in Florida and New Orleans in *Mules and Men* (Philadelphia: J. B. Lippincott, 1935; various reprintings). Hurston says that Old Man Massey was a noted south central Florida hoodoo doctor, though the name is a pseudonym. Hurston adds that, though bested in this story, Aunt Judy Cox also had a local reputation as a powerful hoodoo practitioner. To "throw back" the work of hoodoo practitioners is to create a counterspell that thwarts or even harms them. See story 160 for another legend collected by Hurston. Motifs D2072.0.5.

Aunt Judy Cox was Old Man Massey's rival. She thought so anyway. Massey laughed at the very thought, but things finally got critical. She began to boast about being able to "throw back" his work on him. They had quit speaking.

One evening before sundown, Aunt Judy went fishing. That was something strange. She never fished. But she made her grandchildren fix her up a bait pole and a trout pole and set out to Blue Sink alone.

When it got good and dark and she did not come home, her folks got bothered about her. Then one of the village men said he had heard a woman cry out as he passed along the road near the lake. So they went to look for her.

They found her lying in the lake in shallow water having a hard time holding her old neck above the water for so long a time. She couldn't get up. So they lifted her and carried her home. A large alligator was lying beside her, but dived away when the lantern flashed in his face.

Aunt Judy said that she hadn't wanted to go fishing to begin with, but that something had commanded her to go. She couldn't help herself. She had fished until the sun got very low; she started to come home, but somehow she couldn't, even though she was afraid to be down on the lake after dark. Furthermore, she was afraid to walk home when she couldn't see well for fear of snakes. *But she couldn't leave the lake.* When it was finally dark, she said some force struck her like lightning and threw her into the water. She screamed and called for help, holding her head above the water by supporting the upper part of her body with her hands.

Then the whole surface of the lake lit up with a dull blue light with a red path across it, and Old Man Massey walked to her upon the lake and thousands upon thousands of alligators swam along on each side of him as he walked down this red path of light to where she was and spoke.

"Hush!" he commanded. "Be quiet, or I'll make an end of you right now."

She hushed. She was too scared to move her tongue. Then he asked her: "Where is all that power you make out you got? I brought you to the lake and made you stay here till I got ready for you. I throwed you in, and you can't come out till I say so. When you acknowledge to yourself that I am your top-superior, then you can come out the water. I got to go about my business, but I'm going to leave a watchman, and the first time you holler he'll tear you to pieces. The minute you change your mind—I'll send help to you."

He vanished and the big 'gator slid up beside her. She didn't know how long she had been in the water, but it seemed hours. But she made up her mind to give up root-working all together before she was rescued. The [medical] doctor from Orlando said that she had had a stroke. She recovered to the point where she crept about her yard and garden, but she never did any more "work."

160. Punishing a Wealthy Planter

See the headnote for story 159 for information on Zora Neale Hurston, the collector of this legend, and her folklore work. Motifs Q211, Q285, Q555.

A wealthy planter in Middle Georgia was very arrogant in his demeanor towards his Negro servants. He boasted of being "unreconstructed" and that he didn't allow no niggers to sass him.

A Negro family lived on his place and worked for him. The father, it seems, was the yard man, the mother the cook. The boys worked in the field and a daughter worked in the house and waited on the table.

There was a huge rib-roast of beef one night for dinner. The white man spoke very sharply for some reason to the girl and she sassed right back. He jumped to his feet and seized the half-eaten roast by the naked ribs and struck her with the vertebrate end. The blow landed squarely on her temple and she dropped dead.

The cook was attracted to the dining room door by the tumult. The white man had resumed his seat and was replenishing his plate. He coolly told the mother of the dead girl to "call Dave and you all take that sow up off the floor."

Dave came and the parents bore away the body of their daughter, the mother weeping.

Now Dave was known to dabble in hoodoo. The Negroes around both depended upon him and feared him.

He came back to clear away the blood of the murdered girl. He came with a pail and scrubbing brush. But first he sopped his handkerchief in the blood and put it into his pocket. Then he washed up the floor.

That night the Negro family moved away. They knew better than to expect any justice. They knew better than to make too much fuss about what had happened.

But less than two weeks later, the planter looked out of his window one night and thought he saw Dave running across the lawn away from the house. He put up the window and called to demand what he was doing on his place, but the figure disappeared in the trees. He shut the window and went to his wife's room to tell her about it and found her in laughing hysteria. She laughed for three days despite all that the doctors did to quiet her. On the fourth day she became maniacal and attacked her husband. Shortly it was realized that she was hopelessly insane and she had to be put in an institution. She made no attempt to hurt anyone except her husband. She was gentleness itself with her two children.

The plantation became intolerable to the planter, so he decided to move to more cheerful surroundings with his children. He had some friends in South Carolina, so he withdrew his large account at the bank and transferred it to South Carolina and set up a good home with the help of a housekeeper.

Two years passed and he became more cheerful. Then one night he heard steps outside his window and looked out. He saw a man—a Negro. He was sure it was Old Dave. The man ran away as before. He called and ran from the house in pursuit. He was determined to kill him if he caught him, for he began to fear ambush from the family of the girl he had murdered. He ran back to get his son, his gun and the dogs to trail the Negro.

As he burst into the front door, he was knocked down by a blow on the head, but was not unconscious. His twenty year old son was raving and screaming above him with a poker in his hand. He struck blow after blow, his father dodging and covering himself as best he could. The housekeeper rushed up and caught the poker from behind and saved the man on the floor. The boy was led away weeping by the woman, but renewed his attack upon his father later in the night. This kept up for more than a month before the devoted parent would consent to his confinement in an institution for the criminally insane.

This was a crushing blow to the proud and wealthy ex-planter. He once more gathered up his goods and moved away. But a year later the visitation returned. He saw Dave. He was sure of it. This time he locked himself in his room and asked the housekeeper through the door about his daughter. She reported the girl missing. He decided at once that his black enemies had carried off his daughter Abbie. He made ready to pursue. He unlocked his door and stepped into the hall to put on his overcoat. When he opened the closet door his daughter pointed a gun in his face and pulled the trigger. The gun snapped but it happened to be unloaded. She had hidden in the closet to shoot him whenever he emerged from his room. Her disordered brain had overlooked the cartridges.

So he moved to Baltimore—out in a fashionable neighborhood. The nurse who came to look after his deranged daughter had become his mistress. He skulked about, fearful of every Negro man he saw. At no time must any Negro man come upon his premises. He kept guns loaded and handy, but hidden from his giggling, simpering daughter Abbie, who now and then attacked him with her fists. His love for his children was tremendous. He even contrived to have his son released in his charge. But two weeks later as he drove the family out, the young man sitting in the rear seat attacked him from behind and would have killed him but for the paramour and a traffic officer.

161. Bewitching a Dog

Elizabeth Cloud Seip, who published this legend in the *Journal of American Folklore* in 1901, heard it in Frederick County, Maryland, while attending a session of seasonal apple-butter making. The informant may have been a member of her own family. A *stake-and-rider fence* is a substantial fence of wooden posts and cross pieces. Motif D2072.0.2.6.1*.

The year 1899, though a good apple year, was an off one for peaches. But some friends of mine contrived to get a taste at least, which was more than the most of us had. Coming home late one night, these young men passed a place where the only peaches in the neighborhood were said to be. They all "felt for peaches," as their peculiar idiom has it, and the coincidence of opportunity with capacity struck them all. But the owner of the peaches was likewise the owner of a savage dog, that, howling as he prowled, seemed to realize that eternal vigilance was the price of peaches. But one of the party bethought him how to lay the dog. He took his pocketknife and drove the blade into a stake of the stake-and-rider fence, saying three times, "Dog, keep your mouth shut until I release you."

In the language of an eye-witness, "That dog nearly tore his toenails off getting to the back of the house. And there he stayed, with never a word out of him, until we had all the peaches we wanted. Of course, we only took a few to eat. As Jake pulled the knife out, the dog flew around the house again, raging like mad, and we made good time down the road!"

162. Blood Stopping

The ability to stop the flow of blood from a wound may be thought to stem from magical powers or religious intercession, but belief in this ability is widespread. Usually, the ability is exercised in a community by particular individuals who may have had the power passed on to them by others. This legendary account was written by folklorist Vance Randolph, based on his field research in the Ozarks. Motifs D1504.1, F959.3.

There used to be a woman at West Plains, Missouri, who had a great reputation as a "blood stopper." A wounded man was brought to her home in a wagon. The whole wagon bed seemed to be covered with blood, and the man's friends were unable to stop the bleeding from two deep knife cuts. The woman looked at the patient, then walked out to the barn alone, with a Bible under her arm. In about three minutes the bleeding stopped, and the healer returned to her house. She would take no money for "blood stopping," and she would not discuss the method. She was not a religious woman, and rarely looked at the Bible except when she was asked to stop the flow of blood. The old woman confided to a friend that she had already imparted the secret to three persons, and that if she ever told a fourth the "power" would be taken from her.

163. Curing Rheumatism

"Curing Rheumatism" was told by Alice Kiddney of Florence, New York. Native Americans have often been seen as possessing healing secrets and powers (and indeed Native American healing practices had an important influence on general American folk medicine and scientific medicine); hence, patent medicines in the nineteenth century often were attributed to Native Americans in some way. The healer in this story is a "squaw" (a married female Indian, though today the term is considered an objectionable one). Motifs F950.3(a), F959.

One time there was a little girl who had rheumatism. Her mother heard of an Indian squaw who would cure her. The mother and little girl had to walk to get to the squaw's place. The squaw was very friendly to them. The mother told her why they had come.

The squaw stood the little girl up beside a tree. She marked on the tree how high up the girl came. Then she marked up four inches higher. She cut off a lock of the girl's hair and nailed it at that height. She told the mother to bring the girl back in exactly one year's time. She stood her up against a tree and marked her height again. She told her to bring her back again in a year's time. When she brought her back the next time, the girl reached exactly up to the hair. The squaw took the hair from the tree and gave it to the girl. She told her to put it in her pocket, take it home and keep it. The squaw told the girl to walk away from the tree. She wasn't lame with rheumatism any more. She was cured. The squaw told the girl to put the hair under her pillow every night for three years and the rheumatism would not return again.

164. Blowing the Fire Out of a Burned Arm

This account was recorded in Worthington, Indiana, May 1971, "from a 34-year-old housewife." Motif F959.3.

You know John, don't you? Well, his dad could blow fire. I had a burn, a great big burn on the side of my arm. I stumbled against the heating stove, and it really made a big red burned place on my arm. Anyway, they came out to our house that night. He said, "Is that really hurting you?" I said, "Yes." He said he could blow fire out. He blew in a circular motion, like little bitty circles, like you'd think of a whirlwind, you know. It quit hurting, and the red went away and everything just as soon as he blew on it. I haven't even got a scar, and it was an awful bad burn. He said he had to pass it on to a woman. That was the only way it would work. He told me he would tell me, but he never did. I didn't believe he could do it. He said it didn't matter. But, anyway, it worked.

Omens and Other Strange Events

In American legends, omens—mysterious happenings that presage other events, usually death and disaster—take many forms: personal visions ("A Death's Head"), a voice ("A Voice Calling"), an unseen watch whose ticking is heard ("The Death-Watch Tick"). The popularity of narratives about such omens suggests deeply held beliefs about the interconnectedness of things and in the power of events to communicate with us.

Other legends tell of other remarkable events, and this section includes a number of legends that recount kinds of happenings that do not easily fit into this book's other broad thematic categories of legendry: appearances by werewolves ("A Loup-Garou's Debt"), unexpected salvation ("Saved by Lightning"), indelible impressions made on objects like tombstones ("The Face on the Windowpane," "The Chain on the Tombstone"), inexplicably playing musical instruments ("The Playing Player Piano"), phantom steamboats ("Phantom Steamboat on Devil's Lake"), ineradicable bloodstains ("The Blood Stained Bricks"), as well as various others.

165. The Death-Watch Tick

This story emanates from George Korson's pioneering research into the folklore of American miners. A *fireboss* examines a mine for fire danger and general safety. Motifs D1812.5.1, E761, X1755.1; cf D1812.0.1.

A miner was buried alive by a pillar of coal which he was robbing. After his body was dug out it was discovered that his watch was still in the mine. It was not hanging on a timber in the heading where he usually kept it but was buried in the gob, where it ticked away unseen.

It soon gave evidence of being the most amazing timepiece. Its chief function seemed to be to forecast the approach of death, and so uncannily accurate was it that miners feared it more than the devil. It flitted all through the mine, going from one working place to another and inflicting itself upon this miner or that, depending upon whom fate had marked for death. No one could learn in advance where or when it would appear. Always it announced its arrival by ticking. The ticking was slightly louder than that of an ordinary watch but marked by the same relentlessness. There was no use trying to smash it with one's pick, or to blow it up with a stick of dynamite. Sooner could one smash or blow up one's shadow. The death watch eluded all measures of force and merely mocked men's curses. It was as inevitable as death itself. There were stretches of weeks or months when it kept silent. Then with the suddenness of a fall of top rock, there would come the fateful tick-tock. . . .

One night, while on his accustomed tour of inspection, the fireboss was astounded to hear the death-watch tick. It sounded so weird and awesome in that empty mine! There were fear and pity in his heart for Jim Kelly in whose working place the watch was ticking.

When morning came, the fireboss was in his station along the gangway and waved Jim aside when he came up for his brass check.

"In the name of God, Jim, go back home," he said.

"What's the matter?" asked Jim.

"Now in the name of God, do as I tell ye. You'll be thankful to me later on."

But Jim, with seven hungry little mouths to feed, could not afford to miss a day, and for that reason insisted on knowing why he was being called off.

"Well, if I must tell ye, Jim, I heard the—the death-watch tick in your heading last night as plain as ever I heard anything. Don't go in there or it's kilt you'll be."

"The death-watch tick!"

Jim turned deathly pale. The dinner pail trembled in his hand. He turned back.

Now there was gratitude in Jim's heart for being spared the fate, as he thought, of so many of his fellow miners, and he knew of no better way to celebrate his defeat of the death-watch tick than by attending church. Looking at his watch he found that he could still make the eight o'clock mass and so hurried home to change his clothes. To reach the church from his home he had to go over a railroad grade crossing. When he got there he found the gates down. Rather than wait and take a chance of missing the mass, he ran across the tracks. But he was not fast enough. The 7:55 flyer mowed him down.

166. A Death's Head

The Bay mentioned in this legend is the Chesapeake; the story comes from George Carey's research on Maryland folklore. Motifs D1812.5.1.2.1, E761.

Even stranger was the family legend of Captain B.'s experience aboard his own vessel. Bound up the Bay one summer morning, he looked forward from his position at the helm and on top of the cabin house spied what he thought for sure was the perfect replica of a death's head. Forward of that he witnessed what he swore were the bodies of dead and dying people literally spread all over his deck. No one else saw a thing. But Captain B. knew danger lay ahead and he seemed to know where, for he altered his course. Shortly they came upon an excursion ferry engulfed in flames, the water around it thick with people. Captain B. and his crew pulled as many bodies as they could from the water, and as they turned away from the wreck and headed for Baltimore, the captain once more looked forward to see the picture he had seen that morning: his deck covered with the bodies of the dead and dying.

167. A Dream of Surf and Waves

This legend comes from the Colorado mining country of the Central City district. The terms Cousin Jack and Cousin Jennie refer to people from Cornwall in England. Cornish immigrants to the United States often gravitated to mining because of their experience in the mines in their native English county. Motif D1810.8.3.2.

In August, 1895, probably the worst disaster of the district occurred when fourteen men were drowned in the Sleepy Hollow and Americus mines. Men working in the Americus broke into the Fiske workings which in all lower levels were disused and full of water. (All three mines were on the same vein.) The force of this water surged into the workings of the other mines, trapping unsuspecting workmen and drowning them. Most of the drowned miners were Cousin Jacks, the rest, Italians. The tragedy was made more harrowing because it was months before the bodies could be recovered. Special pumps had to be sent over from Aspen and the whole Gregory-Bobtail incline had to be unwatered. The disaster is remembered not only by miners in the district but by the whole population who remember the tragedy and the prolonged tension that followed before the dead could have decent burial.

It seems that one Cousin Jennie living in Mountain City who had a husband working in the Sleepy Hollow dreamed the night before the disaster of the surf and wild waves pounding in a storm against the high cliffs of Cornwall. In the morning when she awoke, she told her husband she considered this dream a bad omen. She prevailed upon him not to go to work and thereby saved his life.

168. A Voice Calling

The omen in this legend, from a Polish American informant, is as simple as the human voice. Motif D1812.5.0.11.

It was a fall day, the leaves were beautiful, and I had sheets and pillowcases on the line. I looked out the window and there was no wind. There was this one pillowcase, a white one, that was without a clothespin, drooping.

I went outside and went down the steps to hang that pillowcase, and all of a sudden I hear, "Valerie! Valerie!"

And I went running, I went running down the sidewalk, because my father used to like to go to White Eagle Bakery, and he'd put rye bread in my mailbox and just toot [his car horn] or something or yell. So I figured maybe that was him.

I went down there, but there was nobody there, was nobody. So I went down there and said, "*That's* weird. There's no neighbors around—who's calling me?"

I come back up the steps. As I come up the steps, the telephone's ringing like crazy. I went to the telephone, and they said, "Ma got hit by a car, it doesn't look good." She did die afterward.

169. The Dancing Light

This legend, from research conducted by eminent Kentucky folklorist Lynwood Montell into the ghostlore of the foothills of his native state, was recorded from a male informant in Green County, 1966. Motif E761.7.4.

I was traveling alongside a creek on my way to see my father when suddenly a light appeared before me. The creek or branch is called Snake Branch. The light danced along until it was beside me, then it followed me. I ran my horse, but it still stayed by my side. I would think that it could have been the moon, but it was the darkest night I have ever seen.

The light followed me until I was almost to my father's house, then it went out, and it never appeared again. When I reached my father's house, I was told he had died a little while before.

170. The Robed Horseman

Like story 169, this legend was collected by Lynwood Montell in Kentucky, this in 1964 from a female narrator in Green County, who was born in Taylor County. Motifs E421, E423.1.3.4, E575.

Elp Ford lived in Larue County with his wife and his family. His father, mother, and sister lived in Taylor County at the old home place on Little Brush Creek in the Old Mac community. Late one afternoon his father and mother sent for him to come, for his sister was seriously ill. He started about night. When he got to Little Brush Creek, he rode in to let his horse drink.

There was a long, winding hill coming down to the ford of the creek from the opposite direction. Mr. Ford looked up and saw two big white horses and two men riders dressed in white robes. The time was around eleven o'clock at night. The men were singing "A Band of Angels Coming After Me." They came on down to the edge of the creek, turned around; and rode back up the hill and out of sight.

He hurried on, thinking it might be a sign that his sister was worse or dead. When he arrived his sister was better. But after he had been there about an hour, someone from Larue County came and told him that his baby had died at home with the croup about eleven that night.

171. Person Born with Caul Has Second Sight

A *caul*, which figures in this story, is the membrane that envelops a fetus; there is a widespread folk belief that a person born with the membrane still covering his or her face will have psychic powers. This story was collected in May 1972, Cayuga, Indiana, from a retired carpenter. Motifs D1710, D1739; cf T551.8.

My sister was borned with a veil over her face. What I seen, as near as I can remember 'cause she was born in 1903, was that there was fuzz all over her face. She had the power to tell the future, but as far as I know she only used it once. One day her husband went over to the Wabash River to a fishing camp and when he got back he wasn't going to tell her anything about where he had been. But she said to him, "Were you on a boat?" And he said, "No." She said, "Oh yes you were." And she proceeded to tell him that he had been on the Wabash River in a boat taking one or two women for a ride in a boat. Anyway, she told him exactly where he'd been and what he'd been doing and let him know that he couldn't get away with any hanky-panky.

172. Prenatal Fear Causes Birthmark

The idea that a pregnant woman's experiences may cause a particular birthmark to appear on her child is known to many Americans. This legend was collected from a female student, nineteen, Covington, Indiana, November 1972. Motifs F1041.17, T563, T576.

I have heard my grandmother tell this story many times. This happened a long time ago. Well, anyway, in the times when people did their butchering at home, it seems that several members of the family would gather at one house in the early winter and butcher hogs or whatever to last all the winter for everyone. There was a pregnant girl at one of these butcherings. Sometime during the day she left the room, the kitchen, where they were doing a lot of the cutting. One of the guys picked up the hog's head from the table and goes to the doorway where she will reenter the room. Not seeing him, the pregnant girl steps into the room. As she entered the room he shoved the hog's head at her. Terrified, she screamed and put her hand to her face. When her baby was born, it had coarse, hoglike hair on its face in exactly the same place as where the mother touched her own face on the day she was frightened.

173. The Fairy Birth

The idea of close connections between the world of humans and that of fairies is an old one in Europe, but fairy lore, though certainly known in the United States, is not very common in American tradition. This story was recollected from memory by the author of the article from which it is reprinted. He remembered it from the telling of his American-born father who in turn had it from *his* Irish-born mother. The events seem to be set in Ireland. Motif F372.1.

There was a woman in the neighborhood who attended births; most of the people couldn't afford a doctor, and would rather have had the woman even if they could have had the doctor. The woman's name was Brigit. She had great skill in her calling, so that her fame had spread about the country. It was no strange thing for a person to come from miles away in search of her, and she was always willing to make the call. Nor had she ever come to any harm.

One night, when the town was asleep, she was wakened by a knocking. It was not usual for her to be called in the dead of night; and, further, she knew of no event impending in the neighborhood. But she put up a light anyhow, and went to see who was there.

A tall, dark man stood at the door. She had never seen him. He was well dressed, but he had a strange air about him. Though he spoke quietly and with grace when he told her what he wanted her for, he didn't somehow make himself clear enough. Or else it was that Brigit hadn't fully awaked.

His people were in the hills, he said, and one of the women was taken suddenly, and they had no one with them that had Brigit's skill, from what he'd heard tell of it. Would she go with him to attend the birth?

Brigit didn't particularly want to go, because of the stranger's air; and still she did want to go, because of the woman in pain. "All right," she said, "I'll go with you, with the grace of God. And now won't you sit in by the fire until I bring out my horse?" But the stranger declined to enter the house, and said he must keep an eye on his own horse—it was a spirited animal, dark and black-maned as its master.

The two of them, Brigit and the stranger, set off quietly enough toward the hills, all in the light of the full moon. Brigit said little, waiting for the stranger to speak; and he said nothing at all. They had not gone very far when they came to a turn in the path and Brigit suddenly found herself in a part of the country she had never seen before. It was completely strange to her, although she knew every bit of country for miles around. "This is strange country," she said. "Where are your people, anyhow?"

"It's not far to go," said the man; "we'll be there shortly now."

"Indeed, will we," said Brigit. "I'm of a mind to turn back here unless I know where I'm going."

"We are almost there," said the man. He looked at her oddly and then said, "I wasn't going to tell you this—indeed, I'm not supposed to—but I can see you're a good woman. Now, when we come on my people, be just as well spoken to them as they to you; but by no means take food of them when they offer it to you."

Brigit didn't like the sound of this, though she lost some of her fear of the man himself. She had little time to think further, however, for they came now in sight of his people's encampment. "Remember what I told you," the man said. She had no chance to ask "why" because the people flocked to them and made them both very welcome. She herself was treated with great courtliness, and was aided promptly in every way as she went about making her preparations. Yet there seemed something strange about the whole thing, because here it was the dead of night and all were as wide awake as if it were midday and some of the people continued to dance about in a ring and make merry as if nothing at all were going to happen.

Anyhow, she assisted the young woman in question, and brought a boy into the world for her. There was much rejoicing at this, and Brigit felt well pleased. It wouldn't do for the people, though, but that she must sit down to eat a little something with them. They asked her and asked her, and practically begged her to stay awhile to eat; but Brigit remembered what the dark man had warned her against, and she remained firm. At last, the people that asked her stay were almost in tears. Still she refused. Oddly, all the time she felt there was a good deal of laughing going on about her; yet she couldn't tell who was doing it.

Finally, Brigit took horse and went off with the tall stranger by the way she came. As they rode along, she decided to ask him why he had told her to refuse all food. He looked at her for a moment after she asked him and said, "'Tis lucky for you, and unlucky for us, that you ate nothing; for, if you had eaten but one mouthful, you would never return to your own world again. As it is, we have lost you; and you'll go back none the worse."

Then it dawned on Brigit that she had attended a fairy birth, and that she was still in the world of fay. She was about to make the sign of the cross when they came to a turn in the path. Her guide smiled gravely on her, and she suddenly found herself back again where she had entered the land of fay, in plain sight of the town. The man himself had vanished completely, and his horse.

"It was only the grace of God that saved me," she would say in later years.

174. The Playing Player Piano

This story was told by Theodore R. Ebert, a retired miner, August 6, 1957, as part of George Korson's collecting the mining folklore of the Pennsylvania Dutch. Motif E402.1.3.

"The Old Rugged Cross" was my father's favorite hymn and he often played it on our player piano. It was played at his funeral. Well, one night we were all awakened by the player piano giving out with "The Old Rugged Cross." We didn't know of anyone being downstairs so we looked into it. The hymn went on but the roll wasn't moving. Well, we were surely scared. I'd say it played about half-way through and then stopped, and we couldn't understand this. We couldn't sleep so we sat around to try to figure this thing out. We looked in the piano but discovered no mouse or no rats. No, we couldn't find anything.

Three nights later the same song, "The Old Rugged Cross," was heard again, and three nights later it happened again. We gave the piano a good going over and found nothing whatsoever. And while I was examining this, I had a heavy ring on and the ring got caught in one of the strings and broke it. From then on we heard no more of "The Old Rugged Cross."

175. The Blood Stained Bricks

Paul Frazier collected "The Blood Stained Bricks" from a seventy-five-year-old woman of Pennsylvania German descent in Allentown, Pennsylvania. Motif E422.1.11.5.1.

A man had been stabbed to death in a wicked place of merry-making. It was then observed that three bricks in the walk from the house had blood stains on them. When they were washed the blood stains remained. When the three bricks were replaced by others the blood stains were on the new bricks. One night a girl who lived in the residence across the street from the wicked house went on to her front porch and saw a little man about three feet tall who was well dressed in a black suit, a high silk hat, and other excellent clothes. He had sparkling cuff and shirt buttons which shone like the eyes of cats in the dark. He walked out of the wicked house toward the street, the girl became very much frightened and ran into her house and turned up the gas light. She then went back to the door and looked out and did not see the little man. She told no one of this experience at the time. A week later her sister had exactly the same experience.

176. A Lost Stagecoach

This legend, said only to have been collected by J.M. from V.W. of Mora, New Mexico, was part of a collection of New Mexican Hispanic folklore assembled by R. D. Jameson and published by Stanley Robe. Motif F757.

It is said that somewhere north of Mora in Stagecoach Canyon there is intact in a cave an old stagecoach. There are two legends as to how the stagecoach got there. One story is that the stage driver was fleeing from Indians and that he drove his coach into a convenient cave and was trapped. The Indians supposedly took his horses and left the coach intact in the cave. The second theory is that the stage driver and guard were carrying gold and decided to steal the gold, hide the stage-coach so that it could not be easily found, and disappeared.

I have been told by someone who supposedly has seen the coach, that it is still in good condition and the cave into which it was driven now stands fourteen feet above the river bed and it would take a bit of work to recover it.

177. Phantom Steamboat on Devil's Lake

According to Henry Winfred Splitter, who reprints this story from an 1892 news-paper in an article on American phantom ships, phantom ships are less common in American folklore than in that from "foreign ports." Indeed, this story takes place not at sea but on a lake in the American Midwest. Devil's Lake is in east central North Dakota. Although by the mid-twentieth century, farms and ranches surrounded the lake, in the nineteenth century, there were only a government fort and a small settlement on opposite shores; the government ran a small steamer between the two places, though the protagonists in the story are crossing the lake by sailboat. Motif E535.3.

There had been quite a lot of us over at the settlement, and on a Sunday eve we started to return in the sailboat. If I remember rightly there were thirteen in the party, nearly all soldiers from the fort. We had just got rightly started when one of those high winds which suddenly spring up on the lake came down on and it was no time until our sailing gear got out of order, and was useless. When the storm subsided, we were dismantled and drifting. Nearly all the soldiers who were in the boat were on absence leave which expired on Sunday night, and consequently they were in a great state of anxiety over our helpless condition. It grew dark.

As we had no oars we were compelled to sit helpless. There wasn't a drop of anything stronger than the water around us. While we were lying becalmed, somebody heard, or imagined he heard, the puffing of the steam boat. We listened, and what seemed to be the noise of escaping steam was heard distinctly. Instantly the conclusion was reached that somebody at the fort had witnessed our predicament before sunset and had started the steamboat over to our relief. I strained my eyes in the direction from which the sound came, and sure enough, the shadowy outline of a steamboat seemed visible in the darkness.

Everybody was on the alert. The throb of the engines became more distinct. Some of the men saw the lights and detected the glow of the furnace fires. So powerful was this impression, that several of our party hailed the boat, but the cry was unanswered. We watched it go by in the distance till suddenly it disappeared. We managed to get to the fort, landing that night with considerable trouble. The little government steamer lay there with no sign of life about her, and her furnace cold as a January morning. It was evident that she had not been out on the lake within twenty-four hours. The people at the fort verified this.

The story of our experience seemed incredible, but there were plenty of witnesses, and so the phantom steamboat from that hour became one of the mysteries of Devil's Lake. Other people have since claimed to have seen it go puffing up, down the lake in the darkness of moonless nights, the fires making trails of light on the water, while the throb of the ghostly engines was distinctly heard.

178. Going to the Dance Hall

The potential evils of dancing and dance halls is well recognized in American folklore and American popular culture. This legend may be related to a larger cycle of Hispanic American narratives in which the Devil actually appears as a dance partner (see story 195), although here in story 178, the dangers are left more vague with the emphasis simply on the mysterious nature of the event. Motifs D2074.2.1, D2121.1.

Once two girls wanted to go to a dance but they did not have a ride. So they went to visit another girl, thinking that she too might be planning to go to the dance.

Shortly after they got there, they told her about wanting to go to the dance. They wanted to go badly. The girl told them that she could not go but she'd get them a ride.

She stepped into another room. There was no telephone in any part of the house. And soon she came out and told them that someone would come call for them soon. Someone did come. A very handsome young man called for them and off they left for the dance with a man they had never seen before.

On the way, the girls asked who he was. He told them he was just passing by. When they reached the place where he was supposed to let them out, he disappeared. They found themselves standing in the entrance to the dance hall.

179. Finding a Lost Watch

From the Indiana University Folklore Archives, this story was collected from Glen Ward of Walton, Indiana. Motif D1825.4.3.

When I was a kid up in Rochester, I remember a woman that—well, if she wasn't a witch, she's about the closest thing to it I ever saw. Her name was Mrs. Beamendocker and she was real old—and she had this mousey husband. He was the most henpecked man I ever knew, but I always thought he was probably her listener, you know, 'cause he was always hanging around the biddies in town, and then they'd go see Mrs. Beamendocker and she'd tell them all these things she couldn't possibly know unless someone was eavesdropping for her, or she really was a witch.

I remember one time the boy that lived next door to us was out shocking wheat—you probably don't remember what that is. We'd gather up the wheat in bunches and tie up and leave them in the field to dry instead of baling it. Well, Tad had a real nice watch that his old man gave him, and one day when he was out shocking wheat, he lost it. Well, he went to Mrs. Beamendocker and she told him exactly where to find it—under such and such a shock in a certain row, and it was there, just like she said it would be.

180. Saved by Lightning

The "part of the territory" referred to in this Iowa legend is "the bottom lands of the Cedar near its confluence with the Iowa River"; it dates from the late nineteenth century. Motif R341.1.

In the early days of Iowa this part of the territory was inhabited by a wild, desperate class of people, who lived on what they could steal from more industrious neighbors. Horse-stealing was the favorite pursuit of the male portion of this community, and many enterprising men saw the fruits of their toil destroyed for want of livestock which disappeared at the most inopportune times.

Horse-thieves in those days expected no mercy when they had the misfortune to fall into the hands of the settlers; and when one bright June morning in the year 1840, nine of them were caught by a detachment of outraged farmers, they prepared themselves to meet death with bold faces. The gang was conducted to a huge oak tree on the banks of the Cedar River, whose nine branches invited the settlers to finish their work of vengeance. One man after the other was supplied with a hempen neck-tie, and arrangements were made to send them to kingdom come at the same instant.

The signal was given. A fierce stroke of lightning and a deafening roar of thunder followed the command which was to end the earthly existence of nine human beings. Eight bodies dangled in the air. The ninth was lying on the ground, saved by the lightning which had ripped the branch on which he was hanging from the trunk of the tree. It was a miracle, for the man, after recovering from his stupor, proved his innocence to the satisfaction of the "vigilants."

The eight thieves had met their fate, but Providence interfered in a way that could not be misunderstood to save the life of the guiltless. The tree made famous by this incident is still standing—at least it was two years ago.

181. The Face on the Windowpane

This Florida story was collected from Mrs. I. L. Campbell, Panama City, in 1955; like stories 182 and 183, it deals with the idea that meaningful images can be projected on to things through traumatic events. Motifs F782, F968, D992.3.

Once upon a time there was this family who had a very beautiful young daughter. There was to be a big dance one night, and she had planned for many months to go. Since the weather that day and night had been terrible, the family decided that she had better not go.

It made the girl very mad and she ran up to her room. That night she was sitting before her mirror brushing her long hair and crying, when lightning struck and killed her.

From that day until now, one of the windows in her bedroom has the impression of her head and hair on it. They have changed the windowpane time after time but the impression always returns, and now they have painted the impression and completed the picture.

182. The Face on the Tombstone

This legend text comes from the Indiana University Folklore Archives and was collected from Mrs. S. D. Coulter, a practical nurse in her fifties who, according to the collector, "liked to talk about strange happenings," June 20, 1967, Fort Wayne, Indiana. Motifs N270, Q211; cf E422.1.11.2.

This man and woman were married and she was an atheist or agnostic—didn't believe in God—and she and her husband fought all the time.

He was always saying how she made him so mad he could kill her. They lived in some little town up in the north end of Indiana, but out in the country around the town.

Well, one day they had a fight and he threatened to strangle her if she didn't shut up and she told him that if he ever killed her she would get back at him somehow— she would show people how he had killed her.

This made him so mad he kind of went crazy and he did strangle her with his bare hands. He tried to make it look like she had died a natural death and they buried her and he put up a big, expensive tombstone over her grave.

Well, years went by and once in a while he would go to the grave to put some flowers on it or something and he noticed that each time he went it looked a little different, the tombstone. Finally after a couple of years he realized what it was—her face was appearing on the stone and there were hands around her neck.

It got to be so plain that other people could see it too, so he had it removed and some university took it to try to find out what had caused the face. He put up another stone over the grave and thought that was that, but in a couple of more years another picture of her face started coming out on the stone, this time plainer than before. It looked like there were hands around her neck and she was choking to death, her eyes were all rolled back and everything. He tried everything he knew how to keep that face off the stone—soap and water, steel wool, paint, everything, but it showed right through. That was her way of getting back at him because by the time the second face started appearing, people were talking and the police were getting kind of suspicious and they figured she hadn't really died naturally at all.

183. The Chain on the Tombstone

"The Chain on the Tombstone" was collected by William M. Clements from Terry Srygler, Bedford, Indiana, July 14, 1968. In the article about the narrative that he published, Clements includes a photograph of the tombstone of the legend. In this transcription, we see the story emerge as the collector questions his informant, who was locally considered an "expert" on the story. Motifs F840, F855, F863, F900; cf E532, E532(d).

Q. And, Terry, you were gonna tell me something about the tombstone in Bond's Chapel Cemetery. I wonder what makes this tombstone unusual.

A. Well, the tombstone itself isn't unusual. I mean, it's a small tombstone; but when you get up close, you can see what appears to be a chain. And small links of a chain looks maybe engraved in the tombstone to form a cross. Well, let's see, I think it's a Sarah Pruett; and it's not really an old grave—it's 1930 or '40 or something. But at times the links on the chain will vary. I mean, sometimes there'll be seven or eight; sometimes there'll be up to fifteen or sixteen. And, well, nobody knows why it changes. Some people think maybe it's the weather and something in the stone itself; and other people just think it's psy . . . [whistle] supernatural.

Q. Now what do you know about the person that's buried under there?

A. Well, as I said, it was a Sarah Pruett; and she was supposed to have been killed by her husband with a logging chain. And that's why, you know, they called it the chain and all like that. And, well, she was with her lover; and her husband found her and killed her with a chain. And one of the things about the chain is that if you touch it when it has thirteen links on it, you will be killed by a chain. And so, you know, everybody goes out there and looks at it. If it's got thirteen links on it, you know, they stand back. But if you touch it during the time of a full moon, you're supposed to go insane or lose your mind, you know. And there's been several incidents of people touch it, you know, during full moon; and, well, they get chased by a big bright light all the way back to Orleans. I know we were chased one night; but we didn't believe it, you know. We touched it during full moon and got out into the car and started to leave, and the driver looked in the rear view mirror; and that was all, you know. "Look, there's a white light!" [falsetto] Whoom! We were gone.

---

184. The Bride and the Egg Yolk

Folklorist Carol Miller recorded this legend from a Gypsy narrator in 1967 in Seattle, Washington. Miller notes that among American Gypsies, a wedding is a noisy, lively party that takes place over three days; the bride, as in the story, "is often too nervous to eat." *Gaje* are non-Gypsies. Motif E10.

This was in the old days. A young girl was very nervous at her wedding. She didn't eat—there was too much to do. It was a big wedding, lots of people, a big party that lasted into the night. Late that night she peeled an egg, ate the white, and put the yoke in her mouth. She was so nervous she forgot to chew, and the yoke stuck in her throat and she died. So instead of a wedding the people had a funeral.

The next night two *gaje* men who had seen her all dressed up for the wedding with all the gold chains and gold coins came to rob her. They opened her coffin. One of them placed his foot on her chest to yank off the necklaces, and the yolk popped out. Catching her breath, she coughed and said, "What am I doing here?" She frightened the *gaje* away. They didn't get the gold.

Then she walked back to the camp and found her people. They were scared because they knew she had died. She said, "I'm not a ghost, I'm alive." And she lived another forty years.

This is a true story.

185. The Holyoke Dam

Popular writer Clifton Johnson published a book on New England folklore in 1896 in which he included this story about a bursting dam. Motif Q221.4.1.

In 1848 the first Holyoke dam built across the Connecticut was finished. After the escape of the water had been shut off, and the flood was piling up against the new structures, it is said that the builder exclaimed, "God Almighty couldn't sweep that dam away!" The words were no sooner out of his mouth than there was a cracking of timbers, and the whole structure gave way, and crumbled from sight in the torrent of water that then broke loose.

186. The Strange Death of a Slave Master

This legend was uncovered by fieldworkers engaged in a Louisiana collecting project sponsored during the Great Depression by the Federal Writers' Project. Motif Q558.7.

It is said that a certain Mr. Reau used to hang incorrigible slaves in the woods near his plantation. There is a legend that Reau died in a most peculiar fashion. One morning he began to jump up and down in his bed, was at last suspended in midair, eyes and tongue protruding. He had every appearance of having been hanged.

187. Cursed Clock

Zelma Hicks of Marianna, Florida, told this story to a collector in 1949. Motif H252.6; cf E766.1.

At Marianna some years ago a Negro was convicted of a crime and sentenced to be hanged. He pleaded "not guilty" all through the trial, but he was convicted anyway and was hung from the courthouse. Just before they were going to hang him he told them that because he was innocent and they had still done this to him, their clock on the courthouse would never keep good time again. And people living there say that, from that day on, the courthouse clock has indeed been spasmodic—sometimes running, sometimes not, but never correct.

188. A Loup-Garou's Debt

Loup-garou is the French term for a werewolf, that is, a human being trans-formed into a wolf by magical forces; the term is known in parts of the United States where there has been French cultural influence. In this story, the werewolf is a soul who cannot enter heaven because of a debt. New York folklorist Harold Thompson was told the story by Pearl Hamelin, whose great-grandfather (born c. 1820) encountered the werewolf. Motif D113.1.1.

When old Henry, a neighbor, died owing him two dollars, Mr. Hamelin declared that Henry's soul could not enter heaven until it had first come to him begging for the gift of this sum. The declaration was made confidently: an old French belief of Clinton County held that if you die owing money, you cannot enter heaven until your creditor generously informs the Powers Above that he makes your soul a gift of the debt. For several long nights Mr. Hamelin stayed up, grimly awaiting Henry's ghost, but greatly to his annoyance no ghost appeared.

One clear winter night in that same year, Mr. Hamelin was driving his sleigh home to Mooers through a wood under a bright, hard moon. Suddenly he saw a shaggy creature trotting along the road behind his "rig." The first thing that he noticed was the wolf's eyes, gleaming like frozen fire; next he observed with a start that the animal's legs scarcely brushed the snow as he ran.

Reaching for his whip, Mr. Hamelin forced his already trembling horse into a gallop, but the wolf easily kept pace. When the plunging horse slowed to a walk, the strange companion slowed to the same speed. Then it flashed upon Mr. Hamelin that this was a *loup-garou,* Henry's soul prowling the night.

At the edge of the wood the animal spoke: "Joe, Joe, are you going to give me those two dollars?"

Remembering his boasts, Joe roared, "No, I am not!"

Three times the request was repeated, thrice refused. When the barn was reached, the *loup-garou* trotted in and leaped into a manger while Joe unhitched his frightened horse. A stubborn man glared at a stubborn wolf. Then Joe Hamelin did the bravest deed of his life: contemptuously he turned his back upon the super-natural eyes and moved toward the barn-door. With a sudden rush of air a huge body struck his back, bearing him down to the lintel. Hot, furry jaws were at his neck, and a hoarse, furry voice cried, "For the last time—will you give me those two dollars?"

Joe did not take long to decide. "Yes," he said. "I give you the two dollars. Take them with you to a place where they will melt."

At these words the *loup-garou* vanished. With great dignity Joe picked himself up and stalked into the house.

"See, Delphine," he said to his wife. "I give in to no woman and to no man. Tonight for once I have given in, but not until the *loup-garou* had me by the neck."

Delphine looked and shuddered. On the collar of his coat was a savage rent and the white froth from a wolf's jaws.

189. An Oyster-Culling Loup Garou

Stories of *loups garoux* are well known in Cajun Louisiana, the source of this text. In this story, however, the *loup garou* is more vaguely conceived not as a person transformed into a wolf but as some sort of haunting (and potentially helpful) supernatural being. It was collected from Loulan Pitre of Cut Off, Louisiana, by Pat Mire and Maida Owens in the course of producing a video documentary on Louisiana storytelling. Loulan Pitre's son, noted filmmaker Glen Pitre, tells a rather different version of the story, printed in the same published collection from which story 189 is reprinted. *Oyster tongs* are a device with hinged arms for manually lifting oysters from the sea bed; a *dredge* is a large device dragged along the bottom to capture the oysters, put into use in oystering more recently that tongs. Cf motifs D113.1.1, E261.4, E271.

My father was an oyster fisherman because that was his means of a livelihood. And people from his time didn't have anything to do at night. They'd gather—well, it's a gathering of working men instead of old men—and they'd tell each other stories, and they probably told each other stories so often that they'd believe them. They'd actually come to believe them. And this particular story is really amazing.

I don't want to go into the mechanics of the oyster business, but it was a little complicated—not to them but to anyone you want to explain it to.

They used to tong oysters. There were no such things as dredges. *Tong.* And they had these oyster skiffs—were about twenty, twenty-four, twenty-six feet long and maybe ten feet wide. They'd tong oysters, oh, practically all day long and load them up. And that was shells and regular oysters in the rough. And at night, they'd congregate in some bayou. They usually had some little camps or little cabins with the particular fishermen. They sleep on the boats because it was so darn hot—or either so darn cold when it was winter time. And they would gather in one cabin and tell each other stories.

And this particular story stuck in my memory because I actually believed it when they—when my father—related it to me. Anyway, they'd bring these skiffs and tie them up along a big pile of oyster shells. We call this *culling* oysters, not shucking. It's an entirely different system. *Culling* oysters means sitting down in that skiff on a little old bench with a mitten in your hand, with a little hatchet, and get all those oysters as *singles*—single oysters. Every one you had to pass in your hand: if it was too small, throw it away. And then the shells would pile up at your feet and you'd have to shovel those shells onto the big shell pile, so it wouldn't clog up the little stream you were in.

And my father used to say—they call them *loup-garou*. They were a famous topic. The *loup-garou*. They'd pull all kinds of capers. *Loups garoux* would, not the people.

And so it came about that one of these old oystermen would say, "I keep hearing something at night in our oysters." He said, "I keep hearing noises." And they'd listen. Naturally, they wouldn't hear anything. But after a while, another one said, "I hear a noise in our skiffs. Maybe it's a raccoon." And more and more, one and after the other kept hearing [it] and finally they decided the only noise it could be was someone culling the oysters and hitting those clusters with a hatchet.

All night long, this would go. All night long. Next morning, they'd go check out the oysters to get ready to work. And one fisherman would find his skiff: the oysters had all been culled. And none of the others. And, well, they believed in *loups garoux*. They took them for—their existence as a fact. They weren't afraid of them. And this lasted forever. Throughout the winter, and then the following winter, lo and behold, the thing was back again. You see, they just work oysters in the winter time then, when it cool. And so one guy says, "I'm going to stay. I'm going to hide behind a pile of shells and see what's doing that in the moonlight."

So, he was brave enough. He stayed up. And he could see the pile of shells diminishing in the skiff. But he could not see what was doing it. And he could hear the hatchet hitting the clusters. So he kind of went, sneaked over there, and he saw like a shadow, some kind of apparition there. So he took a pole—they used these long poles—that they used to . . . push the skiffs around. They didn't have any engines in them. And he sneaked up on this thing and whapped it across the back of this—more of a shadow than anything physical—and it disappeared. There was nothing. And that night on they never heard another noise, and nobody ever got another oyster culled. And that thing disappeared. And that was the story. . . . And they believed it. They actually got each other to believe it.

The Devil

In European folktales, the Devil is commonly a comic rather than a terrifying figure, a figure who is often outwitted by clever humans. In American legends, he may be frightening or disquieting ("The Devil Appears as a Black Dog," "A Devil Child," "The Devil at the Discotheque"), but even when his appearance terrifies people, the story ultimately may laugh at the terror he inspires ("The Devil in Eisenhower's Saloon," "Raising the Devil," "The Devil and the Card Players"). Indeed, the Devil's function may not be so much to carry people off to Hell as to warn of situations or places potentially evil: the saloon where hymns are parodied, the card game where stakes are gambled, the discotheque or dance hall where men and women gyrate together.

190. The Devil Appears as a Black Dog

This legend was told by James Collison to Joseph B. Higgins as part of a collecting project by students at the New York State College for Teachers, Albany, 1940–1946. Traditionally the Devil was conceived as having cloven hooves for feet, and these make the "cloven marks" referred to. Indeed, in subsequent stories in this section, notice is paid to the Devil's feet being cloven or having other odd and noticeable features. Cf motifs G303.3.1.1, M219.2.

Set back a bit from the banks of the Poestenkill Creek, not far from Troy, there is a house that is deserted now; but not many years ago it was the scene of a visit from Satan in the form of a big black dog, and the evidences of that visit, they tell me, are still to be seen.

It happened this way: a girl was dying in that house and it was decided that her brother should go to get the parish priest; as the boy left, he noticed a black dog going in the house, but he was preoccupied and thought nothing about it. By the time the boy returned with the priest, the dog had found the girl's room and had withstood all efforts to remove him. A few minutes later the priest came hurriedly out of the room and left the house without a word to anyone, but somebody observed that there were long scratches on his neck. As soon as he heard about this, the girl's brother rushed after him. When found, the priest was a badly shaken man; not only had he been physically mauled by the dog, but, far worse, he had been spiritually defeated, for, he explained to the brother, his sister was damned. As soon as the priest had kneeled to pray for the girl, the beast had set upon him and clawed him. He was persuaded to return to the house where they found the sister dead, with red claw-marks on her forehead; and burned into the floor by her bed were cloven marks.

The family moved away and the house has long been empty, but on Good Friday the people still see a black dog prowling about the premises.

191. The Devil Plays Cards

Folklorist Harold Thompson published this story in his widely read book about New York state folklore. Rensselaer County is in upstate New York. Motif G303.6.1.5.

In Rensselaer County there is a story of a group of men playing cards in a hilltown. Late in the evening a stranger who knocked was hospitably invited to join in the game. Toward morning, when he had won every penny in the house, he departed, leaving behind an unspoken question as to his identity which was answered when one of the discomfited players noticed beneath the card-table the dirty mark of a cloven hoof.

192. The Devil and the Card Players

This account of the Devil's appearance was told by Mrs. Frank Bateman to Jane Phillips as part of a collecting project by students at the New York State College for Teachers, Albany, 1940–1946. AT 1187, told as a legend.

In southern Rensselaer County . . . there was a group of cronies who used to get together in a shack out in the woods because they were afraid of their wives, good churchgoing dames, every one of them. One night they were playing a little five-card straight and John Dell was winning, after a long streak of bad luck. Quite unexpectedly there came a rap on the door and they found there a quiet-spoken man who made himself right to home, as though he had been there before; and when one of the boys went home early, the stranger asked if he could sit in on the game. Nobody objected, but John Dell ran his thumb around the candle about halfway down and said that when the flame reached that spot he was going home. They cut the stranger into the game and John's winnings began to melt away until he was digging deep in his pockets. That wasn't all that was making him feel uneasy; the candle wasn't burning down, not so much as a quarter of an inch though they played for an hour or more. And so at last he got up and said he was leaving, and the stranger called him a liar and a cheapskate for not keeping his word, and in a minute they were slugging it out, no holds barred. As they were rolling on the floor, John saw the cloven hoof and he made one long leap, leaving his coat in the stranger's hand; but he was too busy passing Jack rabbits all the way home to miss it.

193. The Devil in Eisenhower's Saloon

George Korson, noted authority on the folklore of coal miners and mining, published this story, noting that it is from "the West End of Schuylkill County," Pennsylvania, where it is much laughed at, especially by miners. Motifs G303, G303.4.8.1.

When miners caroused it was usually done in a saloon, and Eisenhower's saloon in Cherryville, just north of Pine Grove, was one of the places in which they hung out. One evening, a long time ago, there were seven or eight miners in that saloon; Ed Christ was tending bar. At the same time Dunkards were walking home from a church service they called a love feast, and as they passed Eisenhower's saloon they broke into a hymn.

The seven or eight miners, being drunk, decided to hold a mock love feast in imitation of the Dunkards. So they told Ed Christ, the bartender, to go ahead and serve up whiskey and pretzels as substitutes for the communion wine and bread. The drunken miners lifted their glasses, but no liquor touched their lips, for at that very moment all hell broke loose. Smoke suddenly poured through cracks in the floor and filled the saloon. There was the odor of brimstone. A sound like clanking chains announced the arrival of the devil. That awful sight brought the miners to their senses. They quick escaped through the door and windows; or by a stairway leading to the upstairs bedrooms, which was taken by old Ed Christ who locked himself in his room. But the devil just walked through his door. Old Ed was a nervous wreck for weeks afterwards. The devil's cloven feet were burned that deep in the saloon floor that the mark couldn't be removed for a long time. Yah, that was one devil of an experience those miners had.

194. Raising the Devil

"Raising the Devil" was told by Beulah Knapp to Lois Schenck as part of a collecting project by students at the New York State College for Teachers, Albany, 1940–1946. Victor is Victor Tremper, who lived near Stormville Mountain in upstate New York and was reputed locally to be a murderer and to have the power to make the Devil appear. Motifs G303, G303.6.1.2(h).

Well, one rainy afternoon a crowd of the boys were hanging around the general store, looking for some excitement. They got to talking about Victor's power and decided there would never be a better time to prove whether there was any truth in the story. So a group of the hardier souls went sloshing through the rain to the old man's house and asked him point-blank how good a friend of his the Devil was. For reply he led them out to his weather-beaten barn where he cautioned them first to absolute silence, then drew a circle in the middle of the floor. In the breathless quiet he spoke some magic words that none of them understood. They waited for a moment or two, and then he appeared, the Old Boy himself, right out of the middle of the floor. Well, Victor had proved his power, but I reckon the boys didn't stay around very long. I reckon they were satisfied with what they saw.

195. The Devil at the Discotheque

With its discotheque setting, this legend updates a popular legend tradition among Mexican Americans about the sudden appearance of the Devil at a dance or dance hall. It is a story with deep European roots, related to medieval tales of people who dance off following the Devil; see also story 178. Motifs G303.3.1, G303.4.5.3.1, G303.5, G303.10.4.0.1.

This just happened last Saturday, and I really believe it because Mrs C. told my sister this. Mrs C. is very religious and does not make up stories like this. She said that a girl had gone dancing at a disco in McAllen after her mother told her not to go that night. While she was there, she danced with a man that looked like that man who made that dance movie. The man was very handsome and had very dark eyes. He was also the best dancer on the floor that night. There was also something strange about the man, but she couldn't put her finger on it. After it got pretty late, the girl told the man that she had to be going home. The man told her that she could not leave because she was going with him. She thought he was playing but could not help being a little frightened. When she tried to get away from him, he grabbed her and told her to look at his feet so that she would know who she was going with. When she looked down, she saw that the man had a chicken foot and a cow's foot. At that same time her dress caught on fire and a strong smell of sulphur was in the air. Some of the people at the dance floor came to the rescue of the girl, and she was saved from the man but she is still in the hospital. The man disappeared on the spot.

196. A Devil Child

Letitia Humphreys Wrenshall published this brief account in an early twentieth-century issue of the *Journal of American Folklore*. She may have picked up the story from newspaper sources. Motif G303.25.21*.

In January there was great excitement in "little Italy," in New York, over a devil child who inherited a curse, was currently reported to have horns, green eyes that flashed with fire, cloven feet, and, when only two days old, was known to have caused the death of a child next door, whose throat bore the marks of tiny impish fingers.

197. Sold Body and Soul

The subject of this legend, which folklorist Richard M. Dorson reprinted from an earlier source, is General Jonathan Moulton (1726–1787), who in New Hampshire had the reputation of having been in league with the Devil. Moulton fought in both the French and Indian War and the Revolution and was a wealthy land speculator whose business dealings were sometimes suspected as shady. The fire referred to as this narrative opens is the burning-down of his house, and indeed his mansion did burn in 1769. There are a number of legends about Moulton, and he appears in several poems, including one by John Greenleaf Whittier. Motifs F852, G303.22, M210, M219.2.5.

When asked the reason that they did not endeavor to save the old man's effects, which were burning up before them, the inhabitants replied, "He is leagued with the devil, to whom he has sold both his soul and body after death—on condition that he (the general) should be provided with a certain quantity of gold and silver, which should be periodically rained down the chimney into an old boot. The boot," continued they, "was cut off at the bottom by the General, who was not faithful even to the devil—when the latter cried out from the top of the chimney, 'Is not that cursed boot full yet?' 'No!' said the General—and the room was filled, instead of the boot, with gold and silver. When Satan had discovered how he had been imposed upon, he was exceedingly wroth at his unprincipled confederate, and in revenge he burnt his house, when all the General's gains were consumed. But they became friends again, and were seen walking together." . . . .

It was not long after this circumstance that the old General died, and was buried—yes, the coffin was buried, or was ready to be, but the body of the defunct General was not, to all accounts. The deceased, as usual, was laid out and put into the coffin, but on the succeeding day, when all was arranged for the dread solemnities of a great funeral, on lifting the lid to take a last farewell peep—lo! the coffin was empty!

Divine Retribution and Other Miracles

Religion influences legends in a variety of ways. Ultimately, the Devil is a figure drawn from religious contexts. Blood stoppers may call upon divinely given powers or recite prayers. Priests and other ministers are protagonists in legend actions. But perhaps where this influence is seen most directly is in narratives about divine interventions, whether interventions express God's displeasure ("Sunday Mountain," "Retribution") or provide a cure ("Sweet Hour of Prayer") or other miraculous aid ("The Staircase at Loretto").

In American legends, miracles take many forms. The end result may be personal and limited to a single person ("Flowers from the Virgin Mary") and thus somewhat low-key. Or it may affect a whole community ("Statue of St. Joseph Returns") or a key figure upon whom a whole community or more depends ("Three Mysterious Laborers Aid One of Joseph Smith's Protectors").

The attitudes a particular religious group takes toward miracles may have a powerful effect on the circulation of narratives among the members of the group. Thus, Catholics seem to enjoy a wealth of miracle stories, several from New Mexican Hispanic Catholics in particular being included here. And Mormons circulate stories about divine assistance, especially as provided by the Three Nephites (supernatural figures who appear in the *Book of Mormon,* the Mormon sacred text, but who have become in folklore providers of help to the faithful). But miracles are not limited to these groups. "Sweet Hour of Prayer" focuses on events surrounding that standard Protestant hymn. Two of the legends here ("Great Merit," "The Soldier") are from Hasidic Jews in New York.

198. Sunday Mountain

Charles M. Skinner included this legend in one of his popular late nineteenth-century books of American folk stories; he found his material in earlier, published sources. Motif Q223.5(a).

The ideas of supernatural occurrences in these New Hampshire hills obtained until a recent date, and Sunday Mountain is a monument to the dire effects of Sabbath-breaking that was pointed out to several generations of New Hampshire youth for their moral betterment. The story goes that a man of the adjacent town of Oxford took a walk one Sunday, when he should have taken himself to church; and, straying into the woods here, he was delivered into the claws and maws of an assemblage of bears that made an immediate and exemplary conclusion of him.

199. Card-Playing on Sunday

Hops, whose pickers are the characters in this legend, constituted an important crop in New York state, and farmers employed crews to pick them. This story was collected by Neil Van Allen from Carrie Austin of Little Falls, New York. Motif E293.2(d).

She also told me that one Sunday four of the hop-pickers were playing cards. A black dog appeared and began to run around the table, almost dancing on his hind legs. Suddenly the dog fell into the middle of the table, and then disappeared. The men never played cards on Sunday again.

200. Retribution

Folklorist Susie Hoogasian-Villa grew up hearing folktales from her Armenian grandmother in Detroit and between 1940 and 1942 recorded many stories in the Armenian American Delray neighborhood in that city. She listened to the stories in Armenian and wrote out English versions in shorthand. This legend was collected from Mrs. Katoon Mouradian. Motifs A974, A977, D422.1.2, D661, M101, Q223.3, Q551.3.4.

At one time a bridal party was moving toward our village from a far-off town. The people were very thirsty, and the groom said, "If God would grant us a nice cool drink, I would offer Him a *madagh* [sacrifice]." Suddenly, a clear, cool spring appeared at the entrance of the village, and the people drank abundantly of the good water. They looked about and, across the river which gushed from the spring, saw an old shepherd with his many sheep and greeted him.

When they were refreshed, they sat on their horses and crossed to the other side of the river. The groom completely forgot his promise, and had no intention of making a sacrifice. God read his mind and decided to punish him so he turned the whole company into stone. The bride on her horse, the groom on his horse, the parents, the visitors, the gifts and the shepherd with his sheep—all were transformed into stone.

A beautiful cross made of stone appeared at the spring. These stone figures have remained to this day and remind us of the ingratitude of man.

201. Flowers from the Virgin Mary

Included in the holdings of the Indiana University Folklore Archives, this legend was collected March 15, 1967, in Indiana by Gerri Bard from Barbara Haley. Motifs F971.5, V277, V281, V281.1*.

I have an aunt by the name of Aunt Bertha in Dayton, Ohio. She has a son named Ray who is mentally retarded. Now he is about forty-five years old. About five years ago he tried to kill his mother with a butcher knife. Well, she decided to put him in an asylum after that happened. So she did, and one weekend, after he'd been there for about two years, they decided to give him visiting privileges and that he could go home to my Aunt Bertha's for the weekend. During the course of his stay at the asylum, he had become very religious. He had always been very religious, but he had become even more so. And he told my Aunt Bertha that he was praying to the Virgin Mary to make him well. So he came home on a Friday evening, and he went to bed, and the next morning . . . and she heard him screaming, and my Aunt Bertha went running in and said, "What's wrong?" And he said he had seen a vision of the Virgin Mary. So, she didn't believe him and he said, "Well, look at this." And he was holding a rosary given him in his hand—a beautiful wooden rosary. And she knew she hadn't given it to him and she knew no one else had given him anything. And so she thought that he must have gotten it from someone else while he was in the asylum, and that he was just pulling a joke on her, 'cause this would be like him so she really didn't pay any attention to him. Well, he went back to the asylum after that week-end and the next week-end he came home and said that he was still praying to the Virgin Mary; and that he did see her that last week-end and that she left the rosary to prove it. So he was home Friday night and Saturday night and Ray took his nap in the afternoon. And he woke up from the nap screaming and Aunt Bertha raced upstairs again, and he hadn't been out all afternoon, and he said, "I've just had another vision. I saw the Virgin Mary and she told me to keep praying." And Aunt Bertha told him that she didn't believe him again. Well, this was in the winter time and Ray sat there and looked in his lap, and he had been sleeping in one of those lounge chairs. And in his lap were a dozen red roses. Now . . . who put them there? They don't know. There were no flowers in the house. Nothing.

202. Sweet Hour of Prayer

Another Indiana text in the Indiana University Folklore Archives, story 202 was collected by Lenore Bechtel from Mrs. Ermil Hurt, Winslow, Indiana, December 27, 1959. It brings a modern device, an electric fan, into the world of uncanny events. Motif F950.

When, you know, my dad was real sick and he didn't know anything, you know, unconscious or whatever you want to call it, and we didn't have, you know, any hopes for him and neither did the doctor. And we had this electric fan in the bedroom on the dresser right by his bed. And all at once it started playing "Sweet Hour of Prayer"—the music started coming over the fan. And it played for quite a while and I turned it off cause it sort of, you know, made you have a funny feeling. I don't know how it was. And just as I turned it off, why, Dad opened his eyes and he was conscious. And I turned the fan back on and the music was gone, but he was normal.

203. Great Merit

This legend was collected by folklorist Jerome Mintz in the course of his extensive fieldwork among Hasidic Jews in New York. Hasidism is a religious movement within Orthodox Judaism founded in the eighteenth century by Rabbi Israel Ba'al Shem Tov (c. 1700–1760); influenced by the Jewish mystical writings known as the Kabbalah, it stresses emotion over intellect and joyful worship. Members of the group are adherents of a particular teacher (a rebbe); each rebbe's group is a "court." This story was told in English by a narrator identified as a thirty-year-old administrator who belonged to the Stolin Hasidic court. Mintz collected his narratives in 1959–61 and 1963. To drink *lehaim* is to toast; *Shevuos* is a celebration marking the giving of the Torah, the scrolls containing the first five books of the Bible. Motifs D1810.8.2, E720.1, J157.

It was the last day of Passover, and the [Stoliner] Rebbe was conducting the memorial meal. This is a gathering of hasidim the evening after the memorial services said on the holiday. At this gathering the Rebbe used to speak and mention different members who have since departed, and their being mentioned by the table, by the gathering, was for the benefit of their souls. At the gathering on the eve of Passover, the Rebbe called David and asked him to mention a few of our hasidim who had died recently. On the spur of the moment, David thought of a few who were killed in the Israeli war of independence, and later he mentioned another couple of our hasidim. And that was it. The Rebbe drank lehaim and he said that we could benefit the souls by mentioning them here.

A few weeks later it was the second night of Shevuos, and David dreamed that a young man since departed came to him in his dream. And David asked him, "What are you doing here? What do you want from me?"

He said, "Tomorrow night is the memorial meal with the Rebbe, and since you forgot to mention me on Passover, I want you to mention me this evening."

David related this to the Rebbe at the table and the Rebbe said the soul must have had a great merit to be able to come down and remind someone that he should be mentioned at the table.

204. The Soldier

Also from Jerome Mintz's fieldwork with Hasidic Jews in New York (see the previous story), this one was told in Yiddish by an unidentified storyteller who belonged to the Lubavitch Hasidic court. *Habad* is a movement within Hasidism that stresses messianic traditions. Motifs F1088, M185.

The old Rabbi was the first Rebbe who created the movement which we now call Habad. Now the Lubavitcher Rebbe lives in Brooklyn. We are telling a story about this Rebbe. He should be well. One time a soldier went to the Rebbe before he went to Korea. This soldier did not know much about Jewish ways. The Rebbe told him that he should follow all the good deeds that he could, especially the mitsveh [commandment, good deed] of washing before eating. Before a person eats he should wash his hands with a small glass of water and say a prayer. In the beginning the soldier did not know what the Rebbe meant.

And the soldier went to Korea. At that time there was a great big war and he did all the commandments that he knew and also the commandment of washing his hands before eating. One time all the soldiers were sitting around and they wanted to eat. Then all the soldiers took out their food and began to eat, and so did our soldier who went to visit the Rebbe. He took out a little piece of bread and he thought, "I haven't got any water here to wash my hands. What should I do?" It is told that in a person there are two ways—a good way and a bad way. One has nothing to do with the other. So the good side says, "The Rebbe told you to look for water. Go look!" He wanted to go and look as the good side told him. But the other side said, "No. What does the Rebbe mean? Should you look for water in the middle of a desert? The Rebbe thought that if there is a sink with water then you go wash yourself." Just as he was about to begin to eat he caught himself and he said, "If the Rebbe said that I should abide by this law and look for water I should go and look for water." So he went away.

In the middle of the wilderness it was not an easy thing to find water. He went a long way and he found water and he washed in order to eat. He ate a little piece of bread. After that he went back to his troop to be with his comrades. When he came back to all his comrades he saw a strange thing. Where all of his comrades were alive before there was now only smoke. Smoke remained. What had happened was that the enemy came and threw bombs on all the soldiers, and he who went away to look for water to wash his hands, he was the only one left alive. Now he realized what the Lubavitcher Rebbe had told him. He should perform all the commandments and the commandment to wash one's hands.

205. Story of the Holy Child (Santo Niño)

Chimayó, which figures prominently in this legend, is a village north of Santa Fe, New Mexico, and is today an important site for pilgrimage. The shrine there is associated with miraculous healing. This legend recounts the origins of the statue of the Christ Child at the shrine. Stanley Robe, who published this text taken from a collection assembled earlier by another folklore scholar, indicates only that it was collected in northern New Mexico in 1951. Motif D1620; cf H241.

This story began a long time ago when the Christ Child told this man that he must go to a certain place in California and buy his statue. The Christ Child also told this man that he must bring back his statue and build a church or sanctuary in Chimayó, New Mexico.

The old man sold his few belongings to get the money to make the trip to California. He went to the place where the Holy Child would be. There he found it, bought it, and started on his return trip. As in those days they traveled in wagon caravans, they had to stop to camp at night. The old man always put the precious statue by his side when he went to bed. But one night he woke up about midnight. When he looked for the statue of the Holy Child it was gone. He did not know what to do and, thinking someone had stolen it, he resolved to tell the captain of the caravan about it. But the next morning he found the statue beside his pillow where he had placed it. He thought he had had a dream about the Holy Child being lost. But the next night the same thing happened. However, he brought the statue safely to Chimayó and a sanctuary was built for him. Many people make pilgrimages to the Santuario all the time. People take new pairs of baby shoes to the Holy Child. It is believed that the Holy Child walks around at night helping the poor and ill and all those in need of help. It is said that they have found his little shoes worn out completely and that is why they replace his shoes.

I have never been to the Sanctuary, but I know persons who have made pilgrimages to it. They say the Christ Child always grants any favor you ask of him if you visit the church in Chimayó. However, you must really believe and have faith in him.

206. Statue of St. Joseph Returns

Ancient Acoma Pueblo, whose statue of a patron saint is at the center of this narrative, is spectacularly located on top of a mesa west of Albuquerque, New Mexico; Laguna Pueblo consists of six villages nearby and to the northeast of Acoma. This was collected in 1955 by A.L. from "an Indian guide at Acoma Pueblo." Motifs D435.1.1, D1620, D1654.8.1, D2157.

The Acoma Indians were given a statue of Saint Joseph by some of the missionary friars. They experienced a time of great wealth. Their harvests were good and their women bore children. Their neighbors, the Lagunas, on the other hand, experienced many hardships. The Lagunas borrowed the statue from the Acomas. Immediately their luck changed. The Acomas' luck changed also. When they went to get their statue back, the Lagunas would not let them have it. They took the matter to court and the Acomas won the case. The Lagunas were not satisfied and they appealed the case to the supreme court. Again the Acomas won the case. The Acomas sent a company of men after the statue. On the way there they found the statue of Saint Joseph under a piñon tree. Saint Joseph, since he had found out where he rightfully belonged, had started the journey back and was found resting under the piñon tree.

207. Saint Joseph's Day

"Saint Joseph's Day" was collected in northern New Mexico from Mrs. R. by M.R.R.; R. D. Jameson, who assembled a collection of folklore from Hispanic New Mexico, provided with his materials only minimal information, like the initials of collectors and informants, probably out of a desire to protect their privacy, something many earlier folklorists and other field researchers felt obliged to do. Motifs Q212, Q223.1, Q227; cf Q558.6.

There was once a widower who had three sons. Every year it was this man's custom to pay for the mass for Saint Joseph's day. After many years of doing this, and his sons were older, it happened that the eldest son dies on Saint Joseph's day in the evening. And the poor father was so disappointed and sad that for a few days he was angry at Saint Joseph and did not pray to him. But as the months went by, he became comforted and once more when Saint Joseph's feast came along, he offered the mass for him. He could not forget his custom of offering mass. But that same day his second son died suddenly. This time the poor father really became angry with Saint Joseph, so he refused to pay any more masses in his honor.

A year passed and he did not pray or even mention the name of Saint Joseph. One day he went to the forest for wood. He saw two bodies dangling from a pine tree. He was very much surprised to see the two resembled his own deceased sons.

Just then Saint Joseph appeared to him and spoke, "Why do you not offer mass for me on my feast day? And why do you never mention my name any more?"

But the poor man was so astonished that he could not answer. Then Saint Joseph asked, "Do you see those two hanging from this tree? Well, this is what would have been the end of your sons if they had lived. They were destined to become bandits and would have brought you shame and grief. That is why I took them away from you. I left you only your youngest son, who is good and will make you very happy." The old man fell on his knees and thanked Saint Joseph and asked for his forgiveness. From that day on he prayed to him and resumed his old custom of offering mass on his feast day.

208. The Staircase at Loretto

The staircase at Loretto Chapel is located in Santa Fe, New Mexico, and is said by legend to have miraculous origins and construction. The staircase still exists and is in fact a major tourist attraction; the chapel is today part of a hotel. This text was collected by M.R.R. in Santa Fe, 1952. Motifs F789, H976; cf D1620.3.2.

The sisters at Loretto Academy wanted a staircase built in their chapel. For a long time they looked for a carpenter but could find no one to do this work. It is said that they finally prayed to Saint Joseph to send them a carpenter to build the stairway to the choir in their chapel.

One day an old man came to the convent looking for work. He said he was a carpenter, so immediately the sisters put him to work. The old man did his work well but never conversed with anyone. Finally one day he went to the Mother Superior and told her that he had finished. She went to her office to get the money to pay him and left him standing in the hall. When she returned he was gone. She looked for him all over the convent but he had disappeared. No one saw him leave the convent. They claim that it was Saint Joseph who came in answer to the sisters' prayers.

The staircase is truly a wonderful piece of work. It is circular and does not have a single nail. It is said that architects have tried to copy it and have been unable to do so. Many people visit the Academy to see this piece of workmanship that is supposed to have been done by Saint Joseph.

209. How the Wandering Jew Appeared to an Early Settler in Nevada

The Wandering Jew is the legendary man who mocked Jesus on the way to his crucifixion and who was condemned to roam the earth until Jesus should return. This legend took form in the Middle Ages but first appeared in print in the early seventeenth century. The account of his sighting given here was collected December 27, 1939, from Charley Seegmiller, Provo, Utah. Motif Q502.1; cf AT 777.

There was surely a queer incident of that character down on the Muddy here. My brothers Adam and Billy was there—it was before I went down there. One day they was settin' around—kind of a windy day—and all at once they seen a man comin' along the desert. This desert was a plateau above the Muddy Valley, on the east of the Valley, and it was just only covered with evergreens, green bushes, so you could see all over. Well, this man, he come, and they was choppin' some wood there. He said, "How to do," and waited a few minutes and said, "I would like if you would let me have some dry bread and some patches to patch my clothes," and he says, "I am goin' to cross the desert here and I would like to have somet'ing of that kind." My brother Billy looked at him and said, "Do you know what kind o' country you are goin' over? I don't see that you've got much preparation. I've been over that country lots of times and you haven't hardly got anyt'ing to pack water with." He says, "Oh, yes, but I know how to get water." Then they says to him, "What do you want dry bread for? We'll give you some good bread to go over there." "No, I want dry bread, if you got it. Good bread sometimes spoils, but dry bread won't spoil." They talked and finally he says, "I'll be goin' soon." They says, "Well, what might your name be?" So he talked German to them: "Man heisst mich den ewigen Juden"—("They call me the eternal Jew"). Well, they paid no attention to it, but when he got away it come to them, "Well, that must be the rovin' Jew." It was about as far as from here to the Temple (Saint George [Mormon] Temple about eight blocks from Mr. Seegmiller's home), to a drop off the valley. Everyt'ing was clear, and he couldn't make that distance in the time since he left them. They run out to look for him but they couldn't see him anywhere. I've often wondered why they didn't follow his tracks.

210. Three Mysterious Laborers Aid One of Joseph Smith's Protectors

The Nephites are figures mentioned in the *Book of Mormon*, the sacred text of the Church of Jesus Christ of Latter Day Saints, but they have come to play an important role in Mormon oral tradition as mysterious strangers who appear miraculously for some divine purpose. Although the men who appear in this text are not specifically called Nephites, Mormon folklore authority Austin Fife cites it (from John Henry Evans, *One Hundred Years of Mormonism* [Salt Lake City, 1905]) as the earliest known recording of the Nephite legend. Joseph Smith, also called the Prophet, founded Mormonism in upstate New York after obtaining from an angel golden plates that contained the *Book of Mormon*. After violence and persecution, including Smith's murder, Mormons became well established in Utah; this story, of course, takes place earlier, during Smith's lifetime. Motifs H970, H976, N810; cf Q45.1.1.

In the beginning of June [1829] the Prophet removed to Fayette, after having lived at Harmony for about fifteen months, only about two of which Oliver Cowdery had been his scribe [i.e., in the transcription of the Book of Mormon].

Some very interesting details are related concerning this removal. Davil Whitmer informs us that it was in the busiest season of the year when there was so much to do on the farm that word came for him to take Joseph and Oliver from Harmony to Fayette, and he thought the trip would have to be delayed till the work was pretty well over. Nevertheless, he, as well as all the other members of the family, was anxious to hasten rather than to put it off. One morning he got up to do his work as usual when, to his intense surprise, he discovered that during the night about six acres of land had been plowed. On another occasion he found that at the close of a day's harrowing he accomplished more in a few hours than he had usually been able to do in two or three days. Nor was this all. The day following the second circumstance he discovered, on going out to the field to spread some plaster, that the work had already been done. He inquired of his sister, who lived near the field whether she had noticed anyone working there the day before. She replied that she had seen three men at work, but that, supposing he had employed them, she had said nothing about it, though she had observed that they labored with unusual skill and rapidity. These things, of course, hastened the journey and furnished the Whitmer family evidence that something of extraordinary importance was attached to their efforts to aid the Prophet Joseph.

211. Appearance of a Nephite

Folklorist Austin Fife collected this legend from Juanita Brooks, St. George, Utah, August 22, 1939. Fife sees Nephite legends as falling into several categories: those in which a special message is brought; those in which the miraculous manner of their appearance and disappearance is the very point of the narrative; those in which miraculous healing or a providential message is provided; those in which the Nephites give food or a blessing in return for hospitality received; and there are also Nephite stories that do not fit these previous categories. In this story, a message is delivered. The protagonist, at first referred to here only as "he," is Jim Rencher, whose encounter with a Nephite is well known in Mormon folklore. Motif N810; cf E332.3.3.1, Q45.1.1.

He was going from here to his home in Grass Valley with a team and outfit, and as he went up the long summit he met an elderly man afoot. He stopped and offered him a ride, and as they rode along they began discussing one thing and another and talked about the Book of Mormon. Some things that had been troubling him, this man seemed to have quite a clear insight into, and he told him a lot of things that clarified things. As they went through the town of Grass Valley they passed a number of friends and acquaintances who watched them. After they got out of the town and over the hill near his home in Grass Valley he told him he thought he would get out there—he had some friends he wanted to call on in Pinto, so Brother Rencher stopped and he got out, and afterwards Brother Rencher turned around to see him and he couldn't see him. He went back and retraced his steps and he couldn't find the man. The more he thought about it, the more he was convinced it was an unusual occurrence. He inquired of the people he had passed but nobody had seen the man on the wagon with him. His horses were a fractious team of horses but they didn't make any demonstration at all when he picked the man up or when he got out. The more he thought about it the more he was convinced it was one of the Three Nephites. He made it a point to visit Pinto but nobody had been there.

212. Bread for a Missionary

Mormons are notable missionaries, and male Mormons must normally serve some time in the mission field. As a result, the mission experience is the focus for a number of Mormon legends and other stories. Motif N810; cf Q45.1.1.

A missionary was traveling "without purse or script." He was very hungry, and he knelt and prayed to the Lord for food. After walking a short way further he found a loaf of newly-baked bread on the side of the road. He wrote to his mother telling her of the miraculous way in which the Lord had come to his aid.

At the same time that he mailed the letter, one also was being posted to him from his mother in Utah. It told of an experience she had had on the same day and at the same hour that he had found the loaf of bread. She was taking from the oven a "batch" of bread when a man knocked at the door and asked for food. She gave him a loaf of her newly-baked bread, and then went to the window to see if the man was going to ask her neighbors for food. Although the man had not had time to get beyond her front gate, he was not to be seen, nor could she find any trace of him. It is believed that he was one of the Three Nephites sent to secure food for her missionary son.

213. Missionaries Escape a Mob

This legend was collected by Tiare Fullmer, 1981, and is part of the materials assembled and studied by noted Mormon folklorist William A. Wilson. Motifs F1010, K500, R122.

This story happened when two missionaries were in a tough neighborhood some-where in Australia. They came out of the apartment in the rough part of town, and there were at least thirty-five people standing around their car with chains, clubs and knives. The missionaries looked at each other and asked if they should go inside and call the police, go outside and handle the crowd, or just fake it and walk right in and hope nothing happens.

Well, they decided on the latter, and so they walked right through the crowd and opened the car door. They started up the car and drove away. When the car started, the crowd jumped back and scratched their heads. The missionaries drove away and didn't understand what had happened.

They drove some twenty miles, checked in with some missionaries for the evening and returned to their car a few minutes later and found it would not start. On opening the hood, they found that there was no battery. The battery was back with the mob which had apparently removed it to keep the missionaries from leaving. No wonder they jumped back when the car started.

Native Americans

Native Americans, also called Indians, the original inhabitants of America, have played a powerful role in the minds and imaginations of Euro-Americans and African Americans. The extent to which American culture was shaped by Native American contacts is still largely understudied and underrecognized, but in popular culture and, indeed, in folklore, the image of the Native American looms large. Indians are noble helpers and savage foes, givers of the folk knowledge of woodland ways and ignorant fools easily tricked. The legends included here are a sampling of how Native Americans have been depicted in the oral narratives of non-Native America.

There are legends of how groups of Indians "vanished," often through their own warlike actions ("The Legend of Lover's Leap," "The Annihilation of the Pascagoula"), stories sometimes passed off as being of Native American provenance (and the cultural significance of which is discussed in the introduction). And there are those in which non-Natives make their appearance. Daniel Boone uses his wits to defeat his Indian foes ("Daniel Boone's Tricks on Indians"). Or whites may fall in love with Indians, sometimes after being captured. They may stay together ("Wakulla Pocahontas"), or bitter enmities may ultimately ensue ("The Women Who Married Indians"). When it becomes time to finally disappear in a world dominated by whites, a "last" Indian may shove off in his canoe with dignity but finality ("One of the Last of the Mohawks").

214. The Legend of Lover's Leap

Lovers' leap legends—which recount the death of star-crossed lovers from different tribes—are found all over the United States, though they are not from Native American tradition but rather stem from the imagination of Euro-Americans. The introduction includes a brief discussion of these legends. This particular story comes from Nebraska, and it originally appeared in a newspaper, where folklorist Louise Pound found it. Motifs T80, T86.2; cf A968.2, T91.7.2.

Long ago the region of the White Water and the Niobara was the hunting ground of the Cheyenne Indians, who lived in peace with their neighbors the Crows. The Sioux, led by a young chief, Eagle Feather, attacked the camps of the Cheyenne many times. Once, Eagle Feather visited the Cheyenne camp alone in the darkness to spy out the location for a next morning's attack. Drawing near the chief's tepee, he saw the chief's daughter, Crimson Cloud, and fell in love with her. He decided not to attack with his warriors but to come alone and try to capture the maiden. Luck favored him. He arrived with two horses, saw Crimson Cloud, followed her to a stream, grasped her, and, with her consent, carried her off. But he had been seen. The Cheyenne chief was told and gathered his fighting men to follow. They came closer and closer in pursuit of the fleeing pair. In the meantime the Sioux had noted the absence of the chief's son. The lovers, caught between two opposing forces, were driven to the highest point of the hills. Seeing no chance of escape, with their arms about each other they leaped from the high cliff and were crushed to death. And thus Lover's Leap received its name. The Sioux and Cheyenne did not continue their fight but became united against their common enemies and were henceforth as one people.

215. The Legend of Turkey Hill

This legend comes from southern Illinois and was originally published in the 1930s; it is one of many stories in which Native Americans are destroyed through their own actions. Motifs F645, J151, N810, P555; cf C936.

The first white settlers came from West Virginia. They pushed westward down the Ohio to the Mississippi and up to East St. Louis. To the east they noticed a large, well-wooded, gently-sloping hill, and its height impressed them. There were many turkeys on this hill and they found that the hill was a resting-place for these turkeys on their migratory flights, and thus the name Turkey Hill.

Because the land was in the shape of a horse-shoe, the settlers did not notice the Indians living there. The settlers, about twenty families, built their houses. They had quilting-bees and corn-husking parties. A shoemaker stayed with a family for a week and made the shoes for its members, and then went to the next house. The settlers carried their shoes and stockings until they came in sight of the church and then wore them. They were proud of their shoes and carried them in order to save them.

When the settlers discovered Indians on the hill, they expected trouble, but the Indians seemed friendly, and oddly enough they stood in awe of these white settlers who carried rods holding fire and thunder. The Indians told them how to fertilize and plough advantageously and gave them seed to plant. But the settlers noticed something strange about the Indian village. There were many old men and women and many squaws and children but very few braves. And these braves, strange to say, were maimed and crippled and horribly scarred and were no help for protection. The leaders asked the chief the reason for this and this is the story the chief told:

Years before, the Tamaroa Indians had a large town on Turkey Hill. They painted their faces, danced their war-dances, and made war on the other tribes of St. Clair County and the adjoining counties. They were always successful and came home victorious. Of course, they were greatly feared by the other tribes. One day in early spring, an elderly Indian appeared on Turkey Hill. He passed the sentinels quite mysteriously, and no one knew from whence he had come. He was tall and dignified with a goodly appearance and commanded respect. And strangely enough he carried no weapons, only a peace-pipe with a strange insignia. He asked permission to speak around the campfire. The Indians came to the meeting; even the women and children were permitted to stand in the background. The stranger told them that the Great Spirit wanted them to take up farming and to kill wild animals instead of Indians. The old man gave them good advice, telling the Tamaroas to be peaceful and never to go to war. As long as they obeyed this counsel they would be happy and have long lives, but if they disobeyed they would be punished. The Indians agreed to till the soil and stop their warfare. The stranger gave them seed of good vegetables—corn, potatoes, and peas. The wise man stayed with them until fall, and then he disappeared as mysteriously as he had come. For several years the Tamaroas did well and were happy and prosperous and were not molested, but at last they disregarded the sage instruction. After a time the young braves grew tired of this life, for deer hunting seemed to be their only pastime. The young braves, at first secretly and then openly, made ready to go on the warpath. The Indians watched in sadness and sorrow as they departed. For several weeks they did not notice anything. Then they saw several of their braves crawling back to the foot of the hill. Many had died; others were severely wounded and crippled, and some came home to die. From those who returned, the tribe got the story of their torture and defeat at the hands of the Shawnee tribe. And that was why there were so few braves left in the Tamaroa tribe.

216. The Annihilation of the Pascagoula

This story was collected in Mississippi by fieldworkers who did research in the 1930s for the Federal Writers' Project; this government project, which had state affiliates, used writers and other researchers, unemployed because of the Great Depression, to inquire into local folklore and other subjects. As in story 215, Native Americans perish in their own violence. Motifs P555, T80.

The Pascagoula were a gentle tribe of handsome men and shapely women with large dark eyes and small, well-shaped hands and feet. The Biloxi, on the other hand, were a tribe calling themselves the "first people" and extremely jealous of their position. Miona, a princess of the Biloxi tribe, though betrothed to Otanga, a chieftain of her people, loved Olustee, a young chieftain of the Pascagoula, and fled with him to his tribe. The spurned and enraged Otanga led his Biloxi braves to war against Olustee and the neighboring Pascagoula, whereupon Olustee begged his tribe to give him up for atonement. But the Pascagoula swore they would either save their young chieftain and his bride or perish with them.

However, when thrown into battle against terrible odds, they soon lost hope of victory. Faced with the choice either of subjection to Otanga or death, they chose suicide. With their women and children leading the way into the river, the braves followed with joined hands, each chanting his song of death until the last voice was hushed by the engulfing dark waters.

217. The Women Who Married Indians

This legend is from a group of narratives recorded in Virginia in the 1930s and 1940s by fieldworkers of the Virginia affiliate Federal Writers' Project (see headnote to story 216), the Virginia Writers' Project. It was collected by Emory L. Hamilton from Polly Johnson, Wise County, August 29, 1940. Cf motifs R13.1.6, R227.2.

One time there's two girls and a boy. One of the girls and the boy was brother and sister and the other was a friend to the girl and the brother's sweetheart. They were out walking one day and were captured by Indians. They were taken to the Indian nation. They were took to the place where the old chief was. They tied the boy up and put him under the guard of the old chief and his squaw. They built up a brush heap to burn the boy. The girls were told to lay down and sleep. The Indians went out to hunt some pine knots. They was going to stick the splinters in the boy and set them afire and torture him.

While they was gone the old chief started dozing. His head kept drooping lower and lower, 'til finally he went to sleep. It was getting dark and neither one of the girls had gone to sleep. They was watching the old chief. The boy's sister said to the other girl, "Shhhh, be quiet. I'm going to let my brother loose." The old chief had a knife in his hand that he'd been whittling with before he went to sleep. She got up easy like and slipped the knife from his hand and cut the ropes from her brother and let him loose. She slipped the knife back in his [the chief's] hand and laid down again. When the Indians come and found him gone they waked up the old chief and squaw and asked who turned him [the boy] loose. They said if the girls has done it we'll kill 'em. The old squaw said, "No, they didn't do it. They've been asleep all the time." The Indians said, "Whooeee, white man gone."

Two of the Indians asked the girls which they'd druther do—be burned in the brush heap alive, stabbed and killed, shot, or marry me and be dressed in silk and have good things to eat. One of the girls said, "I'd druther marry you," and the other one said the same. They married the Indians and lived with them three years. They done what they said and dressed them in silk. They wore fine beaded moccasins and beads around their necks. The boy's sister had learned to love the Indian she married.

One day they said to the old squaw, "Mama, we're going to go get some grapes." They had lived with the Indians three years and they trusted them to go anywhere now. They got their silk aprons full of grapes and set down on a log to rest. One of the girls, the one who was the boy's sweetheart said, "I'm gone, I'm going back to my people." The one who loved her Indian husband says, "I'm not going. I'm going to stay." The other'n said, "I'm going. You can stay if you want to." And she started out. The other girl watched her out of sight and then throwed [down] her grapes and hollered, "I'm coming too."

They traveled 'til night, running and walking. When the Indians come in they started out hunting for them. The Indians had a fiest [feist; that is, mongrel] dog and the two girls heard it coming after them barking. One of them jumped into a sink hole and covered herself with leaves. The other one crawled in a hollow log. The fiest dog come up and run in the log. She grabbed it and smothered it to death with her clothes. They heard the Indians coming. The husband of the one in the sink hole was hollering "Honey's gone, Oh, Honey's lost." They said when she heard him hollering she come very nigh making herself known. They come up to the log and hacked on it with their tomahawks, and said, "Whooee, Honey's gone. We'll go back and take a soon start in the morning and find them and kill 'em."

As soon as the Indians got gone they crawled out and went on. They traveled 'til they come to a river, and on the other side was houses. They hollered and a man come out. He saw them and said, "There's my sister." He got a boat and come across after them. Just as they got on the other side the Indians come, and the white men killed them.

218. Wakulla Pocahontas

Pocahontas, of course, was the now-famed Indian "princess" who according to legend saved the life of Captain John Smith in early colonial Virginia. This parallel Florida story was told by Inez Walker, Wakulla County, 1949. Motifs R110, T32.1; cf T121.3.1.

Approximately four miles up the Wakulla River from its confluence with the St. Marks River occurred a real Pocahontas story, when a daughter of an Indian chief, Prophet Francis, by her entreaties saved a young Georgia soldier from being burned at the stake.

It is said that the young man was stationed at a fort between the Chattahoochee and Flint rivers, just across the Georgia line. With nothing much to do, he begged his commander to allow him to go into the woods hunting. While so engaged, he was seized by some of Francis's Indians and carried to their town on the Wakulla.

The chief said that the white man had been guilty of trespassing on his land and deserved death. The soldier was fastened to a stake, and lightwood knots piled around him. A torch was lighted, and the fire in another minute would have been consuming his body, when Malee, the Indian princess and daughter of Francis, with tears in her eyes begged for the soldier's life.

Her piteous pleas finally affected her father.

He said to her, "I will let him go if he will go to St. Marks and get me two demijohns of firewater."

You may be sure the soldier went into St. Marks under heavy guard. When he reached the fort, the commander allowed him to have the liquor on credit. In due time it reached Prophet Francis at his town on the Wakulla.

Many who told the story said that the young soldier later married the princess.

I don't know, but it is said that she was awarded a pension by the government for the part she played in saving this young soldier's life.

219. Daniel Boone's Tricks on Indians

Pioneer Daniel Boone (1734–1820) opened Kentucky to exploration and settlement, and particularly after the publication of his *Adventures* in 1784, enjoyed great fame as a woodsman. The legendary tricks played on Indians by pioneers are often attributed to various historical figures including, as here, Daniel Boone. This story was collected from Joe Hubbard by James M. Hylton, Wise County, Virginia, October 12, 1940. Motifs K551.29*, K621, K1111; cf AT 38, AT 73.

Daniel Boone and a Stuart fellow that lived by him each had two girls a piece. Boone had taught his girls to keep a ball of red yarn handy so that if the Indians carried them off they could leave bits of yarn for him to track them by. One day the Indians carried off Boone's girls and the two Stuart girls too. They went to hunt for them and Boone tracked them by the bits of red yarn and found all four of them, and seven Indians that stole them.

They killed the seven Indians and took the girls back home.

One time Daniel Boone was re-hanging some tobacco in his barn loft and was busy with the tobacco and wasn't watching out for the Indians. Four Indians come up on him and took him unawares. They had their guns on him and said, "We've got you now!" He stood looking at them, and all the time he was crumblin up tobacco leaves in his hands. All at once he threwed the crumbled tobacco in their eyes. And while they's getting it out he run off.

One time Boone's out splittin' rails and five Indians come up on him and throwed their guns on him. He told them he'd go with them, but first he had some deer meat on cooking and wanted them to eat some first. He had a log partly split open—gluts [wedges] drove in it. He told them to take hold and help him pull the log open and they'd eat and then he'd go with them. The Indians put their fingers down in the split place to pull the log open, and then Boone knocked the gluts out and the log closed back on their fingers and held them so tight they couldn't get them out. He took his axe and cut all five's brains out.

220. One of the Last of the Mohawks

The Mohawk Indians are one of the Iroquois groups and have hardly disappeared, as this legend seems to suggest, though perhaps it comments only on the withdrawal of the Mohawks from the geographical area of the narrative. Certainly the story, from a collection published by noted New York state folklorist Louis C. Jones, concentrates on the tragic figure of the "vanishing red man." *Dorp* is a remnant of colonial Dutch meaning town. Cf motif E425.2.4.

In Schenectady they tell of one of the last Mohawks in that area who died in 1789. His name has not survived, but men have remembered that in two of the ways of the white man he excelled his teachers; he could outshoot them and outdrink them. With these arts mastered he had long moved among the men of the Dorp with austere familiarity. Now and then during the year he would bring to town some meat or fish to exchange for the few articles his simple way of life required. While he was there he would practice a little drinking and then drift back to his cabin on the Hill of Strawberries. On the August day of which I write he made a present of his mess of fish to an old friend, refusing anything for it. His explanation was simple and pointed: "Great Spirit call. Indian no need." For once he shunned the tavern and getting into his canoe he started up the Mohawk. Boys who were swimming off a sand bar reported a strange thing later: the canoe moved against the current, driven by no visible power, for the Indian sat in the stern, his head erect, his arms folded serenely across his chest. They were the last to see him alive. No one ever found his body, but the canoe they did find the next day, drifting empty far down the river.

A week later a white man who had known the Indian was fishing among the river islands when he glanced up and saw the old Mohawk warrior sitting on the high bank. His arms were clasped around his knees and his face was turned toward his departed people. The white man thought merely that the Indian wanted a lift to the mainland and so he rowed close to the island and invited him to get in the boat. At the first word, the Mohawk slowly turned his head and faded from view. Afterward many others saw him, sitting by the river's edge, always in the same position, his knees hugged to his chin and his eyes watching the upper reaches of the valley.

Folk Heroes, Local Characters, and Wild People

Legends commonly form around the personalities of particular individuals, often though not necessarily historical persons, who become protagonists in cycles of stories about their actions, real or imputed. That may make them folk heroes or merely local characters and curiosities. This process, generally, is a purely local one, and when a folk hero like Johnny Appleseed or John Henry becomes someone of national note, that character's popularity has stemmed from influences beyond folklore: books or newspapers or the mass media. Johnny Appleseed ("Johnny Appleseed"), the historical John Chapman, was the subject of oral stories in nineteenth-century Ohio, but it was through literary sources that he became widely known. Although the folklore of John Henry ("John Henry") probably was widely dispersed throughout the South (among whites as well as blacks), he too achieved national prominence through novels and plays and other popular sources. Someone like Molly Mulhollun ("Molly Mulhollun, the Cabin Builder") or Ben Lilly ("Ben Lilly, Strongman of Morehouse Parish") have remained largely in local tradition.

Local tradition will also preserve stories about local figures who do not reflect heroic virtues so much as amusing or "colorful" traits. Billy Hazard ("Billy Hazard") is an exiled aristocrat who cooks his meals in old tomato cans. Of course, what is "heroic" to a local community may not always seem so to outsiders. George Magoon ("George Magoon Escapes the Wardens") was a local hero in rural Maine because he hunted illegally at a time when locals felt oppressed by new game laws. And, of course, there is a whole range of American outlaw heroes like Jesse James (see the section "Outlaws, Crime, and Criminals") who enjoy a romantic mystique but who may have been seen quite differently in their own time and place. Then too, some local figures are just disquieting, like those who turn into wild people in the wilderness ("The Wild Girl of the Santa Barbara Channel Island"), negating the norms of civilization.

221. Johnny Appleseed

Johnny Appleseed is the nickname given to John Chapman (1774–1845), a Massachusetts-born investor in Western lands who also established apple orchards, notably in Ohio. Primarily through literary sources, he came to be seen as a sort of happy hermit who wandered through Ohio and Indiana dispensing apple seeds to settlers. There were stories about him in nineteenth-century Ohio, but twentieth-century oral narratives concerning him, like this one, are unusual; the account given here probably was influenced by written sources. It was narrated by Nancy C. Wooding to Bessie A. Scales, Danville, Virginia, March 4, 1941. Motifs A2602, F556.

Many many years ago a little sail-boat came sailing in from the ocean and landed on a shore that was afterwards named Virginia. In this boat came a queer, blue-eyed man with long hair hanging to his shoulders, barefooted and wearing ragged clothes. The first people he saw were the Indians, who treated him kindly, dressed him in clothes made of skins, and helped him on his way. His friends were the animals he met and one day he was seen playing with three bear cubs, while their mother looked-on greatly pleased.

On his back he carried a big sack of apple-seed, brought from nobody knew where, and everywhere he went he planted appleseed. For ten long years he journeyed far into the mountains planting his appleseed everywhere 'til they all gave out. Then he started back in the way he had come. Apple trees had sprung up everywhere, hundred of acres were a-bloom, and the people were all rejoicing at the sight of the beautiful apple blossoms, soon to turn to fruit, and they were all talking about the strange man who had brought them such beauty and such luscious fruit—they called him Johnny Appleseed.

Everywhere Johnny Appleseed was welcomed by the grateful people. When he sat down at table with them he would not eat until he was sure that there was plenty of food for the children. After he had eaten he would stretch himself out on the floor, take out the Bible he always carried in his sack, and read aloud what he called "news fresh from heaven." His voice was loud as the roar of the wind and waves, then soft and soothing as the balmy air.

One day he walked along for twenty miles to reach the home of a friend. He sat down on the doorstep to eat his evening meal of bread and milk. Then he read aloud from his Bible for a while. Then he went to sleep stretched out on the floor, and he did not wake up.

And all the folks bless Johnny Appleseed, for they know that when spring comes to the land there will be many acres of pink and white apple blossoms.

222. Molly Mulhollun, the Cabin Builder

This story of Molly Mulhollun was recollected by Mary E. W. Smith, Alleghany County, Virginia, as part of the Federal Writers' Project folklore investigations from the American New Deal period. Mulhollun's "indenture" refers to the practice in colonial times of a person's being legally bound to work for another for a specified period of time in exchange for some payment, such as funds for emigrating to America. Motifs K1831, K1837.

When Virginia was being settled land from the King of England was granted through the governor to those who transported future citizens to the colony. It sometimes happened that there would be among the passengers one or more who would serve in the household of the person who brought them from foreign shores.

There was, in what is now Alleghany County, one such personage by the name of Molly Mulhollun. She was brought to Staunton and became a servant in the home of a Mr. Bell.

Benjamin Borden was the possessor of a large tract of land. He was very ambitious in regard to the encouragement of settlements along the James River, the Cowpasture, and the Jackson River. As an incentive he made known far and near that for every cabin built he would give the builder a plot of ground. This happened during the closing year of Molly Mulhollun's indenture [and], Molly being possessed of the adventurous spirit, [she] was very impressed with the Borden proposition. The desire of owning a home with surrounding land made her determined to enter the arena of cabin building.

Upon the end of her servitude in the Bell home she trekked out from Staunton to the site of the city of Covington. Undaunted, she donned the wearing apparel of men over her own clothing, and, equipped with tools, she began viewing the surroundings. Molly lost no time in starting work on her future abode. In due time the first cabin was built. The builder was known as John Mulhollun in her new role. Time passed, [and] with it there came into existence thirty cabins on the site of what has developed into an outstanding manufacturing town in Allegheny County.

When Borden arrived on the place where he supposed one cabin had been built, he was astounded to see houses for a small sized settlement, all built by one "man." These he was viewing [were] something unthought of. He admitted he had not made any bargain with anyone by the name of John Mulhollun.

People became suspicious as to the reality of the person who had built the thirty cabins. It happened that Molly Mulhollun visited Staunton wearing her adopted attire of leather shirt, pants, and moccasins. She was recognized by people who had known her when she served in the home of Mr. Bell. She, finally, was prevailed upon to acknowledge her identity. She afterward discarded the masculine garb and appeared among her old acquaintances as Molly Mulhollun who [had] paid her transportation [to America] by working in the capacity of a servant.

223. John Henry

John Henry is best known through the ballad and work songs ("hammer songs") about him and through a variety of publications and productions that feature him—novels, plays, children's books, radio shows—which followed in the wake of the early research on him and the songs by folklorists, notably Guy Johnson and Louis Chappell. He was probably a real person, and a recent book (Scott Reynolds Nelson, *Steel Drivin' Man: John Henry, The Untold Story of an American Legend* [New York: Oxford University Press, 2006]) makes a detailed case for this, but his historical existence has been uncertain; though he has generally been seen as an African American folk hero, some accounts claim he was white, and the ballad about him has been recorded in Anglo-American tradition. The story of how he engaged in a contest with a steam drill while working at tunneling for a railroad (the Big Bend Tunnel, constructed in the 1870s in West Virginia, is most often mentioned), won that contest, and then tragically died has had great appeal as a tale of man against machine. Although the story is told primarily through the ballad, Johnson and Chappell turned up other traditions about him, including the texts given here. The first (no. 1 here) is a written account sent to Johnson by an African American student, the other two from informants of Louis Chappell. The first of these (given as no. 2 here) was provided by George Johnston, Lindside, West Virginia, and the second (given as no. 3 here) by Pete Sanders, "an old Negro" who lived in Fayetteville, West Virginia. Although John Henry sometimes has been depicted as driving railroad spikes, his job was to horizontally drive a steel drill, positioned by another worker called a shaker, into rock for tunneling. Motifs F610, F660, H1540.

1. It happens that every summer I go away to work in order to return to school the next fall. Last summer I went to Brooklyn, N.Y., and obtained a job in the Arbuckle Sugar Co. It was there that I met a hard working fellow who sang this song ["John Henry"] every day, and as a boy I adopted it. The history is thus: John Henry, a spike driver, was working in the North at the time the steam driller was invented. It was taking work from all the drivers, and John Henry bet his boss he could drive the spike faster than the newly invented machine. The people heard about it and came from town to see it. He hummed a tune and drove the spike, he beat the machine but fell dead afterwards in his tracks. His pal continued to sing and ended the song.

2. John Henry was the best driver on the C and O [Chesapeake and Ohio Railroad]. He was the only man that could drive steel with two hammers, one in each hand. People came for miles to see him use his two 20 lb. hammers he had to drive with.

It seems that two different contracting companies were meeting in what is called Big Bend Tunnel. One had a steam drill while the other used man power to drill with. When they met everyone claimed that the steam drill was the greatest of all inventions, but John Henry made the remark he could sink more steel than the steam drill could. The contest was arranged and the money put up. John Henry was to get $100.00 to beat the steam drill.

John Henry had his foreman to buy him 2 new 20 lb. hammers for the race. They were to drill 35 minutes. When the contest was over John Henry had drilled two holes 7 feet deep, which made him a total of 14 feet. The steam drill drilled one hole 9 feet which of course gave the prize to John.

When the race was over John Henry retired to his home and told his wife that he had a queer feeling in his head. She prepared his supper and immediately after eating he went to bed. The next morning when his wife awoke and told him it was time to get up she received no answer, and she immediately discovered that he had passed to the other world some time in the night. His body was examined by two Drs. from Baltimore and it was found that his death was caused from a bursted blood vessel in his head.

3. I didn't drive no steel in Big Bend Tunnel. Uncle Jeff and Eleck did though, and saw John Henry drive against the steam drill, and died in five minutes after he beat it down. They said John Henry told the shaker how to shake the steel to keep it from getting fastened in the rock so he couldn't turn it. He told him to give it two quick shakes and a twist to make the rock dust fly out of the hole.

I heard the song of John Henry driving steel against the steam drill when they were still working on the C and O. It was all amongst us when I was a boy. When we boys there in Franklin County worked on the extension of the railroad up in Pocahontas County, we carried the song with us there and carried it back home when we went. It was the leading railroad song, but they've tore it all to pieces and sp'iled it. I heard it the other day on the machine [phonograph], but it ain't noways like it used to be.

They said Big Bend Tunnel was a terrible-like place, and many men got killed there. Mules too. And they throwed the dead men and mules and all together there in that fill between the mountains. Uncle Jeff and me come in West Virginia together when I first come, and he showed me the big fill and said they tried to put John Henry there first, but didn't do it and put him somewhere else. The dumper at the fill was the man that knowed all about it. Uncle Jeff said one day a long slab of rock that hung down from the roof fell and killed seven men. He said he seen 'em killed, and they put 'em in the fills. The people in the tunnel didn't know where they went.

224. Ben Lilly, Strongman of Morehouse Parish

"Ben Lilly, Strongman of Morehouse Parish" was recorded by C. Renée Harvison, September 14, 1990, from James B. Rider of Bastrop, Louisiana; because it was collected (as part of a state-sponsored storytelling project) at a storytelling event at a local festival, members of Rider's audience add to the telling about Ben Lilly. Theodore Roosevelt, in his account of hunting in north Louisiana in 1907, writes of Lilley (as Roosevelt spells the name), locally famed as a hunter and woodsman. Roosevelt says that Lilley "equalled Cooper's Deerslayer in woodcraft, in hardihood, in simplicity—and also in loquacity," referring to James Fennimore Cooper's literary hero. In Louisiana, counties are called parishes. Motifs F610, F685; cf A526.2.

Ben Lilly, around Mer Rouge, was always entertaining people. He was supposedly a tremendously strong man. People that have been witnesses to the things he did—

according to what's been written on him, he once stood on the sidewalks of Mer Rouge and got in a barrel. And without touching the barrel, just flat-footed, jumped out of the barrel onto the sidewalk.

They said it was many times that he could pick up a hundred pound steel anvil from the ground and just extend it out at arm's length and just hold it there.

They said that he once picked up a five-hundred-pound bale of cotton and walked off with it.

Lilly made his own knives. He once said that, he showed a knife to a fellow one time out West and said that he had killed, in so-called hand-to-hand combat, six bears with this knife. He held it up and showed that he had stabbed those bears to death. They weren't all black bears. One or two were supposed to be grizzlies. Pretty tough customers.

Ben Lilly would not do any kind of work on Sunday, no matter what. If his cows got out, he wouldn't let anybody herd those cows up. They might stay lost for days. On Monday morning he'd go hunt them, but not on Sunday. He read his Bible on Sunday. He tried to adhere to the Bible as near as he could.

Audience member: Mr. Rider, I have heard that he organized a hunting expedition for Roosevelt. For President Roosevelt. Is that true? Have you found that to be true in your research?

James B. Rider: That was Theodore Roosevelt. Teddy Roosevelt. Roosevelt came down to Tensas Parish, around Transylvania down there, and he wanted to kill a bear. So they hired Ben to come over with his dogs to run bear. And he hunted with Teddy.

Audience member: And I've also been told, since I'm a Mer Rouge resident, and because so many people enjoy talking about Ben Lilly, that he had such a keen sense of smell and keen sense of hearing, they say he was more animal than human. But he could be a gentleman when the occasion arose. Didn't they say something about how he could lay on the ground and tell you how the grass was growing, he had such a keen sense of smell?

James B. Rider: He said that. He told that. He was, like you were talking about, he was a gentle man, too. When he did come back to Mer Rouge on one of his hunts, he'd play with the children. He just spent a lot of time playing with children, no matter whose they were.

He had all kind of idiosyncrasies. He believed if you got wet, naturally out in the rain, that nothing would happen to you if you just kept wearing your clothes till they dried. You might get sick if you took them off and took a bath and dried off real good and put on dry clothes. You'd probably get sick. So what he did, he'd even go to bed with his wet clothes on. If he come in wet, and he wanted to go to bed, he'd just crawl in bed and pull the covers up and sleep wet. He had a belief, he stuck with it.

Audience member: They say he believed in bathing. He'd even bathe in the snow!

James B. Rider: One time, him and another fellow had been out in the woods for a long time. They hadn't taken a bath in months. They decided they'd take a bath. Ben said, "Let's take a bath."

This guy said, "Well, you know, it's about thirty degrees." Only thing they had was this stream to take a bath in. He'd heard that Ben didn't mind. He'd pull off his clothes and wade on in, start taking a bath. This guy didn't want to do that. So Ben took his bath in that cold water. It didn't make him any matter. It was just like when he was tracking a bear or a cougar. He'd pull off everything but his pants. He'd take his rifle and knife and take off. No food, no nothing. He might hunt two days without a bite to eat. Sometimes when he'd eat, he would just go out in somebody's corn field and pull two ears of corn.

225. Billy Hazard

Workers for the Works Progress Administration, the agency that sponsored the Federal Writers' Project and its folklore collecting activities during the New Deal period, wrote down the story of "Billy Hazard" in Indiana. Burke's Peerage Register refers to a directory of British nobility. Motif T93.2.

William (Billy) Hazard was one of Salem's most colorful residents in the early 1900s. Billy, it seems, had a place in Burke's Peerage Register, but he became infatuated with one of his mother's maids and eloped with her. Finally she deserted him, and he lived alone in Salem for the rest of his life. He died in the county asylum in 1913.

Billy lived as a recluse in an old brick house at the north end of Salem. Its walls were lined with cordwood, and there were no carpets on the floors. He cooked his meals in old tomato cans on a little rusty iron stove that he might have rescued from a junk dealer's pile.

Billy was very well educated, and there appears to be no doubt of his aristocratic British ancestry. Because of his eccentricities, he could truly be called a legend in his own time.

226. Ziba King

This account of Florida cattle baron Ziba King was collected from Sara Crittenden, Arcadia, Florida, 1950. Motifs F513.1.2.2*, F628.1.2.3*, F632, N6.4*.

One of the pioneers of Fort Ogden, settled during the Civil War, was Judge Ziba King.

He was a colorful character and known all over the state as the Cattle King of South Florida. He stood six feet six in his stocking feet, weighed two hundred twenty-five pounds, and could out-eat all competitors. Ziba didn't "rile" easily, but once when a wild steer attacked him he swung a haymaker from the floor and it struck the six-hundred-pound animal near the heart, killing it instantly.

Ziba was never known to be beaten at stud poker. When some cardsharps from Savannah got wind of this Florida Cattle King named King who had plenty of money and a liking for cards, they packed up and came south. Ziba's former storekeeper tells of the procession of gamblers who would inquire for Ziba. He would direct them to the ranchhouse, and after several hours they would return broke and downhearted. The storekeeper, it is said, had standing orders from Ziba to advance the gamblers enough money to get back home on. There was one time when there wasn't enough money to pay the schoolteachers in the county and Ziba handed over enough gold to pay their salaries for six months. One of Ziba's sons, Bet, is a character in his own right. It is said that his teeth are filled with diamonds instead of gold.

227. George Magoon Escapes the Wardens

George Magoon (1851–1929) is the subject of a number of stories in his native Maine. Magoon grew up in a culture where hunting was a way of life and where men supplemented their income by market hunting, selling deer meat to the Boston market in particular. Under pressure from conservation and sports hunting interests, Maine hunting laws were changed in the 1880s; market hunting became illegal, much to the resentment of Maine backwoodsmen. Hence, these stories of Magoon's resistance to game wardens present him as a local folk hero. The stories are taken from the Northeast Archives of Folklore and Oral History, University of Maine. The first was told by Grace Seavey, Crawford, Maine, October 13, 1963; the second by Harold Day, Wesley, Maine, July 24, 1971; the third by Carroll Ellsmore, Garland, Maine, July 31, 1964. Motifs J1180, J1650.

1. It seems that one day George was busy digging a trench in front of his house when he spotted the wardens coming. He yelled to his wife, "Etta, keep those wardens busy talking while I make some tracks for them." In a flash George was out of the trench, and he made tracks because the wardens couldn't even think of catching him as he had gotten so far away from them.

2. Yes, [the wardens] they come right down that lane driveway, down across the field. There was an old rail fence there, see. Well, he'd walk on that until he got out of sight or something, and [then] he'd make a jump-spring right out into the snow . . . quite a distance. He'd find a place where it wasn't all clear . . . so that his tracks would be hid. Ah, he had all kinds of tricks.

3. A warden who was active in chasing him was Penny Longfellow. One time Penny went out to arrest Magoon for poaching. It was a mean, cold, snowy night and Magoon was setting in front of his fire in his stocking feet. When he heard a knock at the door, he sent Etta his wife to see who it was. As soon as he heard the warden's voice, he took right out the back door into the snow in his stocking feet and didn't come back for hours until he was sure the warden was gone. Yes sir, he was a hardy man, that Magoon.

228. The Wild Girl of the Santa Barbara Channel Islands

Austin Fife, noted folklorist of the American West, was told this story by Los Angeles artist Joseph Henniger as they rode along a California coastal highway from which the Channel Islands that figure in the legend could be seen, and Henniger later repeated the story for it to be written down. Henniger had been told it earlier by an accountant named Waddie. Motifs N764, R1.

The man who told this story was just loaded full of California folklore. He knew California history as well as anyone with whom I have come in contact. He was telling us one night that there was a very curious story told about a wild girl who was found here in California. All of this was apropos of the stories of children raised by wolves in India.

A group of sportsmen living up at Santa Barbara decided to go over to hunt wild goats on one of the islands off the coast. No one had gone to this island for a number of years because it was very hard to reach. These men finally made the island, anchored the boat offshore, and went ashore, in a small boat. They hunted for the day and in returning to the boat came across a curious creature who was running along the beach stark naked and tore up the side of the mountain as fast as a goat could go. One of the men asked the fellows if they had noticed this thing running along the beach; he would have sworn it was a young woman completely nude. The other fellows hadn't noticed it, but the man was so insistent that they climbed up the side of the mountain and found a cave and with their lights went in. They found this cave loaded full of bones—goats' bones, rabbits' etc. In the back of the cave they found this wild young girl.

They tied her up and took her back to boat and took her to the mainland. She couldn't speak any English. When they got to shore they put her in the hands of medical authorities who said she had been wild for several years. They delved back into the records of missing persons and [found that] in the year 1901 or 1902 a sailboat had set out from Santa Barbara with a man, his wife, and daughter a little over two. Several weeks later pieces of the boat were washed ashore but there were no sign of the bodies, and so these men concluded that what had happened was that child had survived the storm. She had been old enough to walk and apparently had existed since that time on the island. She was removed to a hospital and the authorities did everything they could to cover up her predicament, hide her from the curious.

Panthers, Snakes, and Other Beasts

The dangers posed by wild beasts such as mountain lions and wolves seemed very real to early explorers and settlers of the American continent, and it is hardly surprising that accounts of encounters with wild animals figure in legendry. Panthers (a term commonly used for large wildcats such as cougars, mountain lions, and pumas), with their strangely human cries, figure prominently in stories ("The Panther"), but so too do snakes. Several mythical snakes that have poisonous, horny tails ("The Poisoned Tree") or can enter human bodies and be enticed out by milk ("Milk Snakes") have been popular in American lore since colonial times. And fantastic sea serpents have been spotted off American coasts, though lakes provide homes for legendary creatures as well ("A Lake Serpent," "The Beast of Busco").

229. The Panther

From a collection of Georgia folk narratives, "The Panther" was told by Yvonne White Turner and recorded by her daughter, Carol Ann Turner, 1974. The story's setting was said to be the Florida Panhandle. Motif D672.

Years ago, people would settle on what they called a section. Now, I don't even know how big that is; but anyway, it was probably over two or three hundred acres. And there was a young couple married and settled in a part of the country that the girl had never lived in. And anyway, they told her when they built their cabin that panthers roamed that area. And the first year they didn't take in too much land, because of course they didn't have the tools they do now to clear with; but they had a good-sized field. And they told the girl if she ever heard a noise like a woman screaming that it would be a panther, and to pull off her clothes one piece at a time and run as hard as she could, because the panther would stop and tear whatever you put down to shreds.

And said one day she used that knowledge to very great advantage. Said she took some water down to her husband in the field, and when she got about halfway home she heard this scream and she knew it was a panther. So she had on a big bonnet. She pulled that off first and threw it down, and she ran a little further and pulled off a jacket that she had, and then she pulled off an apron, and she pulled off her skirt, and then her blouse, running just as hard as she could.

Said when she got home she was stark naked, but she beat the panther and saved her life. And she did get to see him, and he was a giant of an animal.

230. Dick the Slave Boy and Wolves

Another legend collected in Virginia by Federal Writers' Project workers, this was collected from Harold Pugh by Susie Spoles, Grayson County, Virginia. Motif K551.3.1.

In early pioneer days the people would gather together for house raisings and things of that kind. In this instance the house raising was on Smythe County side of Iron Mountain, while the family to whom the slave boy belonged lived on the Grayson County side. The entire family had been invited, so they had gone on in the early morning leaving Dick to care for things during the day and to lock up that night before he came on. The reason for his going was that at night after the work of the day had been completed, the host gave the participants a party, or frolic, as they were called in those days. Dick was one of the best fiddlers in the country, so of course he had to go over to help make the music.

He started out in the early afternoon to complete his work so that he might be able to start on his journey before nightfall. As the cows had strayed away, he had to spend some time hunting them. Finally, however, they were found and safely housed.

After seeing that everything was safe under lock and key he snatched up his violin and started on his way. He traveled rapidly for he was fleet of foot and covered much ground in just a short time. But before he could reach the mountaintop dark overtook him. He was growing tired because of the mountain climb, but he knew he must press onward because the people would be waiting for him to come. And then he also knew there were many wolves on the mountain, and if they were to get on his track that he might perish before he could get assistance or before he could reach his destination.

Just as he was reaching the top of the mountain he heard behind him the long drawn out howl of a wolf. Then, on the opposite side, he heard the howl of a fellow creature and in a second he heard the howl of two or three of the beasts on the other side of the mountain. He knew by instinct that they were on his track, and that they would gather in force as they came on after him.

He started in a run down the mountain, but he could tell by their howls they were gaining on him. He knew of an abandoned house not far down the mountain that if he could reach he might thereby save his life. He was by this time very tired, but his seeing the house revived him, and with the wolves close behind him he made one last effort to get there before they could overtake him.

The door had rubbish piled up against it from the inside but with one superhuman effort he pushed the door open, all the time clinging to his violin. Then he slammed the door shut just as the wolves came up. He laid his violin upon some planks that lay across the joists of the house and then he barricaded the door as best he could.

By this time the pack of wolves had surrounded the house and he knew if they found the door they could with their strength soon push it open. So as soon as possible he climbed to the top of the joists and, settling himself in on the planks with his feet hanging down he tremblingly waited.

It was not long before the leader found the door and, aided by his followers, they soon pushed it open. It made the pack angry when they saw their prey just out of reach. They commenced jumping up, but could not reach him. Finally one of the beasts jumped up and landed on the back of another of the pack, and in that way bit at Dick's trousers, which nearly pulled him off into the midst of the howling wolves. This frightened Dick very much, and he quickly pulled his legs up and crouched in a sitting position on the planks.

The animals were making fearful leaps now and were about to get to him when suddenly he picked up his violin and drew the bow sharply across the strings. This frightened the beasts away for the time being. He succeeded with this stratagem but a few times, for they soon got used to the noise and would not leave.

Suddenly one of the beasts jumped up so high that he caught with one paw on the plank. But he could not hold on. This was very serious for Dick, and he racked his brain to find some device to drive the animals away.

Presently he thought of the way wolves would jump on anything when it was covered with blood. Taking out his knife, he opened it and held it in readiness to cut the next wolf that had the audacity to put his paw on the plank. He soon had this opportunity and the beast fell back among his fellow creatures. They, seeing the blood, turned on the one that had been cut and soon had him torn to pieces. In the melee another of the companions jumped on him as soon as they had finished the first one.

By this time the day was beginning to break into the darkness, and just at that moment Dick heard someone calling, "Dick, oh Dick!" This was a crowd of men who were hunting for him. Dick's heart beat with joy and gladness as he answered, "Heah I is, boss! In the old cabin, an' ah is powerful glad yuh is come!"

This conversation caused the wolves to run out of the cabin and away into the woods. Many of them were killed by the men who were hunting Dick. And then they came on to the cabin where they found Dick, who had just climbed down from the joists. When he told them of his adventure, they all exclaimed in unison, "You have had a narrow escape, Dick, a narrow escape!"

231. The Poisoned Tree

From Frank C. Brown's great North Carolina collections, "The Poisoned Tree" was told by Clara Hearne, Chatham County, North Carolina, 1922–23. Motif B765.11.

Many years ago the people in the neighborhood near Pittsboro had assembled at the church for service. Before the service began, a man out in the grove encountered a large snake. He looked for something with which to defend himself. The snake ran toward him, and the man to protect himself dodged behind a tree. The snake at once threw himself against the tree fastening himself to the tree by the horn on the end of his tail. There he hissed at the man, who struck him with a pole until the snake was killed. The man left him there in the tree and went into the church. When the service was over, he found that the leaves on the tree had withered and later the tree died.

232. Milk Snakes

Legendary accounts of snakes attracted to milk have been popular in the United States for many years, the story given here coming from nineteenth-century New England. Motifs B765.5, B765.6.1; cf B765.4, B784.1.1.

Many still believe that in drinking from brooks one runs the risk of swallowing a young snake, which is liable to grow in the stomach, and become large and troublesome. In support of this idea, it is related that once there was a certain child that took large quantities of food, in particular a great deal of milk, yet became more and more emaciated. One night when the child was sitting at the table with a bowl of milk before it, of which it had not eaten, a great snake put its head out of the child's mouth. Apparently it was hungry, had scented the milk, and came up out of the child's stomach to get it. The child's father was by, and he gripped the snake by the neck, and pulled it out. It was four feet long.

Some say that instead of a bowl of milk on the table, it was a pailful on the kitchen-floor fresh from the cow.

Another telling of the story has it that a woman swallowed the snake. As it grew she was in great distress, so that finally she could not eat. At length her friends laid her down with her stomach on a chair, and put a basin of steaming hot food on the floor before her. That brought out the snake, and the woman got well.

233. The Coach-Whip Snake

This North Carolina story was among the many gathered by Frank C. Brown, and it recounts another of the legendary snakes that are part of American folk tradition. Motif B765.10.

An old man in our neighborhood told of being chased by a coach-whip. He was working south of Kingstree, when he was a youth of seventeen years, living with his brother. One night he took a foot path that led across a swamp to see some girls. He left for home about eleven o'clock and walked very fast as he knew many snakes were in the swamp. Presently he heard something rattling in the bushes, then something like a bull whip crack. He glanced back. He heard it again still nearer. He began to run; so did it, popping that whip. He fell in his brother's porch exhausted when he reached there. Next day they both went to investigate. They found his tracks from six to eight feet apart, and the trail of a coach-whip behind, but the trail did not go far out in the clearing. The snake ran after others and was at last shot and killed by hunters.

234. A Lake Serpent

Richard M. Dorson heard this story during his fieldwork in 1946 in the Upper Peninsula, the part of Michigan separated from the rest of the state by Lakes Michigan and Huron. Motifs G308, G308.2.

Angus Steinhoff and Van Dein were lifting gill nets on the west side of Trout Bay from near Black Point along the Grand Island shore. Angus was a young fellow then working for Van Dein, the owner of the boat, a man about sixty. They were coming toward Munising, and sighted a creature swimming fast. They took after it in their boat, the "Viva," a gas boat; it made eight and a half to nine miles an hour. The creature zigzagged back and forth. A good part of it was out of the water; it had an angled head, looked like a big snake or serpent, made quite a wake. It was broad daylight so they could see it clearly. Nothing in the lake could go that fast. Van Dein said something similar in the Old Country, Sweden, took after him once when he got too close. So they turned the boat across the bay and went by the Thumb home.

Van Dein said he always hated to tell anyone about it because they wouldn't believe it. I heard Angus tell it two or three times though.

235. The Beast of Busco

This legend, collected in Terre Haute, Indiana, May 1970, from a nineteen-year-old student, is centered on Churubusco, a town that is today a suburb of Fort Wayne, Indiana. There is a town festival that whimsically celebrates the "mythical" beast that features in the legend; for more information, see John Gutowski, *The Beast of 'Busco: An American Tradition* (*Midwestern Folklore* 24, nos. 1/2, 1988). Motifs B875.3, H1331.

There is a lake in Churubusco, Indiana, called Blue Lake. One time two old guys were out there fishing and saw what they believed to be a huge sea monster. The noise that it made was kind of a sucking sound. The people in the town formed a vigilante group to investigate and to keep watch on the lake at night. They found large footprints around the lake and felt that whatever it was walked on two legs.

The men patrolled the lake at night and would hear these strange noises, but they didn't see anything. During the day they would find fresh footprints. There was always someone who reported that they had seen the monster. Some said it was a hairy thing that would come out of the water, kill small animals and return to the water. Others thought it a great sea serpent. Many who discount the monster story believe the tracks belong to a huge turtle that lives in the lake. Every few years tracks are found, and the search begins again. The last time the "Beast of Busco" stories kicked up again was in 1967. Churubusco has an annual parade called the Beast of Busco parade.

Hidden Treasure and Lost Mines

Legends about treasure and other wealth lost and discovered are found in many parts of the world, and the United States enjoys a vital tradition of such stories. Buried pirate loot is often spoken of in regions where pirates like Jean Lafitte are known to have once operated ("Bluebeard's Treasure," "Buried Treasure of Jean Lafitte"). In the West in particular, lost mines have long held a fascination, offering the promise of gold or other precious metals to those who can find and work these mines anew. A legend may tell of a treasure's origins, but usually the focus is on attempts to find it.

The possible cultural significance of treasure stories is discussed in the introduction, but in fact in American legend, the treasure is often *not* found by the searchers. A valuable mine may be discovered once but never again because the landscape has changed when searchers go back ("The Metate Rocks of Loma Linda"). And buried treasure is often guarded by spirits who frighten diggers away ("Frightened Away from Captain Kidd's Treasure," "Phantom Pigs Guard a Treasure"), though sometimes a ghost actually guides people to treasure, and the treasure brings them unexpected wealth ("Bluebeard's Treasure" and story 136).

236. Bluebeard's Treasure

The pirate Edward Teach (died 1718), usually known as Blackbeard but sometimes as Bluebeard (probably a confusion with the fairytale character of that name), had his headquarters in the Outer Banks of North Carolina. In the early eighteenth century, he operated mostly along the coast of the Southeastern American colonies; he was finally killed in an attack by British naval forces, though tales of his treasure have persisted since then. This account was told by a woman from Rehobeth, Maryland, who had grown up on Tangier Island and heard the story in the 1920s. Motifs E371, E373, E545.12; cf E371.1, N538.

My mother used to tell us this, told it to her grandchildren too, and she used to keep them spellbound with the story of Bluebeard. It went something like this:

One time there was a very poor man and he had four children. Nothing he ever tried amounted to anything and the harder he worked, the less he seemed to have. So one night he was sitting around the local store over there on the island, and the men got to talking about pirates, mostly about this pirate Bluebeard and how he used to go around hijacking ships and taking the cargo for himself. They told how he got richer than anyone could imagine and just before he was captured, he took all that treasure and buried it. And they said his spirit was still wandering around the island trying to find someone to tell where the treasure was 'cause his spirit couldn't rest until he'd given away all his gold.

Well, this fellow listened and he wished he could have some of that gold. On his way home he had to pass this old deserted house. But before he got there the wind started to whine and moan in the trees, and as he got near the house, he heard this voice whispering in his ear and it said, "Can I speak with you?" Well, this man was scared out of his wits and he started to run along the road, but he heard the voice very close by say again, "Please let me speak with you."

So this man stopped and stuttered and said, "What do you want with me?"

And the voice said, "I'm the spirit of Bluebeard the Pirate and I want you to have my money; I must give it to someone before I can rest, so if you will come to this old deserted house at midnight Saturday, I'll meet you here and you will never want for anything more as long as you live."

Now that old fella, he ran all the way home as fast as he could, but he never told a soul what he'd heard out there on the marsh, but all week he kept thinking about meeting that ghost out there by that deserted house. But he kept telling himself he just had to do it for his family.

He thought Saturday would never come, but when it did it was cloudy and cold and dismal. The family went to bed early and after everyone was asleep he crept out of bed and put on his clothes and buttoned up his raggedy old coat around his neck and pulled this old felt hat down over his eyes and started out for that place.

When he got there, he crouched down near an old tree and waited. All of a sudden the sky got dark and the wind began to howl and he felt this hot breath against the back of his neck.

Well, he just couldn't take it; with the last bit of strength he had, he gave a screech and jumped to his feet and took off for home. And when he got there, he crawled into bed and never let anyone know what had happened that night.

So that ended that little episode. But one of the children in the family was a boy about twelve years old. He was sort of retarded and couldn't attend school, and he used to wander in the woods a lot, and almost everyday he would come home with all these gold pieces and throw them on the table and say, "Look at these shiny things, aren't they pretty."

And his father would say, "Where did you get this?"

And he'd say, "A dark man with a long blue beard gave it to me and he told me to come back and he'd always give me some more every time I returned."

And so that man knew it was really Bluebeard who was giving the boy the money he was too frightened to take away.

237. Buried Treasure of Jean Lafitte

Jean Lafitte (1780?–1826) operated for a number of years as smuggler, slave trader, and pirate, based on the island of Grand Terre at the mouth of Barataria Bay in Louisiana. In 1815, he and his men helped Andrew Jackson's defense against the invading British at the Battle of New Orleans for which he received a pardon for his crimes, though he soon returned to illegal activities. Stories of his buried treasure abound along the Gulf Coast. This story was collected by C. Renée Harvison, June 28, 1990, from Arthur Irwin of DeQuincy, Louisiana. Motif N511; cf N513, N513.5.

One of the most famous stories here is after the War of 1812. Jean Lafitte, the pirate, was still active here. He helped the United States in the Battle of New Orleans when Jackson defeated the British. They let him go, and he went to Galveston. The city of Galveston was founded by Jean Lafitte. He moved, supposedly, all his operations and headquarters outside the jurisdiction of the United States. But his biggest market, of course, was New Orleans. He would ply his piracy and his trade there.

At night, they knew all these swamps and innerland that the U.S. didn't know, the Coast Guard didn't know. And he would slip his stuff in through Barataria Bay and peddle it to New Orleans. One time one of his sloops or ships was apprehended, almost apprehended, by the U.S. Coast Guard. When they got to what they thought was waters outside of the United States, they turned into Sabine Lake [on the Texas–Louisiana border]. But it wasn't at that time outside of the United States. The Coast Guard was so close behind them that they scuttled their ship and sank it. There's always been a claim that they buried whatever they had somewhere in that area. People still look for the money there.

238. Phantom Pigs Guard a Treasure

Ozarks folklorist Vance Randolph uncovered this story during his field collecting. In legends, treasures are frequently guarded by spirits, though phantom pigs are unusual. Motif E291.2.2.

In Stoddard county, Missouri, near Bloomfield, stood the ruin of an old house, so dilapidated that there was not much left save the big stone chimney. There was a neighborhood story that gold and silver were buried somewhere about the place. People who tried to dig for the treasure were all driven away by pigs—dozens of wild pigs which came squealing and dashing back and forth over the site of the old building. They were ghost pigs, not affected by stones or bullets. One man fired repeatedly with a shotgun at very close range, but the animals paid no attention. The general impression was that the phantom swine were somehow stationed there to drive off treasure hunters.

239. Frightened Away from Captain Kidd's Treasure

William Kidd (1645–1701) was hanged for piracy after a rather ill-fated career at sea, including forays into the Indian Ocean. Stories of his buried treasure have long been popular along the coasts of New York, New England, and the Atlantic provinces of Canada; this particular story comes from Connecticut. Motifs E291, E422.1.1, N556, N576; cf N557.

Charles Island, near Milford, Connecticut, was dug into, one night, by a company from that town that had learned of Kidd's visit to it—and what could Kidd be doing ashore unless he was burying money? The lid of an iron chest had been uncovered when the figure of a headless man came bounding out of the air, and the work was discontinued right then. The figure leaped into the pit that had been dug, and blue flames poured out of it. When the diggers returned, their spades and picks were gone and the ground was smooth.

240. Larsen's Vein

The setting for "Larsen's Vein" is the Upper Peninsula of Michigan, where Richard M. Dorson collected folklore in 1946 (see also the headnote to story 234). The narrator for this tale was Jim Hodge. Motifs N557, N596; cf N541.

A fellow named Larsen was traveling north of Teal Lake, Negaunee, picking berries—lots of berries on the hills. He picked up a piece of quartz, attracted by the specks in it. If he'd been a mining man, he would have known there was gold in it. He put it in his pocket, and cut across the hills back to town, to his brother's saloon. There was a mining man present; he said, "Show it to me." After he looked at it he said, "I'd like to show that to a friend of mine." He sent the piece to an assayer at Houghton, and it was assayed at two hundred dollars a ton in gold.

But when Larsen went back to look for the quartz he couldn't find the spot, or even the hill.

Geologists have been intensively surveying the country all around, and they admit there is gold. Some day they will probably find Larsen's vein.

241. The Treasure of Cacapan

Published in an English folklore journal in 1888, this legend tells of mysterious foreigners of unknown origin who once mined a now-lost mine not far from Washington, D.C. By *Vaudos*, W. H. Babcock, who collected and published the story, probably means practitioners of Voodoo or Voudou, the African American religion associated with an array of magical practices. Motifs N576, N596.

Cacapan creek is one of the minor affluents of the Potomac while that river passes through the Alleghany ridges; and one of the minor folds of those ridges parallel with the creek is known as Cacapan mountain. Walking over this beside a mountaineer some years ago, I heard from him a local legend which sounded to me like something fresh from the old world. I had asked him if there were any mines of valuable metals thereabout. After some information of a commonplace kind, he added that as to gold and silver there was plenty of them in the mountains as everybody knew; and the place had been found. A lot of foreign men, who acted very queerly, and kept to themselves, and who spoke a language which nobody about them could understand, had settled along that mountain, and dug into it, and found gold there. They worked at night mostly; and at last left suddenly, and covered the hole with a stone, and put a spell on it. For a long time nobody could find the spot; but a man out hunting came on it in a thicket and tried to raise the stone, but failed. He went for help, but could not lead them back to where it was. Afterward a man looking for sheep or cattle discovered it; but he could not lift it either, and proved a bad pilot likewise. These men had described it as marked with very strange letters. Now in that neighborhood there was a negro who pretended to that kind of magic which is commonly supposed to belong to Vaudos or other heathen rites, although most of those who practise it claim to be Christians. He determined to set *his* black lore against that of the foreigners; and succeeded not only in finding the stone but in partly lifting it also. Then there was a sudden rush of enemies whom he could not see, and he felt blows falling all over him as he was fleeing headlong down the mountain-side. Nobody has ever found the magically-anchored stone since that day.

242. The Metate Rocks of Loma Linda

This Texas story is one of many about lost treasures and mines in the American West. A *metate* is the flat stone used for grinding corn; a *plata* is a map. Motif N511; cf N511.1.3, N557.

Just west of the Hill of Seven Rocks towers in primeval roughness Loma Alta, the highest point in the whole country. John Murphy told me this story connected with it. An early settler named Drummond had a squat near the foot of the mountain. One time an old Mexican came to him looking for some bullion that he claimed had been buried in the vicinity by ancient *parientes* (kinsmen) in flight from the Indians. His *plata* called for a mesquite tree on the southeast slope of Loma Alta marked by a certain sign. Murphy thinks that the sign was a cross but does not well remember. The *plata* called also for a line of smooth, oblong rocks that bore a resemblance to the stones used for grinding corn on the *metate*. They had been culled from the hillside and laid to point to the hidden bullion. Drummond and the Mexican found the tree but rode around for days without being able to find the rocks. They finally decided that generations of horses and cattle had scattered them so that they could no longer be recognized as forming a line, and gave up the search.

The Mexican left, Drummond died, and years passed. Then one day while Murphy was holding down a wormy calf out in the pasture to doctor it, he raised his eyes and saw three or four of the *metate*-like rocks lined up in some thick chaparral. He was down on his knees, so that he could see under the brush. He thought of the tale that Drummond had told him, and looking about further, he found, badly scattered, yet preserving a kind of line, other such rocks. But he could never settle on a place to dig, and so far as he knows no one has ever dug on that side of Loma Alta.

243. The Lost Red Blanket Mine

Frank Robertson, who collected this legend from A. B. Ruzicka, a Polish American forestry station lookout who had spent earlier days as a prospector, places the setting for the story as California. Although this story mentions Oregon, the collector published it as part of a group of California legends. Motifs N500, N596.

Up in eastern Oregon near Cannonville there lived an old miner by the name of Shefflin. He was a peculiar old man who lived all by his self and mingled with no one. During the week he would take a red blanket off someplace into the hills and not come back until he had mined enough gold or ran out food. He would sleep alongside his claim in the red bedroll, and at the end of the week he would roll up all the gold ore he could carry in his red blanket and return to his cabin. Every Saturday he would hike down from the hills into town to get his grub for the following week. People made up stories about the old man who came down from the hills only to get food and wondered what he had up on his property.

Several weeks had passed and the old man hadn't made his weekly appearances in town. The store keeper got a couple of guys to go up the mountain to find the old miner and see if he was sick or something. When the men reached the miner's cabin they found him dead. He was wrapped up in a blue blanket.

Many townspeople had seen Shefflin return wrapped up in this red blanket, so the men immediately began to search the cabin for either the gold the old miner had hidden away, or the red blanket they thought it would be wrapped up in.

The searchers found plenty of gold in the cabin but the blanket was gone. They knew that the old man must have left the blanket at his mine and if they could find the red blanket next to his claim they would find wealth enough to last them a life-time. Practically the whole town was searching for the lost mine, but the old miner died with the secret that no one has found out to this day.

244. The Lost Haystack Mine

"The Lost Haystack Mine" comes from the Big Bend country of south Texas, where it was narrated by Mary Ella Vannoy of Alpine, Texas. Motifs N500, N596; cf N557.

In the days when there was much mining and prospecting around Alpine, a Negro man would show up about once a year, take a burro, and go for a camping trip in the mountains. Before long people began to notice that, although he seemed to have very little money before the camping trip, when he returned he would have plenty of money to do anything he wanted.

Naturally people were curious, so one night several of the men in Alpine bought the Negro drinks enough to make him very talkative. They asked him many questions, but they were able to get him to say only that he had found enough riches to last him the rest of his life.

After finding this out, the men tried to follow the Negro on his excursions, but he always managed to lose himself in the mountains. It is believed that the lost mine is somewhere in the vicinity of Haystack Mountain, but in order to get away from his followers, the Negro would sometimes travel as far as Fort Davis before turning back in that direction. When their following the Negro didn't lead them to the mine, many people set out to find it by searching the mountains on their own.

The only man who ever knew the secret of the mine's location was the Negro, and he carried the secret to his death. Ironically, not only the mine's whereabouts is unknown, but the whereabouts of the Negro himself became a mystery. The last time the man was seen—by that time he was quite old—was the day he left on his last burro trip to the mine. When he did not return in several weeks, a search party was formed. Although the burro was found, the old Negro had completely disappeared. It is said that if the Lost Haystack Mine is ever found, the remains of the lost Negro will be found also.

Slavery and the Civil War

Slavery was a centerpiece of American life until ended by the Emancipation Proclamation and the Civil War, and in some legends, slavery and the War are inextricably bound together. In "What Caddy Did When She Heard That Lee Had Surrendered," the protagonist links the end of the War and the end of her servitude, and in "James Bowser, Emancipation Hero," we hear of the protagonist's attitudes toward slaves and his actions during the War. Slavery is particularly remembered in African American tradition, where stories of escapes from slavery ("The Escape of John Bennett") or of cleverly outwitting slave owners and their agents are characteristic forms.

Legendary accounts of the Civil War itself dwell not on grand battles but on less prominent events remembered in local communities or in families: escape from capture by Confederate or Federal forces ("The Buss"), dispatching marauders who invade homes ("Blood on the Floor"), guns kept from or taken in battle ("Morgan's Raiders"). Lincoln's assassination is remembered not as a monumental event in itself but through its connection with a local spy ("A Confederate Spy"). And in part, the War is remembered through the Union and Confederate ghosts who linger long after the fighting ("Yankee Ghosts in New Orleans," "A Confederate Soldier").

---

245. The Escape of John Bennett

The story of John Bennett's escape was recorded from James A. Coker in Michigan by Richard M. Dorson. Dorson collected folk material in Michigan in 1952, particularly in Calvin Township, a community settled by black freedmen before the Civil War. Fred Steele, who is addressed by the narrator in this selection at one point, had brought Dorson to see James Coker, who recounted this story of escape from an unnamed slaveholding Southern state to Ohio. Motifs R211.4, S110; cf S139.2.2.3.

I've talked to lots of them ex-slaves. John Bennett, whose boy Ed lives in Calvin now, used to tell me how he escaped; he was half white, tall and freckled, and wore his hair long. A hostler boy, a roustabout, crossed and mixed too, had a little education. He forged his own press, printed free papers, and wrote the magistrate's name on them. Then he stole a riding horse and rode to Kelbyware, sold it there, 'cause he needed money, and set out walking to Ohio. He'd sleep in the daytime, and travel at night, following the North Star. One night he got a chicken, cooked and ate it, started on, and saw he wasn't very far from Ohio. So he stopped in a cornfield by a spring, started to eat an ear, when he heard a dog a-barking. He knew he was on his trail. He ran and clumb a tree about one-fourth a mile off, to get away from the bloodhound. A man came along with the dog and said, "Come on down." "Don't shoot me." "I won't, but if you run you'll bite lead." John had an old double-barreled pistol himself. They went back to the spring together. The man set the gun down by the tree to get a gourd for a drink, and John walked around and grabbed it, and shot him with his own gun, "Pow." Then he shot the dog.

Next day he saw a colored man walking along the banks of the Ohio. He spoke to Bennett and said, "I'm a free man; I'm helping you fellows across." He rowed him across to a little house, which was a station on the underground railway. About ten of the farmers came around and gave Bennett little presents. The colored man rowed down a ways, then cut back to the Kentucky side. When John Bennett said he had shot that slave-hunter, they all cheered—so John Bennett said.

They sent him up to the next station, about twenty miles north. He made his way to Philadelfy, worked there a while, saved $150, came to Michigan, and settled on that farm across the creek, Mr. Steele. He told me that settin' right there. He said, "I don't care who knows I killed a man."

246. The Tombstone

Folklorist Ruth Ann Musick recorded this legend from Herschel Conoway, Fairmont, West Virginia, 1959; he had the story from his grandfather, who had heard it from the son of the slave owner in the legend. Motifs E234.3, E402, E413.

My story about a cruel slaveowner was related to my grandfather by his father. My grandfather was a good friend of the slaveowner's son and told me that the son always had large groups of men working, literally at nothing, and that he paid them large salaries. The son said that his father had cheated people out of money all his life, and he, the son, was just trying to pay some of it back.

As the story goes, one day Mr. Soames, the slaveowner, was inspecting one of his favorite plots of ground. An old Negro had been told to hoe a potato patch in that part of the estate, but instead he was sitting in the shade of a tree. Upon seeing this, the owner flew into a rage and beat the old man to death with the hoe. Two years later the slaveowner fell dead on the exact spot where he had killed the Negro. Two local doctors could not find any cause for his death, and as far as anyone knew, he was in perfect health. HERE LIES MR. SOAMES was all that was put on his tombstone.

Some three or four months later a young boy happened to be passing the grave at night and heard a sound like someone using a chisel. The boy could see no one at the tombstone or near it. He reported the incident to the son, and the son looked at the tombstone the next morning.

A much larger epitaph had been chiseled into the rock. Below HERE LIES MR. SOAMES were now the following lines:

He stole from the poor;
He robbed from the rich;
Gone to hell,
The son of a b_____.

247. James Bowser, Emancipation Hero

Collected May 18, 1937, by Emmy Wilson and Claude Anderson from Virginia Hayes Shepherd, Norfolk, Virginia, this story was one of a number gathered by workers for the state affiliate of the Federal Writers' Project. Nathan Hale, who is referred to, was executed by the British as a spy and was a great hero of the Revolutionary War. Motif Q421.

I want to tell you about undertaker Hale's grandfather. I'll bet he doesn't know this about his grandfather. This man's name was James Bowser. James Bowser was a free Negro who lived in Nansemond County during slavery times. Now you know free Negroes had to be very careful of mixing with slaves or white folks in those days because both races were always watching them, especially the whites. Some white folks watched all the time, to keep them from mixing with the slaves. Consequently Bowser did his best to avoid trouble in any shape or form. He had five daughters who were in the courting stage. He wouldn't let them entertain any male slave company and allowed very few female slaves to come visiting. His policy was no slaves in his home any longer than possible. If he came in the house and a strange Negro was sitting there, he would ask, "Who are you? Are you your own man?" Generally the conversation would run, "No sir." "Well, then whom do you belong to?" "I belong to so and so." "I'm sorry, you'll have to go home. I can't entertain you. I got enough trouble of my own." When he finished, another young lovesick buck slave was sent back to his master's plantation. Such attitude and action made Bowser very unpopular among the slaves. Bowser hated the fact that his own people despised him, but there was nothing else to do to protect himself from the white man's wrath. He had no redress in court. He owned property which they desired and he knew association with slaves could be used as an excuse for attacking him by jealous white neighbors, one Phelps especially. The slave had protection; Bowser had none. He detested slavery because it kept him bound. As long as slavery existed, Bowser knew he could never be absolutely free; so whenever he could, he threw a monkey wrench in the machinery of slavery.

He did it once too often however. The Civil War began and the Yankees came down to free the Negroes. Because they were in strange country the Yankees needed information. Free Negroes aided them a great deal. Bowser began to act as a spy for the Yankees and give them all the information he knew about his section of the country. He gave it gladly. He saw his chance to deliver a telling blow at slavery and took it.

Soon the news leaked out to the whites. That was all the cause they wanted. Led by Phelps, an envious white man, a band of white planters attacked the Bowser home one night and demanded that Bowser and his son come forth. They came out, were seized by the mob and carried into the woods between Driver and Suffolk. After severely beating both father and son, the horde made Bowser lie on the ground and stretch his neck over a log like a chicken on a chopping block. Then someone cut his head off. The plan was to kill the boy in the same manner, but the more thought-ful ones disagreed. They suggested that he be left to carry the news of this ghastly example back to the other Negroes. The mob gave in. The boy went home, got a cart, and returned for his father's body. The family was stunned by the news and remained as meek as lambs. A quiet funeral was held and the body of James Bowser was laid to rest in the family plot while a few miles away slaves chuckled gleefully in their quarters. Big hat Bowser had got what he deserved at last.

After the war the daughters, all five of them, Ruth, Mary, Evaline and the other two married. The Bowser family was one family that never felt the blight of dis-grace on their fair name. Their father had reared them too well. Colored spies were common during the rebellion, but very few of them are credited in today's history. Bowser should be ranked with [Nathan] Hale.

248. A Confederate Spy

The story that President Abraham Lincoln's assassination stemmed from the execution of a Confederate spy named John Beall (he is called Bell in this leg-end) was probably begun by a partisan newspaper and was well known at one time. This legendary version of that story was collected by Mary Smith from Harriet G. Miller, Mathews County, Virginia, as part of the Virginia Writers' Project folklore collecting. The Bay referred to is the Chesapeake.

In an old home situated on the Bay, I heard an interesting tale of Civil War days. During the war a Confederate spy by the name of Bell came to the home of Mr. William Hudgins near Fitchett's Wharf and asked for refuge. While he was there some Yankee soldiers prowling through that section of the county came upon a Confederate cap in the vicinity of the Hudgins' home.

They immediately started to the house to search, but in the meantime Bell had gone out into a dense woods nearby to hide.

The mistress of the house saw the soldiers coming and ran up to Bell's room to see if any of his belongings had been left there. Nothing seemed to be in the room which would reveal his presence in the house except some letters, which she grabbed quickly and just had time to slip them inside of the dress of a doll which her little girl was holding. She put the child on the porch telling her to sit there and hold the doll tight in her arms.

As soon as the soldiers reached the porch, one of them picked the little girl up in his arms to talk to her. But she remembered her mother's warning and held her doll baby close to her side. So the letters were not discovered.

Mr. Hudgins took Bell in a sail boat at night to Gwynne's Island, where he hid in the woods. At times the Yankees were so near that they could hear them breath-ing. Later Mr. Hudgins took Bell to Eastern Shore, Virginia, where he remained for a while. His mother was living in New York and he was very anxious to see her. It was during a visit to her that he was finally captured.

[John Wilkes] Booth, who was an old friend and school-mate of Bell's, sent word to Lincoln that if Bell were hung, he (Lincoln) would die. Bell was hung, but before he died he wrote a beautiful letter to the man in Virginia who had befriended him. In this letter Bell wrote about the beauty of the morning of the day before he died, and of how much he wanted to live. He also expressed beautifully his appreciation of the great kindness of Mr. Hudgins and his family. This letter was destroyed by mistake, greatly to the distress of the present members of the family, who would have liked to have preserved it.

Many people believed that the hanging of Bell was one of the causes of the assassination of President Lincoln.

249. The Buss

This family legend comes from southern Illinois and was originally published in the 1930s. Cf motif K551.10.

I can tell you a real story about the Civil War. My grandfather, Joshua G. Burch, sympathized with the South, and when Southern soldiers came along, he took them in and hid them. He would let them rest and then send them along. One time a Confederate soldier came along in disguise. He was a stranger. My grandfather took him in. Folks found it out some way, and the officers came to arrest J. G. Burch. They took him to the home of a man named Clark on the other side of the river near Prairie Du Rocher. They promised to let Burch stand trial, but they were going to kill him. He found it out from one of the girls who was waiting on the table.

Grandfather was always full of fun. He told the girl that she was so pretty that he wanted to give her a buss. (He always said buss for kiss.) She found out that they were going to kill Grandfather on the bluff not far off. She told the officers that she wouldn't wait on them if they didn't take their guns off because they made her nervous. They took off their guns and laid them down on the floor and put a man to guard Grandfather, who was in a room. The men had a good dinner and they forgot about their prisoner, for they were having a good time.

The apron that the girl wore had a big pocket, and she stole a gun and hid it in the pocket. They didn't notice because she flirted with the officers. She managed to steal the key to the handcuffs, too. Then she slipped to the room that Grandfather was in. She unlocked the handcuffs and gave him the gun and told him that there was a horse in the field.

As Grandfather had one leg through the window, he turned around and kissed the girl. She said to him, "Go on, you fool!"

He said, "I'm no fool. I've just kissed the prettiest girl in the country."

He got away and went home. Then he sent word to the officers to come and get him, but they never bothered him.

250. Blood on the Floor

"Blood on the Floor" is a legend from Florida, told by Gordon Louis Tillery of Winter Haven, 1955. The idea that a stain on the floor of a house is that of a Yankee soldier killed there is part of the lore of a number of Southern houses. Motifs E422.1.11.5.1, K834, K910; cf K818.

During the days of the Civil War many of the men were fighting around Winter Haven. Often these men would slip home for a good meal and to spend the night with their wives. One afternoon while the war was being hard fought, a Yankee slipped into the house of one of the southerners and said he would kill both the wife and the small child if the woman of the house wouldn't cook him a good meal and allow him to spend the night with her. Being a good southerner, she felt this might be her chance to do her share in helping fight for the South. She didn't know exactly how she was going to kill this intruder, since he had demanded that she give him the gun she had in the house for her protection, but she knew that if she was going to do her part she would have to find some way to kill him.

She acted very pleasant toward him. After she had pushed her fear and hate far down inside of her, she seated this man in front of the fire to warm himself; it was cold outside and she knew that this man would want the warmth of the fire. As she began stirring around in the kitchen the man's eyes were always on her. She thought about running out to the neighbors, but had to dismiss this idea from her mind. She knew that the man wouldn't let her out of the house, and, too, the neighbors' house was too far away for her to make it with the baby.

After a short time the man saw that the woman wasn't going to try to get away and, because she had been so nice to him, he trusted her fully. He then allowed himself to go slowly to sleep in the chair by the fire. Only a short time later the woman slipped to the side of the fire, picked up the axe used for cutting firewood, and with one quick hard blow sunk the axe deep into the man's head. The blood from the head fell on the floor by the fireside, and the house stands today, with the Yankee blood still on the floor.

251. Morgan's Raiders

Morgan's Raiders were Confederate cavalry who invaded Indiana during the Civil War. Folklorist Donald A. Bird recorded folklore, including this legend, from Benjamin A. Kuhn of Hartsville, Indiana, November 1968. Cf motifs X1122, X1122.3, X1122.3.1, X1122.5*.

Now when the people of Madison learned that Morgan's Raiders was coming through they hid their horses, see? Morgan's boys pushed them so hard that they needed new ones every time they came through. Well, there was this man that was a noted squirrel hunter. Yes sir, he could shoot better than any of them farmers. But mainly because he had this wonderful rifle, see? It was the best gun around. Made special for squirrels. Well, this farmer was going to shoot one of Morgan's boys. But Morgan's boy tricked the farmer in this way. "Ah" he says, "that's sure a good looking rifle you got there." "Sure is," bragged the farmer. Well Morgan's man said he could make it so he could shoot over the hill with it. There was a sapling tree there by the road. And he just wrapped her around the tree. And you know, it just bent the barrel like a rainbow! (Laughter) Then he handed it back to him. "Now," he says, "you can shoot over the hill with it," now he says, "cause it is curved with it." And they done them kind of tricks, Morgan's army did. I think they was headed pretty near to Cincinnati. They went through Cassels over there; but, I think they was going to Cincinnati.

252. Yankee Ghosts in New Orleans

Drawn from a volume about Louisiana folklore, material for which was assembled by workers for the Federal Writers' Project in the 1930s, this story relates to a house in New Orleans at 1447 Constance Street in what is today called the Lower Garden District. The authors of the book include other stories about the house and its haunting by Yankee ghosts. Motifs E275, E281, E334.4, E402.1.1.4; cf E334.5.

At one time a widow took a portion of the dwelling as an apartment. Sitting sewing one afternoon a drop of blood fell from the ceiling on her arm. Another. She stared upward. Blood dripped from a spot in the ceiling, one drop at a time. Then she heard someone singing:

John Brown's body lies a-moulding in his grave,
John Brown's body lies . . .

The next day, when the widow moved, two young men in the blue uniforms of the Union Army appeared at an upstairs window, looked down and smiled.

Patrolman William Fleming remembered visiting the house as a small boy, taking two other boys and a pair of dogs. The floor had been ripped up in an upper chamber and the youngsters walked the joists. Suddenly a door swung open slowly, and an icy draft blew in. One of the dogs fell through the floor and was instantly killed. The other cried and carried on strangely. The boys made a hasty departure. Behind them came the song in a deep baritone:

John Brown's body lies a-moulding in his grave,
John Brown's body lies a-moulding in his grave,
John Brown's body lies a-moulding in his grave,
But his soul keeps marching on.

Oh, we'll hang Jeff Davis to a sour-apple tree,
Oh, we'll hang Jeff Davis to . . .

The story is that two Federal officers in New Orleans during the occupation of General Ben Butler stole army funds, and when accused of the crime, hid themselves in this house. Then, one night, they lay side by side on the bed, and each placing his revolver over the other's heart, they pulled the triggers. There were two shots, as one. Then no sound but the drip, drip, drip of their mingling blood. This happened more than three quarters of a century ago, yet still they walk, singing their old Yankee song.

253. A Confederate Soldier

This legend was collected from Eleanor Harper, Parsons, West Virginia, 1967. Motifs E279.2, E279.3, E281.3, E337.

One of the best-known ghost tales of Tucker County was told by Lewis Kittle, who lived on the Indian Fork of Clover Run. His reputation among his neighbors and acquaintances was above reproach, and the following story is an account of the facts as he knew and understood them. Mr. Kittle was not a superstitious man and was not a believer in spiritualism.

In 1867 Lewis Kittle, with several others, was mining coal near the ground on which the battle of Rich Mountain was fought. He and a cousin named Daniel Courtright boarded with a Mr. Hart, whose house was adjacent to the battlefield and had been used as a hospital during the battle. In the course of the battle a soldier had been shot in the room later occupied by Kittle and his cousin. The first night in the room they heard a weird and continuous noise. They supposed it was only the wind, but one day they were told by a fellow miner that the room was haunted.

One Saturday night soon after this, Courtright was absent, and Kittle slept in the room alone. Along in the night he was awakened by a strange coldness and a dim light that outlined the furniture in the misty air. The silence was broken only occasionally by a low sound that seemed to be the echo of a night breeze. Drawn by some unseen, irresistible power, Kittle arose from the bed and moved near the door. He said that he felt no fear and was struck with a sense of solemnity. Almost immediately he saw eight forms materialize, clad in Confederate uniforms. Silently they approached the bed on which Kittle had been sleeping and removed the covers, throwing them over the footboard. Four of them leaned over the bed and raised something up, as if lifting a weight.

The object, which Kittle could not see, was laid down carefully upon apparently nothing. Two of those who had lifted the object from the bed then took a place in front of the four, and the other two stepped behind. In this order they slowly marched toward the door, and as they filed out, Kittle saw lying between the pall-bearers the body of a handsome young man. His coat and vest had been removed, but he was wearing butternut trousers. The figures made no sound until they had reached the hallway, where a noise resembling the knock of a crutch on a wooden floor was heard. This was followed by the closing of a door.

Kittle collected the covers and returned to bed. He said that there was not any possibility of his being mistaken about what he saw. He was in perfect health, wide awake, and not frightened. Kittle spoke to several men staying in the house who said that other people who had occupied the room had had similar experiences.

On another occasion, when Mr. Courtright was present, the covers were removed from the bed several times in quick succession. Finally, both men got up, clutching their bedclothes tightly. The same cold, clammy light entered the room and the weird wind was again heard as the two men were pushed out of the way and up against the wall. Then a calm and quiet settled over the room, and the gray air rolled like a fog in a slight breeze. The forms began to emerge slowly at first and then suddenly stood in bold view. Again they approached the bed. In a few moments they solemnly took up their burden and enacted the same scene.

These nocturnal visits became so frequent that Kittle and Courtright finally got used to it. When they first became aware of the cold light and weird echo, they would wrap their blankets tightly around them and say, "Here come them rebels again."

254. What Caddy Did When She Heard That Lee Had Surrendered

Caddy Gordon (1833 or 1834–1919), the protagonist here, was the maternal great-grandmother of folklorist Kathryn L. Morgan, who recorded this version of the story from her own daughter, Susan. Caddy Gordon was born free in Virginia but kidnapped and sold into slavery in 1842; she became "a midwife, a farmer, a tradeswoman, a 'wheeler and dealer'" and is the central figure in a number of stories in Morgan's mother's family. Motif J1250.

Caddy had been sold to a man in Goodman, Mississippi. It was terrible to be sold in Mississippi. In fact, it was terrible to be sold anywhere. She had been put to work in the fields for running away again. She was hoeing a crop when she heard that General Lee had surrendered. Do you know who General Lee was? He was the man who was working for the South in the Civil War. When General Lee surrendered that meant that all the colored people were free! Caddy threw down that hoe, she marched herself up to the big house, then, she looked around and found the mistress. She went over to the mistress, she flipped up her dress and told the white woman to do something. She said it mean and ugly. This is what she said: "Kiss my ass!"

Outlaws, Crime, and Criminals

The American fascination with outlaws and other badmen and with murders and other crimes certainly is reflected in legends. Outlaws intrigue us, perhaps because they embody some rebellious spirit to be admired. But legends about them often are rather low-key: family stories about an ancestors' being visited by a famous robber ("Jesse James Spent the Night near Terre Haute"), local stories about a hideout maintained by some celebrated gangster ("Al Capone's Hideout Near Edwardsport"). Jesse James, Dillinger, Al Capone have their legends, but much lesser-known outlaws may also be remembered in local or family legend, men like Lewis the Robber ("Lewis the Robber Helps a Poor Widow") and Eugene Bunch ("Eugene Bunch, the Robin Hood of Southeast Louisiana"). Outlaws in legend are apt to be Robin Hood figures, sympathizing with the poor. They are often tricksters, as when they steal from an authority figure about to foreclose on a poor widow's property, give the widow the money to pay off her debt, then steal it back (told here about both Lewis the Robber and Eugene Bunch). And the African American badman Railroad Bill actually takes on supernatural powers to thwart those who would pursue him ("How Railroad Bill Chased Himself to His Girl's House").

But if outlaws enjoy a certain romance, crime as such may simply fill us with fear and a wish to see criminals punished. Waylaying poor pioneer migrants on the road to the West ("Winn Parish Night Riders") or enticing men with offers of marriage, then robbing and killing them ("Belle Gunness") is simply wrong and chilling. The Frankie Silver of folklore ("Frankie Silver") is hanged for the murder of her husband, as was the actual Frankie in 1833; that her father may have had a hand in the crime and went unpunished, as the account given here suggests, remains unsettling, a possibility never resolved.

255. Jesse James Spent the Night Near Terre Haute

Jesse James (1847–1882) was probably the most famous nineteenth-century American outlaw, celebrated in balladry and dime novels (and in films and on television in the twentieth and twenty-first centuries). A Confederate guerilla during the Civil War, after the war James and his gang robbed banks and trains in many parts of the West. This story about his possible appearance was collected in Terre Haute, Indiana, from a forty-seven-year-old man who was a florist, April 1971. Cf motifs K650, K1800, K1817.

My father likes to tell a story that happened to his grandparents. I don't know how many years ago it was, but it was back in the pioneer days, more or less, in this part of Indiana. They ran a roadside inn south of Terre Haute about ten miles, which is east of the present [Highway] 41, and at that time it was the main road between Terre Haute and Louisville. At that time the transportation was horses; there weren't many buggies, if any, and travelers would stop and stay the night at this inn, similar to the way they stay at motels today.

This one night, just a little while before dark, some man rode in on a big white horse. The horse was all lathered up as though he had been ridden very hard. The man wanted to stay all night, so they put his horse in the barn and give the man his supper, and he went to bed, and so did they. The way the inn worked, the meals were included with the room and figured in the price. And the next morning they all had breakfast. They didn't have customers every night, or a lot of them, and they ate breakfast at the family breakfast table. And so they were having their breakfast as usual, and somebody in the family noticed two pearl-handled pistols sticking out of this man's coat that was hanging on the coat peg in the hallway. This was kind of unusual, particularly two pearl-handled pistols, big ones like they were, but they didn't think too terribly much about it. So the man had his breakfast and took off on his big white horse.

This was early in the morning. About noon that day the lawmen came through looking for Jesse James. They had word that Jesse James had traveled this way. They had no way of ever knowing that the man that had stayed with my father's grandparents at their inn was Jesse James, but Jesse James was supposed to have ridden a big white horse and was always wanted by the law, and it seemed probable that this was Jesse James that stayed at this inn. It just so happens that we built our house right on the very location where this inn was, where Jesse James was supposed to have stayed one night.

256. Butch Cassidy's Escape

Deirdre Murray Paulsen collected the stories of her grandfather, Rowland W. Rider, a former cowboy and skilled raconteur, for a book they published together, which included this story of Butch Cassidy. Butch Cassidy (1866–?), whose real name was Robert LeRoy Parker, gained notoriety as a cattle rustler and train and bank robber; he may have perished in South America, where he had robbed banks after the American West became too settled for outlaws, though some have claimed he returned to the United States and lived under other names. He gained particular fame from the 1969 Hollywood film *Butch Cassidy and the Sundance Kid*. Motifs K500, K550.

I knew Butch Cassidy's brother, Bill Parker, and Bill Parker told me that when the sheriff got the drop on Butch when he went to visit his home in Circle Valley,

Cassidy said, "I'll come with you, sheriff, but just give me a chance to kiss my mother goodbye." Her picture was hanging on the wall across the room and the sheriff said, "Go ahead." So Cassidy went over there and acted like he was going to kiss that picture and he put his hand around back of the picture and got his six-shooter and had the drop on the sheriff—and he got away. Took the sheriff's gun. And they never caught him.

257. Eugene Bunch, the Robin Hood of Southeast Louisiana

> This story was recorded in Clinton, Louisiana, June 24, 1990, from Carl Bunch, a relative of Eugene Bunch, the little-known Louisiana/Texas outlaw who is the subject of the family legends given here. Cf motif J1269.8.

Eugene's daddy's name was James Bunch. James Bunch's father and my grandfather, my grandfather was Thomas Clarence Bunch and his daddy was Alexander H. Bunch. He's buried at Kentwood today and his wife, too. His wife was Martha R. Bunch. That's Alexander, my great-grandfather. This James Bunch is my great-grandfather's brother. He come from Tennessee years ago down into Mississippi. James, when he come into Mississippi—the Bunches loved women. I don't know why, but they always did—he met a girl by the name of Martha R. McDonald, a wealthy, wealthy farmer in Mississippi's daughter. James and Martha had these children. Eugene and T.C. was brothers.

In later years, when they sold out in Mississippi, the boll weevils eat them up, so they was hunting new territory. They come north of Bogalusa over here to Angie, Louisiana, and they bought another big farm. So he sent his kids through every school he could send them to at that time. James and his wife sent Eugene and Tom up here to the best schools. Like I said, he had ten kids, James did. And my grandfather, Tom Bunch, had ten kids. They liked a lot of help, I guess.

But anyway, to make it short, these boys went through school and finished school. When the Civil War started, they both volunteered. They got out of the service. T.C. went back and he run for clerk of court. He was clerk of court in Washington Parish—T.C. was, after the Civil War. And Eugene went back to teaching school. He was a schoolteacher in Washington Parish. He taught school for a good many years, and he had a lot of friends in Washington Parish. About all this same time, the railroad came through. It went right through the middle of his daddy's field. Cotton and all, they tore it up. Lord, did he hate the railroad. What's so sad about it is that it turned a well-educated man into the worst criminal the state of Louisiana has ever known.

He left there teaching school, and he started robbing trains. He pulled the biggest train robbery ever pulled in the state of Louisiana by himself—from New Orleans going up to around Angie and Bogalusa. By himself, he robbed it. What he did with the money, he'd go back into Honey Island and hide out. When the taxes on these people's property came due and they couldn't pay it, he'd pay their taxes. So the money started showing up in the sheriff's office.

One of his close friends, an old lady, was fixing to lose her place over there. She was a young girl, in her twenties; they were going to lose their property. Eugene went there and said, "I'm going to give you the money." She got the word to Eugene when [the sheriff] was coming. So that afternoon, when the sheriff got the money and gave her her receipt, on his way back to town, he robbed the sheriff. This is the God's truth, he robbed the sheriff! They couldn't arrest him in Washington Parish. He taught school in Washington and Tangipahoa Parish, and everybody loved him. And they'd hide him out and feed him. They got real hot after him.

He left Louisiana, they got so bad after him. He went to Texas. He was a newspaper editor in Texas. He went to Waco, Texas, and opened up his own newspaper. The people really liked him over there. They liked him so well, he run for clerk of court and won for three terms in a row. In Cook County in Texas.

But what happened to him, he started drinking some. They began to miss him in town and for a few days he'd be gone. He was the clerk of court at this time. He was robbing trains while he was clerk of court! He was recognized in a bar as Eugene Bunch. A Texas ranger recognized him as Eugene Bunch and walked up to him and said, "I'm going to arrest you."

And [Eugene] said, "And you fixing to die." He always had a pistol in his coat and he'd shoot right through his coat. He said, "You going to die. If you don't get up and get out of here, you going to die." So the ranger got up and left.

So that night, he left. The next they heard of him was four years later. He was pulling robberies in Colorado and Wyoming. He made it back to Honey Island, and he contacted some of his friends over there. He was really planning this big one that time. He was going to really get it. And he got it. This train robbery, this last one, he said, "I want to rob it with these detectives sitting on the train." He had ten detectives riding the train. He boarded the train at New Orleans. Colonel Hobgood had the horses. He had a man with him with the horses who was a colonel. He was up at this creek by Sheridan, Louisiana, with the horses hid. So Eugene goes to New Orleans and boards the train. When he got closer, he eased on up and got the engineer, went back to the express car, got all the money, which was forty-eight thousand dollars. The detectives never knew the robbery took place until he came out there and waved goodbye and jumped out the window with the forty-eight thousand dollars.

He hid out at Honey Island. They had implanted a man in his gang. They killed [Eugene] sleeping. In this country, we all knew Judge Horace Reeves. Judge Horace Reeves' daddy [known as R.R. Reeves] tried the man in the gang over at the courthouse in Franklin. . . . They tried the man that shot [Eugene]. And they had a seven-year-old boy for a witness, and it really turned into a long, drawn out trial. But they convicted the man. You had a lot of people who wanted to claim credit for killing him.

What was so funny, while he was in Cook County, they were remodeling the courthouse. They had to move the clerk's office down to the jail. They moved the clerk's office down to the jail and he was sitting down there. He had this friend of his, "You know, I should be behind bars, but this is the closest I'll ever become to be put in jail in my life." He never was arrested at all. His daddy owned a big plantation over in Mississippi. Cotton caused all his trouble.

258. How Railroad Bill Chased Himself to His Girl's House

Best known from the folksong that bears his name, Railroad Bill was an African American badman of the 1890s whose real name was Morris Slater. Although the legend text given here (from Depression-era Virginia Writers' Project collections) was collected in Virginia and provides a North Carolina provenance for the story, Railroad Bill was especially well known in Florida and southern Alabama, sometimes celebrated as a Robin Hood figure. Motifs A527.3.1, D135, D141, D313.1; cf J1269.8.

Railroad Bill has been a popular fellow among the Negroes living in the little cabins among the dark North Carolina pines for a long time. Everywhere, if you listen hard enough you can hear a whispering about him. White folks say his real name was not Railroad Bill, but black boys and girls who tell stories and sing songs about him have never known him by any other name.

He still lives, they say, in the North Carolina woods near the railroad. Sometimes when a poor old black woman opens her cabin door in the morning she finds a little pile of canned foods on her door-step. "God bless Railroad Bill," she says, as she hides away the cans, because she knows Railroad Bill has taken the cans of food, sacks of flour and sugar, and all kinds of things out of the freight cars to divide them with all the poor black folks he knows.

Nobody could ever catch up with him, but all the black folks know why. One time, as the sheriff and a large crowd of white men who were looking for him raced through a clearing in the woods, they saw a little black sheep standing there watching them run. Some of them don't believe to this day that the little black sheep was Railroad Bill. But it was.

Another time the sheriff and his men rode a train to a lonesome place where they thought he was hiding, but Bill was in the car behind them all the time. And when they got off the train and went looking for him, he just stayed on the train and collected up all the canned goods, which he gave away to all the poor folks all over the countryside that night.

Another time the sheriff and his men were looking for Bill in a dense wood. They spied a red fox run out of an old hollow tree, and fired twice. But neither of the shots hit the red fox. And when he ran away off to the top of a hill he looked back and laughed out loud at all this crowd of men trying to catch one poor little red fox who turned into a man right before their eyes, but he was too far off for them to do anything about it.

When that story got out it made the sheriff mighty mad and he swore he would catch him yet. That sheriff sent way off to Mississippi and rented some blood-hounds, saying he knew he would catch the varmint now. He found one of Railroad Bill's old shoes in the road, and when he gave the dogs the scent, they started right off following a track straight to a cabin where his girl lived on the other side of the mountain. When they got to the cabin of Bill's best girl the sheriff saw her on the porch. But she told him she hadn't seen Bill in a month. After searching all around he couldn't find Railroad Bill. All at once he asked, "Did I start with three dogs or four?" Nobody seemed to be able to remember, but now there were four dogs on the trail. And one of them was a black bloodhound.

The dogs seemed to want to go on and so the sheriff and his men followed them. But now the sheriff noticed there were only three bloodhounds on the trail. The black one was gone. The sheriff never really did know that the black dog was Railroad Bill, who had chased himself all the way out to his girlfriend's house and had just stayed when the sheriff and his men left. White folks say that the sheriff finally caught Railroad Bill, but the black folks who live in the cabins in the woods just laugh when they hear that. And they tune up their banjos and sing a song called Railroad Bill.

---

259. Lewis the Robber Helps a Poor Widow

David Lewis (1788?–1820) carried out a career of thievery in central Pennsylvania, where he is still remembered as Lewis the Robber. The story given here is a widely told one, attributed to Robin Hood, Jesse James, and other outlaws (including Eugene Bunch in story 257) who "steal from the rich and give to the poor." This account is taken from the 1853 edition of *The Confessions or Narrative of David Lewis,* an anonymous account of Lewis's crimes allegedly by Lewis himself and originally published soon after his death; it is quoted from the informative study of Lewis by folklorist Mac Barrick. Cf motif J1269.8.

The following incident is said to have happened in Mifflin county: Having failed of carrying into execution some of his deeply laid schemes for robbing several wealthy farmers, during one of his marauding expeditions, and his finances getting uncomfortably low, he determined on making an effort to replenish at the first opportunity. Coming across a house that promised security from molestation, no other being near, he called at the door, and was admitted by an elderly female, of respectable appearance. Lewis, to ascertain where her money was kept, asked her to change a five dollar note. "That unfortunately I am unable to do," replied the woman, "for

I have not a dollar in the house; and, what is worse," she added despondingly, as she caught a glimpse of a man coming through the woods some distance from the house, "there comes the constable to take my cow for the last half-year's rent. I don't know what to do without her." "How much is due?" inquired Lewis, hurriedly. "Twenty dollars, sir." "Have you no one to help you?" "No one," she replied. "Then I will," replied the robber as he drew from his pocket the exact sum, and threw it upon the table. "Pay that fellow his demand, *and take his receipt,* but don't say anything about me." Lewis had just time to make good his escape unobserved, when the worthy official arrived. He was proceeding without more ado to drive away the cow, when the woman came forward, paid him the money and took his receipt. He immediately set out on his return, but had not proceeded far, when Lewis bounded into the road and accosted him with, "How d'ye do, stranger? Got any spare change about you?" "No!" simpered the frightened constable. "Come, shell out old fellow or I'll save you the trouble," returned Lewis, as he presented a pistol at him. This argument convinced the constable that the fellow was up to his business, and he handed over his money as quickly as possible. Lewis got his own twenty back, and forty dollars in addition. He often boasted that the loan of the twenty dollars was one of the best investments he had ever made.

260. Winn Parish Night Riders

This legend was collected by C. Renée Harvison from J. Maxwell Kelley of Winnfield, Louisiana, June 19, 1990. In Louisiana, counties are called parishes; Winn Parish is in western Louisiana, and the Harrisonburg Road was an important artery for settlers and others moving west. Motif S100.

You ever heard about the night riders? Earlier I told you about this trail, Harrisonburg Road. There was a group of men back in the late 1860s, after the Civil War, mainly two families, the West family and the Kimbrell family. A guy by the name of John West and a guy by the name of Lars Kimbrell. They were mainly from the Montgomery area, which is in Grant Parish now, but at that time it was part of Winn Parish.

Anyway, they were Masons; they were respected people in the community. But they devised a scheme to take advantage of these disenfranchised people who were traveling the Harrisonburg Road going west. Their scheme was simply to murder them and take what they had.

They really ravaged that road for many, many years. They took what money they had. They took what valuable possessions they had, pianos or whatever. Right out here in Winn Parish! Besides Lafitte the Pirate, it's really the only other outlaw band that ever established a foothold in Louisiana.

This went on for many, many years. No telling how many people they killed all along the Harrisonburg Road. Their territory was like Vidalia, Louisiana, all the way to the Texas line. They used to call it No Man's Land in Sabine Parish, Zwolle, that area. They really ravaged that whole countryside. No one ever suspected these people. No one ever knew that it was them that was doing these atrocities. Like I said, they were Masons!

They had an outlet for the sale of all these goods. The person who was in the gang was a retail merchant, and they just sold these pianos or whatever came in. They got the cash and divvied up the cash.

Anyway, even Lars Kimbrell's mother was involved in this. She had a boarding house. They would kind of woo people in to stay with them, and they'd probably never walk back out the door. There's an account told of Ma Kimbrell, they called her, of even throwing an infant into the air and grabbing a butcher knife and letting the infant land on the butcher knife.

261. Robbery and Murder of a Traveler

Noted Kentucky folklorist Lynwood Montell collected this legendary account for his study of murder and justice in one region of the American South. He provides pseudonyms for all his informants but gives "Ish Christie's daughter" as the source for this text. These events took place "sometime after the Civil War" in the country along the Kentucky–Tennessee border, where the "lingering effects" of the war were one cause of "the violent character that came to be a hallmark" of the area. Here the aftermath of the murder has supernatural implications in that groaning sounds suggest the victim may haunt the place where the body was disposed of. Motifs E275, E402.1.1.2, E547.1, S110; cf E234.3.

[Bart Billings] was a pretty rough customer, according to what I heard his wife tell my mother one time. She said at one time they was a woman that come to their house to stay all night. She was going through to Washington and was walking. Bart said, "I know a nearer way that we can go through here. I can take you out up toward the top of the mountain and cut off a lot of ground."

Said next morning her and Bart started out. His wife told my mother that that woman was never seen tell or heard of any more. They was a big hole up on the head of Buffalo Hollow. She said that that woman was killed and put in that hole. . . . Said she had money.

And Garland [Boyer] and Gary Boyer used to keep hogs back on the mountain. The mountain was covered in mast, all kinds of acorns and everything. Well, they'd buy up a bunch of hogs in the fall of the year and take them back there on the mountain and turn loose, you know. And they would camp around out there and take care of them and see after them.

And these Talbots—Annis Talbot and Cleve Talbot—watched after these hogs when they wasn't around. Garland said they was camping one night not too far from where this hole was and he said there was some of the most pitiful groaning and hollering and taking on that he ever heard in his life in that hole. He said that they never did camp there any more. That was years and years after the woman had disappeared.

262. Al Capone's Hideout Near Edwardsport

Al Capone (1899–1947) controlled bootleg liquor distribution and other illegal vice operations in Chicago during the era of Prohibition in the 1920s; he became the most famous of American gangsters in his day through wide media exposure. He was known for his ruthlessness, and his celebrity continued in films and television shows long after his death. This legend about one of his hideouts was collected in Lyons, Indiana, December 1970, from a store manager, a fifty-seven-year-old man.

Al Capone had a hideaway in the river bottoms in the southern part of the state west of a little town on Highway 67 called Edwardsport. This hideaway was built as a double corncrib out in the commons where it wasn't likely anyone would happen around. The corn would be in the cribs on each side, but in the middle of the crib or the driveway was two rooms. One was for the automobile, and the other was for Al's comfort while dodging the police. It has been said that Al's places of hiding were very plush and elaborate and had all the facilities that there could be this far out in the country. People nearby knew what the corncrib was really for, and out of their own good judgment for their safety would not relay the information to the police. This is supposed to be one of Capone's hideaways that never was bothered.

263. Dillinger's Long Penis in the Smithsonian

John Dillinger (1903–1934) captured the imagination of the American public in the 1930s as he and a gang robbed banks and police arsenals in the Midwest. This legend about his anatomy was recorded from a male salesclerk, twenty-three, Terre Haute, Indiana. Motif F547.3.1.

At work we started talking about some of the greatest lovers of all time, and Phil happened to mention the fact that John Dillinger was not a lover even though he had a 23-inch penis, soft. He said they called him Wailing Willy. So I asked him why he wasn't a great lover with a penis that big. He said he didn't have enough blood to support an erection. He said every time it got hard he passed out from lack of blood to the brain. I asked him if this was true, and he said that it was and that John

Dillinger's penis is in a glass case located in the Smithsonian Institution. I asked him if he had seen it, and he said no, but his wife and Mike, a friend of theirs, saw it when they were in high school. I asked him how he found out about it, and one person offered it as part of the information when they were playing Jeopardy, and another supported it as being true.

264. Belle Gunness

Belle Gunness (1859–1908) moved to a farmhouse near LaPorte, Indiana, in 1901; when her house burned in 1908 and various bodies were discovered on her property, it was realized that she had been luring men to her farm through matrimonial advertisements and then murdering them for their money. Although she presumably perished in the 1908 fire, many believed that she escaped and lived elsewhere. Gunness has been written about extensively, and the *Guinness Book of World Records* listed Gunness as the "modern murderess" with the greatest number of victims ascribed to her. This account was collected in LaPorte, 1970, from a male, middle-aged informant. Gunness is the subject of a study by folklorist Janet L. Langlois, *Belle Gunness, the Lady Bluebeard* (Bloomington: Indiana University Press, 1985). Motifs K640, S110.

There is a farm in LaPorte on McClung Road where a woman named Belle Gunness lived. It was about 50 years ago because I can remember my folks telling about her. She was a very large woman—big and strong and not nice looking at all. She would advertise in out-of-state newspapers for male companions. She said she was lonely. Since she owned this 80-acre farm, one of the stipulations in the ad was that the man have some money. They would come; she would take their money and kill them. When she was found out and they started digging on the farm they found seventeen bodies. They were all cut up and put in gunnysacks. Belle had a daughter that graduated from high school in LaPorte and was supposedly sent off to college. But no one ever saw her after that. They think that one of the bodies that they dug up was her daughter.

The way she was found out was a brother of one of the victims was suspicious because he never heard from his brother after he left for Indiana. So he came to LaPorte to find him. The house on the farm burned down, and the body of a woman was found in the ashes. But a local dentist said it wasn't Belle. The bridgework of the body they found was not that of Belle Gunness. It is thought that she killed someone and planted the body in the house and set fire to it. It was believed but never proven that a local attorney and possibly even the sheriff helped her escape for money.

The neighbors said that she was a very good-hearted person and did a lot for other people. It was the neighbor lady who felt later that she had done something to the daughter. I don't think she ever married any of the men.

265. Drinks on the House

In researching the folklore of American coal mining, George Korson collected this legend. The Molly Maguires ("the Mollies") were a group of Irish immigrant coal miners in Pennsylvania in the 1860s and 1870s who fought for better working conditions in the mines and who often have been considered early partisans of the American labor movement. Several Mollies were executed for murders committed in the violence that attended their activities, and at the time, many people considered them criminals. Certainly here they appear unsavory at best.

Anthony McAndrew and his wife were returning from Ashland to the Rapp (Rappahannock, a small mining patch near Girardsville), a distance of approximately five miles. McAndrew was carrying a hundred of flour on his back. At a saloon on the road, McAndrew stopped to have a drink, and leaving Mrs. McAndrew outside to watch the flour, entered the place. It was filled with Mollies, the place being a meeting place of the secret order. When McAndrew ordered the drink, the saloonkeeper gave everyone in the place a drink at the same time, and when McAndrew attempted to pay for his own drink, was told the drink just served all the others had been charged to him, McAndrew. When [he] asked what the cost was, he was informed it totaled $20. McAndrew knew there was no use of his making a protest against this highhanded business, as he had been very outspoken against the Mollies at a previous time and knew that had he protested or refused to pay that he would have suffered bodily injury or possibly worse.

266. Frankie Silver

Frankie Silver, who was hanged in 1833 in North Carolina for the murder of her husband, is best known in folklore for a widely collected murder ballad about her crime, "Frankie Silvers" (the name has been rendered both Silver and Silvers). The account here was told by Bobby McMillon. McMillon is related to Silver by descent and marriage and became interested in her story and spent years looking into it. His recounting of it here is a combination of various traditions of historical legendry and his own research. The "Frankie and Johnny" song referred to is a different ballad also known as "Frankie and Albert," known primarily in African American tradition but also from popular sources. Motifs D1817.0.3, K521.4.1.1, S110, S118.

Well, my great-great-grandfather was a first cousin to Charlie Silvers that got his head cut off. Charlie's wife, Frankie, cut his head off, cut his body up, and burned it all night. Hid part of his remains in a log—his lights, the guts, the parts that won't burn, under a rock. He was buried in a little family cemetery up on the ridge above where she killed him, what was left of him, what they could find. And she was the first woman ever hanged in North Carolina, or legally anyway. My mother was raised just about a half a mile from where that happened. Oh Lordy, I've heard that all my life. Well, I tell you, it's even been put in books.

I tell it to you like my uncle Latt told me because he told it different than anybody else. He said it wasn't Frankie that started it, it was her daddy. I don't know what they had against Charlie, but he was a trapper. This was way back before the Civil War, a long time ago. It was nearly Christmas and Charlie had been out cutting wood all that day to burn all during Christmas. There was a big snow on the ground. They lived in a little shantylike cabin that just had two rooms, a kitchen-livingroom where the fireplace was, and a back bedroom. And they had a daughter—she couldn't have been more than a year old; she was still crawling.

So anyway, my great-great-uncle Latt told me that her daddy was down to supper that night and Charlie had got through cutting that tree down. He had piled up the wood and come in and eaten supper. And they said that when Charlie got in, he said, "I'm beat, I think I'll lay down." And Frankie said, "Well, I fixed a pallet for you by the fireplace. I thought you might want to take a nap before you got ready to go to bed." [Laughs] I don't know why he wanted to take a nap before he got ready to go to bed to sleep again. But anyway, he got the baby and laid down there in front of the fireplace and went to sleep. And when he got to sleep, my great-uncle said that her daddy said, "Now's your chance, Frankie."

And they said she went and laid the baby in the back room. Then she took the ax that Charlie had brought in and come back in there. Charlie was laying on his back, and they said everytime she'd come back to take a swing at him, he would smile at her in his sleep. And she swung about three times and her arm about give out. "Well," she said, "I just can't do it. I can't kill him like this." And her pap said, "If you don't kill him, I'll kill you and him both." So I reckon she figured she better go ahead. And they said that finally she come down and give one hit in the head. They claim that he jumped up and screamed, "God bless the child." And she run back there in the bedroom and jumped under the covers and hid. She was so scared. Well, according to my uncle Latt, when she went in there her daddy took the ax and he come back and cut Charlie's head square off. They said he hit him so hard that his head bounced against the rafters of the cabin.

And they said about that time the baby got up and was crawling, and they said it crawled in its own dad's blood. And they said it got over there to the table where it tried to stand itself up with its hands, and it left blood prints on the table. They said you couldn't wash them off or nothing. You couldn't get them off.

So Uncle Latt said Frankie's daddy cut him up and done all that dirty work hisself. And he used all that wood Charlie had cut up to last through Christmas and burned his body all night long. And they said he took Charlie's head and put it under a stump, an old hollow stump, and that he put on his boots to carry the rest of him and put it under a rock. I've seen that rock a hundred times. And then he went down to the river, the Toe River that runs by the foot of that holler, about half a mile down the road there. And he walked in the snow down there and then backtracked up. And of course it was put out that Frankie claimed that Charlie had went across the river for his Christmas liquor and hadn't come back.

It got to be two or three days, and everybody was wondering what had happened to him. They said this old man, I forget his name—I think they called him Dickie Collins—lived over cross the mountain somewhere and had been a' noticing Charlie's dog. It had always been with Charlie, and he said the dog would go up to the house and holler and just bark and go on. And Dickie just got suspicious, so one day when Frankie was out he went down there to the house and got to looking around. And he found some bloody chips and things around the fireplace, and he lifted up the floor boards and found blood down under there. So word got out that he had been killed. I mean that was evidence enough to know.

And they always told something about how his daddy had went over to Tennessee where they had this New Guinea slave that had what they called a conjure ball, or something. You'd ask it a question and it would swing. And however it was that they was asking it, they said it would swing right toward the house. When they come back they arrested Frankie. I reckon they got her to confess to killing him.

At that time the county seat was in Morganton, North Carolina, almost fifty miles away on the east side of the Blue Ridge Mountains. You had to go plum over there to the courthouse. They took her over there where they had her trial and they found her guilty and sentenced her to be hung.

I don't know if she bribed the jailer or who it was, but anyway, her family slipped her out and was trying to get back over the mountains. They had her hair cut off short like a man's and she was wearing a big old hat and walking alongside a haywagon. Her uncle was up in the haywagon driving. The sheriff comes up and says, "Where are you going, Frankie?" And she turned around and tried to put on a man's voice and said, "Thank you, sir, but my name is Tom." And they said her uncle turned around and said, "Yes sir *her* name is Tom." And so they knew right then who it was and took her back in to jail.

Before they hung her she was supposed to have sung this song, an old ballad that they sing back up there now. They just call it "Frankie Silvers' Ballad." I don't know whether she did sing it or not. They claim up there that that's how the Frankie and Johnny story got started. Course the Frankie and Johnny song ain't nothing like the song that she sung. But I reckon it just rolled over.

According to the best I ever heard, when they were taking her body back across the mountains to bury her—you know, they didn't have no embalming in them days—that she just got to stinking so bad that finally they had to bury her on the way, somewhere close to where Lake James is now. And they got her husband Charlie's remains and buried him in the graveyard up on the hill with the Silvers family.

People never could figure out why she done it, unless it was jealousy. In the song there's a rhyme that says "the jealous thought that first gave strife." They don't know why she was jealous. One of [Charlie's] brothers who lived to be way up in his nineties told years and years later that there wasn't never nothing bad come out on him. And in communities like that nothing happened that wasn't found out and told, you know. My grandmammy's uncle was the only one that I ever heard say that her daddy was there eating supper with them that evening, and that he done it. He's way up in his eighties, or close to eighty anyway now, and it's not been a year ago since he told me that.

But they did always say that before she hung she was about to tell something and her mother or her daddy either one hollered out, "Die with it in you, Frankie." They say she just didn't say anything.

Frankie's daughter, the little baby, I think her mother kept it for a while, but most of them moved off. But her girl married somebody from Madison County, I think. And then her daughter, Frankie's granddaughter, married my grandmother's uncle. Anyway that's about all I know about it.

Horrors

Many legends evoke negative emotions and certainly some of those in other sections may fill us with a sense of horror. But some seem to especially hinge on the frisson of the horrible: cannibalism ("The Cannibal Couple"), devoured babies ("The Faithful Dog"), reptiles that kill pregnant women ("The *Chirrionera*").

267. The Cannibal Couple

This story was collected in 1969 by Claudia Wells from Suzie Petty of Atlanta. Motif G20.

When I was a little girl, my mother used to tell us stories. She told me one time about her grandmother, her mother, and her great-grandmother having to travel for miles and miles and miles from one "country" to the other, because they were trying to get to Atlanter. My grandfather and my mother's grandfather had died, and they just traveled and traveled.

So, one night they stopped at this farmhouse, and they asked could they work, you know, so that they could get food and travel on the next day. And said they stayed there that night, and got food fer to go on to the next li'l farm.

Said when they went to the next farm it took 'em days and days to get there, because houses wasn't close together. She said she got to the farmhouse an' she knocked on the door, an' said a man came to the door, and she asked could they spend the night. And they told her to come on in. Well, she went on in, and Great-great-grandmother and Great-grandmother all went on in. Said she set down; the old lady was cookin' supper, said she had collards. And said Grandmother had a little apron on; and said she was eatin' away on them collards, and said she found a forefinger in the collards! Said she didn't say nothing to nobody; said she just raked it out in her lap, and wrapped it up in a little handkerchief she had, and stuck it in her apron pocket.

So the man and woman got ready to go to bed, and said when they went to bed there were two teenage boys there who stayed to wash the dishes. The two teenage boys told 'em, "Don't y'all stay here tonight"; say, "they'll kill y'all like they did our mother and daddy, and salt ye down like hogs!"

So the grandmother and them got so scared; they told the two boys, said, "Well, we'll hitch up and we'll leave, and we'll take you with us." And they was afraid, you know, that they make enough noise to get the people up; so they slipped out and went on to get the mule and wagon, and they drove on off.

They rode for days and days and got to the next farmhouse, but the next farmhouse was a sheriff—he lived there. And on that plantation it was four or five houses, you know, that the farmers lived on. So, Grandma she walked up and knocked on the door, and the man came to the door. She was kindly scared then, but when he told her that he was a sheriff she wadn't scared anymore. So she said that Great-grandmother an' all of 'em got out of the wagon, and they told the man what had happened. And the little boys told about them killing their mother and their daddy, and they had 'em down in the basement, salted down; just had a lot of people down there, salted down like hogs. And said that he had a horn—they called it bugles back then—and he blowed it, and when he blowed that bugle the men and women knew some'in' was wrong and they all came, and they got on mules. They went and took Grandma and the two boys and all of 'em back to the farm where they had come from, and the old lady and the old man was there. When they went to searchin', they found all these bodies where they had salted 'em down and put 'em in the basement. They found even little babies; they had killed little babies and salted them down. They said that was the "young meat," and when they killed old people they called it "old meat," see.

And she said that when they found all that, this woman and man tried to get away, but they couldn't get away because it was so many there. And they caught 'em and they tied 'em up, and then they tarred and feathered 'em, and took 'em to a stake, and burnt 'em, just set fire to 'em. Back then, they did that.

And that was it. They come to Atlanter, where they had started.

268. The Faithful Dog

From the Federal Writers' Project folklore collecting activities in Virginia, this was recorded from C. Wentz Carter by James Taylor Adams, Wise County, September 24, 1940. AT 178, related as fact.

There was a man lived away back in the woods one time. They just had one little baby. They had a big dog an' the dog wouldn't let any thing come near the baby. His wife worked out an' they would leave the baby in a box in the house an' the dog would lay right by it and mind it.

One day they was apiece from the house an' the baby had been left at the house with the dog. That day when they come in, the dog met 'em in the door and he was just a-growlin' and actin' like he was goin' to jump on 'em. He was just as bloody as he could be, an' he was a-lickin' his lips.

They was scared nearly to death. And the man, he kicked the dog out of his way an' run in an' there lay the baby, killed an' nearly eat up. He jus' reached up over the door an' picked up his gun an' shot the dog's brains out. They looked under the bed and there laid the biggest panther they'd ever seed in their life, tore all into pieces. The panther had killed the baby an' the dog had killed it.

They made two coffins, one for the baby an' one for the dog.

An' they buried him by the baby and put up a tombstone for him, just like they did for the baby.

269. Death from Fright

Behind this legend is the widespread belief that people can die of fright. The story was collected May 1968 from a twenty-one-year-old woman employed as a secretary, Shelburne, Indiana. Motifs F1041.7, N384.

Two men were driving along a country road near here when they had car trouble. As they were going for help a terrible storm blew up, so they decided to take cover in a nearby church. The sky grew darker and darker until it looked more like night than day. The men were just sitting inside the church when one of them got up and walked over to the window. Lightning flashed, but the man could see nothing out the window because the rain was so heavy. The sky grew even darker than before. The man was looking out into the darkness. Suddenly lightning flashed, and there at the window was a horrible face grinning terribly in at the man. As it turned out, the "face" belonged to an escaped inmate of the insane asylum. But the man that had been looking out the window died of fright; his hair had turned completely white.

270. The Yankee Soldiers and the Baby

This legend that recounts Civil War–period events was collected in Fall 1978 by David Brogdon from Retha Payne of Atlanta, who grew up in Piedmont, Alabama. Motif S100.

My great-grandfather told my grandmother something that happened back during the Civil War. A lady he knew that lived down the road from them was in her cabin with her baby, and some Yankee soldiers came riding up. She started to hide [in the loft], and she didn't have time to hide the baby. She figured that the soldiers wouldn't bother the baby, so she left it down there.

And she could hear them; and she heard the baby laughing, and after a little while she heard it crying, and then it didn't make any sounds at all and she could hear it kicking.

So when the soldiers left she came out of her hiding place. And they had been throwing the baby up, and that was causing it to laugh; and one of them had taken a bayonet and stuck it through the baby and pinned it to the ceiling, and the baby was kicking the ceiling as it was dying. And that's what she heard, the kicking.

271. The *Chirrionera*

Folklorist Rosan A. Jordan recorded this legendary account in the course of her fieldwork among Mexican Americans in Texas. The term *chirrionera* may refer to the axolotl, the larval stage of a salamander. Jordan recorded a number of stories from Mexican American women about serpents that sexually aggress against women. Cf motif G477.

And there's this type of snake. It has many different names, and the people in West Texas call them *chirrioneras*. And this is a real funny snake—grows real long and likes women. And they whistle, you know, like regular men—wolf whistle, you know. They whistle to women as they go by.

And there's this story that was told also, about this lady that was pregnant. And this was a bunch of families that lived out in the country. These families lived out in the country, and the men would work out in the fields. And the ladies would stay at home and take care of the children and, oh, at a certain hour they would go and take their husbands their lunch. So all the women would walk together, and as they went by a certain tree out in the woods, there was one of these snakes, you know, *chirrioneras*. And it would whistle at the women as they went by. And so they didn't like that, and they would tell their husbands. They said, "Well, stay together and he won't bother you."

So this lady that was pregnant, she was getting pretty fat and she couldn't walk as fast as the other ladies, and so every day she would get a little further behind. So toward the end before she had her baby, she was walking and all the ladies walked faster, so they left her behind because she walked too slowly. And they got over there where the men were, and her husband said, "Where's my wife?" And they said, "Well, she was walking too slow and so we just left her behind because we were going to be late"—you know, if they didn't hurry. So he said, "Where did you leave her?" And they said, "Well, just as we went through the woods. As we were going through the woods she got behind, so we just came on without her."

So he went out to the woods to look for his wife, and when he got to that tree he could see that she was laying down under that tree that they complained that the snake would whistle at. And so when he got there . . . the baby had been born, and the snake had choked the baby, was wrapped around the baby. And she was dead.

Place Names and Other Origins

To know how something began is to understand something essential about it. How a ghost came to exist or how a buried treasure happened to be hidden is explained by legends included in other sections, for example, and questions about how things began continue to intrigue us. Legends may explain origins of various kinds. Countless localities bear names that seem puzzling or obscure and often there are legends (which may or may not enjoy historical accuracy) to explain those place names. "How Mother Leather Coat Mountain Was Named" and "How the Rock Got Its Name" are but two examples. Other legends tell of the origins of phenomena like mysterious lights ("Prairie Lights") or well-known flora ("The Legend of the Dogwood Tree"). It's doubtful that legends like the one about dogwood are ever taken seriously as being even possibly true, but some have been very popular; the dogwood legend, like a few others, even appears on widely available postcards.

272. How Mother Leather Coat Mountain Was Named

This place-name legend, featuring none other than George Washington, was written down by Susan R. Morton "from her own recollection," Prince William County, Virginia, February 22, 1941. Motif A1617.

One of the peaks in the Bull Run Mountains to the west of Thoroughfare Gap is called "Mother Leather Coat." (This is proved by old records, indentures, etc.) Tradition says that it was given this name by George Washington who as a very young man surveyed there for his friend, Fairfax.

There was an old woman who lived on the southerly side of the mountain and who, both winter, and summer, wore [a] leather apron and jacket. She offered food and lodging for any traveler who happened by, and it was at her cabin that youthful Washington sought hospitality during his sojourn in that section. She had a reputation for being a very fine cook, and in appreciation of her kindly ministrations to him and his party, he named that peak in her honor. Until a few years ago there were a few rotting logs of her cabin that could be seen among the thick undergrowth.

273. How the Rock Got Its Name

James Few, an African American student, wrote out this account in Fall 1965; his family came from Lamar County, Georgia. Motif A1617.

My paternal family lived in a community that was rich in historical sites. One of the most interesting is The Rock, Georgia. This village received its name from a very large rock found in the middle of the area. My great-grandfather and his friends told a very interesting story about this particular rock.

It is said that the slaves used this rock as a hiding place for a book that was shared secretly by them. They also hid notes that they had written to each other. This story states that the slave masters did not allow the slaves or their children to learn to read and write, but many of them did learn. They had a book that was passed from one to another. When one person had completed use of the book, it was hidden by the rock for another slave. The plan was discovered when the slaves began to say to each other, "Look by the r-o-c-k and find the b-o-o-k." According to stories told by former slaves, this is how the village apparently got its name.

274. The Legend of the Dogwood Tree

Emory L. Hamilton, Wise County, Virginia, recollected this legend about the dogwood from his own memory and wrote it down December 10, 1938, in connection with Federal Writers' Project folklore research. Motifs A2711.2, A2751.3.2.

The legend about the dogwood tree is quite widely known in the Cumberlands, as elsewhere in the state of Virginia. Since the dogwood is our state flower and we have begun to have Dogwood Festivals around us, the legend is perhaps just now in the cradle of its infancy and is due much more popularity in the future. Anyone who has ever studied the dogwood flower can readily see the symbols in the flower that are mentioned in this legend. Whether the legend be true or false, one is lead [led] to believe that it is pretty near the truth. This legend runs that during and before the time of Christ, the dogwood tree grew to the height and dimensions of the oak, maple, and other larger forest trees. The wood was so firm and strong that it was the chosen tree to make the cross of crucifixion of the Savior. The trees were greatly distressed at having been chosen for such a cruel purpose, and Jesus, sensing their regret for his great suffering, gave them this promise:

"Never again shall the dogwood grow large enough for a cross. Henceforth it shall be slender, bent, and twisted; and its blooms shall be in the form a cross, two long and two short petals, and in the center of the outer edge of each petal there shall be nailprints, brown with rust and stained by blood. And in the center of the flower will be a crown of thorns, so that all those who see it shall know that it was on a dogwood tree that I was crucified. It shall not be mutilated or destroyed, but protected and cherished as a reminder of my agony and death upon the cross."

275. The Jack o' Lantern

The area of central Pennsylvania from which this legend comes was settled successively by Swedish, Dutch, German, and English people. Motif A2817; cf A2817.1.

There was a man named Jack-o'-Lanthorn, who was noted for his wickedness. It was agreed that he should do whatever he wished in this world, and at his death he was to go to the Devil. When he died he first went to the portals of Heaven and asked for admission, but was refused. He then went to Hell, but there he was told that he was so very bad that he would make the evil ones there unmanageable. So he was turned away, and sent to wander the bogs and marshes, and was given this mysterious light to guide him in his wanderings.

276. Prairie Lights (La Luz del Llano)

Collected from Mexican Americans on the vast King Ranch in south Texas, this legend accounts for a natural phenomenon, a mysterious light that appears on the local prairies. Cf motif A2817.2.

La luz del llano (the prairie light) is a mysterious red light which appears at night on the prairies, and sometimes in the hills. I myself have seen this *luz* several times. It can be seen only at a distance. When you ride towards it, you will not be able to see it after you get within a hundred yards of it.

. . . .

It is a good thing for a fellow to know just how the prairie lights came into existence. José Reyna, a boy who used to be *remudero* [horse wrangler] here, says that there was once an old woman who had twin daughters. This old woman loved her daughters so much that she would do anything for their happiness. They were on the verge of starvation, and the old woman was willing to do anything to save them. One day she met an old wizard. The wizard asked her if she was in trouble. She said, "Yes, my twin daughters are starving. I am trying to get food to save them."

"Very well," said the wizard, "I will provide food for them if you will promise me that when they are sixteen years of age, you will give them to me."

The old woman did not want to make such a promise, but it seemed to be the only way to keep her daughters alive, and as the daughters were only twelve years old at the time and sixteen was still a long way off, she made the agreement with the wizard.

So the wizard provided food for them for those four years; then he came and took them away, on their sixteenth birthday. He told the old woman not to hunt for them, for he would burn her if she did. The old woman could not stand the loss. When her daughters were gone, she could not keep from seeking them. She began searching for them all over the prairies and hills and valleys. The wizard was displeased and caught her, saying, "I told you what I would do if you searched for your children." Thereupon he kindled a great fire, tied the old woman's hands and feet, and threw her into the flame, burning her alive.

The blazes of the fire which burnt her went up in a bundle and remained in mid-air. It was the spirit of the old woman which held them together. The bundle of fire moved over the prairie, still searching for the lost children. It moved and moved, over hills, and over valleys, and through the thickets, and still it moves, seeking the lost daughters. And now people see it and call it *la luz del llano*.

277. Origin of Packenham's Rum (The Corpse in the Cask)

This legend, which goes back to events of the War of 1812, was heard from Helen Weaver of Tallahassee in the 1950s and published by Florida folklorist J. Russell Reaver; she had the story from her father. Motifs A1427,3*, C624.1*, S160.6*.

We hear a lot about General Jackson in this part of Florida around Tallahassee. Jackson was our commander at the Battle of New Orleans. The English commander was Packenham. My great-grandfather had a cousin, Henry Hunter, who was a soldier in that battle, and it is likely that he fired the shot that killed General Packenham.

When my father was a boy of ten, old Henry was ninety and blind. He would sit for hours telling of fighting the Indians and hunting for bear and deer. As you know from your history books, General Jackson's men were made up of frontiersmen from Tennessee and Kentucky, men who were expert at shooting the long rifles. Henry Hunter was one of these men. His home was in west Tennessee.

While the battle was raging, the English general could be seen walking back and forth on the breastworks waving a sword and urging his men on. With his red coat, white ruffled shirt front, and white trousers, he made a splendid target. Now I quote old Henry: "My officer came to me and said, 'Hunter, can you see the General?' 'Of course,' I said. 'Do you think you could bring him down from there?' 'Well,' I said, 'I've killed many a deer on Half Pone (a small mountain in west Tennessee) as far away as he is!' 'Well, load your gun heavy and take careful aim, and see if you can get him.' I did load heavy and got a good bead on his chest. When I fired he fell. Of course, others were shooting, and I never could be sure, but I heard afterwards that there was a wound right where I held."

It was the general's express wish that should he be killed in battle his body should be sent to England for burial, for he did not want to lie dead in rebel soil. In those days sailors were superstitious about carrying a corpse on board, so the officer in charge smuggled the body on board the ship. As no embalming was done in those days, they drew out about two-thirds of the contents from a barrel of rum, removed the corpse's head [since the body was too long to fit in the barrel], placed the body of the general inside, and placed the head beside the body. After this odoriferous work was finished, the barrel was hidden deep in the hold of the ship sailing for England.

The passage was long and rough. The weather was stormy, the grog was not plentiful, and food was limited. The unhappy sailors did a lot of complaining.

Finally an old salt went prowling around down in the ship and found the barrel in which the general was hidden. He reported to his mates as to how the officers were holding out on the men and hiding a whole barrel of rum for their own use. Since the men were just as smart as any officer, they soon had a gimlet, bored a hole in the barrel, and drew out enough each day for a little nip all around—on the sly, of course.

The poor old general was almost dry when he was opened up for the funeral. When the sailors found out what had happened, they were sorry they had been so eager to doubt the motives of their officers.

Anyway, it is said that all around the Gulf Coast that particular kind of rum is called "Packenham."

Occupational Legends

Those who share a particular occupation may also share folklore particular to the group, including legends that comment on the group's activities, outlook, and concerns. Thus, "A. Philip Randolph's Blank Check" is a statement of occupational (as well as ethnic) pride in the integrity of a famous union official, while "Death in the Mines" expresses something of the fears that miners may share. Occupational dangers are spoken about also in "Buying More Wind," while "The Resident's Stamp" and "Sleeping on the Night Shift" take a more lighthearted perspective.

278. Death in the Mines

Jim Hodge related this story to folklorist Richard M. Dorson during Dorson's collecting trip to Michigan's Upper Peninsula in 1946 (see the headnotes to stories 234 and 240 for more information).

Dad told me how the first man was killed in the Negaunee mine, in 1888. He and a partner were working two hammers on a drill, while George was twisting the drill. Father heard something fall, although the stope had been trimmed of loose rock. He went one way and his partner went another to see what it was; George said, "I'll sit down here and wait for you." A rock came down and killed George right where he was sitting.

. . . . .

Captain Dick Edwards sealed a burning mine, when the men were within seeing distance. He saved the mine, but didn't figure about the men.

There was a similar disaster at the Hartford mine in May, 1911. The Captain ordered the water turned down the shaft, and the fumes and smoke suffocated the men. One miner on the surface offered to break the connection to the timber shaft so that the trapped men wouldn't be choked by the fumes when the firemen turned the hose down the main shaft. They wouldn't let him, although he knocked down the mine captain and the company clerk. Eleven men were lost. Sam Steinaway carried his son on his back half a mile, and saved him, but gave his own life. (Young boys went down to the mines then; I went down when I was only thirteen. Now you have to be twenty-one.)

279. Buying More Wind

Patrick Mullen, the folklorist who recorded this story, undertook fieldwork among fishermen along the Texas coast in 1967, 1971, and 1975; this legend was recorded from Doc Moots, a shrimp boat captain originally from Georgia (where the story has its setting). Motif F963; cf D1543.

This is a true story, and this was sailing-boat days, back there when that's all there was. And this fellow had his wife and two kids on the boat, the way it was told to me. Now that's just a story that was handed down, but it's supposed to be true. And we had a place that we called Hell's Gate; I don't know where it got its name, but that's the name of that. It's where the (pause) Big Ogeechee and the Little Ogeechee come down and went into the sound. It was a cut there, and they called it Hell's Gate; it was just a cut you could go through. And this fellow down in a sailboat, and he throwed two bits overboard. He said, Old Man, give me a quarter's worth of wind. And it breezed up a little bit, and he said, "Aw, give me fifty cent's worth." And he threw fifty cents overboard, and it breezed up a little more. And he said, "If we're getting this much—" he said, "give me a dollar's worth." And he threw a dollar overboard. And when he got to Hell's Gate, and he made the turn, the boat capsized, and he was the only one saved out of the bunch. He lost his wife and kids. Now that is supposed to be a true saying. It happened at Hell's Gate. But I mean that's an old, old story.

280. The Last Train Robbery

"The Last Train Robbery" was collected from an anonymous informant during fieldwork with Southern Railway employees.

I couldn't tell ya the exact date of the last robbery but it was when the steam engines were still around. The robbers got on the train at Pervis. They sneaked on the coal car and snuck up on the three men in the engine—the engineer, fireman, and brakeman. There were three robbers. They uncoupled the engine and express car from the rest of the train and told the engineer to drive to Okalhola Crossing just to the north of Pervis. Here they cleaned out the express car and got away with it all. None of the crew was hurt but they didn't catch the robbers right off. They caught 'em because one of the robbers promised his girl friend a dress made out of one hundred dollar bills if the robbery was successful. He got his girl friend the dress like he promised and one day soon after the robbery she wore it to a dance. Then they knew who the robbers were and brought 'em in. They let 'em go easy though 'cuz no one was hurt in the robbery.

281. A. Philip Randolph's Blank Check

A. Philip Randolph (1889–1979) was president of the Brotherhood of Sleeping Car Porters, the union that came to represent the African American men who worked aboard railroad sleeping cars. Randolph and his organization played important roles not only in labor history but in the struggle for rights for American blacks. This story about his incorruptibility is well known among union members. Motif J1110.

After the brotherhood had won the right to organize the porters, the Pullman Company found that they had been defeated. And to make themselves look good, they sent A. Philip Randolph a check, a signed check, and all he had to do was put the amount of money he wanted in the check, and on the bottom it said, "Not to exceed a million dollars." I said it'd be hard to find a man or woman, or any person as far as that's concerned, who wouldn't have accepted that check and drawn a reasonable amount of money off of it. But Randolph made a photostatic copy of that check and framed it and hung it on his wall and sent the original back to the Pullman Company and told them Negro principles were not for sale.

282. The Resident's Stamp

This was collected from a medical resident at Charity Hospital, New Orleans. Charity Hospital, virtually destroyed during the floods following Hurricane

Katrina and the levee failures in 2005, was a huge state-run operation that served vast numbers of emergency patients.

In the admit room at Charity when it gets crowded late at night, the resident in charge has a stamp which he uses to mark charts: "Not An Emergency, Return Between 7:00 a.m. and 7:00 p.m." Some residents, especially in a rush, get very cavalier in using this stamp. One night, a drunk came in with a seemingly trivial complaint. Since it was busy, the resident, who was probably out of patience—pardon my pun—stamped right on the drunk's forehead "Not An Emergency" and sent him away. The next morning the patient was found dead behind the hedges near the emergency ramp. When the resident left for home, there was a nurse's aide scrubbing the stamp mark off before the meat wagon came.

283. Sleeping on the Night Shift

This was written out for a folklore collector by an anonymous Louisiana police officer.

Several years ago it was common practice for members of the Shreveport Police Department, on the night shift, to take a nap. Some beats were not very busy and the officers that worked them had more time to sleep. Officer B. A. Warren was one of those officers that slept very soundly. In his briefcase he carried an alarm clock to make sure he did not oversleep and fail to return to the station on time. One of the busiest shopping centers in Shreveport was located in the middle of Warren's beat. One very quiet night, just before Christmas, Warren backed his patrol unit into a dark spot on the parking lot of this shopping center. He set his alarm clock and dozed off. Officers from another beat found him asleep in the car. They turned off his alarm clock and covered his patrol unit with Christmas trees. Officer Warren woke up, about his usual time, but due to the trees on the car, thought it was still night and went back to sleep. About ten o'clock that morning the lot was full of Christmas shoppers. Officer Warren heard the noise and became alarmed. He started the patrol unit and drove across the lot still covered with trees. Never again did Officer Warren sleep on a shopping center lot.

"Urban" Legends

Americans have become much aware of the stories called urban (or sometimes, contemporary) legends: tales about scary, uncanny, bizarre, or ironic events, usually said to have taken place recently and nearby, perhaps involving a "friend of a friend" (folklorists sometimes call them FOAF—for friend of a friend—tales). The *urban* name seems to stem not from the action of the stories taking place solely in cities but because these narratives reflect life in the modern, "urban" world (and, indeed they are a global phenomenon, not just an American one). Although certainly many people may doubt the veracity of these stories, they are indeed legends, "told for true," the events supposedly having actually taken place.

In urban legends, insects destroy us ("The Bouffant Hair-Do"), and snakes pop up in department store bins or amusement parks ("Snakes in the Fun House Tunnel"). Killers stalk the innocent ("The Hook," "The Roommate's Death," "The Boy Friend's Death"), and other threatening characters invade our personal spaces ("The Killer in the Back Seat," "The Choking Doberman"). In other urban legends, however, the problems have more of an ironic twist, as when a body disappears ("The Runaway Grandmother") or unbridled jealousy goes wrong ("The Concrete-Filled Cadillac"). Urban legends are a kind of discourse on the vagaries and dangers of contemporary life and perhaps in part serve as warnings about the frightening or problematic things that can (supposedly) happen to people today.

284. The Hook

Among the best known of urban legends, this version of "The Hook" was narrated by Diane Diggins, who told the story to her roommate, Gerri Bard, at Indiana University, Bloomington, May 20, 1967. Motif Z500.

I heard this story at a fraternity party. I heard this. This guy had this date with this really cool girl, and all he could think about all night was taking her out and parking and having a really good time, so he takes her out in the country, stops the car, turns the lights off, puts the radio on, nice music; he's really getting her in the mood, and all of the sudden there's this news flash comes on over the radio and says to the effect that a sex maniac has just escaped from the state insane asylum and the one distinguishing feature of this man is that he has a hook arm, and in the first place this girl is really, really upset, 'cause she's just sure this guy is going to come and try and get in their car, so the guy locks all the doors and says it'll all be okay, but she says he could take his arm and break through the window and everything and she just cries and cries and goes just really frantic and the guy finally consents to take her home, but he's really mad 'cause you know he really had his plans for this girl, so he revs up the car and he goes torquing out of there and they get to her house, and he's really, really mad and he's not even going to get out of the car and open the door for her, and she just gets out on her own side of the car and as she gets out she turns around and looks and there's a hook hanging on the door.

285. The Cadaver Arm

This Florida version of "The Cadaver Arm" was told by the Osborne sisters, Miami, 1950. Like story 269, it suggests belief in the dire consequences of being frightened. Motif N384.0.1.1.

There was a girl at some university which also had a medical school on the campus. She was known by all of the students for her practical jokes, and everyone soon became tired of them.

Once a bunch of students got together and decided to end her pranks once and for all. One of them was a medical student; so they went over to the laboratory and got a human arm. They took it up to her room and tied it to her light cord late one afternoon.

The next day they looked for her on campus to see how she took it. Since no one saw her that day or the next, they decided to go to her room.

Finding the door locked, they became alarmed and went to the housemother. They got her to bring the passkey, and when they went inside of the room they found the girl sitting in the middle of the floor chewing on the arm. She had literally been frightened out of her mind.

286. Snakes in the Fun House Tunnel

The setting for this legend from Maryland, Echo Park, is a national park that, unusually, includes an amusement park, northwest of Washington, D.C. Motif Z500.

The first time I heard about the snakes was on a trip to Glen Echo to go swimming. I was about twelve [this would make it about 1957] and some of my friends and I were going to Glen Echo. We walked by the old fun house and saw that it was abandoned—just a stone shell of a building. There was a stream that flowed through the building. This started a discussion as to why Glen Echo no longer had a fun house and somebody said—I forget who it was—the reason for the closing was that at one time a girl and her date were riding in one of the boats through the fun house and she was trailing her hand in the water. Shortly after the ride began, the girl was bitten on the wrist by a water moccasin. Since the boat was just starting its trip through the fun house there was no way to get any help or medical attention. The couple had to continue the ride through the dark fun house. By the time the ride was finished, the girl had died of the snake bite. The fun house was closed at that time and they found a leak from the Chesapeake and Ohio Canal into the stream that went into the fun house. The snakes came into the fun house to get into the warmer water.

287. The Roommate's Death

This story was collected by Sylvia Grider from Melissa Warner, February 21, 1973. Motifs S139.2, Z500.

The time is Christmas vacation, which is a very desolate time in the dormitory. And there are two girls who are roommates and they come back to the dorm early before anyone else is in the area. And they're sorta joking around, you know, about how funny it is to be the only people in this great building with all these empty rooms around them. And they're just sitting around talking and doing things and they had their radio on and they hear that a man, a murderer has escaped from a prison and that he is armed and dangerous and people in the area should be on the lookout for this person and they shouldn't go into any desolate areas or be out late at night or do anything that might open them to this man. And the girls hear this story and they think, "Oh, I doubt if anything's gonna happen; maybe we should just, you know, lock the door and stay inside and not worry about it too much."

So they were sitting inside and one of the girls got hungry. And she said, "I'm gonna go downstairs to the Coke machine and get a Coke and something to eat." And the other girl said, "Oh, I'm not too sure. Maybe we should just stay in here at least until morning; it's kinda late." The other girl said, "Oh, no, you're just being ridiculous; there's nothing that's going to happen."

So she went downstairs. Time went by. First it was five minutes and then ten minutes and then the other girl was getting a little bit worried because there was no reason why her roommate should be gone so long just to go downstairs, three flights. And she was waiting. Sat around, and after about forty-five minutes she heard a noise. And it was just this drag and then a "klunph" and a klunking noise like a chain being dragged up stairs, a similar noise to that. And she could not figure out what it was and she was absolutely petrified. She just waited and waited and she kept hearing this noise. She couldn't decide what to do. She was too scared to go outside and she didn't know who to call because there was no one in the area and there was no one she could . . . no other human beings around. And she decided she was going to turn on the radio and just make some noise and try to block out this sound. And she tried but she just could not stand it. And after she heard this klunking noise and then she didn't hear it for awhile. And it went away and she thought, "Oh, great, this is all over with."

And then she heard another noise. A sliding noise. And then scratching began on her door. And she just thought that this was too much. That if somebody was pulling a joke on her she didn't like it. She thought it was her roommate. After awhile . . . that it was somebody doing . . . she was trying to scare her a little bit. So she started asking her, saying, "C'mon, just cut it out." She heard nothing. The noise just went on. She kept getting more scared and more scared. And finally called the police. And they thought, you know, that she was probably just exaggerating and was a scared girl but they said, "O.K. we'll come and check it out for you." And, uh, after about fifteen minutes they arrived and she heard noises coming up the stairs and a lot of voices outside and somebody told her, "Everything's all right. We're gonna be in there in a few minutes. Just stay inside and we'll come in and get you, take you out of there."

And the girl was just thrilled to hear a human voice because she had been alone for all this time and she was so scared that she threw open the door. And when she opened the door she saw the body of her roommate lying on the floor and she had had her legs cut off and had dragged herself all the way up the stairs trying to get back to her roommate and she had been scratching on the door and had died while she was waiting outside.

288. The Bouffant Hair-Do

Puffy bouffant hair-dos were popular in the 1950s, and the legend probably dates from that time period, though it may indirectly trace back to medieval tales about human vanity. This particular version comes from Maryland. Motif Z500.

When I was fifteen or sixteen years old, bouffant hair styles were very much the rage. It was almost as if it were a contest to see which girl could rat her hair the highest and pour the most hair spray on it. One day I went to the beauty shop to have my hair done. My hairdresser told me this story, and she swore that it really happened to a friend of her niece's.

There was this girl who had ratted her hair so high, and put so much hair spray on it, that she never took it down and combed it out or washed it. One day a spider fell into her hair. When the baby black widow spiders hatched, they bit her scalp and she died. I heard this story all over northern and southern California. When I moved to Baltimore, I met people who had heard the same story. They said it happened to a girl who had been a dancer on the Buddy Dean Show, on Baltimore television. These people said that a bee had gotten into the girl's head and stung her and she died from the bee sting because the doctors couldn't get to her head in time, due to her hair.

289. The Fried Rat

"The Fried Rat" legend may suggest our doubts about the quality of fast food. Sometimes told more elaborately, this version (told by a nineteen-year-old female, April 1977) suggests how simple legend narration can be. Motif Z500.

There was a wife who didn't have anything ready for supper for her husband. So she quick got a basket of chicken and tried to make her dinner look fancy with the pre-prepared chicken. Thus, she fixed a candlelight dinner, etc. when her and her husband started eating the chicken, they thought it tasted funny. Soon to find out it was a fried rat.

290. The Choking Doberman

This Louisiana version of an urban legend certainly known elsewhere sets the story in Metairie, an affluent suburb of New Orleans. The fact that the intruder in the story is black may suggest that the story comments on racial tension as well as fear of crime. Motif Z500.

This is supposed to be a true story that happened in Metairie. She said that the woman had gotten a Doberman Pinscher, was frightened of living alone, and she left it in the apartment, and she went to work. This is the first day she had the dog, OK? And she came back from work. She went in, and she couldn't find the dog. So she called the dog and it didn't come. So, finally she looked all over the house, and she went into the bedroom and there was the dog, and it was choking. So she quick called the veterinarian, and he was just about to close. So he says, "Put the dog in the car and come down here right away, if it's choking." So she did. And so, the dog was still choking (hand around throat—cough, cough) and so he said, "I think you better leave it here overnight. You go on home before it gets any later. I'll go ahead and work on it." So, she went back on home, and when she entered, the phone was ringing when she got back to the apartment. And he said, "Leave your apartment immediately and call me back." And she said, "What are you talking about? Who is this?" And he said, "This is Dr. So-and-So, the veterinarian." And he said, (emphasis) "Get out of that apartment. Go to another telephone. Go to a neighbor or friend or something like that." She said, "You must be out of your mind!" So he said, "All right, if you won't leave any other way." He said, "Would you like to know what was choking that dog? (Emphasis) Two black fingers." And she panicked, and she dropped the phone and ran over to a neighbor and called him back, and said, "All right, I'm over at the neighbors. Did you say two black fingers?"

"Yes." he said, "Call the cops."

So she called the cops. They searched the house. In her closet was a black dude. He had passed out from loss of blood. He was jammed way back up in the closet, and he was missing two fingers. He had gotten into that apartment and he was waiting for her, and they caught him.

And she said she'd never, ever part with that dog.

291. The Boy Friend's Death

One of several urban legends that tie in with the practice of parking in "lovers' lanes," this story was recorded by Jackie Brigl from Terry Brigl, Bloomington, Indiana, January 18, 1968. Motif Z500.

Don Smith told me this story; actually a friend of his told him it, so you are getting it second-hand. There was this local Moses Lake couple who went out and parked one night. They were in the country on a road that leads to a dead-end right under a big weeping willow tree. It is about four or five miles from town, and there is no one around. The tree was the only one there, it was standing all alone. They were there until late in the morning, and a . . . when they decided to leave the car wouldn't start, they were out of gas. The young man decided that it would be best if he went back and a got some gas. He told her to lie down on the seat, and not to look up, and keep all the doors locked and the windows rolled up . . . an' everything . . . an' he left. And a . . . she was very scared most of the night, she was very scared, and she blew up everything out of proportion. She heard all sorts of strange things, like things on the roof . . . all sorts of sounds, but she didn't look up. Toward morning she saw the shadow of some sort of liquid on the window shield. But she still didn't look up. Just after, the sun had risen, she heard the sound of a siren, someone had seen the car parked out under the weeping willow tree, and reported it to the police, they had been looking for the two kids all that night. Her parents had called because they were worried about the pair. The police came up to the car, they told her to unlock the doors, come out and go with them. The police told her not to look back, but she did anyway. And there on the branch of the willow tree was her boy friend, his hand was dangling in the breeze scraping the top of the car with his finger nails. He was hanging upside down, but he didn't have a head, it was as if it had been tore off. The police looked around for feet prints, but they only saw the footprints of the boy. I heard it when I was back in Washington, probably around the first part of this last December. Don Smith heard it from this chick, who it supposedly happened to. I really believed that it happened. This girl is so afraid of boys now that she won't go out with anyone.

292. The Killer in the Back Seat

"The Killer in the Back Seat" was told by Erin Buckner, who heard it in Bloomington, Indiana, from Mary Lee Memmott of Ogden, Utah.

There was once a high school girl who lived in a suburb of Ogden, Utah, and on the opening night of the school play, in which she had a main part, her parents were fated suddenly with a mild illness, forcing her to drive to the school alone at night. This she did and the production was a success. When starting her journey home, she noticed that some man had parked directly behind her and had started his motor up about the same time she had started hers up. This didn't bother her because many people were leaving at this time.

On the highway, she glanced through the side view mirror (her rear view mirror was broken or something) and saw that same car. This time it did occur to her that perhaps she was being followed. However, she still had to turn off on a vacated country road, and she felt sure that surely he wouldn't be going in that direction because hardly anyone knew about this short-cut . . . and that if he did turn on it also . . . then she would be certain that she was being followed.

Her suspicions were strengthened as the trailing automobile crept up behind her and also turned off onto the road. She was just frantic and kept driving at a very high, increasingly dangerous speed . . . but then again so did he!

All of a sudden for no reason at all, she felt this blinding light hitting her in the face, and she realized that he had turned on his brights. She was tempted to believe that this was just a temporary thing . . . but after they had been off awhile . . . here they came back on again . . . as bright as ever. As the story goes, he kept turning his brights on and off at strangely unexplainable intervals . . . very rapidly . . . just quick enough to startle her for a moment, leaving her petrified.

Finally she reached her driveway and sure enough, he pulled in right after her, turned off his motor, but left his bright lights on. She dashed into her house, told her parents, who in turn telephoned the police.

When the police arrived the car was still in the driveway with the brights on. The cops went up to the car and tried to arrest the man, but he just resisted the arrest by saying, "I'm sorry, but I'm not the man you want." Then he pointed to the car the girl was driving in and said, "I believe the one you're looking for is up there."

And sure enough, in the back seat of the car the girl was driving a small man was crouched down. As the first man later explained, this tiny man would creep up on the girl driving the car and would attempt to strangle her, but at this time the first man, who had seen the tiny guy slip into the car at the schoolyard but who didn't have enough time to alert the girl, would blink on his brights and the strangler would dart back down into the back seat! Thus the tiny man was arrested and the girl, as well as all the kids going to Mary Lee's high school, learned to lock their car doors and to look into the back seat of their cars before entering.

293. The Crazy Baglady Who Ate Her Hair

The first version of this urban legend, probably not as well known as some, was recorded in Lawrence, Kansas, November 16, 1991; the second in Normal, Illinois, July 19, 1991. Both Lawrence and Normal are college towns, and versions of the story, including one of these, do portray the protagonist as a failed professor.

1. This crazy old broad goes walking around the streets carrying a bag. And she ain't got no hair, you know—I mean, she ain't bald or anything, but her hair's real short, like it's been chopped off. That's 'cause the woman was starving, and the only way she could stay alive was by eating it. It's got lots of protein in it. Her name's supposed to be Deborah or Diane or something like that with a D. And I heard she talks a lot, too, like she's possessed or something.

2. She was a biology professor out in Colorado somewhere, and she didn't get tenure. That's when she went nuts and cut all her hair off. Then she decided she had to leave town, and she's been a baglady ever since, just roaming from place to place. And the reason her hair never grows back is because she keeps cutting it off and

eating it. A friend of mind actually saw her get thrown out of a restaurant downtown, where she tried to steal some food. And supposably [sic] she's always talking to herself, too. She must really be whack.

294. The Runaway Grandmother

Folklorists have called this legend "The Runaway Grandmother," perhaps something of a misnomer, as no one runs away in the story; rather, a body is stolen and disappears. This version was told by Carolyn Hinkle, Indianapolis, 1966.

I first heard this story in Columbus, Indiana, in the fall of 1963. It was supposed to have happened to the brother of a local doctor and his family—the "grandmother" being his mother-in-law. The family, consisting of the brother and his wife, their children, and, of course, the grandmother, took a vacation to the Upper Peninsula of Michigan. Loaded down with a camping gear and all the necessary baggage, the family made its way to an isolated area and proceeded to set up a campsite. On the second night, maybe from unfamiliar physical activity, the grandmother had a heart attack and died.

Miles away from civilization, the grief stricken family had to get the body to an undertaker. It was inconceivable that the body ride in the back of the station wagon with the children, who had been very close to their grandmother, so, placed in a sleeping bag, it was strapped to the luggage carrier on top.

After riding many hours, they finally came to a town large enough to have a mortuary. No member of the nearly hysterical family wanted to remain with the car and they all went in, leaving the car and corpse unattended. When they finally emerged, they found to their horror that the car and all its contents had been stolen. The stripped car was found a few weeks later without the corpse and at the time I heard the story it was still missing.

295. The Concrete-Filled Cadillac

One of the urban legends in which foolish actions lead to ironic turns of events, this particular version is from Florida. Motifs K2110.1, T75.2.2*, X757*.

A worker in a concrete factory drove home unexpectedly one morning to find a Cadillac parked outside his house. When he looked through the kitchen window, he saw his wife standing close to a strange man.

To get revenge for his wife's secret affair, he went back to the factory, loaded his concrete-mixer truck with concrete, and dumped it on the Cadillac.

Later that night, his wife explained with tears in her eyes that the man in the kitchen had been a car salesman, who had brought the Cadillac as a surprise birthday gift for him.

296. John F. Kennedy Is Still Alive in Dallas

Perhaps tied into older stories of the slain hero who will one day return, legends about how President John Kennedy was in fact still alive popped up in the later 1960s. This one was narrated by a twenty-year-old female office worker, February 1969, Bedford, Indiana. Motif A580.

Did you know that President Kennedy is still alive? That's what I said. President John F. Kennedy is still alive today! Oh, he's not really a human being anymore. In fact, he's really nothing more than a vegetable. You see, I have this friend who works with me in my office here in Bedford who has a cousin who lives in St. Louis who has a friend that works in the library in Dallas, Texas. Well, this girl who works in the library is a friend of a nurse and an orderly who work in the Parkland Hospital in Dallas—you know, the one where Kennedy was taken after he was shot.

Well, anyway, this nurse and this orderly had heard that Kennedy had not died in November 1963. What happened was that his brain was severely damaged, but the doctors were able to keep his body alive. In other words, the doctors were able to keep Kennedy alive, but only as a vegetable. He just exists. They had also heard that doctors there were working on research so that one day other brain cells might be transplanted into the damaged parts of Kennedy's brain.

They had also heard that Kennedy was being kept on the third floor of the hospital. Well, the orderly didn't believe a word of it. You know what I mean—it does sound rather fantastic. And besides, everyone had seen Kennedy buried over television. So this orderly decided to disprove this rumor by going up on the third floor of the hospital. When he got off the elevator, he was met by two plainclothesmen. One identified himself as a member of the Secret Service, and the other was from the Central Intelligence Agency—the CIA, you know. Well, they asked this orderly to see his pass. He replied that he didn't have a pass, but that he worked at the hospital. They then told him that no one could be on that floor without a special pass, and that if they ever caught him up there on the third floor again without one of these passes, he would be in serious trouble with the Federal Government of the United States. So the orderly quickly got back into the elevator and went down and told the nurse what had happened.

After this incident, the nurse and orderly were on their toes noticing who got in the elevator and went up to the third floor. Then one day the nurse saw a lady wearing a big hat and sunglasses enter the hospital and approach the elevator. There was something very familiar about this woman, but the nurse could not put her finger on it. The nurse continued to watch the woman as she approached the elevator, and as the woman took off her sunglasses to see which floor the elevator was on, the nurse recognized her—it was Jacqueline Kennedy. After Mrs. Kennedy got in the elevator, the nurse ran over to the elevator to see where she went. And, sure enough, the elevator stopped on the third floor and then came back down, without Mrs. Kennedy.

After this, the nurse and orderly saw Mrs. Kennedy come into the hospital and go up to the third floor many times. The last time she visited the hospital was in November 1969. And this time she was with a man—a man they recognized as Aristotle Onassis from his pictures which appeared in the papers after his summer marriage to Jacqueline. They stayed up on the third floor about an hour, and then they came back down and left.

Well, anyway, this story makes me doubt whether John F. Kennedy is really dead or not. You can see that this story comes from very reliable sources. My friend who works with me here in Bedford hasn't talked to her cousin in St. Louis who has a friend that works in the library in Dallas who is a friend of the nurse and orderly who work in the Parkland Hospital in Dallas for a couple of months. But I just wish she would because I'm just dying to know if Jacqueline or Onassis have made any more trips to the third floor of the Parkland Hospital. And some day when the doctors complete the transplants on Kennedy's brain and he's able to leave the hospital, this fantastic story will be made known to the general public. But you'll always remember that it was me who first told you that John F. Kennedy is not dead.

Story Credits

This page constitutes a continuation of the copyright page.

1. From Jeremiah Curtin, *Seneca Indian Myths* (New York: E. P. Dutton, 1923), pp. 70–75.

2. From Jeremiah Curtin, *Myths of the Modocs: Indian Legends of the Northwest* (Boston: Little, Brown, 1912), pp. 51–59.

3. From Jeremiah Curtin and J. N. B. Hewitt, "Seneca Fiction, Legends and Myths," *Thirty-second Annual Report of the Bureau of American Ethnology* (1910–11), pp. 84–86.

4. From George A. Dorsey, *Traditions of the Skidi Pawnee* (Boston: Houghton Mifflin for the American Folklore Society, Memoirs of the American Folklore Society 8, 1904), pp. 80–88.

5. From Elaine Jahner, "Stone Boy: Persistent Hero," in Brian Swann, ed., *Smoothing the Ground: Essays on Native American Oral Literature* (Berkeley: University of California Press, 1983), pp. 179–85. Used by permission.

6. From F. A. Golder, "Tales from Kodiak Island," *Journal of American Folklore* 16 (1903): 95–98.

7. From Barre Toelken, *The Anguish of Snails: Native American Folklore in the West* (Logan: Utah State University Press, 2003), pp. 134–35. Reprinted with permission of Utah State University Press.

8. From Archie Phinney, *Nez Perce Texts* (New York: Columbia University Press, 1934), pp. 282–85. Reprinted with permission of Columbia University Press.

9. From Frank Russell, "Myths of the Jicarilla Apaches," *Journal of American Folklore* 11 (1898): 265–66.

10. From Robert Lowie, "Myths and Traditions of the Crow Indians," *Anthropological Papers of the American Museum of Natural History* 25, part I [1918]: 115–17.

11. From Henry Hull St. Clair and Leo J. Frachtenburg, "Traditions of the Coos Indians of Oregon," *Journal of American Folklore* 22 (1909): 27–28.

12. From Jeremiah Curtin and J. N. B. Hewitt, "Seneca Fiction, Legends and Myths," *Thirty-second Annual Report of the Bureau of American Ethnology* (1910–11), pp. 460–62.

13. "The Siege of Courthouse Rock," from *American Indian Myths and Legends* by Richard Erdoes and Alfonso Ortiz, pp. 254–55. © 1984 by Richard Erdoes and Alfonso Ortiz. Used by permission of Pantheon Books, a division of Random House, Inc.

14. From *Swapping Stories: Folktales from Louisiana,* edited by Carl Lindahl, Maida Owens, and C. Renée Harvison (Jackson: University Press of Mississippi, 1997), pp. 93–98, where some of the original Koasati text is included. Reprinted with permission of University Press of Mississippi.

15. From Mary Kawena Pukui, with Laura C. S. Green, *Folktales of Hawai'i/ He Mau Ka'ao Hawai'i* (Honolulu: Bishop Museum Press, 1995), pp. 81–82; this original publication includes the text in Hawaiian. Used by permission of the Bishop Museum Press.

16. From W. D. Westervelt, *Hawaiian Legends of Volcanoes* (Boston: Ellis Press, 1916), pp. 31–32.

17. From Thos. G. Thrum, *Hawaiian Folk Tales* (Chicago: A.C. McClurg, 1917), pp. 39–42.

18. From Donald J. Waters, *Strange Ways and Sweet Dreams: Afro-American Folklore from the Hampton Institute* (Boston: G.K. Hall, 1983), pp. 194–96.

19. Reprinted by permission of the publisher from *Negro Folktales in Michigan,* collected and edited by Richard M. Dorson, p. 40, Cambridge, Mass.: Harvard University Press. © 1956 by the President and Fellows of Harvard College.

20. From Carl Lindahl, *American Folktales from the Collections of the Library of Congress* (Armonk, N.Y.: M.E. Sharpe, in association with the Library of Congress, Washington, D.C., 2004), I: 191–93. Reprinted with permission of Martha Suggs Spencer.

21. From Arthur L. Campa, "Spanish Traditional Tales in the Southwest," *Western Folklore* 6 (1947): 323–25. Reprinted with permission of the Western States Folklore Society.

22. From Isabel Gordon Carter, "Mountain White Folk-Lore: Tales from the Southern Blue Ridge," *Journal of American Folklore* 38 (1925): 341–43. Used by permission of the American Folklore Society, www.afsnet.org.

23. From Leonard Roberts, *South from Hell-fer-Sartin: Kentucky Mountain Folk Tales* (Lexington: University of Kentucky Press, 1955), pp. 21–22. Used by permission of the University Press of Kentucky.

24. From Vance Randolph, *Who Blowed Up the Church House? and Other Ozark Folk Tales* (New York: Columbia University Press, 1952), pp. 48–50. Reprinted with permission of Columbia University Press.

25. From Isabel Gordon Carter, "Mountain White Folk–Lore: Tales from the Southern Blue Ridge," *Journal of American Folklore* 38 (1925): 349. Used by permission of the American Folklore Society, www.afsnet.org.

26. From Leonard Roberts, *South from Hell-fer-Sartin: Kentucky Mountain Folk Tales* (Lexington: University of Kentucky Press, 1955), pp. 35–38. Used by permission of the University Press of Kentucky.

27. From Ruth Ann Musick, *Green Hills of Magic: West Virginia Folktales from Europe* (Lexington: University of Kentucky Press, 1970), pp. 248–50. Used by permission of Daniel and Patricia Musick.

28. From Ralph Steele Boggs, "Folktales Current in the 1820s," *Journal of American Folklore* 47 (1934): 319. Used with permission of the American Folklore Society, www.afsnet.org.

29. From Isabel Gordon Carter, "Mountain White Folk-Lore: Tales from the Southern Blue Ridge," *Journal of American Folklore* 38 (1925): 360–61. Used by permission of the American Folklore Society, www.afsnet.org.

30. From Richard M. Dorson, "Polish Wonder Tales of Joe Woods," *Western Folklore* 8 (1949): 47–50. Reprinted with permission of the Western States Folklore Society.

31. "Mutsmag" from *The Grandfather Tales: American English Folktales*, selected and edited by Richard Chase, pp. 40–50. © 1948; copyright renewed 1976 by Richard Chase. Reprinted by permission of Houghton Mifflin Company. All rights reserved.

32. From W. W. Newall, "Lady Featherflight: An English Folk-Tale," *Journal of American Folklore* 6 (1893): 54–60.

33. From Vance Randolph, *The Devil's Pretty Daughter and Other Ozark Folk Tales* (New York: Columbia University Press, 1955), pp. 63–65. Reprinted with permission of Columbia University Press.

34. From Arthur L. Campa, "Spanish Traditional Tales in the Southwest," *Western Folklore* 6 (1947): 326–28. Reprinted with permission of the Western States Folklore Society.

35. From "English Folk-Tales in America," *Journal of American Folklore* 2 (1889): 213–14.

36. From Alcée Fortier, *Louisiana Folk-Tales* (Boston: Houghton Mifflin for the American Folklore Society, Memoirs of the American Folklore Society 2, 1895), pp. 117–19.

37. From Marie Campbell, *Tales from the Cloud Walking Country* (Bloomington: Indiana University Press, 1971), pp. 241–42. Used by permission of Indiana University Press.

38. From Marie Campbell, *Tales from the Cloud Walking Country* (Bloomington: Indiana University Press, 1971), pp. 98–100. Used by permission of Indiana University Press.

39. From Calvin Claudel, "Three Spanish Folktales," *California Folklore Quarterly* 3 (1944): 21–22. Reprinted with permission of the Western States Folklore Society.

40. From George Reinecke, "A Louisiana Black Creole Version of 'The Land and Water Ship,'" *Louisiana Folklore Miscellany* 9 (1994): 22–25. Used by permission of the Louisiana Folklore Society.

41. From Vance Randolph, *Sticks in the Knapsack, and Other Ozark Folk Tales* (New York: Columbia University Press, 1958), pp. 108–109. Reprinted with permission of Columbia University Press.

42. From Bertha McKee Dobie, "Tales and Rhymes of a Texas Household," in *Texas and Southwestern Lore*, edited by J. Frank Dobie (Austin: Publications of the Texas Folklore Society 6, 1927), pp. 45–47. Used by permission of the Texas Folklore Society.

43. From Leonard Roberts, *Old Greasybeard: Tales from the Cumberland Gap* (Detroit: Folklore Associates, 1969), pp. 109–15. Used by permission.

44. From Isabel Gordon Carter, "Mountain White Folk-Lore: Tales from the Southern Blue Ridge," *Journal of American Folklore* 38 (1925): 355–57. Used with permission of the American Folklore Society, www.afsnet.org.

45. "Jack and the King's Girl" from *The Jack Tales: Folk Tales from the Southern Appalachians*, selected and edited by Richard Chase, pp. 83–88. © 1943; copyright renewed 1971 by Richard Chase. Reprinted by permission of Houghton Mifflin Company. All rights reserved.

46. From Charles C. Jones, Jr., *Negro Myths from the Georgia Coast* (Boston: Houghton Mifflin, 1888).

47. From Américo Paredes, *Folktales of Mexico* (Chicago: University of Chicago Press, 1970), pp. 127–33. © 1970 by The University of Chicago.

48. From Vance Randolph, *Who Blowed Up the Church House? And Other Ozark Folk Tales* (New York: Columbia University Press, 1952), pp. 6–7. Reprinted with permission of Columbia University Press.

49. From Arthur Huff Fauset, "Negro Folk Tales from the South," *Journal of American Folklore* 40 (1927): 259–60. Used with permission of the American Folklore Society, www.afsnet.org.

50. From Vance Randolph, *Who Blowed Up the Church House? And Other Ozark Folk Tales* (New York: Columbia University Press, 1952), pp. 143–44. Reprinted with permission of Columbia University Press.

51. From Elizabeth Johnston Cooke, "English Folk-Tales in America," *Journal of American Folklore* 12 (1899): 126–30.

52. From Norman Studer, "Yarns of a Catskills Woodsman," *New York Folklore Quarterly* 11 (1955): 188–89. Used by permission of the New York Folklore Society.

53. From Vance Randolph, *The Devil's Pretty Daughter, and Other Ozark Folk Tales* (New York: Columbia University Press, 1955), pp. 15–19. Reprinted with permission of Columbia University Press.

54. "All These are Mine," p. 214, from *Mules and Men* by Zora Neale Hurston. © 1935 by Zora Neale Hurston; copyright renewed 1963 by John C. Hurston and Joel Hurston. Reprinted by permission of HarperCollins Publishers.

55. From Richard M. Dorson, *American Negro Folktales* (Greenwich, Ct.: Fawcett, 1967), pp. 75–76. Used by permission of Roland Mercer Dorson.

56. From Calvin Claudel and J.-M. Carrière, "Three Tales from the French Folklore of Louisiana," *Journal of American Folklore* 56 (1943): 41–42. Used with permission of the American Folklore Society, www. afsnet.org.

57. From J. Russell Reaver, "Lithuanian Tales from Illinois," *Southern Folklore Quarterly* 14 (1950): 162–63.

58. From Leonard Roberts, *Sang Branch Settlers: Folksongs and Tales of a Kentucky Mountain Family* (Austin: University of Texas Press for the American Folklore Society, 1974), pp. 225–28. Used by permission.

59. From Mary A. Owen, "Coyote and Little Pig," *Journal of American Folklore* 15 (1902): 64–65.

60. From David S. McIntosh, "Blacksmith and Death," *Midwest Folklore* 1 (1951): 51–53.

61. From Ethel LaBorde Smith and Ethelyn Orso, "Roquelaure: An Acadian Trickster," *Louisiana Folklore Miscellany* 3, no. 3 (1973): 25–27. Used by permission of the Louisiana Folklore Society.

62. From Ralph Steele Boggs, "North Carolina White Folktales and Riddles," *Journal of American Folklore* 47 (1934): 308. Used with permission of the American Folklore Society, www.afsnet.org.

63. From Emma M. Backus, "Tales of the Rabbit from Georgia Negroes," *Journal of American Folklore* 12 (1899): 113–14.

64. From J. Mason Brewer, "John Tales," in *Mexican Border Ballads and Other Lore,* edited by Mody C. Boatright (Austin: Publications of the Texas Folklore Society 21, 1946), pp. 87–88. Used by permission of the Texas Folklore Society.

65. From Emma M. Backus, "Folk-Tales from Georgia," *Journal of American Folklore* 13 (1900): 25–26.

66. From Mrs. William Preston Johnston, "Two Negro Tales," *Journal of American Folklore* 9 (1896): 195–96.

67. From Daryl Cumber Dance, *Shuckin' and Jivin': Folklore from Contemporary Black Americans* (Bloomington: Indiana University Press, 1978), pp. 187–89. Used by permission of Indiana University Press.

68. From Ralph Steele Boggs, "North Carolina White Folktales and Riddles," *Journal of American Folklore* 47 (1934): 306. Used with permission of the American Folklore Society, www.afsnet.org.

69. From Herbert Halpert, "The Cante-Fable in New Jersey," *Journal of American Folklore* 55 (1942): 138–39. Used with permission of the American Folklore Society, www.afsnet.org.

70. Used with the permission of Routledge Publishing Inc–Books, from Barry Jean Ancelet, *Cajun and Creole Folktales: The French Oral Tradition of South Louisiana* (Jackson: University Press of Mississippi, 1994), pp. 82–84, where the original French text is also included. Permission conveyed through Copyright Clearance Center, Inc.

71. From Thomas B. Stroup, "Analogs to the Mak Story," *Journal of American Folklore* 47 (1934): 380. Used with permission of the American Folklore Society, www.afsnet.org.

72. From Herbert Halpert, "Tales of a Mississippi Soldier," *Southern Folklore Quarterly* 8 (1944): 113.

73. From Carl Lindahl, Maida Owens, and C. Renée Harvison, *Swapping Stories: Folktales from Louisiana* (Jackson: University Press of Mississippi with the Louisiana Division of the Arts, Baton Rouge, 1997), p. 203. Reprinted with permission of University Press of Mississippi.

74. From Carl Lindahl, Maida Owens, and C. Renée Harvison, *Swapping Stories: Folktales from Louisiana* (Jackson: University Press of Mississippi with the Louisiana Division of the Arts, Baton Rouge, 1997), p. 196. Reprinted with permission of University Press of Mississippi.

75. From George Korson, *Minstrels of the Mine Patch: Songs and Stories of the Anthracite Industry* (Philadelphia: University of Pennsylvania Press, 1938), pp. 73–74. Used by permission of Betsy Korson Glazer.

76. From Daryl Cumber Dance, *Shuckin' and Jivin': Folklore from Contemporary Black Americans* (Bloomington: Indiana University Press, 1978), p. 61. Used by permission of Indiana University Press.

77. From Helen Zunser, "A New Mexican Village," *Journal of American Folklore* 48 (1935): 175. Used with permission of the American Folklore Society, www.afsnet.org.

78. From Norman Studer, "Yarns of a Catskills Woodsman," *New York Folklore Quarterly* 11 (1955): 191–92. Used by permission of the New York Folklore Society.

79. From Carl Lindahl, *American Folktales from the Collections of the Library of Congress* (Armonk, N.Y.: M.E. Sharpe, and the Library of Congress, Washington, D.C., 2004), I: 155–58. Reprinted with permission of Rosa Hicks.

80. Used with the permission of Routledge Publishing Inc–Books, from Barry Jean Ancelet, *Cajun and Creole Folktales: The French Oral Tradition of South Louisiana* (Jackson: University Press of Mississippi, 1994), p. 105, where the original French text is also printed. Permission conveyed through Copyright Clearance Center, Inc.

81. From Vance Randolph, *The Talking Turtle, and Other Ozark Folk Tales* (New York: Columbia University Press, 1957), pp. 24–25. Reprinted with permission of Columbia University Press.

82. From Vance Randolph, *The Talking Turtle, and Other Ozark Folk Tales* (New York: Columbia University Press, 1957), pp. 39–41. Reprinted with permission of Columbia University Press.

83. From Daryl Cumber Dance, *Shuckin and Jivin': Folklore from Contemporary Black Americans* (Bloomington: Indiana University Press, 1978), pp. 105–06. Used by permission of Indiana University Press.

84. From Donald J. Waters, *Strange Ways and Sweet Dreams: Afro-American Folklore from the Hampton Institute* Boston: G.K. Hall, 1983), pp. 336–37.

85. From *Tales and Songs of Southern Illinois,* collected by Charles Neely, edited by John Webster Spargo (Carbondale: Southern Illinois University Press, 1998; Crossfire Press, 1989; originally published 1938, copyright 1938 Julia Jonah Neely), pp. 64–65.

86. From Richard M. Dorson, *Negro Tales from Pine Bluff, Arkansas, and Calvin, Michigan* (Bloomington: Indiana University Press, Indiana University Publications Folklore Series 12, 1958), pp. 51–52. Used by permission of Indiana University Press.

87. From Ralph Steele Boggs, "North Carolina White Folktales and Riddles," *Journal of American Folklore* 47 (1934): 296 Used with permission of the American Folklore Society, www.afsnet.org.

88. From Fanny D. Bergen, "English Folk-Tales in America," *Journal of American Folklore* 2 (1889): 60–62.

89. Used with the permission of Routledge Publishing Inc–Books, from Barry Jean Ancelet, *Cajun and Creole Folktales: The French Oral Tradition of South Louisiana* (Jackson: University Press of Mississippi, 1994), pp. 75–76, where the original French text is included. Permission conveyed through Copyright Clearance Center, Inc.

90. From Mody C. Boatright, *Tall Tales from Texas Cow Camps* (Dallas: Southern Methodist University Press, 1982; originally published Dallas: Southwest Press, 1934), pp. 64–67. Reprinted with permission of Southern Methodist University Press.

91. Reprinted by permission of the publisher from *Negro Folktales in Michigan,* collected and edited by Richard M. Dorson, pp. 191–192, Cambridge, Mass.: Harvard University Press. © 1956 by the President and Fellows of Harvard College.

92. From Vance Randolph, *The Devil's Pretty Daughter, and Other Ozark Folktales* (New York: Columbia University Press, 1955), pp. 91–92. Reprinted with permission of Columbia University Press.

93. From Mody C. Boatright, *Tall Tales from Texas Cow Camps* (Dallas: Southern Methodist University Press, 1982; originally published Dallas: Southwest Press, 1934), pp. 60–64. Reprinted with permission of Southern Methodist University Press.

94. From K. Bernice Stewart and Homer A. Watt, "Legends of Paul Bunyan, Lumberjack," *Transactions of the Wisconsin Academy of Sciences, Arts, and Letters* 18 (1916): 645.

95. From Dan G. Hoffman, "Folk Tales of Paul Bunyan: Themes, Structure, Style, Sources," *Western Folklore* 9 (1950): 315. Reprinted with permission of the Western States Folklore Society.

96. From Herbert Halpert and Emma Robinson, "'Oregon' Smith, an Indiana Folk Hero," *Southern Folklore Quarterly* 6 (1942): 165.

97. Folktale from *Body, Boots, and Britches* by Harold W. Thompson, p. 138. © 1939 by Harold W. Thompson; copyright renewed 1967 by Dr. Marion Thompson. Reprinted by permission of HarperCollins Publishers.

98. From Sue Gates, "Windy Yesterdays," in *Coyote Wisdom,* edited by J. Frank Dobie, Mody C. Boatright and Harry H. Ransom (Austin: Publications of the Texas Folklore Society 14, 1938), p. 264. Used by permission of the Texas Folklore Society.

99. From Calvin Claudel, "Spanish Folktales from Delacroix, Louisiana," *Journal of American Folklore* 58 (1945): 221–22. Used with permission of the American Folklore Society, www.afsnet.org.

100. From C. Grant Loomis, "A Tall Tale Miscellany, 1830–1866," *Western Folklore* 6 (1947): 38, reprinting a piece from an 1833 Boston newspaper.

101. From Herbert Halpert, "Tales Told by Soldiers," *California Folklore Quarterly* 4 (1945): 375. Reprinted with permission of the Western States Folklore Society.

102. From Richard M. Dorson, "Maine Master-Narrator," *Southern Folklore Quarterly* 8 (1944): 282.

103. From Ruth Ann Musick, *Green Hills of Magic: West Virginia Folktales from Europe* (Lexington: University Press of Kentucky, 1970), pp. 260–61. Used by permission of Daniel and Patricia Musick.

104. From Mody C. Boatright, *Gib Morgan, Minstrel of the Oil Fields* (n.p.: Publications of the Texas Folklore Society 20, 1945), pp. 73–74. Used by permission of the Texas Folklore Society.

105. From Robert D. Bethke, *Adirondack Voices: Woodsmen and Woodslore* (Urbana: University of Illinois Press, 1981), p. 41. Used by permission of Robert D. Bethke.

106. From William Hugh Jansen, *Abraham "Oregon" Smith: Pioneer, Folk Hero and Tale-Teller* (New York: Arno Press, 1977), p. 271. Used by permission of Ayer Company Publisher.

107. From Richard M. Dorson, "Maine Master-Narrator," *Southern Folklore Quarterly* 8 (1944): 282.

108. From Vance Randolph, *The Talking Turtle, and Other Ozark Folk Tales* (New York: Columbia University Press, 1957), pp. 41–43. Reprinted with permission of Columbia University Press.

109. From Vance Randolph, *Pissing in the Snow and Other Ozark Folktales* (Urbana: University of Illinois Press, 1976), pp. 95–96.

110. From Mariella Glenn Hartsfield, *Tall Betsy and Dunce Baby: South Georgia Folktales* (Athens: University of Georgia Press, 1987), pp. 116–18. © 1987 by the University of Georgia Press, Athens, Georgia 30602. All rights reserved.

111. From Daryl Cumber Dance, *Shuckin' and Jivin': Folklore from Contemporary Black Americans* (Bloomington: Indiana University Press, 1978), pp. 72–73. Used by permission of Indiana University Press.

112. From Charles L. Perdue, Jr., *Outwitting the Devil: Jack Tales from Wise County Virginia* (Santa Fe: Ancient City Press, 1987), p. 6. Reprinted with permission of Charles L. Perdue, Jr.

113. Used with the permission of Routledge Publishing Inc–Books, from Barry Jean Ancelet, *Cajun and Creole Folktales: The Oral Tradition of South Louisiana* (Jackson: University Press of Mississippi, 1994), pp. 66–67, where the original French text is provided. Permission conveyed through Copyright Clearance Center, Inc.

114. From Ruth Ann Musick, *Green Hills of Magic: West Virginia Folktales from Europe* (Lexington: University Press of Virginia, 1970), pp. 20–23. Used by permission of Daniel and Patricia Musick.

115. From Sylvia Trop, "An Italian Rip Van Winkle," *New York Folklore Quarterly* 1 (1945): 101–05. Used by permission of the New York Folklore Society.

116. From Emelyn E. Gardner, "Two Ghost Stories," *Journal of American Folklore* 58 (1945): 155. Used with permission of the American Folklore Society, www.afsnet.org.

117. From George Carey, *Maryland Folk Legends and Folk Songs* (Centreville: Tidewater Publishers, 1971), p. 7. Reprinted with permission of Tidewater Publishers.

118. From Cornelius J. Laskowski, "Polish Tales of the Supernatural Collected in Albany, N.Y.," *New York Folklore Quarterly* 10 (1954): 174–75. Used by permission of the New York Folklore Society.

119. From Caroline Bancroft, "Folklore of the Central City District, Colorado," *California Folklore Quarterly* 4 (1945): 327. Reprinted with permission of the Western States Folklore Society.

120. From Caroline Bancroft, "Folklore of the Central City District, Colorado," *California Folklore Quarterly* 4 (1945): 327–28. Reprinted with permission of the Western States Folklore Society.

121. From Linda Dégh, "The Negro in the Concrete," *Indiana Folklore* 1, no. 1 (1968): 61. Used with permission of the Indiana University Folklore Archives.

122. From Frank Goodwyn, "Folk-Lore of the King Ranch Mexicans," in *Southwestern Lore,* edited by J. Frank Dobie (Austin: Southwest Press, Publications of the Texas Folklore Society 9, 1931), p. 50. Used by permission of the Texas Folklore Society.

123. From W. J. Hoffman, "Folk-Lore of the Pennsylvania Germans," *Journal of American Folklore* 2 (1889): 33–34.

124. From J. Hampden Porter, "Notes on the Folk-Lore of the Mountain Whites of the Alleghanies," *Journal of American Folklore* 7 (1894): 109.

125. From Eileen Thomas, "Ghosts in Widow Mary's Place," *New York Folklore Quarterly* 5 (1949): 289–90. Used by permission of the New York Folklore Society.

126. From Newman Ivey White, general editor, *The Brown Collection of North Carolina Folklore* (Durham: Duke University Press, 1952) I: 676–77. Reprinted with permission of Duke University Press.

127. From Emelyn E. Gardner, *Folklore from the Schoharie Hills, New York* (Ann Arbor: University of Michigan Press, 1937), p. 90.

128. From J. Hampden Porter, "Notes on the Folk-Lore of the Mountain Whites of the Alleghanies," *Journal of American Folklore* 7 (1894): 110–11.

129. From D. K. Wilgus, "Wyoming's Headless Horseman," *Western Folklore* 14 (1955): 207. Reprinted with permission of the Western States Folklore Society.

130. From Vance Randolph, *Ozark Superstitions* (New York: Columbia University Press, 1947), p. 224. Reprinted with permission of Columbia University Press.

131. From A. M. Bacon and E. C. Parsons, "Folk-Lore from Elizabeth City County, Virginia," *Journal of American Folklore* 35 (1922): 289.

132. From S. P. Bayard, "Witchcraft Magic and Spirits on the Border of Pennsylvania and Virginia," *Journal of American Folklore* 51 (1938): 54–55. Used with permission of the American Folklore Society, www.afsnet.org.

133. From W. Stuart Rogers, "Irish Lore Collected in Schenectady," *New York Folklore Quarterly* 8 (1952): 25. Used by permission of the New York Folklore Society.

134. From Doret Meeker, "Back to the Blanket: Lore of Steuben County," *New York Folklore Quarterly* 8 (1952): 175. Used by permission of the New York Folklore Society.

135. From Emelyn E. Gardner, "Two Ghost Stories," *Journal of American Folklore* 58 (1945): 155–56. Used with permission of the American Folklore Society, www.afsnet.org.

136. From Charles L. Sonnichsen, "Mexican Spooks from El Paso," in *Straight Texas: A Book of Texas Folk-lore,* edited by J. Frank Dobie and Mody Boatright (Austin: The Steck Company, Publications of the Texas Folklore Society 13, 1937), pp. 122–23. Used by permission of the Texas Folklore Society.

137. Rosan A. Jordan, "The Folklore and Ethnic Identity of a Mexican-American Woman," Ph.D. dissertation, Indiana University, 1975, p. 221. Copyright 1975 by Rosan Augusta Jordan. Used by permission.

138. From Stanley Robe, *Hispanic Folktales from New Mexico: Narratives from the R. D. Jameson Collection* (Berkeley: University of California Press, University of California Publications, Folklore and Mythology Series 31, 1977), pp. 464–65. © 1977 by The Regents of the University of California.

139. From Richard K. Beardsley and Rosalie Hankey, "The Vanishing Hitchhiker," *California Folklore Quarterly* 1 (1942): 325. Reprinted with permission of the Western States Folklore Society.

140. From Lyle Saxon, Edward Dreyer and Robert Tallant, *Gumbo Ya-Ya: A Collection of Louisiana Folk Tales* (Boston: Houghton Mifflin, 1945), p. 286. Reprinted with permission of the State Library of Louisiana.

141. From Ruth Dodson, "The Ghost Nun," in *Backwoods to Border,* edited by Mody C. Boatright and Donald Day (Dallas: University Press in Dallas, Southern Methodist University; Austin: Publications of the Texas Folklore Society no. 18, 1943), p. 138. Used by permission of the Texas Folklore Society.

142. From Grace Partridge Smith, "Folklore from 'Egypt,'" *Journal of American Folklore* 54 (1941): 54–55. Used with permission of the American Folklore Society, www.afsnet.org.

143. From J. Hampden Porter, "Notes on the Folk-Lore of the Mountain Whites of the Alleghanies," *Journal of American Folklore* 7 (1894): 110.

144. From Ruth Ann Musick, *The Telltale Lilac Bush and Other West Virginia Ghost Tales* (Lexington: University Press of Kentucky, 1965), p. 157. Used by permission of the University Press of Kentucky.

145. From Janet Langlois, "Mary Whales I Believe in You: Myth and Ritual Subdued," *Indiana Folklore* 11 (1978): 5–34. Used with permission of the Indiana University Folklore Archives.

146. From Jesse Harris and Julia Neely, "Southern Illinois Phantoms and Bogies," *Midwest Folklore* 1 (1951): 178.

147. From A. M. Bacon and E. C. Parsons, "Folk-Lore from Elizabeth City County, Virginia," *Journal of American Folklore* 35 (1922): 286–87.

148. From Clifton Johnson, *What They Say in New England: A Book of Signs, Sayings and Superstitions* (Boston: Lee and Shepard, 1896), pp. 235–36.

149. From Wheaton P. Webb, "Witches in Cooper County," *New York Folklore Quarterly* 1 (1945): 130. Used by permission of the New York Folklore Society.

150. From Henry M. Wiltse, "In the Field of Southern Folklore," *Journal of American Folklore* 13 (1900): 209–10.

151. From Fanny Bergen, "Two Witch Stories," *Journal of American Folklore* 12 (1899): 68.

152. From A. M. Bacon and E. C. Parsons, "Folk-Lore from Elizabeth City County, Virginia," *Journal of American Folklore* 35 (1922): 284.

153. From A. M. Bacon and E. C. Parsons, "Folk-Lore from Elizabeth City County, Virginia," *Journal of American Folklore* 35 (1922): 285.

154. From F. A. de Caro, "The Butter Witch," *Indiana Folklore* 1, no. 1 (1968): 17–18. Used with permission of the Indiana University Folklore Archives.

155. From Millard F. Roberts, "The Wizard of Remsen," *New York Folklore Quarterly* 3 (1947): 42–43. Used by permission of the New York Folklore Society.

156. From "Indiana Witch Tales," *Journal of American Folklore* 65 (1952): 57–58. Used with permission of the American Folklore Society, www.afsnet.org.

157. From S. P. Bayard, "Witchcraft Magic and Spirits on the Border of Pennsylvania and West Virginia," *Journal of American Folklore* 51 (1938): 48–49. Used with permission of the American Folklore Society, www.afsnet.org.

158. From S. P. Bayard, "Witchcraft Magic and Spirits on the Border of Pennsylvania and West Virginia," *Journal of American Folklore* 51 (1938): 51–52. Used with permission of the American Folklore Society, www.afsnet.org.

159. From Zora Neale Hurston, "Hoodoo in America," *Journal of American Folklore* 44 (1931): 404–05. Used with permission of the American Folklore Society, www.afsnet.org.

160. From Zora Neale Hurston, "Hoodoo in America," *Journal of American Folklore* 44 (1931): 408–10. Used with permission of the American Folklore Society, www.afsnet.org.

161. From Elisabeth Cloud Seip, "Witch-Finding in Western Maryland," *Journal of American Folklore* 14 (1901): 44.

162. From Vance Randolph, *Ozark Superstitions* (New York: Columbia University Press, 1947), pp. 122–23. Reprinted with permission of Columbia University Press.

163. From Mildred R. Larson, "Lore from Snow County," *New York Folklore Quarterly* 11 (1955): 264. Used by permission of the New York Folklore Society.

164. From Ronald L. Baker, *Hoosier Folk Legends* (Bloomington: Indiana University Press, 1982), p. 99. Used by permission of Indiana University Press.

165. From George Korson, *Minstrels of the Mine Patch: Songs and Stories of the Anthracite Industry* (Philadelphia: University of Pennsylvania Press, 1938), pp. 159–60. Used by permission of Betsy Korson Glazer.

166. From George Carey, *Maryland Folk Legends and Folk Songs* (Centreville: Tidewater Publishers, 1971), pp. 23–24. Reprinted with permission of Tidewater Publishers.

167. From Caroline Bancroft, "Folklore of the Central City District, Colorado," *California Folklore Quarterly* 4 (1945): 324–5. Reprinted with permission of the Western States Folklore Society.

168. From Deborah Anders Silverman, *Polish-American Folklore* (Urbana: University of Illinois Press, 2000), pp. 84–85.

169. From Lynwood Montell, *Ghosts along the Cumberland: Deathlore in the Kentucky Foothills* (Knoxville: University of Tennessee Press, 1975), p. 53. Reprinted with permission of University of Tennessee Press.

170. From Lynwood Montell, *Ghosts along the Cumberland: Deathlore in the Kentucky Foothills* (Knoxville: University of Tennessee Press, 1975), p. 49. Reprinted with permission of University of Tennessee Press.

171. From Ronald L. Baker, *Hoosier Folk Legends* (Bloomington: Indiana University Press, 1982), p. 103. Used by permission of Indiana University Press.

172. From Ronald L. Baker, *Hoosier Folk Legends* (Bloomington: Indiana University Press, 1982), p. 39. Used by permission of Indiana University Press.

173. From James Travis, "Three Irish Folktales," *Journal of American Folklore* 54 (1941): 200–01. Used with permission of the American Folklore Society, www.afsnet.org.

174. From George Korson, *Black Rock: Mining Folklore of the Pennsylvania Dutch* (Baltimore: Johns Hopkins Press, 1960), pp. 302–03. Used by permission of Betsy Korson Glazer.

175. From Paul Frazier, "Some Lore of Hexing and Powwowing," *Midwest Folklore* 2 (1952): 106.

176. From Stanley Robe, *Hispanic Folktales from New Mexico: Narratives from the R. D. Jameson Collection* (Berkeley: University of California Press, University of California Publications, Folklore and Mythology series 31, 1977), pp. 493–94. © 1977 by The Regents of the University of California.

177. "New Tales of American Phantom Ships," *Western Folklore* 9 (1950): 203–04.

178. From Stanley Robe, *Hispanic Folktales from New Mexico: Narratives from the R. D. Jameson Collection* (Berkeley: University of California Press, 1977), pp. 449–50. © 1977 by The Regents of the University of California.

179. From F. A. de Caro, "Finding a Lost Watch," *Indiana Folklore* 1, no. 1 (1968): 25. Used with permission of the Indiana University Folklore Archives.

180. From G. W. Weippiert, "Legends of Iowa," *Journal of American Folklore* 2 (1889): 289.

181. From J. Russell Reaver, *Florida Folktales* (Gainesville: University Presses of Florida, 1987), p. 96. Reprinted with permission of the University Press of Florida.

182. From F. A. de Caro and C. Richard K. Lunt, "The Face on the Tombstone," *Indiana Folklore* 1, no. 1 (1968): 34–35. Used with permission of the Indiana University Folklore Archives.

183. From William M. Clements, "The Chain," *Indiana Folklore* 2, no. 1 (1969): 91. Used with permission of the Indiana University Folklore Archives.

184. "The Bride and the Egg Yolk" from *Gypsy Folktales* (San Diego: Harcourt Brace Jovanovich, 1989), p. 50. © 1989 by Diane Tong, reprinted by permission of Harcourt, Inc.

185. From Clifton Johnson, *What They Say in New England: A Book of Signs, Sayings and Superstitions* (Boston: Lee and Shepard, 1896), p. 139.

186. From Lyle Saxon, Edward Dreyer and Robert Tallant, *Gumbo Ya-Ya: A Collection of Louisiana Folk Tales* (Boston: Houghton Mifflin, 1945), p. 234. Reprinted with permission of the State Library of Louisiana.

187. From J. Russell Reaver, *Florida Folktales* (Gainesville: University Presses of Florida, 1987), p. 66. Reprinted with permission of the University Press of Florida.

188. Folktale from *Body, Boots, and Britches* by Harold W. Thompson, pp. 116–17. © 1939 by Harold W. Thompson; copyright renewed 1967 by Dr. Marion Thompson. Reprinted by permission of HarperCollins Publishers.

189. From Carl Lindahl, Maida Owens, and C. Renee Harvison, *Swapping Stories: Folktales from Louisiana* (Jackson: University Press of Mississippi, 1997), pp. 273–74. Reprinted with permission of University Press of Mississippi.

190. From Louis C. Jones, "The Devil in York State," *New York Folklore Quarterly* 8 (1952): 6–7. Used by permission of the New York Folklore Society.

191. Folktale from *Body, Boots, and Britches* by Harold W. Thompson, p. 114. © 1939 by Harold W. Thompson; copyright renewed 1967 by Dr. Marion Thompson. Reprinted by permission of HarperCollins Publishers.

192. From Louis C. Jones, "The Devil in York State," *New York Folklore Quarterly* 8 (1952): 14–15. Used by permission of the New York Folklore Society.

193. From George Korson, *Black Rock: Mining Folklore of the Pennsylvania Dutch* (Baltimore: Johns Hopkins Press, 1960), pp. 297–98. Used by permission of Betsy Korson Glazer.

194. From Louis C. Jones, "The Devil in York State," *New York Folklore Quarterly* 8 (1952): 10. Used by permission of the New York Folklore Society.

195. From Mark Glazer, "'El Diablo en el Baile': Cultural Change, Tradition and Continuity in a Chicano Legend," *Contemporary Legend* 4 (1994): 37. Used by permission of Mark Glazer.

196. From Letitia Humphreys Wrenshall, "Incantations and Popular Healing in Maryland and Pennsylvania," *Journal of American Folklore* 15 (1902): 274.

197. From Richard M. Dorson, *Jonathan Draws the Long Bow* (Cambridge: Harvard University Press, 1946), pp. 52–53; drawn from an earlier source.

198. From Charles M. Skinner, *Myths and Legends of Our Own Land* (Philadelphia: J. B. Lippincott, 1896): II: 332.

199. From Neil Van Allen, "Aunt Carrie and the Hop-Pickers," *New York Folklore Quarterly* 6 (1950): 166. Used by permission of the New York Folklore Society.

200. Reprinted from Susie Hoogasian-Villa's "Retribution," *100 Armenian Tales and their Folkloristic Relevance* (Detroit: Wayne State University Press, 1966), p. 413, with the permission of Wayne State University Press. © 1966 by Wayne State University Press, Detroit, Michigan 48202. All rights reserved.

201. From F. A. de Caro, "Indiana Miracle Legends," *Indiana Folklore* 2, no. 1 (1969): 37–38. Used with permission of the Indiana University Folklore Archives.

202. From F. A. de Caro, "Indiana Miracle Legends," *Indiana Folklore* 2, no. 1 (1969): 44. Used with permission of the Indiana University Folklore Archives.

203. From Jerome R. Mintz, *Legends of the Hasidim: An Introduction to Hasidic Culture and Oral Tradition in the New World* (Chicago: University of Chicago Press, 1968), p. 316. Used by permission of Betty Mintz.

204. From Jerome R. Mintz, *Legends of the Hasidim: An Introduction to Hasidic Culture and Oral Tradition in the New World* (Chicago: University of Chicago Press, 1968), pp. 330–31. Used by permission of Betty Mintz.

205. From Stanley Robe, *Hispanic Folktales from New Mexico: Narratives from the R. D. Jameson Collection* (Berkeley: University of California Press, University of California Publications, Folklore and Mythology Series 31, 1977), pp. 511–12. © 1977 by The Regents of the University of California.

206. From Stanley Robe, *Hispanic Folktales from New Mexico: Narratives from the R. D. Jameson Collection* (Berkeley: University of California Press, University of California Publications, Folklore and Mythology Series 31, 1977), p. 516. © 1977 by The Regents of the University of California.

207. From Stanley Robe, *Hispanic Folktales from New Mexico: Narratives from the R. D. Jameson Collection* (Berkeley: University of California Press, University of California Publications, Folklore and Mythology Series 31, 1977), pp. 522–23. © 1977 by The Regents of the University of California.

208. From Stanley Robe, *Hispanic Folktales from New Mexico: Narratives from the R. D. Jameson Collection* (Berkeley: University of California Press, University of California Publications, Folklore and Mythology Series 31, 1977), pp. 527–28. © 1977 by The Regents of the University of California.

209. From Austin E. Fife, "Popular Legends of the Mormons," *California Folklore Quarterly* 1 (1942): 124–25. Reprinted with permission of the Western States Folklore Society.

210. Quoted by Austin E. Fife, "Popular Legends of the Mormons," *California Folklore Quarterly* 1 (1942): 105.

211. From A. E. Fife, "The Legend of the Three Nephites among the Mormons," *Journal of American Folklore* 53 (1940): 29–30. Used with permission of the American Folklore Society, www.afsnet.org.

212. From A. E. Fife, "The Legend of the Three Nephites among the Mormons," *Journal of American Folklore* 53 (1940): 38. Used with permission of the American Folklore Society, www.afsnet.org.

213. From William A. Wilson, "Mormon Folklore: Cut from the Marrow of Everyday Experience," *Brigham Young University Studies* 33 (1993): 532. Used by permission of Brigham Young Studies.

214. From Louise Pound, "Nebraska Legends of Lovers' Leaps," *Western Folklore* 8 (1949): 310–11, quoting a 1936 Nebraska newspaper account.

215. From *Tales and Songs of Southern Illinois,* collected by Charles Neely, edited by John Webster Spargo (Carbondale: Southern Illinois University Press, 1998; Crossfire Press, 1989; originally published 1938, copyright 1938 Julia Jonah Neely), pp. 16–18.

216. From Federal Writers' Project, *Mississippi: A Guide to the Magnolia State* (New York: Hastings House, 1949), pp. 287–88.

217. From Thomas E. Barden, *Virginia Folk Legends* (Charlottesville: University Press of Virginia, 1991), pp. 146–48. © 1991. University of Virginia Press.

218. From J. Russell Reaver, *Florida Folktales* (Gainesville: University Presses of Florida, 1987), pp. 52–53. Reprinted with permission of the University Press of Florida.

219. From Thomas E. Barden, *Virginia Folk Legends* (Charlottesville: University Press of Virginia, 1991), pp. 181–82. © 1991. University of Virginia Press.

220. From Louis C. Jones, *Things That Go Bump in the Night* (New York: Hill and Wang, 1967), pp. 121–23. Used with permission.

221. From Thomas E. Barden, *Virginia Folk Legends* (Charlottesville: University Press of Virginia, 1991), pp. 188–89. © 1991. University of Virginia Press.

222. From Thomas E. Barden, *Virginia Folk Legends* (Charlottesville: University Press of Virginia, 1991), pp. 183–84. © 1991. University of Virginia Press.

223. [version 1] Guy Johnson, *John Henry: Tracking Down a Negro Legend* (Chapel Hill: University of North Carolina Press, 1929), p. 9. Reprinted with permission of University of North Carolina Press. [versions 2 and 3] *John Henry: A Folk-Lore Study* (Jena: Frommannsche Verlag, 1933), pp. 32–34.

224. From Carl Lindahl, Maida Owens and C. Renée Harvison, *Swapping Stories: Folktales from Louisiana* (Jackson: University Press of Mississippi, 1997), pp. 238–239. Reprinted with permission of University Press of Mississippi.

225. From Ronald L. Baker, *Hoosier Folk Legends* (Bloomington: Indiana University Press, 1982), p. 144. Used by permission of Indiana University Press.

226. From J. Russell Reaver, *Florida Folktales* (Gainesville: University Presses of Florida, 1987), p. 62. Reprinted with permission of the University Press of Florida.

227. All versions from Edward D. Ives, *George Magoon and the Down East Game War: History, Folklore, and the Law* (Urbana: University of Illinois Press, 1988), p. 164.

228. From Austin E. Fife, "The Wild Girl of the Santa Barbara Channel Islands," *California Folklore Quarterly* 2 (1943): 150. Reprinted with permission of the Western States Folklore Society.

229. From John Burrison, *Storytellers: Folktales & Legends from the South* (Athens: University of Georgia Press, 1989), p. 226. © 1989 by the University of Georgia Press. Athens, Georgia 30602. All rights reserved.

230. From Thomas E. Barden, *Virginia Folk Legends* (Charlottesville: University Press of Virginia, 1991), pp. 295–98. © 1991. University of Virginia Press.

231. From Newman Ivey White, general editor, *The Frank C. Brown Collection of North Carolina Folklore* (Durham: Duke University Press, 1952), I: 637. Reprinted with permission of Duke University Press.

232. From Clifton Johnson, *What They Say in New England: A Book of Signs, Sayings and Superstitions* (Boston: Lee and Shepard, 1896), pp. 98–99.

233. From Newman Ivey White, general editor, *The Frank C. Brown Collection of North Carolina Folklore* (Durham: Duke University Press, 1952), I: 637. Reprinted with permission of Duke University Press.

234. Reprinted by permission of the publisher from *Bloodstoppers and Bearwalkers: Folk Traditions of the Upper Peninsula,* by Richard M. Dorson, p. 247, Cambridge, Mass.: Harvard University Press. © 1952 by the President and Fellows of Harvard College; © 1980 by Richard M. Dorson.

235. From Ronald L. Baker, *Hoosier Folk Legends* (Bloomington: Indiana University Press, 1982), p. 126. Used by permission of Indiana University Press.

236. From George Carey, *Maryland Folklore* (Centreville: Tidewater Publishers, 1989), pp. 57–58. Reprinted with permission of Tidewater Publishers.

237. From Carl Lindahl, Maida Owens, and C. Renée Harvison, *Swapping Stories: Folktales from Louisiana* (Jackson: University Press of Mississippi, 1997), p. 262. Reprinted with permission of University Press of Mississippi.

238. From Vance Randolph, *Ozark Superstitions* (New York: Columbia University Press, 1947), p. 227. Reprinted with permission of Columbia University Press.

239. From Charles M. Skinner, *Myths and Legends of Our Own Land* (Philadelphia: J.B. Lippincott, 1896), II: 268–69.

240. Reprinted by permission of the publisher from *Bloodstoppers and Bearwalkers: Folk Traditions of the Upper Peninsula,* by Richard M. Dorson, pp. 216–17, Cambridge, Mass.: Harvard University Press. © 1952 by the President and Fellows of Harvard College; © 1980 by Richard M. Dorson.

347

241. From W. H. Babcock, "Folk-Tales and Folk-Lore Collected in and Near Washington, D.C.," *Folk-Lore Journal* 6 (1888): 88–89.

242. From J. Frank Dobie, "Treasure Legends of McMullen County," in *Legends of Texas,* edited by J. Frank Dobie (Austin: Publications of the Texas Folklore Society 3, 1924), pp. 39–40. Used by permission of the Texas Folklore Society.

243. From Frank Robertson, "Lost Mines of California," *Western Folklore* 10 (1951): 31. Reprinted with permission of the Western States Folklore Society.

244. Copied with permission from Elton Miles, *Tales of the Big Bend* (College Station: Texas A&M University Press, 1976), pp. 147–48.

245. Reprinted by permission of the publisher from *Negro Folktales in Michigan,* collected and edited by Richard M. Dorson, pp. 86–87, Cambridge, Mass.: Harvard University Press. © 1956 by the President and Fellows of Harvard College.

246. From Ruth Ann Musick, *The Telltale Lilac Bush and Other West Virginia Ghost Tales* (Lexington: University Press of Kentucky, 1965), pp. 88–89. Used by permission of the University Press of Kentucky.

247. From Thomas E. Barden, *Virginia Folk Legends* (Charlottesville: University Press of Virginia, 1991), pp. 69–70. © 1991. University of Virginia Press.

248. From Thomas E. Barden, *Virginia Folk Legends* (Charlottesville: University Press of Virginia, 1991), pp. 72–73. © 1991. University of Virginia Press.

249. From *Tales and Songs of Southern Illinois,* collected by Charles Neely, edited by John Webster Spargo (Carbondale: Southern Illinois University Press, 1998; Crossfire Press, 1989; originally published 1938, © 1938 Julia Jonah Neely), pp. 30–31.

250. From J. Russell Reaver, *Florida Folktales* (Gainesville: University Presses of Florida, 1987), p. 57. Reprinted with permission of the University Press of Florida.

251. From Donald A. Bird, "Morgan's Raiders: 'That's Sure a Good Looking Rifle You Got There,'" *Indiana Folklore* 2, no. 1 (1969): 124. Used with permission of the Indiana University Folklore Archives.

252. From Lyle Saxon, Edward Dreyer, and Robert Tallant, *Gumbo Ya-Ya: A Collection of Louisiana Folk Tales* (Boston: Houghton Mifflin, 1945), pp. 283–84. Reprinted with permission of the State Library of Louisiana.

253. From Ruth Ann Musick, *Coffin Hollow and Other Ghost Tales* (Lexington: University Press of Kentucky, 1977), pp. 51–53. Used by permission of the University Press of Kentucky.

254. From Kathryn L. Morgan, *Children of Strangers: The Stories of a Black Family* (Philadelphia: Temple University Press, 1980), p. 18.

255. From Ronald L. Baker, *Hoosier Folk Legends* (Bloomington: Indiana University Press, 1982), pp. 150–51. Used by permission of Indiana University Press.

256. From Rowland W. Rider and Deirdre Murray Paulsen, *The Roll Away Saloon: Cowboy Tales of the Arizona Strip* (Logan: Utah State University Press, 1985), p. 22. Reprinted with permission of Utah State University Press.

257. From Carl Lindahl, Maida Owens, and C. Renée Harvison, *Swapping Stories: Folktales from Louisiana* (Jackson: University Press of Mississippi, 1997), pp. 235–37. Reprinted with permission of University Press of Mississippi.

258. From Thomas E. Barden, *Virginia Folk Legends* (Charlottesville: University Press of Virginia, 1991), pp. 170–72. © 1991. University of Virginia Press.

259. From Mac E. Barrick, *Lewis the Robber: A Pennsylvania Folk Hero in Life and Legend* (*Midwestern Folklore* 20, no. 2, 1994), pp. 116–17, taken from the 1853 edition of the *Confession or Narrative of David Lewis.*

260. From Carl Lindahl, Maida Owens, and C. Renée Harvison, *Swapping Stories: Folktales from Louisiana* (Jackson: University Press of Mississippi, 1997), p. 232. Reprinted with permission of University Press of Mississippi.

261. From William Lynwood Montell, *Killings: Folk Justice in the Upper South* (Lexington: University Press of Kentucky, 1986), pp. 18–19. Used by permission of the University Press of Kentucky.

262. From Ronald L. Baker, *Hoosier Folk Legends* (Bloomington: Indiana University Press, 1982), pp. 154–55. Used by permission of Indiana University Press.

263. From Ronald L. Baker, *Hoosier Folk Legends* (Bloomington: Indiana University Press, 1982), p. 162. Used by permission of Indiana University Press.

264. From Ronald L. Baker, *Hoosier Folk Legends* (Bloomington: Indiana University Press, 1982), p. 165. Used by permission of Indiana University Press.

265. From George Korson, *Black Rock: Mining Folklore of the Pennsylvania Germans* (Baltimore: Johns Hopkins Press, 1960), pp. 346–47. Used by permission of Betsy Korson Glazer.

266. From *A Collection of American Family Folklore: Tales and Traditions from the Smithsonian Collection,* edited by Steven J. Zeitlin, Amy J. Kotkin, and Holly Cutting Baker (New York: Pantheon, 1982), pp. 104–08. An even longer version of this account is found in Daniel W. Patterson, *A Tree Accurst: Bobby McMillon and Stories of Frankie Silver* (Chapel Hill: University of North Carolina Press, 2000), pp. 174–77. Used by permission of Bobby McMillon.

267. From John Burrison, *Storytellers: Folktales & Legends from the South* (Athens: University of Georgia Press, 1989), pp. 228–29. © 1989 by the University of Georgia Press. Athens, Georgia 30602. All rights reserved.

268. From Thomas E. Barden, *Virginia Folk Legends* (Charlottesville: University Press of Virginia, 1991), p. 46. © 1991. University of Virginia Press.

269. From Ronald L. Baker, *Hoosier Folk Legends* (Bloomington: Indiana University Press, 1982), p. 51. Used by permission of Indiana University Press.

270. From John Burrison, *Storytellers: Folktales & Legends from the South* (Athens: University of Georgia Press, 1989), p. 227. © 1989 by the University of Georgia Press. Athens, Georgia 30602. All rights reserved.

271. Rosan A. Jordan, "The Folklore and Ethnic Identity of a Mexican-American Woman," Ph.D. dissertation, Indiana University, 1975, pp. 202–203. Copyright 1975 by Rosan Augusta Jordan. Used by permission.

272. From Thomas E. Barden, *Virginia Folk Legends* (Charlottesville: University Press of Virginia, 1991), p. 223. © 1991. University of Virginia Press.

273. From John Burrison, *Storytellers: Folktales & Legends from the South* (Athens: University of Georgia Press, 1989), p. 225. © 1989 by the University of Georgia Press. Athens, Georgia 30602. All rights reserved.

274. From Thomas E. Barden, *Virginia Folk Legends* (Charlottesville: University Press of Virginia, 1991), pp. 61–62. © 1991. University of Virginia Press.

275. From J. G. Owens, "Folk-Lore from Buffalo Valley, Central Pennsylvania," *Journal of American Folklore* 4 (1891): 124.

276. From Frank Goodwyn, "Folk-Lore of the King Ranch Mexicans," in *Southwestern Lore,* edited by J. Frank Dobie (Dallas: Southwestern Press; Austin: Publications of the Texas Folklore Society 9, 1931), pp. 53–54. Used by permission of the Texas Folklore Society.

277. From J. Russell Reaver, *Florida Folktales* (Gainesville: University Presses of Florida, 1987), pp. 29–30. Reprinted with permission of the University Press of Florida.

278. Reprinted by permission of the publisher from *Bloodstoppers and Bearwalkers: Folk Traditions of the Upper Peninsula,* by Richard M. Dorson, pp. 222–23, Cambridge, Mass.: Harvard University Press. © 1952 by the President and Fellows of Harvard College; © 1980 by Richard M. Dorson.

279. From *I Heard the Old Fisherman Say: Folklore of the Texas Gulf Coast* by Patrick B. Mullen, © 1978. Courtesy of the University of Texas Press.

280. From Mary Ann Oalmann, "Southern Railroad Folklore," *Louisiana Folklore Miscellany* 3, no. 5 (1975): 30. Used by permission of the Louisiana Folklore Society.

281. From Jack Santino, *Miles of Smiles, Years of Struggles: Stories of Black Pullman Porters* (Urbana: University of Illinois Press, 1989), p. 8.

282. From Yvette L. Trahant, "The Oral Tradition of the Physician," *Louisiana Folklore Miscellany* 5, no. 1 (1981): 46. Used by permission of the Louisiana Folklore Society.

283. From A. S. Barnes, "Policelore," *Louisiana Folklore Miscellany* 5, no. 2 (1982): 40. Used by permission of the Louisiana Folklore Society.

284. From Linda Dégh, "The Hook," *Indiana Folklore* 1, no. 1 (1968): 92. Used with permission of the Indiana University Folklore Archives.

285. From J. Russell Reaver, *Florida Folktales* (Gainesville: University Presses of Florida, 1987), p. 99. Reprinted with permission of the University Press of Florida.

286. From George Carey, *Maryland Folk Legends and Folk Songs* (Centreville: Tidewater Publishers, 1971), p. 75. Reprinted with permission of Tidewater Publishers.

287. From Sylvia Grider, "Dormitory Legend-Telling in Progress: Fall 1971–Winter 1973," *Indiana Folklore* 6 (1973): 28–29. Used with permission of Sylvia Grider.

288. From George Carey, *Maryland Folk Legends and Folk Songs* (Centreville: Tidewater Publishers, 1971), p. 87. Reprinted with permission of Tidewater Publishers.

289. From Gary Alan Fine, *Manufacturing Tales: Sex and Money in Contemporary Legends* (Knoxville: University of Tennessee Press, 1992). Reprinted with permission of University of Tennessee Press.

290. From Ethelyn G. Orso, "The Choking Doberman Legend," *Louisiana Folklore Miscellany* 5, 3 (1983): 49–50. Used by permission of the Louisiana Folklore Society.

291. From Linda Dégh, "The Boy Friend's Death," *Indiana Folklore* 1, no. 1 (1968): 101–02. Used with permission of the Indiana University Folklore Archives.

292. From Carlos Drake, "The Killer in the Back Seat," *Indiana Folklore* 1, no. 1 (1968): 107–08. Used with permission of the Indiana University Folklore Archives.

293. Thomas E. Murray, "The Ontogeny of a Midwestern Legend: The Case of the Crazy Baglady Who Ate Her Hair," *Midwestern Folklore* 18 (1992): 52. Used by permission.

294. From Linda Dégh, "The Runaway Grandmother," *Indiana Folklore* 1, no. 1 (1968): 69. Used with permission of the Indiana University Folklore Archives.

295. From J. Russell Reaver, *Florida Folktales* (Gainesville: University Presses of Florida, 1987), p. 113, from newspaper sources. Reprinted with permission of the University Press of Florida.

296. From Ronald L. Baker, *Hoosier Folk Legends* (Bloomington: Indiana University Press, 1982), pp. 132–34. Used by permission of Indiana University Press.

Index of Tale Types and Motifs

Tale type and motif numbers are used by folklorists to provide information by which various versions of a story (tale type) or plot or character elements of different stories (motifs) can be compared; by referring to the master indexes, similar stories or elements can be located. The indexes are Stith Thompson and Antti Aarne, *The Types of the Folktale: A Classification and Bibliography* (Helsinki: Suomalainen Tiedeakatemia Academia Scientiarum Fennica, Folklore Fellows Communications, 184, 1961); Stith Thompson, *Motif-Index of Folk Literature,* 6 vols. (Bloomington: Indiana University Press, n.d.); and Ernest W. Baughman, *Type and Motif Index of the Folktales of England and North America* (The Hague: Mouton, Indiana University Folklore Series 20, 1966). For motifs, an asterisk indicates a new motif established for a particular story and not appearing in Thompson and/or Baughman.

Aarne-Thompson (AT) Tale Types

AT number and title: story number

15, The Theft of Butter (Honey) by Playing Godfather: 55
38, Claw in Split Tree: 219
73, Blinding the Guard: 219
124, Blowing the House In: 59
130, The Animals in Night Quarters: 18
155, The Ungrateful Serpent Returned to Captivity: 20
157, Learning to Fear Man: 19
175, The Tarbaby and the Rabbit: 55
178, The Faithful Animal Rashly Killed: 268
300, The Dragon-Slayer: 21
301A, Quest for a Vanished Princess: 22
303, The Twins or Blood-Brothers: 23

312, The Giant-killer and His Dog (Bluebeard): 33
313C, The Girl as Helper plus the Forgotten Fiancée: 32
326, The Youth Who Wanted to Learn What Fear Is: 26
327B, The Dwarf and the Giant: 31
328, The Boy Steals the Giant's Treasure: 24
330A, The Smith and the Devil: 60
332, Godfather Death: 60
366, The Man from the Gallows: 87
402, The Mouse (Cat, Frog, etc.) as Bride: 25
425C, Beauty and the Beast: 35
440, The Frog King or Iron Henry: 92
480, The Spinning-Women by the Spring: 36
501, The Three Old Women Helpers: 37
507A, The Monster's Bride: 38
511, One-Eye, Two-Eyes, Three-Eyes: 39
513B, The Land and Water Ship: 40
550, Search for the Golden Bird: 34
563, The Table, the Ass, and the Stick: 42
571, Making the Princess Laugh: "All Sticks Together": 45
577, The King's Tasks: 43
593, Fiddevav: 53
670, The Animal Languages: 41
750A, The Wishes: 91
766, The Seven Sleepers: 115
769, Dead Child's Friendly Return to Parents: 113
777, The Wandering Jew: 209
812A*, The Devil's Riddle: 51
813, A Careless Word Summons the Devil: 114
817*, Devil Leaves at Mention of God's Name: 114
851, The Princess Who Cannot Solve the Riddle: 47
853A, The Hero Catches the Princess with Her Own Words: "No": 47, 48
859D, "All of These Are Mine": 54

Motifs

Motif number and description: story number

Frank de Caro received his Ph.D. in folklore from Indiana University and is Professor Emeritus of English at Louisiana State University. His previous books include *The Folktale Cat, Folklife in Louisiana Photography: Images of Tradition,* and *Re-Situating Folklore: Folk Contexts in Twentieth Century Literature and Art* (co-author). He taught at the University of Texas and the University of Indore in Central India. He currently lives in New Orleans.